James Martin, Karl Friedrich Keil

Biblical commentary on the prophecies of Ezekiel

Vol. 1

James Martin, Karl Friedrich Keil

Biblical commentary on the prophecies of Ezekiel
Vol. 1

ISBN/EAN: 9783337719074

Printed in Europe, USA, Canada, Australia, Japan

Cover: Foto ©Lupo / pixelio.de

More available books at **www.hansebooks.com**

CLARK'S

FOREIGN

THEOLOGICAL LIBRARY.

FOURTH SERIES.
VOL. XLIX.

Keil on the Prophecies of Ezekiel.

VOL. I.

EDINBURGH:
T. & T CLARK, 38 GEORGE STREET.
1876.

PRINTED BY MURRAY AND GIBB,

FOR

T. & T. CLARK, EDINBURGH.

LONDON,	HAMILTON, ADAMS, AND CO.
DUBLIN,	ROBERTSON AND CO.
NEW YORK,	SCRIBNER, WELFORD, AND ARMSTRONG.

BIBLICAL COMMENTARY

ON THE

PROPHECIES OF EZEKIEL.

BY

CARL FRIEDRICH KEIL, D.D.,
DOCTOR AND PROFESSOR OF THEOLOGY.

Translated from the German

BY

REV. JAMES MARTIN, B.A.

VOL. I.

EDINBURGH:
T. & T. CLARK, 38 GEORGE STREET.
MDCCCLXXVI.

THE whole of this Commentary, with the exception of the first 99 pages of Vol. i., has been translated by Rev. JAMES MARTIN, B.A.

F. C.

UNIVERSITY, ST. ANDREWS.

CONTENTS.

INTRODUCTION.

	PAGE
I. The Person of the Prophet,	1
II. The Times of the Prophet,	2
III. The Book of Ezekiel,	7

EXPOSITION.

FIRST HALF.—THE PROPHECIES OF JUDGMENT.
CHAP. I.–XXXII.

The Consecration and Calling of Ezekiel to the Office of Prophet (Chap. i.–iii. 21),	17
The Destiny of Jerusalem and its Inhabitants (Chap. iii. 22–v. 17),	61
The Judgment upon the Idolatrous Places, and on the Idol-worshippers (Chap. vi.),	93
The Overthrow of Israel (Chap. vii.),	99
Vision of the Destruction of Jerusalem (Chap. viii.–xi.),	111
Departure of the King and People; and Bread of Tears (Chap. xii.),	155
Against the False Prophets and Prophetesses (Chap. xiii.),	164
Attitude of God towards the Worshippers of Idols, and Certainty of the Judgments (Chap. xiv.),	177
Jerusalem, the Useless Wood of a Wild Vine (Chap. xv.),	191
Ingratitude and Unfaithfulness of Jerusalem. Its Punishment and Shame (Chap. xvi.),	194
Humiliation and Exaltation of the Davidic Family (Chap. xvii.).	236
The Retributive Justice of God (Chap. xviii.),	246
Lamentation for the Princes of Israel (Chap. xix.),	258

	PAGE
The Past, Present, and Future of Israel (Chap. xx.),	263
Prophecy of the Burning Forest and the Sword of the Lord (Chap. xx. 45 to Chap. xxi. 32 (Heb. Chap. xxi.)),	286
The Sins of Jerusalem and Israel (Chap. xxii.),	309
Oholah and Oholibah, the Harlots Samaria and Jerusalem (Chap. xxiii.),	320
Prediction of the Destruction of Jerusalem both in Parable and by Sign (Chap. xxiv.),	339
PREDICTIONS OF JUDGMENT UPON THE HEATHEN NATIONS (CHAP. XXV.-XXXII.),	353
Against Ammon, Moab, Edom, and the Philistines (Chap. xxv.),	360
AGAINST TYRE AND SIDON (CHAP. XXVI.–XXVIII.),	370
The Fall of Tyre (Chap. xxvi.),	370
Lamentation over the Fall of Tyre (Chap. xxvii.),	383
Against the Prince of Tyre (Chap. xxviii. 1-19),	405
Prophecy against Sidon, and Promise for Israel (Chap. xxviii. 20-26),	425

THE PROPHECIES OF EZEKIEL.

INTRODUCTION.

I. THE PERSON OF THE PROPHET.

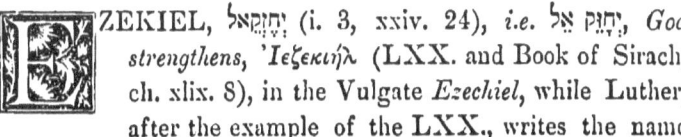ZEKIEL, יְחֶזְקֵאל (i. 3, xxiv. 24), *i.e.* יְחַזֵּק אֵל, *God strengthens,* Ἰεζεκιήλ (LXX. and Book of Sirach, ch. xlix. 8), in the Vulgate *Ezechiel,* while Luther, after the example of the LXX., writes the name *Hesekiel,* was the son of Busi, of priestly descent, and was carried away captive into exile to Babylon in the year 599 B.C.,—*i.e.* in the eleventh year before the destruction of Jerusalem,—along with King Jehoiachin, the nobles of the kingdom, many priests, and the better class of the population of Jerusalem and of Judah (i. 2, xl. 1; cf. 2 Kings xxiv. 14 ff.; Jer. xxix. 1). He lived there in the northern part of Mesopotamia, on the banks of the Chaboras, married, and in his own house, amidst a colony of banished Jews, in a place called Tel-Abib (i. 1, iii. 15, 24, viii. 1, xxiv. 18). In the fifth year of his banishment, *i.e.* 595 B.C., he was called to be a prophet of the Lord, and laboured in this official position, as may be shown, twenty-two years; for the latest of his prophecies is dated in the twenty-seventh year of his exile, *i.e.* 572 B.C. (xxix. 17). Regarding the other circumstances and events of his life, as also of his death, nothing is known. The apocryphal legends found in the Fathers and in the Rabbinical writings, to the effect that he was put to death by a prince of his own nation for rebuking his idolatry, and was buried in the tomb of Shem and Arphaxad, etc. (cf. Carpzov, Introd. ii. p. 203 ff.), are without any historical value. So much

alone is certain, that he ended his life among the exiles, where God had assigned him his sphere of labour, and did not, like his contemporary Daniel (comp. Dan. i. 21, x. 1), outlive the termination of the Captivity and the commencement of the redemption of Israel from Babylon, as his prophecies do not contain the slightest allusion to that effect.

II. THE TIMES OF THE PROPHET.

Ezekiel, like Daniel, is a prophet of the exile, but in a different fashion from the latter, who had been already carried away prisoner before him to Babylon on the first capture of Jerusalem by Nebuchadnezzar in the reign of Jehoiakim, and who lived there upwards of seventy years at the Babylonian and Medo-Persian court, and who held from time to time very important offices of State. Daniel was placed by God in this high position, which afforded him a view of the formation and evolution of the world-kingdom, in order that from this standpoint he might be enabled to see the development of the world-kingdoms in the struggle against the kingdom of God, and to predict the indestructible power and glory of the latter kingdom, which overcomes all the powers of the world. Ezekiel, on the other hand, was appointed a watcher over the exiled nation of Israel, and was in this capacity to *continue* the work of the earlier prophets, especially that of Jeremiah, with whom he in several ways associates himself in his prophecies; to preach to his contemporaries the judgment and salvation of God, in order to convert them to the Lord their God.—Rightly to understand his work as a prophet, the ripe fruit of which lies before us in his prophetic writings, we must not only keep in view the importance of the exile for the development of the kingdom of God, but also form a clear conception of the relations amidst which Ezekiel carried on his labours.

What the Lord had caused to be announced by Moses to the tribes of Israel while they were yet standing on the borders of the Promised Land, and preparing to take possession of it, viz. that if they should persistently transgress His commands, He would not only chastise them with heavy punishments, but would finally drive them out of the land which they were about to occupy, and disperse them among all nations (Lev. xxvi. 14–45; Deut. xxviii. 15–68),—this threatening, repeated by all the prophets after Moses, had been already executed by the Assyrians upon the ten tribes, who had revolted from the house of David, and was now in process of fulfilment by the Chaldeans upon the kingdom of Judah also. In the reign of Jehoiakim, Nebuchadnezzar, king of Babylon, for the first time invaded Judah, captured Jerusalem, made Jehoiakim tributary, and carried away to Babylon a number of Israelitish youths of noble birth and of the blood-royal, amongst whom was Daniel, along with a portion of the vessels of the temple, in order that these youths might be trained up for the service of his court (Dan. i. 1–7). With this invasion of the Chaldeans begin the seventy years of Chaldean servitude and exile in Babylon, predicted by Jeremiah. As Jehoiakim, so early as three years afterwards, revolted against Nebuchadnezzar, the latter, after a lengthened siege, took Jerusalem a second time, in the third month of the reign of Jehoiachin, and carried away into captivity to Babylon, along with the captive monarch and the members of his court, the nobles of Judah and Jerusalem, a great number of priests, warriors, carpenters, and smiths, leaving behind in the land only the meaner portion of the people, over whom he appointed as his vassal King Mattaniah, the uncle of the banished monarch, whose name he changed to Zedekiah (2 Kings xxiv. 10–17; Jer. xxix. 2). By this removal of the heart and strength of the nation the power of the kingdom of Judah was broken; and although Nebuchadnezzar did not at that time *destroy* it, but still allowed it to remain as a subject kingdom under his sway, yet its existence could not be of any long duration. Judah had fallen too deeply to recognise in the calamities which she had suffered the chastening hand of her God, and to bow herself repentantly under His mighty arm. Instead of listening to the voice of the prophet Jeremiah, and bearing the Chaldean yoke in patience (2 Chron. xxxvi. 12), both monarch and people placed their trust in the assistance of Egypt, and Zedekiah broke the oath of fealty which he had sworn to the king of Babylon. To punish this perfidy, Nebuchadnezzar again marched against Jerusalem, and by the capture and burning of the city and temple in the eleventh year of Zedekiah's reign put an end to the kingdom of Judah. Zedekiah, who had fled from the beleaguered city, was taken by the Chaldeans, and brought with his sons to Riblah into the presence of King Nebuchadnezzar, who first caused the sons of Zedekiah to be put to death before the eyes of their father; next, Zedekiah himself to be deprived of sight, and then commanded the blind monarch to be conducted in chains to Babylon (2 Kings xxv. 1-21; Jer. lii. 1-30). Many military officers and priests of rank were also put to death at Riblah; while those who had been taken prisoners at Jerusalem, along with the deserters and a great portion of the rest of the people, were led away into exile to Babylon (2 Kings xxv. 1-21; Jer. lii. 1-30). By this catastrophe the Old Testament theocracy lost its political existence; the covenant people were now driven out of their own land amongst the heathen, to bear the punishment of their obstinate apostasy from the Lord their God. Nevertheless this dispersion among the heathen was no entire rejection of Israel; it was merely a *suspension*, and not an *annihilation*, of the covenant of grace. Man's unfaithfulness cannot destroy the faithfulness of God. "In spite of this terrible judgment, brought down upon them by the heaviest transgressions, Israel was, and remained,"—as Auberlen (*The Prophet Daniel*, p. 27, 2d ed.) well remarks,— "the chosen people, through whom God was still to carry out His intentions towards humanity. His gifts and calling may not be repented of" (Rom. xi. 29). Even *after* the Babylonian exile the theocracy was not again restored; the covenant people did not after their return again recover their independence, but remained, with the exception of the short period when under the Maccabees they won for themselves their freedom, in constant dependence upon the heathen world-rulers, until, after the destruction of Jerusalem by the Romans, they were completely dispersed among all the nations of the earth. The kingdom of God, however, was not *really* to perish along with the external theocracy; it was only to pass into a new phase of development, which was intended to be the medium of transition towards its renewal and perfection in that kingdom of God which was to be founded by Christ. To pave the way to this end, and at the same time to serve as a witness to the exiles, that Israel, notwithstanding its dispersion among the heathen, still remained God's people, the Lord raised up in Ezekiel, the son of a priest, a prophet of uncommon power and energy in the midst of the captives, "one who raised his voice aloud, like a trumpet, and showed to Israel its misdeeds,—whose whole manifestation furnished the most powerful testimony that the Lord was still amongst His people; who was himself a temple of the Lord, before whom the visible temple, which yet remained standing for a short time at Jerusalem, sank back into its nothingness; a spiritual Samson, who seized with mighty arm the pillars of the idol temple, and dashed it to the ground; a powerful, gigantic nature, which was fitted by that very qualification to effectually subdue the Babylonian spirit of the time, which delighted in powerful, gigantic, and grotesque forms; standing alone, but equal to a hundred of the sons of the prophets" (Hengstenberg's *Christol.* II. p. 531).

The call of Ezekiel to the prophetic office took place in the fifth year of the reign of Zedekiah, in the fourth month of the year (i. 1, 2), at a point of time when, amongst those who had remained behind in the land, as well as amongst those who had been carried to Babylon, the hope of the speedy downfall of the Babylonian monarchy, and of the return of the exiles to their native country, which was then to follow, was very strong, and was powerfully encouraged by the lying statements of false prophets; cf. Jer. xxix. In the same year and month prophesied Hananiah, a prophet from Gibeon, in the temple at Jerusalem, before the eyes of the priests and the whole people, saying that Jehovah would break the yoke of the king of Babylon, and within two years bring back to Jerusalem all the temple-vessels carried away by Nebuchadnezzar, as well as King Jechoniah and all the captives who had been brought to Babylon, Jer. xxviii. 1–4. And the prophet Jeremiah, who with the word of the Lord rebuked and opposed those lying predictions and empty hopes, and foretold that the Babylonian servitude would be of long duration, was violently assailed and persecuted by the lying prophets, even by those of them who were to be found in Babylon; cf. Jer. xxviii. 5–17, xxix. 21–32. This delusion regarding the political condition of affairs, this spirit of resistance to the decree of the Lord, had seized not only upon the people, but also upon the nobles and the king, so that they formed and eagerly carried on conspiracies against the king of Babylon. The meeting of the kings of Edom, Moab, Ammon, Tyre, and Sidon, with Zedekiah in Jerusalem, had no other object than this (Jer. xxvii. 3). The embassy, moreover, sent by Zedekiah to Babylon (Jer. xxiv. 3), as well as his own journey thither in the fourth year of his reign (Jer. li. 59), were intended merely to deceive the king of Babylon, by assurances of devotion and fidelity, in order that the intended revolt might be carried out. But this baseless hope of a speedy liberation from the Babylonian yoke was ignominiously disappointed: in consequence of the treacherous rebellion of Zedekiah, Nebuchadnezzar, after a blockade and siege of a year and a half, captured Jerusalem, burnt the city and temple to the ground, and destroyed the kingdom of Judah. By this blow all the supports upon which the God-alienated nation had vainly relied were broken. The delusive statements of the false prophets had proved to be lies; the predictions of the Lord's prophets, on the contrary, had been strikingly justified as divine truth. The destruction of Jerusalem, the burning of the temple, and the downfall of the kingdom, form accordingly a turning-point for the prophetic labours of Ezekiel. Hitherto, prior to the calamity, he had to announce to the people (animated with the hope of speedy liberation from exile) the judgment of the downfall of Jerusalem and Judah, although such preaching found little acceptance. The time, however, had now arrived when, in order to preserve from despair the nation languishing in exile, and given over to the scorn, contempt, and tyranny of the heathen, he was able to open up the sources of comfort by announcing that the Lord, in requital of the ignominy heaped upon His people, would overwhelm all the heathen nations with destruction, but that, if His people whom they had oppressed would repent and return to Him, He would again gather them out of their dispersion; would make of them a holy nation, walking in His commands and yielding Him a willing service; would conduct them back to their own land; would give them His servant David for a prince, and once more gloriously establish His kingdom.

III. THE BOOK OF EZEKIEL.

The collection of the prophecies placed together in this book, as forming a complete unity, falls into two main divisions:— I. Announcements of judgment upon Israel and the heathen nations, ch. i.-xxxii.; II. Announcements of salvation for Israel, ch. xxxiii.-xlviii. Each of these main divisions is subdivided into two sections. The first, namely, contains the prophecies of judgment (*a*) upon Jerusalem and Israel, ch. iii. 22-xxiv.; (*b*) upon the heathen nations, ch. xxv.-xxxii. The second main division contains (*c*) the predictions of the redemption and restoration of Israel, and the downfall of the heathen world-power, ch. xxxiii.-xxxix.; (*d*) the prophetic picture of the re-formation and exaltation of the kingdom of God, ch. xl.-xlviii.; and the entire collection opens with the solemn dedication of Ezekiel to the prophetic office, ch. i. 1–iii. 21. The prophecies of the first, third, and fourth parts are throughout arranged in chronological order; those of the second part—the threatenings predicted against the heathen nations—are disposed according to their actual subject-matter. This is attested by the chronological data in the superscriptions, and confirmed by the contents of the whole of the groups of prophecies in the first three parts. The first part contains the following chronological notices: the fifth year of the captivity of Jehoiachin (i. 2) as the time of Ezekiel's call to the office of prophet, and of the first predictions regarding Jerusalem and Israel; then the sixth (viii. 1), seventh (xx. 1), and ninth years of the captivity of that monarch (xxiv. 1). The second part contains the predictions against seven foreign nations, of which those against Tyre fall in the eleventh (xxvi. 1), those against Egypt in the tenth (xxix. 1), twenty-seventh (xxix. 17), eleventh (xxx. 20 and xxxi. 1), and twelfth years of the exile. Of the two last parts, each contains only one chronological notice, namely, ch. xxxiii. 21, the twelfth year of the captivity, *i.e.* one year after the destruction of Jerusalem; and ch. xl. 1, the twenty-fifth year of the captivity, or the fourteenth after the destruction of Jerusalem. The remaining prophecies, which bear at their head no note of time, connect themselves closely as to their contents with those which are furnished with chronological data, so that they belong to the same period with those. From this it appears that the prophecies of the first part wholly, those of the second part to a great extent, date before the destruction of Jerusalem; those of the third and fourth parts proceed from the time after this catastrophe. This chronological relationship is in favour of the view that the prophecies against foreign nations, ch. xxv.–xxxii., are not —as the majority of expositors suppose—to be assigned to the second, but rather to the first half of the book. This view is confirmed, on the one hand, by the contents of the prophecies, inasmuch as these, without an exception, announce only the downfall of the heathen nations and kingdoms, making no reference to the future forgiveness and conversion of the residue of these nations, and through this very peculiarity connect themselves closely with the prophecies of threatening against Israel in the first part; on the other hand, by the resemblance which exists between ch. xxx. 1-20 and ch. iii. 16-21, compared with ch. xviii. 19-32, and which leaves no doubt upon the point that ch. xxxiii. 1-20 marks out to the prophet the task which was to occupy his attention after the destruction of Jerusalem, and consequently forms the introduction to the second half of his prophecies.—For further remarks upon the contents and subdivisions of the book, see the expositions in the introductory observations to the individual sections and chapters.

Ezekiel's *style of prophetic representation* has many peculiarities. In the first place, the clothing of symbol and allegory prevails in him to a greater degree than in all the other prophets; and his symbolism and allegory are not confined to general outlines and pictures, but elaborated in the minutest details, so as to present figures of a boldness surpassing reality, and ideal representations, which produce an impression of imposing grandeur and exuberant fulness. Even the simplest prophetic discourse is rich in imagery, and in bold, partly even strange, comparisons, and branches out into a copiousness which strives to exhaust the subject on all sides, in consequence of which many peculiar expressions and forms are repeated, rendering his language diffuse, and occasionally even clumsy. These peculiarities of his style of representation it has been attempted, on the one hand, to explain by the influence of the Babylonian spirit and taste upon the form of his prophecy; while others, again, would regard them as the result of a literary art, striving to supply the defect of prophetic spirit, and the failing power of the living word, by the aid of learning and an elaborate imitation of actual life. The supposed Babylonian spirit, however, in the forms of our prophet's symbolism, has no existence. The assertion of Hävernick, that "the whole of these symbols has a colossal character, which points in many ways to those powerful impressions experienced by the prophet in a foreign land,—Chaldea,—and which here are grasped and given out again with a mighty and independent spirit," remains yet to be proved. For the observation that these symbols, in reference to form and contents, resemble in many respects the symbols of his contemporary Daniel, is not sufficient for the purpose, and cannot in itself be accepted as the truth, by reference to the picture of the eagle, and the comparison of rich men to trees, cedars, in ch. xvii., because these pictures already occur in the older prophets, and lions as as well as cedars are native in Palestine. Just as little are Babylonian impressions to be recognised in the visions of the field with the dead men's bones, ch. xxxvii., and of the new temple, ch. xl., so that there only remains the representation of the cherubim with four faces, in ch. i. and x., which is peculiar to Ezekiel, as presumptive evidence of Chaldean influence. But if we leave out of account that the throne, upon which the Lord appears in human form, indisputably forms the central point of this vision, and this central point has no specific Babylonian impress, then the representation of the cherubim with faces of men, lions, oxen, and eagles, cannot be derived from the contemplation of the Assyrian or Chaldean sculptures of human figures with eagle heads and wings, or winged oxen with human heads, or sphinxes with bodies of animals and female heads, such as are found in the ruins of ancient Nineveh, inasmuch as the cherubim of Ezekiel were not pictures of oxen with lions' manes, eagles' wings, and human countenances furnished with horns,—as W. Neumann has still portrayed them in his treatise upon the tabernacle,— but had, according to Ezekiel, ch. i. 5, the *human* form. There are indeed also found, among the Assyrian sculptures, winged human figures; but these Ezekiel had no reason to copy, because the cherubic images in human form, belonging to Solomon's temple, lay much nearer to his hand. The whole of Ezekiel's symbolism is derived from the Israelitish sanctuary, and is an outcome of Old Testament ideas and views. As the picture of the ideal temple in ch. xl. ff. is sketched according to the relations of Solomon's temple, which was burnt by the Chaldeans, so the elements for the description of the majestic theophany, in ch. i. and x., are contained in the throne of Jehovah, which was above the cherubim, who were over the covering of the ark of the covenant; and in the phenomena amid which was manifested the revelation of the divine glory at the establishment of the covenant on Sinai. On the basis of these facts, Isaiah had already represented to himself the appearance of the Lord, as a vision, in which he beholds Jehovah in the temple, sitting on a high and lofty throne, and, standing around the throne, seraphim with six wings, who began to sing, "Holy, holy" (Isa. vi.). This symbolism we find modified in Ezekiel, so as to correspond with the aim of his vocation, and elaborated to a greater extent. The manner in which he works out this vision and other symbols certainly gives evidence of his capacity to describe, distinctly and attractively in words, what he had beheld in spirit; although the symbolism itself is, just as little as the vision, a mere product of poetic art, or the subjective framework of a lively fancy, without any real objective foundation; for it rests, in harmony with its contents and form, upon views which are *spiritually* real, *i.e.* produced by the Spirit of God in the soul of the prophet, in which the art of the author is reduced to a faithful and distinct reproduction of what had been seen in the spirit.— It is only the abundance of pictures and metaphors, which is in this respect *characteristic* of Ezekiel, and which betrays a lively imagination, and the many-sidedness of his knowledge. These qualities appear not merely in the sketch of the new temple (ch. xl. ff.), but also in the description of the widespread commerce of Tyre (ch. xxvii.), and of the relations of

Egypt (ch. xxix. and xxxi.), as well as in the endeavours manifest in *all* his representations,—not merely in the symbolical descriptions and allegorical portraits (ch. xvi. and xxiii.), but also in the simple discourses, in the rebukes of the current vices and sins, and in the threatenings of punishment and judgment,—to follow out the subject treated of into the most special details, to throw light upon it from all sides, to penetrate through it, and not to rest until he has exhausted it, and that without any effort, in so doing, to avoid repetitions. This style of representation, however, has its foundation not merely in the individuality of our prophet, but still more in the relations of his time, and in his attitude towards that generation to whom he had to announce the counsel and will of the Lord. As symbolism and the employment of parables, pictures, and proverbs is, in general, only a means for the purpose of presenting in an attractive light the truths to be delivered, and to strengthen by this attractiveness the impression made by speech and discourse, so also the copiousness and circumstantiality of the picture, and even the repetition of thoughts and expressions under new points of view, serve the same end. The people to whom Ezekiel was now to preach repentance, by announcing the divine judgment and salvation, was "a rebellious race, impudent and hard-hearted" (ch. iii. 7-9, 26, xii. 2, etc.). If he was faithfully and conscientiously to discharge the office, laid upon him by the Lord, of a watcher over the house of Israel, he must not only punish with stern words, and in drastic fashion, the sins of the people, and distinctly paint before their eyes the horrors of the judgment, but he must also set forth, in a style palpable to the senses, that salvation which was to bloom forth for the repentant nation when the judgment was fulfilled.

Closely connected with this is the other peculiarity of Ezekiel's style of prophecy, namely, the marked prominence assigned to the divine origin and contents of his announcements, which distinctly appears in the standing form of address

—" Son of man"—with which God summons the prophet to speech and action; in the continual use of אֲדֹנָי יהוה; in the formulae כֹּה אָמַר יְיָ or נְאֻם יְיָ; in the introduction to almost every discourse of God's requirement to him to prophesy or to do this and that; and in the formula which recurs frequently in all the discourses,—" Ye shall know that I am Jehovah." The standing address, "Son of man," and the frequent call to speech and action, are likewise regarded by modern critics as a token of the failure of the prophetic spirit-power. Both phrases, however, could only be held to convey so much, if—in conformity with the view of Ewald, who, agreeably to the *naturalistic* representation of prophecy, assumes it to be a result of high poetic inspiration—they had been selected by Ezekiel of his own free choice, and employed with the intention of expressing the feeling of his own profound distance from God, and of imparting to himself courage to prophesy. If, on the contrary, according to the *Scriptural* conception of prophecy, God the Lord addressed Ezekiel as " son of man," and called him, moreover, on each occasion to utter predictions, then the use of the God-given name, as well as the mention of the summons, as proceeding from God only, furnishes an evidence that Ezekiel does not, like the false prophets, utter the thoughts and inspirations of his own heart, but, in all that he says and does, acts under a *divine* commission and under *divine* inspiration, and serves to impress the rebellious nation more and more with the conviction that a prophet of the Lord is in their midst (ii. 5, xxxiii. 33), and that God had not departed with His Spirit from Israel, notwithstanding their banishment among the heathen. In favour of the correctness of this view of the expressions and phrases in question, there speak decisively the manner and fashion in which Ezekiel was called and consecrated to the prophetic office; not only the instruction which God communicates to him for the performance of his calling (ii. 1–3, 21),—and which, immediately upon the first act of his prophetic activity, He supplements to the effect of enjoining upon him dumbness or entire silence, only then permitting him to open his mouth to speak when He wishes to inspire him with a word to be addressed to the rebellious people (iii. 26, 27; cf. xxiv. 27 and xxxiii. 22),—but also the theophany which inaugurated his call to the prophetic office (ch. i.), which, as will appear to us in the course of the exposition, has unmistakeably the significance of an explanation of a reality, which will not be dissolved and annihilated with the dissolution of the kingdom of Judah, and the destruction of Jerusalem, and of the temple of that covenant of grace which Jehovah had concluded with Israel.

It is usual, moreover, to quote, as a peculiarity of Ezekiel's prophecies, the prominence given to his priestly descent and disposition, especially in the visions, ch. i., cf. ch. x., ch. viii.–xi. and xl.–xlviii., and in individual traits, as iv. 13 ff., xx. 12 ff., xxii. 8, xxvi. 24, 16 ff., etc., etc., which Ewald explains as "a result of the one-sided literary conception of antiquity according to mere books and traditions, as well as of the extreme prostration of spirit intensified by the long duration of the exile and bondage of the people;" while de Wette, Gesenius, and others would see in it an intellectual narrowness on the part of the prophet. The one view is as groundless and perverse as the other, because resting upon the superficial opinion that the copious descriptions of the sacred articles in the temple were sketched by Ezekiel only for the purpose of preserving for the future the elevating recollection of the better times of the past (Ewald). When we recognise, on the contrary, the symbolical character of these descriptions, we may always say that for the portrayal of the conception of the theophany in ch. i. and x., and of the picture of the temple in ch. xl., no individual was so well fitted as a priest, familiar with the institutions of worship. In this symbolism, however, we may not venture to seek for the products of intellectual narrowness, or of sacerdotal ideas, but must rise to the conviction that God the Lord selected a priest, and no other, to be His prophet, and permitted him to behold the future of His kingdom on earth in the significant forms of the sanctuary at Jerusalem, because this form was the symbolical covering which presented the closest correspondence to the same.—Still less do the passages iv. 13 ff., xx. 12 ff., and others, in which stress is laid upon the ceremonial commands of the law, and where their violation is mentioned as a cause of the judgment that was breaking over Israel, furnish evidence of priestly one-sidedness or narrowness of spirit. Ezekiel takes up towards the Mosaic Law no other position than that which is taken by the older prophets. He finds impressed on the precepts, not only of the Moral, but also of the Ceremonial Law, divine thoughts, essential elements of the divine holiness, attesting itself in and to Israel; and penetrated by a sense of the everlasting importance of the whole law, he urges obedience to its commands. Even the close adherence to the Pentateuch is not at all peculiar to him, but is common to all the prophets, inasmuch as all, without exception, criticize and judge the life of the nation by the standard of the prescriptions in the Mosaic Law. Ezekiel, with his nearest predecessor Jeremiah, is in this respect only distinguished from the earlier prophets, that the verbal references to the Pentateuch in both occur with greater frequency, and receive a greater emphasis. But this has its ground not so much in the descent of both from a priestly family, as rather in the relations of their time, especially in the circumstance that the falling away of the nation from the law had become so great, in consequence of which the penal judgments already threatened in the Pentateuch upon transgressors had fallen upon them, so that the prophets of the Lord were obliged, with all their energy, to hold up before the rebellious race not merely the commandments, but also the threatenings of the law, if they were faithfully to discharge the office to which they had been called.

The *language* of Ezekiel is distinguished by a great number of words and forms, which do not occur elsewhere, and which, probably, were for the greater part coined by himself (see an enumeration of these in the *Manual of Historico-Critical Introduction*, § 77, Rem. 6), and shows a strong leaning towards the diction of the Pentateuch. It has, however, been unable to resist the influences of the inaccurate popular dialect, and of the Aramaic idiom, so that it betrays, in its many anomalies and corruptions, the decline and commencement of the dying out of the Hebrew tongue (cf. § 17 of the *Historico-Critical Manual*), and reminds us that the prophet's residence was in a foreign country.

The *genuineness* of Ezekiel's prophecies is, at the present day, unanimously recognised by all critics. There is, moreover, no longer any doubt that the writing down and redaction of them in the volume which has been transmitted to us were the work of the prophet himself. Only Ewald and Hitzig, for the purpose of setting aside the predictions which so much offend them, have proposed very artificial hypotheses regarding the manner and way in which the book originated; but it appears unnecessary to enter into a closer examination of these, as their probability and trustworthiness depend only upon the dogmatic views of their authors.

For the exegetical literature, see the *Historico-Critical Manual*, vol. i. p. 353 (new ed. p. 254), where is also to be added, as of very recent date, *Das Buch Ezechiels*. Uebersetzt und erklärt von Dr. Th. Kliefoth. Zwei Abtheilungen. Rostock, 1864 and 1865.

EXPOSITION.

FIRST HALF.—THE PROPHECIES OF JUDGMENT.

CHAP. I.–XXXII.

CHAP. I.–III. 21.—THE CONSECRATION AND CALLING OF EZEKIEL TO THE OFFICE OF PROPHET.

N a vision of God, Ezekiel beholds in a great cloud, through which shone the splendour of fire, and which a tempestuous wind drives from the north, the glory of the Lord above the cherubim upon a majestic throne in human form (ch. i.), and hears a voice, which sends him as a prophet to Israel, and inspires him with the subject-matter of his announcements (ii. 1–iii. 3). He is thereafter transported in spirit to Tel-abib on the Chebar, into the midst of the exiles, and the duties and responsibilities of his calling laid before him (iii. 4–21). By this divine appearance and the commission therewith connected is he consecrated, called, and ordained to the prophetic office. The whole occurrences in the vision are subdivided into the copious description of the theophany, ch. i., by which he is consecrated for his calling; and into the revelation of the word, ch. ii. 1–3, 21, which prepares him for the discharge of the same. From these contents it clearly appears that these chapters do not constitute the *first section* of the book, but the *introduction* to the whole, to which the circumstantial notices

of the time and place of this revelation of God at the commencement, i. 1-3, also point.

Chap. i. THE APPEARANCE OF THE GLORY OF THE LORD.—Vers. 1-3. Time and place of the same.—Ver. 1. *Now it came to pass in the thirtieth year, in the fourth (month), on the fifth (day) of the month, as I was among the captives by the river of Chebar, that the heavens were opened, and I saw visions of God.* Ver. 2. *On the fifth day of the month, it was the fifth year of King Jehoiachin's captivity,* Ver. 3. *The word of the Lord came to Ezekiel the priest, the son of Busi, in the land of the Chaldeans by the river Chebar; and the hand of the Lord was there upon him.*

Regarding וַיְהִי at the beginning of a book, as *e.g.* in Jonah i. 1, cf. the note on Josh. i. 1. The two notices of the year in vers. 1 and 2 are closely connected with the twofold introduction of the theophany. This is described in verse first, according to its form or phenomenal nature, and then in verses second and third, according to its intended purpose, and its effect upon the prophet. The phenomenon consisted in this, that the heavens were opened, and Ezekiel saw visions of God. The heaven opens not merely when to our eye a glimpse is disclosed of the heavenly glory of God (Calvin), but also when God manifests His glory in a manner perceptible to human sight. The latter was the case here. מַרְאוֹת אֱלֹהִים, " visions of God," are not " *visiones præstantissimæ*," but visions which have divine or heavenly things for their object; cf. Isa. vi. 1; 1 Kings xxii. 19; 2 Kings vi. 17. Here it is the manifestation of Jehovah's glory described in the following verses. This was beheld by Ezekiel in the thirtieth year, which, according to verse second, was in the fifth year of the captivity of Jehoiachin. The real identity of these two dates is placed beyond doubt by the mention of the same day of the month, " on the fifth day of the month " (ver. 2 compared with ver. 1). The fifth year from the commencement of Jehoiachin's captivity is the year 595 B.C.; the thirtieth year, consequently, is the year 625 B.C. But the era, in accordance with which this date is reckoned, is matter of dispute, and can no longer be ascertained with certainty. To suppose, with Hengstenberg, that the reference is to the year of the prophet's own life, is forbidden by the addition " in the fourth month, on the fifth day of the month," which points to an era generally recognised. In the year 625 B.C., Nabopolassar became king of Babylon, and therefore many of the older expositors have supposed that Ezekiel means the thirtieth year of the era of Nabopolassar. Nothing, however, is known of any such era. Others, as the Chaldee paraphrast and Jerome, and in modern times also Ideler, are of opinion that the thirtieth year is reckoned from the eighteenth year of the reign of Josiah, because in that year the book of the law was discovered, and the regeneration of public worship completed by a solemn celebration of the Passover. No trace, however, can elsewhere be pointed out of the existence of a chronology dating from these events. The Rabbins in *Seder Olam* assume a chronology according to the periods of the years of jubilee, and so also Hitzig; but for this supposition too all reliable proofs are wanting. At the time mentioned, Ezekiel found himself בְּתוֹךְ הַגּוֹלָה, "in the midst of the exiles," *i.e. within the circuit of their settlements,* not, *in their society;* for it is evident from ch. iii. 15 that he was alone when the theophany was imparted to him, and did not repair till afterwards to the residences of the settlers. Ver. 3. By the river *Chebar*, in the land of the Chaldees, *i.e.* in Babylon or Mesopotamia. The river כְּבָר, to be distinguished from חָבוֹר, the river of Gosan, which flows into the Tigris, see on 2 Kings xvii. 6, is the Mesopotamian *Chaboras,* Ἀβόῤῥας (Strabo, xvi. 748), or Χαβώρας (Ptolem. v. 18, 3), خابور (Edrisi Clim. iv. p. 6, ii. p. 150, ed. Jaubert and Abulf. Mesopot. in the *N. Repertor.* III. p. xxiv.), which according to Edrisi takes its rise from " nearly three hundred springs," near the city *Ras-el-'Ain*, at the foot of the mountain range of Masius, flows through Upper Mesopotamia in a direction parallel with its two principal streams, and then, turning westward, discharges itself into the Euphrates near Kirkesion. There the hand of Jehovah came upon Ezekiel. The expression (אֶל) יַד יְיָ הָיְתָה עַל always signifies a miraculous working of the power or omnipotence of God upon a man,—the hand being the organ of power in action,—by which he is placed in a condition to exert superhuman power, 1 Kings xviii. 46, and is the regular expression for the supernatural transportation into the state of ecstasy for the purpose of beholding and announcing (cf. 2 Kings iii. 15), or undertaking, heavenly things; and so throughout Ezekiel, cf. iii. 22, viii. 1, xxxiii. 22, xxxvii. 1, xl. 1.

Vers. 4–28. Description of the theophany seen by the spirit of the prophet.—Ver. 4. *And I saw, and, lo, a tempestuous wind came from the north, a great cloud, and a fire rolled together like a ball, and the brightness of light round about it, and out of its midst, as the appearance of glowing metal from the midst of the fire.*—The description begins with a general outline of the phenomenon, as the same presented itself to the spiritual eye of the prophet on its approach from the north. A tempestuous wind brings hither from the north a great cloud, the centre of which appears as a lump of fire, which throws around the cloud the brightness of light, and presents in its midst the appearance of glowing metal. The coming of the phenomenon from the north is, as a matter of course, not connected with the Babylonian representation of the mountain of the gods situated in the extreme north, Isa. xiv. 13. According to the invariable usage of speech followed by the prophets, especially by Jeremiah (cf. *e.g.* i. 14, iv. 6, vi. 1, etc.), the north is the quarter from which the enemies who were to execute judgment upon Jerusalem and Judah break in. According to this usage, the coming of this divine appearance from the north signifies that it is from the north that God will bring to pass the judgment upon Judah. אֵשׁ מִתְלַקַּחַת, "fire rolled together like a ball," is an expression borrowed from Ex. ix. 10. לוֹ refers to עָנָן, and אֵשׁ to מָתוֹכָהּ, as we see from the words in apposition, מִתּוֹךְ הָאֵשׁ. The fire, which formed the centre of the cloud, had the appearance of חַשְׁמַל. The meaning of this word, which occurs again in ver. 27 and ch. viii. ver. 2, is disputed. The Septuagint and Vulgate translate it by ἤλεκτρον, *electrum, i.e.* a metal having a bright lustre, and consisting of a mixture of gold and silver. Cf. Strabo, III. 146; Plin. *Hist. Nat.* xxxiii. 4. To the explanation of Bochart, that it is a compound of נְחֹשֶׁת, "brass," and the Talmudic word מלל or מללא, "*aurum rude*," and signifies "rough gold ore," is opposed the fact that the reading מללא in the Talmud is not certain, but purports to be ממלא (cf. Gesen. *Thesaur.* p. 535, and Buxtorf, *Lexic. Talmud*, p. 1214), as well as the circumstance that raw gold ore has not a lustre which could shine forth out of the fire. Still less probability has the supposition that it is a compound of חֻשׁל, in Syriac "*conflavit, fabricavit*," and חשם, "*fricuit*," on which Hävernick and Maurer base the meaning of "a piece of metal wrought in the fire." The word appears simply to be formed from חשם, probably "to glow," with ל appended, as כַּרְמֶל from כרם, and to denote "glowing ore." This meaning is appropriate both in ver. 27, where עֵין חַשְׁמַל is explained by מַרְאֵה־אֵשׁ, as well as in ch. viii. 2, where זֹהַר, "brilliancy," stands as parallel to it. חַשְׁמַל, however, is different from נְחֹשֶׁת קָלָל in ver. 7 and in Dan. x. 6, for חַשְׁמַל refers in all the three places to the person of Him who is enthroned above the cherubim; while נְחֹשֶׁת קָלָל in ver. 7 is spoken of the feet of the cherubim, and in Dan. x. 6 of the arms and feet of the personage who there manifests Himself. In verse fifth the appearance is described more minutely. There first present themselves to the eye of the seer four beings, whom he describes according to their figure and style.

Vers. 5–14. *The four cherubim.*—Ver. 5. *And out of its midst there prominently appeared a figure, consisting of four creatures, and this was their appearance: they had the figure of a man.* Ver. 6. *And each had four faces, and each of them had four wings.* Ver. 7. *And their feet were upright-standing feet; and the soles of their feet like the soles of a calf, and sparkling like the appearance of shining brass.* Ver. 8. *And the hands of a man were under their wings on their four sides; and all four had faces and wings.* Ver. 9. *Their wings were joined one to another; they turned not as they went; they went each one in the direction of his face.* Ver. 10. *And the form of their faces was that of a man; and on the right all four had a lion's face; and on the left all four had the face of an ox; and all four had an eagle's face.* Ver. 11. *And their faces and their wings were divided above, two of each uniting with one another, and two covering their bodies.* Ver. 12. *And they went each in the direction of his face; whithersoever the spirit was to go, they went; they turned not as they went.* Ver. 13. *And the likeness of the creatures resembled burning coals of fire, like the appearance of torches: it (the fire) went hither and thither amongst the beings; and the fire was brilliant, and from the fire came forth lightning.* Ver. 14. *And the beings ran hither and thither in a zig-zag manner.*

From out of the fiery centre of the cloud there shows itself the form (דְּמוּת, properly "resemblance," "picture") of four חַיּוֹת, *animantia*, "living creatures;" ζῶα, Apoc. iv. 6; not θηρία, "wild beasts," as Luther has incorrectly rendered it, after the *animalia* of the Vulgate. These four creatures had דְּמוּת אָדָם, "the figure of a man." Agreeably to this notice, placed at the head of the description, these creatures are to be conceived as presenting the appearance of a human body in all points not otherwise specified in the following narrative. Each of them had four faces and four wings (אֶחָת without the article stands as a distributive, and כְּנָפַיִם are "pinions," as in Isa. vi. 2, not "pairs of wings"). Their feet were רֶגֶל יְשָׁרָה, "a straight foot;" the singular stands generically, stating only the nature of the feet, without reference to their number. We have accordingly to assume in each of the four creatures two legs, as in a man. יָשָׁר, "straight," *i.e.* standing upright, not bent, as when sitting or kneeling. רֶגֶל is the whole leg, including the knee and thigh, and כַּף רֶגֶל, "sole of the foot," or the under part of the leg, with which we tread on the ground. This part, not the whole leg, resembled the calf's foot, which is firmly planted on the ground. The legs sparkled like the appearance of נְחֹשֶׁת קָלָל. The subject of נֹצְצִים is not "the כְּרוּבִים, which are understood to be intended under the חיות in verse fifth" (Hitzig), for this subject is too far distant, but רַגְלֵיהֶם, which is here construed as masculine, as in Jer. xiii. 16. In this sense are these words apprehended in the Apocalypse, i. 15, and נְחֹשֶׁת קָלָל there translated by χαλκολίβανος. On this word see Hengstenberg and Düsterdieck on the Apoc. i. 15. נח' קלל probably signifies "light," *i.e.* "bright, shining brass," as the old translators have rendered it. The Septuagint has ἐξαστράπτων; the Vulgate, *aes candens;* and the Chaldee paraphrast, *aes flammans.* The signification "smoothed, polished brass" (Bochart), rests upon uncertain combinations; cf. Gesen. *Thes.* p. 1217, and is appropriate neither here nor in Dan. x. 6, where these words precede, "His face had the appearance of lightning, and his eyes were as a flame of fire." Under the four wings were four hands on the four sides of each cherub, formed like the hands of a man. The wings accordingly rested upon the shoulders, from which the hands came forth. The *Chetib* וידו may certainly be defended if with Kimchi and others we punctuate וְיָדוֹ, and take the suffix distributively and אָדָם elliptically, "his (*i.e.* each of the four creatures) hands were (the hands of) a man;" cf. for such an ellipsis as this, passages like that in Ps. xviii. 34, רַגְלַי כָּאַיָּלוֹת, "my feet as the (feet) of hinds;" Job xxxv. 2, מֵאֵל, "before the righteousness of God." It is extremely probable, however, that ו is only the error of an old copyist for י, and that the *Keri* וִידֵי is the correct reading, as the taking of אדם elliptically is not in keeping with the broad style of Ezekiel, which in its verbosity verges on tautology. The second half of ver. 8 is neither, with Hävernick, to be referred to the following ninth verse, where the faces are no more spoken of, nor, with Hitzig, to be arbitrarily mutilated; but is to be taken as it stands, comprising all that has hitherto been said regarding the faces and wings, in order to append thereto in ver. 9 sqq. the description of the use and nature of these members. The definite statement, that "the wings were joined one to another," is in ver. 11 limited to the two upper wings, according to which we have so to conceive the matter, that the top or the upper right wing of each cherub came in contact with the top of the left wing of the neighbouring cherub. This junction presented to the eye of the seer the unity and coherence of all the four creatures as a complete whole—a חַיָּה, and implied, as a consequence, the harmonious action in common of the four creatures. They did not turn as they went along, but proceeded each in the direction of his face. אֶל־עֵבֶר פָּנָיו, "over against his face." The meaning is thus rightly given by Kliefoth: "As they had four faces, they needed not to turn as they went, but went on as (*i.e.* in the direction in which) they were going, always after the face." In the closer description of the faces in ver. 10, the face of the man is first mentioned as that which was turned towards the seer, that of the lion to the right side, the ox to the left, and that of the eagle (behind). In naming these three, it is remarked that all the four creatures had these faces: in naming the man's face, this remark is omitted, because the word פְּנֵיהֶם (referring to all the four) immediately precedes. In ver. 11, it is next remarked of the faces and wings, that they were divided above (מִלְמַעְלָה, "from above," "upward"); then the direction of the wings is more precisely stated. The word וּפְנֵיהֶם is neither to be referred to the preceding, "and it was their faces," nor, with Hitzig, to be expunged as a gloss; but is quite in order as a statement that not only the wings but also the faces were divided above, consequently were not like *Janus*' faces upon one head, but the four faces were planted upon four heads and necks. In the description that follows, חֹבְרוֹת אִישׁ is not quite distinct, and אִישׁ is manifestly to be taken as an abbreviation of אִשָּׁה אֶל־אֲחוֹתָהּ in ver. 9: on each were two wings joining one another, *i.e.* touching with their tops the tips of the wings of the cherub beside them, in accordance with which we have to conceive the wings as expanded. Two were covering their bodies, *i.e.* each cherub covered his body with the pair of wings that folded downwards; not, as Kliefoth supposes, that the lower wings of the one cherub covered the body of the other cherub beside him, which also is not the meaning in ver. 23; see note on that verse. In ver. 12, what is to be said about their movements is brought to a conclusion, while both statements are repeated in ver. 9*b*, and completed by the addition of the *principium movens*. In whatever direction the רוּחַ " was to go, in that direction they went;" *i.e.* not according to the action of their own will, but wherever the רוּחַ impelled them. רוּחַ, however, signifies not "impulse," nor, in this place, even " the wind," as the vehicle of the power of the spiritual life palpable to the senses, which produced and guided their movements, (Kliefoth), but spirit. For, according to ver. 20, the movement of the wheels, which was in harmony with the movements of the cherubim, was not caused by the wind, but proceeded from the רוּחַ הַחַיָּה, *i.e.* from the spirit dwelling in the creature. On the contrary, there is not in the whole description, with the exception of the general statement that a tempestuous wind drove from the north the great cloud in which the theophany was enwrapped, any allusion to a means of motion palpable to the senses. In the 13th and 14th verses is described the entire impression produced by the movement of the whole appearance. וּדְמוּת הַחַיּוֹת precedes, and is taken absolutely " as regards the form of the creatures," and corresponds to the דְּמוּת אַרְבַּע חַיּוֹת in ver. 5, with which the description of the individual figures which appeared in the brightness of the fire was introduced. Their appearance was like burning coals of fire, like the appearance of torches. הִיא refers to אֵשׁ as the principal conception. Fire, like the fire of burning coals and torches, went, moved hither and thither amongst the four creatures. This fire presented a bright appearance, and out of it came forth lightnings. The creatures, moreover, were in constant motion. רָצוֹא, from רָצָא, an Aramaising form for the Hebrew רוּץ, to run. The *infin. absol.* stands instead of the *finite verb.* The conjecture of יָצׂא, after Gen. viii. 7 (Hitzig), is inappropriate, because here we have not to think of "coming out," and no reason exists for the striking out of the words, as Hitzig proposes. The continued motion of the creatures is not in contradiction with their perpetually moving on straight before them. "They went hither and thither, and yet always in the direction of their countenances; because they had a countenance looking in the direction of every side" (Kliefoth). בָּזָק signifies not "lightning" (=בָּרָק), but comes from בָּזַק; in Syriac, "to be split," and denotes "the splitting," *i.e.* the zigzag course of the lightning (Kliefoth).

Vers. 15–21. *The four wheels beside the cherubim.* — Ver. 15. *And I saw the creatures, and, lo, there was a wheel upon the earth beside the creatures, towards their four fronts.* Ver. 16. *The appearance of the wheels and their work was like the appearance of the chrysolite; and all four had one kind of figure: and their appearance and their work was as if one wheel were within the other.* Ver. 17. *Towards their four sides they went when they moved: they turned not as they went.* Ver. 18. *And their felloes, they were high and terrible; and their felloes were full of eyes round about in all the four.* Ver. 19. *And when the creatures moved, the wheels moved beside them; and when the creatures raised themselves up from the earth, the wheels also raised themselves.* Ver. 20. *Whithersoever the spirit was to go, they went in the direction in which the spirit was to go; and the wheels raised themselves beside them: for the spirit of the creatures was in the wheels.* Ver. 21. *When the former moved, the latter moved also; when the former stood, the latter stood; and when the former raised themselves from the ground, the wheels raised themselves beside them: for the spirit of the creatures was in the wheels.*—The words, " and I saw the creatures," prepare the way for the transition to the new object which presented itself in these creatures to the eye of the seer. By the side of these creatures upon the ground he sees a wheel, and that at the four fronts, or front faces of the creatures. The singular suffix in לְאַרְבַּעַת פָּנָיו can neither be referred, with Rosenmüller, to the chariot, which is not mentioned at all, nor, with Hitzig, to the preposition אֵצֶל, nor, with Hävernick, Maurer, and Kliefoth, to אוֹפָן, and so be understood as if every wheel looked towards four sides, because a second wheel was inserted in it at right angles. This meaning is not to be found in the words. The suffix refers *ad sensum* to חַיּוֹת (Ewald), or, to express it more correctly, to the figure of the cherubim with its four faces turned to the front, conceived as a unity—as *one* creature (הַחַיָּה, ver. 22). Accordingly, we have so to represent the matter, that by the side of the four cherubim, namely, beside his front face, a wheel was to be seen upon the earth. Ezekiel then saw four wheels, one on each front of a cherub, and therefore immediately speaks in ver. 16 of wheels (in the plural). In this verse מַרְאֶה is *adspectus*, and מַעֲשֶׂה " work;" *i.e.* both statements employing the term " construction," although in the first hemistich only the appearance, in the second only the construction, of the wheels is described. תַּרְשִׁישׁ is the chrysolite of the ancients, the topaz of the moderns,—a stone having the lustre of gold. The construction of the wheels was as if one wheel were within a wheel, *i.e.* as if in the wheel a second were inserted at right angles, so that without being turned it could go towards all the four sides. גַּבֵּיהֶן, in ver. 18, stands absolutely. "As regards their felloes," they possessed height and terribleness, —the latter because they were full of eyes all round. Hitzig arbitrarily understands גֹּבַהּ of the upper sides; and יִרְאָה, after the Arabic, of the under side, or that which lies towards the back. The movement of the wheels completely followed the movement of the creatures (vers. 19–21), because the spirit of the creature was in the wheels. הַחַיָּה, in vers. 20 and 21, is not the "principle of life" (Hävernick), but the cherubic creatures conceived as a unity, as in ver. 22, where the meaning is undoubted. The sense is: the wheels were, in their motion and rest, completely bound by the movements and rest of the creatures, because the spirit which ruled in them was also in the wheels, and regulated their going, standing, and rising upwards. By the רוּחַ הַחַיָּה the wheels are bound in one with the cherub-figures, but not by means of a chariot, to or upon which the cherubim were attached.

Vers. 22–28. The throne of Jehovah.—Ver. 22. *And over the heads of the creature there appeared an expanse like the appearance of the terrible crystal, stretched out over their heads above.* Ver. 23. *And under the expanse were their wings, extended straight one towards another: each had two wings, covering to these, and each two (wings), covering to those, their bodies.* Ver. 24. *And I heard the sound of their wings, as the sound of many waters, like the voice of the Almighty, as they went: a loud rushing like the clamour of a camp: when they stood, they let down their wings.* Ver. 25. *And there came a voice from above the expanse which was above their heads; when they stood, they let their wings sink down.* Ver. 26. *Over the expanse above their heads was to be seen, like a sapphire stone, the figure of a throne: and over the figure of the throne was a figure resembling a man above it.* Ver. 27. *And I saw like the appearance of glowing brass, like the appearance of fire within the same round about; from the appearance of his loins upwards, and from the appearance of his loins downwards, I saw as of the appearance of fire, and a shining light was round about it.* Ver. 28. *Like the appearance of the bow, which is in the clouds in the day of rain, was the appearance of the shining light round about. This was the appearance of the likeness of the glory of Jehovah. And I saw it, and fell upon my face, and I heard the voice of one that spake.*—Above, over the heads of the figures of the cherubim, Ezekiel sees something like the firmament of heaven (ver.

22 sq.), and hears from above this canopy a voice, which re-echoes in the rushing of the wings of the cherubim, and determines the movement as well as the standing still of these creatures. The first sentence of ver. 22 literally signifies: "And a likeness was over the heads of the creature,—a canopy, as it were, stretched out." רָקִיעַ is not the genitive after דְּמוּת, but an explanatory apposition to it, and before רָקִיעַ; neither has כְּ fallen out (as Hitzig supposes), nor is it to be supplied. For דְּמוּת denotes not any definite likeness, with which another could be compared, but, properly, *similitudo*, and is employed by Ezekiel in the sense of "something like." רָקִיעַ, without the article, does not mean the firmament of heaven, but any expanse, the appearance of which is first described as resembling the firmament by the words כְּעֵין הַקֶּרַח. It is not the firmament of heaven which Ezekiel sees above the heads of the cherubim, but an expanse resembling it, which has the shining appearance of a fear-inspiring crystal. נוֹרָא, used of crystal, in so far as the appearance of this glittering mass dazzles the eyes, and assures terror, as in Judg. xiii. 6, of the look of the angel; and in Job xxxvii. 22, of the divine majesty. The description is based upon Ex. xxiv. 10, and the similitude of the crystal has passed over to the Apocalypse, iv. 6. Under the canopy were the wings of the cherubim, יְשָׁרוֹת, standing straight, *i.e.* spread out in a horizontal direction, so that they appeared to support the canopy. אִשָּׁה אֶל־אֲחוֹתָהּ is not, with Jerome and others, to be referred to the cherubim (הַחַיָּה), but to בְּנַפְיהֶם, as in ver. 9. The לְאִישׁ which follows does refer, on the contrary, to the cherub, and literally signifies, "To each were two wings, covering, namely, to these and those, their bodies." לָהֵנָּה corresponds to לְאִישׁ, in a manner analogous to לְאַחַת לָהֶם in ver. 6. By the repetition of the לָהֵנָּה, "to these and those," the four cherubim are divided into two pairs, standing opposite to one another. That this statement contradicts, as Hitzig asserts, the first half of the verse, is by no means evident. If the two creatures on each side covered their bodies with the two wings, then two

other wings could very easily be so extended under the canopy that the tops of the one should touch those of the other. As the creatures moved, Ezekiel hears the sound, *i.e.* the rustling of their wings, like the roaring of mighty billows. This is strengthened by the second comparison, "like the voice of the Almighty," *i.e.* resembling thunder, cf. x. 5. The קוֹל הֲמֻלָּה that follows still depends on אֶשְׁמַע. הֲמֻלָּה, which occurs only here and in Jer. xi. 6, is probably synonymous with הָמוֹן, "roaring," "noise," "tumult." This rushing sound, however, was heard only when the creatures were in motion; for when they stood, they allowed their wings to fall down. This, of course, applies only to the upper wings, as the under ones, which covered the body, hung downwards, or were let down. From this it clearly appears that the upper wings neither supported nor bore up the canopy over their heads, but only were so extended, when the cherubim were in motion, that they *touched* the canopy. In ver. 25 is also mentioned whence the loud sound came, which was heard, during the moving of the wings, from above the canopy, consequently from him who was placed above it, so that the creatures, always after this voice resounded, went on or stood still, *i.e.* put themselves in motion, or remained without moving, according to its command. With the repetition of the last clause of ver. 24 this subject is concluded in ver. 25. Over or above upon the firmament was to be seen, like a sapphire stone, the likeness of a throne, on which sat one in the form of a man—*i.e.* Jehovah appeared in human form, as in Dan. vii. 9 sq. Upon this was poured out a fiery, shining light, like glowing brass (עֵין חַשְׁמַל, as in ver. 4) and like fire, בֵּית־לָהּ סָבִיב, "within it round about" (בֵּית = מִבֵּית, "within," and לָהּ, pointing back to דְּמוּת כִּסֵּא). This appears to be the simplest explanation of these obscure words. They are rendered differently by Hitzig, who translates them: "like fire which has a covering round about it, *i.e.* like fire which is enclosed, whose shining contrasts so much the more brightly on account of the dark surroundings." But, to say nothing of the change which would then be necessary of בֵּית into בֵּית, this meaning seems very far-fetched, and cannot be accepted for this reason alone, that מַרְאֶה אֵשׁ, neither in the following hemistich (ver. 27b) nor in viii. 2, has any such or similar strengthening addition. The appearance above shows, as the centre of the cloud (ver. 4), a fiery gleam of light, only there is to be perceived upon the throne a figure resembling a man, fiery-looking from the loins upwards and downwards, and round about the figure, or rather round the throne, a shining light (נֹגַהּ, cf. ver. 4), like the rainbow in the clouds, cf. Apoc. iv. 3. This [הוּא, ver. 28, does not refer to הַנֹּגַהּ, but to the whole appearance of him who was enthroned,—the covering of light included, but throne and cherubim (x. 4, 19) excluded (Hitzig)] was the appearance of the likeness of Jehovah's glory. With these words closes the description of the vision. The following clause, "And I saw, etc.," forms the transition to the word of Jehovah, which follows on the second chapter, and which summoned Ezekiel to become a prophet to Israel. Before we pass, however, to an explanation of this word, we must endeavour to form to ourselves a clear conception of the significance of this theophany.

For its full understanding we have first of all to keep in view that it was imparted to Ezekiel not merely on his being called to the office of prophet, but was again repeated three times,—namely, in ch. iii. 22 sqq., where he was commissioned to predict symbolically the impending siege of Jerusalem; ch. viii. 4 sqq., when he is transported in spirit to the temple-court at Jerusalem for the purpose of beholding the abominations of the idol-worship practised by the people, and to announce the judgment which, in consequence of these abominations, was to burst upon the city and the temple, in which it is shown to him how the glory of the Lord abandons, first the temple and thereafter the city also; and in ch. xliii. 1 sqq., in which is shown to him the filling of the new temple with the glory of the Lord, to dwell for ever among the children of Israel. In all three passages it is expressly testified that the divine appearance was like the first which he witnessed on the occasion of his call. From this Kliefoth has drawn the right conclusion, that the theophany in ch. i. 4 sqq. bears a relation not to the call only, but to the whole prophetic work of Ezekiel: "We may not say that God so appears to Ezekiel at a later time, because He so appeared to him at his call; but we must say, conversely, that because God wills and must so appear to Ezekiel at a later time while engaged in his prophetic vocation, therefore He also appears to him in this form already at his call." The intention, however, with which God so appears to him is distinctly contained in the two last passages, ch. viii.–xi. and ch. xliii : " God withdraws in a visible manner from the temple and Jerusalem, which are devoted to destruction on account of the sin of the people: in a visible manner God enters into the new temple of the future; and because the whole of what Ezekiel was inspired to foretell was comprehended in these two things,—the destruction of the existing temple and city, and the raising up of a new and a better;—because the whole of his prophetic vocation had its fulfilment in these, therefore God appears to Ezekiel on his call to be a prophet in the same form as that in which He departs from the ancient temple and Jerusalem, in order to their destruction, and in which He enters into the new edifice in order to make it a temple. The form of the theophany, therefore, is what it is in i. 4 sqq., because its purpose was to show and announce to the prophet, on the one side the destruction of the temple, and on the other its restoration and glorification." These remarks are quite correct, only the significance of the theophany itself is not thereby made clear. If it is clear from the purpose indicated why God here has the cherubim with Him, while on the occasion of other appearances (*e.g.* Dan. vii. 9; Isa. vi. 1) He is without cherubim; as the cherubim here have no other significancy than what their figures have in the tabernacle, viz. that God has there His dwelling-place, the seat of

His gracious presence; yet this does not satisfactorily explain either the special marks by which the cherubim of Ezekiel are distinguished from those in the tabernacle and in Solomon's temple, or the other attributes of the theophany. Kliefoth, moreover, does not misapprehend those diversities in the figures of the cherubim, and finds indicated therein the intention of causing it distinctly to appear that it is the one and same Jehovah, enthroned amid the cherubim, who destroys the temple, and who again uprears it. Because Ezekiel was called to predict both events, he therefore thinks there must be excluded, on the one hand, such attributes in the form of the manifestation as would be out of harmony with the different aims of the theophany; while, on the other, those which are important for the different aims must be combined and comprehended in one form, that this one form may be appropriate to all the manifestations of the theophany. It could not therefore have in it the ark of the covenant and the mercy-seat; because, although these would probably have been appropriate to the manifestation for the destruction of the old temple (viii. 1 sqq.), they would not have been in keeping with that for entering into the new temple. Instead of this, it must show the living God Himself upon the throne among "the living creatures;" because it belongs to the new and glorious existence of the temple of the future, that it should have Jehovah Himself dwelling within it in a visible form. From this, too, may be explained the great fulness of the attributes, which are divisible into three classes: 1. Those which relate to the manifestation of God for the destruction of Jerusalem; 2. Those which relate to the manifestation of God for entering into the new temple; and, 3. Those which serve both objects in common. To the last class belongs everything which is essential to the manifestation of God in itself, *e.g.* the visibility of God in general, the presence of the cherubim in itself, and so on: to the first class all the signs that indicate wrath and judgment, consequently, first, the coming from the north, especially the fire, the lightnings, in which God appears as He who is coming to judgment; but to the second, besides the rainbow and the appearance of God in human form, especially the wheels and the fourfold manifestation in the cherubim and wheels. For the new temple does not represent the rebuilding of the temple by Zerubbabel, but the economy of salvation founded by Christ at His appearing, to which they belong as essential tokens; to be founded, on the one hand, by God's own coming and dwelling upon the earth; on the other, to be of an œcumenic character, in opposition to the particularities and local nature of the previous ancient dispensation of salvation. God appears bodily, in human form; lowers down to earth the canopy on which His throne is seated; the cherubim, which indicate God's gracious presence with His people, appear not merely in symbol, but in living reality, plant their feet upon the ground, while each cherub has at his side a wheel, which moves, not in the air, but only upon the earth. By this it is shown that God Himself is to descend to the earth, to walk and to dwell visibly among His people; while the œcumenic character of the new economy of salvation, for the establishment of which God is to visit the earth, is represented in the fourfold form of the cherubim and wheels. The number four—the sign of the œcumenicity which is to come, and the symbol of its being spread abroad into all the world—is assigned to the cherubim and wheels, to portray the spreading abroad of the new kingdom of God over the whole earth. But how much soever that is true and striking this attempt at explanation may contain in details, it does not touch the heart of the subject, and is not free from bold combinations. The correctness of the assumption, that in the theophany attributes of an opposite kind are united, namely, such as should refer only to the destruction of Jerusalem and of the temple, and such as relate only to the foundation and nature of the new economy of salvation, is beset with well-founded doubts. Why, on such a hypothesis, should the form of the theophany remain the same throughout in all three or four cases? This question, which lies on the surface, is not satisfactorily answered by the remark that Ezekiel had to predict not only the destruction of the old, but also the foundation of a new and much more glorious kingdom of God. For not only would this end, but also the object of showing that it is the same God who is to accomplish both, have been fully attained if the theophany had remained the same only in those attributes which emblemize in a general way God's gracious presence in His temple; while the special attributes, which typify only the one and the other purpose of the divine appearance, would only then have been added, or brought prominently out, where this or that element of the theophany had to be announced. Moreover, the necessity in general of a theophany for the purpose alleged is not evident, much less the necessity of a theophany so peculiar in form. Other prophets also, *e.g.* Micah, without having seen a theophany, have predicted in the clearest and distinctest manner both the destruction of Jerusalem and the temple, and the raising up of a new and more glorious kingdom of God. The reason, then, why Ezekiel witnessed such a theophany, not only at his call, but had it repeated to him at every new turn in his prophetic ministry, must be deeper than that assigned; and the theophany must have another meaning than that of merely consecrating the prophet for the purpose of announcing both the judgment upon Jerusalem and the temple, and the raising up of a new and more glorious economy of salvation, and strengthening the word of the prophet by a symbolical representation of its contents.

To recognise this meaning, we must endeavour to form a distinct conception, not merely of the principal elements of our theophany, but to take into consideration at the same time their relation to other theophanies. In our theophany three elements are unmistakeably prominent,—1st, The peculiarly formed cherubim; 2d, The wheels are seen beside the cherubim; and, 3d, The firmament above, both with the throne and the form of

God in human shape seated upon the throne. The order of these three elements in the description is perhaps hardly of any importance, but is simply explicable from this, that to the seer who is on earth it is the under part of the figure which, appearing visibly in the clouds, first presents itself, and that his look next turns to the upper part of the theophany. Especially significant above all, however, is the appearance of the cherubim under or at the throne of God; and by this it is indisputably pointed out that He who appears upon the throne is the same God that is enthroned in the temple between the cherubim of the mercy-seat upon their outspread wings. Whatever opinion may be formed regarding the nature and significance of the cherubim, this much is undoubtedly established, that they belong essentially to the symbolical representation of Jehovah's gracious presence in Israel, and that this portion of our vision has its real foundation in the plastic representation of this gracious relation in the Holy of Holies of the tabernacle or temple. As, however, opinions are divided on the subject of the meaning of these symbols, and the cherubim of Ezekiel, moreover, present no inconsiderable differences in their four faces and four wings from the figures of the cherubim upon the mercy-seat and in the temple, which had only one face and two wings, we must, for the full understanding of our vision, look a little more closely to the nature and significance of the cherubim.

While, according to the older view, the cherubim are angelic beings of a higher order, the opinion at the present day is widely prevalent, that they are only symbolical figures, to which nothing real corresponds, — merely ideal representations of creature life in its highest fulness.[1] This modern view, how-

---

[1] Compare the investigation of the cherubim in my *Handbuch der Biblischen Archæologie*, I. pp. 86 sqq. and 113 sqq.; also Kliefoth's *Abhandlung über die Zahlensymbolik der heiligen Schrift* in der *Theolog. Zeitschrift von Dieckhoff und Kliefoth*, III. p. 381 sqq., where especially the older view— that the cherubim are angelic beings of a higher rank—is defended in a thorough manner, and the daring hypothesis of Hofmann signally refuted;

ever, finds in the circumstance that the cherubim in the Israelitish sanctuary, as well as in Ezekiel and in the Apocalypse, are symbolical figures of varying shape, only an apparent but no real support. The cherubim occur for the first time in the history of Paradise, where, in Gen. iii. 22–24, it is related that God, after expelling the first human pair from Paradise, placed at the east side of the garden the cherubim and the flame of a sword, which turned hither and thither, to guard the way to the tree of life. If this narrative contains historical truth, and is not merely a myth or philosopheme; if Paradise and the Fall, with their consequences, extending over all humanity, are to remain real things and occurrences,—then must the cherubim also be taken as real beings. "For God will not have placed symbols — pure creations of Hebrew fancy — at the gate of Paradise," Kliefoth. Upon the basis of this narrative, Ezekiel also held the cherubim to be spiritual beings of a higher rank. This appears from ch. xxviii. 14–16, where he compares the prince of Tyre, in reference to the high and glorious position which God had assigned him, to a cherub, and to Elohim. It does not at all conflict with the recognition of the cherubim as real beings, and, indeed, as spiritual or angelic beings, that they are employed in visions to represent super-sensible relations, or are represented in a plastic form in the sanctuary of Israel. "When angels," as Kliefoth correctly remarks in reference to this, "sing the song of praise in the holy night, this is an historical occurrence, and these angels are real angels, who testify by their appearance that there are such beings as angels; but when, in the Apocalypse, angels pour forth sounds of wrath, these angels are figures in vision, as elsewhere, also, men and objects are seen in vision." But even this employment of the angels as "figures" in vision, rests upon the belief that

---

lastly, Ed. C. Aug. Riehm, *De naturâ et notione symbolicâ Cheruborum, Commentat. Basil.* 1864, who, proceeding from the view—adopted by Bähr, Hengstenberg, and others—that the cherubim were only symbolical figures, has sought to determine more minutely the meaning of these symbols.

there are actually beings of this kind. Biblical symbolism furnishes not a single undoubted instance of abstract ideas, or ideal creations of the imagination, being represented by the prophets as living beings. Under the plastic representation of the cherubim upon the mercy-seat, and in the most holy and holy place of the tabernacle and the temple, lies the idea, that these are heavenly, spiritual beings; for in the tabernacle and temple (which was built after its pattern) essential relations of the kingdom of God are embodied, and all the symbols derived from things having a real existence. When, however, on the other hand, Hengstenberg objects, on Apoc. iv. 6, " that what Vitringa remarks is sufficient to refute those who, under the cherubim, would understand angels of rank,—viz. that these four creatures are throughout the whole of this vision connected with the assembly of the elders, and are distinguished not only from the angels, but from *all* the angels, as is done in ch. vii. 11,"—we must regard this refutation as altogether futile. From the division of the heavenly assembly before the throne into two choirs or classes (Apoc. v. and vii.),—in which the ζῶα (cherubim) and the elders form the one (v. 8), the ἄγγελοι the other choir (ver. 11),—an argument can be as little derived against the angelic nature of the cherubim, as it could be shown, from the distinction between the στρατιὰ οὐράνιος and ἄγγελος, in Luke ii. 13, that the "multitude of the heavenly host" were no angels at all. And the passage in Apoc. vii. 11 would only then furnish the supposed proof against the relationship of the cherubim to the angels, if πάντες ἄγγελοι in general—all angels, how numerous soever they may be— were spoken of. But the very tenor of the words, πάντες οἱ ἄγγελοι, "all the angels," points back to the choir of angels already mentioned in ch. v. 11, which was formed by πολλοὶ ἄγγελοι, whose number was ten thousand times ten thousand, and thousands of thousands.[1] From the distinction between

---

[1] See on this distinction Winer's *Grammar of New Testament Greek* (Moulton's translation), p. 137, where, among other remarks, it is observed

the ζῶα and the ἄγγελοι in the Apocalypse, no further inference can be deduced than that the cherubim are not common angels, "ministering spirits, sent forth to minister" (Heb. i. 14), but constitute a special class of angels of higher rank. More exact information regarding the relationship of the cherubim to the other angels, or their nature, cannot indeed be obtained, either from the name *cherubim* or from the circumstance that, with the exception of Gen. iii., they occur always only in connection with the throne of God. The etymology of the word כְּרוּב is obscure: all the derivations that have been proposed from the Hebrew or any other Semitic dialect cannot make the slightest pretensions to probability. The word appears to have come down from antiquity along with the tradition of Paradise. See my *Biblical Archæology*, p. 88 sqq. If we take into consideration, however, that Ezekiel calls them חַיּוֹת, and first in ch. x. employs the name כְּרוּבִים, known from the tabernacle, or rather from the history of Paradise; since, as may be inferred from x. 20, he first recognised, from the repetition of the theophany related in ch. x., that the living creatures seen in the vision *were* cherubim,—we may, from the designation חַיּוֹת, form a supposition, if not as to their nature, at least as to the significance of their position towards the throne of God. They are termed חַיּוֹת, "living," not as being "ideal representatives of all living things upon the earth" (Hengstenberg), but as beings which, among all the creatures in heaven and earth, possess and manifest life in the fullest sense of the word, and on that very account, of all spiritual beings, stand nearest to the God of the spirits of all flesh (who lives from eternity to eternity), and encircle His throne. With this representation harmonises not only the fact, that after the expulsion of the first human beings from Paradise, God commanded them to guard the way to the tree of life, but also the form in which

that "πᾶσαι γενεαί are all generations, whatever their number; πᾶσαι αἱ γενεαί (Matt. i. 17), *all the* generations,—those which, either from the context or in some other way, are familiar as a definite number."

they were represented in the sanctuary and in the visions. The cherubim in the sanctuary had the form of a man, and were only marked out by their wings as super-terrestrial beings, not bound by the earthly limits of space. The cherubim in Ezekiel and the Apocalypse also preserve the appearance of a man. Angels also assume the human form when they appear visibly to men on earth, because of all earthly creatures man, created in the image of God, takes the first and highest place. For although the divine image principally consists in the spiritual nature of man,—in the soul breathed into him by the Spirit of God,—yet his bodily form, as the vessel of this soul, is the most perfect corporeity of which we have any knowledge, and as such forms the most appropriate garment for rendering visible the heavenly spiritual being within. But the cherubim in our vision exhibit, besides the figure of the human body with the face of a man, also the face of the lion, of the ox, and of the eagle, and four wings, and appear as four-sided, square-formed beings, with a face on each of their four sides, so that they go in any direction without turning, and yet, while so doing, they can always proceed in the direction of one face; while in the vision in the Apocalypse, the four faces of the creatures named are divided among the four cherubim, so that each has only one of them. In the countenance of man is portrayed his soul and spirit, and in each one also of the higher order of animals, its nature. The union of the lion, ox, and eagle-faces with that of man in the cherubim, is intended, doubtless, to represent them as beings which possess the fulness and the power of life, which in the earthly creation is divided among the four creatures named. The Rabbinical dictum (*Schemoth Rabba*, Schöttgen, *Horæ Hebraicæ*, p. 1168): *Quatuor sunt qui principatum in hoc mundo tenent. Inter creaturas homo, inter aves aquila, inter pecora bos, inter bestias leo*, contains a truth, even if there lies at the foundation of it the idea that these four creatures represent the entire earthly creation. For in the cherub, the living powers of these four creatures are actually united. That the eagle, namely, comes into consideration only in reference to his power of flight, in which he excels all other birds, may be concluded from the circumstance that in Apoc. iv. 7 the fourth ζῶον is described as resembling an eagle flying. According to this principle, the ox and the lion are only to be considered in reference to their physical strength, in virtue of which the ox amongst tame animals, the lion amongst wild beasts, take the first place, while man, through the power of his mind, asserts his supremacy over all earthly creatures.[1] The number four, lastly, both of the cherubim and of the four faces of each cherub in our vision, is connected with their capacity to go in all directions without turning, and can contribute nothing in favour of the assumption that these four indicate the whole living creation, upon the simple ground that the number four is not essential to them, for on the mercy-seat only two cherubim are found. That they are also represented in the vision as higher spiritual beings, appears not only from Ezek. x. 7, where a cherub stretches forth his hand and fetches out fire from between the cherubim, and places it in the hands of the angel clothed in white linen, who was to accomplish the burning of Jerusalem; but, still more distinctly, from what is said in the Apocalypse regarding their working. Here we observe them, as Kliefoth has already pointed out, " in manifold activity: they utter day and night the Tersanctus; they offer worship, iv. 8, 9, v. 8, xix. 4; they repeat the Amen to the song of praise from all creation, v. 14; they invite John to see what the four first seals are accomplishing, vi. 1, 3, 5, 7; one of them gives to the seven angels the seven phials of wrath, xv. 7."

[1] This has been already rightly recognised by Riehm, *l.c.* p. 21 ff., who has drawn from it the inference: *quaternis igitur faciebus eximiae vires atque facultates significantur cherubis a deo ad munus suum sustinendum impertitae*, which is connected with the erroneous representation that the cherubim are intended to bear the throne of God, and to carry the Lord of the world.

Besides this activity of theirs in the carrying out of the divine counsel of salvation, we must, in order to gain as clear a view as possible of the significance of the cherubim in our vision, as well as in Biblical symbolism generally, keep also in view the position which, in the Apocalypse, they occupy around the throne of God. Those who are assembled about the throne form these three concentric circles: the four ζῶα (cherubim) form the innermost circle; the twenty-four elders, seated upon thrones, clothed in white garments, and wearing golden crowns upon their heads, compose the wider circle that follows; while the third, and widest of all, is formed by the many angels, whose number was many thousands of thousands (Apoc. iv. 4, 6, v. 6, 8, vii. 11). To these are added the great, innumerable host, standing before the throne, of the just made perfect from among all heathens, peoples, and languages, in white raiment, and with palms in their hands, who have come out of great tribulation, and have washed their robes, and made them white in the blood of the Lamb, and now, before the throne of God, serve Him day and night in His temple (vii. 9, 14, 15). Accordingly the twenty-four elders, as the patriarchs of the Old and New Testament congregation of God, have their place beside God's throne, between the cherubim and the myriads of the other angels; and in the same manner as they are exalted above the angels, are the cherubim exalted even above them. This position of the cherubim justifies the conclusion that they have the name of ζῶα from the indwelling fulness of the everlasting blessed life which is within them, and which streams out from the Creator of spirits—the King of all kings, and Lord of all lords—upon the spiritual beings of heaven, and that the cherubim immediately surround the throne of God, as being representatives and bearers of the everlasting life of blessedness, which men, created in the image of God, have forfeited by the Fall, but which they are again, from the infinitude of the divine compassion, to recover in the divine kingdom founded for the redemption of fallen humanity.

It is easier to recognise the meaning of the wheels which in our vision appear beside the cherubim. The wheel serves to put the chariot in motion. Although the throne of God is not now expressly represented and designated as a chariot-throne, yet there can be no doubt that the wheels which Ezekiel sees under the throne beside the cherubim are intended to indicate the possibility and ease with which the throne can be moved in the direction of the four quarters of the heavens. The meaning of the eyes, however, is matter of controversy, with which, according to i. 18, the felloes of the wheels, and, as is expressly mentioned in ch. x. 12, and also noted in Apoc. iv. 6, the cherubim themselves are furnished all round. According to Kliefoth, the eyes serve the purpose of motion; and as the movement of the cherubim and wheels indicates the spreading abroad over the whole earth of the new economy of salvation, this mass of eyes in the cherubim and wheels must indicate that this spreading abroad is to take place, not through blind accident, but with conscious clearness. The meaning is not appropriate to Apoc. iv. 6, where the cherubim have no wheels beside them, and where a going forth into all countries is not to be thought of. Here therefore, according to Kliefoth, the eyes only serve to bring into view the moral and physical powers which have created and supported the kingdom of God upon earth, and which are also to bring it now to its consummation. This is manifestly arbitrary, as any support from passages of the Bible in favour of the one view or the other is entirely wanting. The remark of Rosenmüller is nearer the truth, that by the multitude of the eyes is denoted *Coelestium naturarum perspicacia et ὀξυωπία*, and leads to the correct explanation of Apoc. v. 6, where the seven eyes of the Lamb are declared to be τὰ ἑπτὰ πνεύματα τοῦ Θεοῦ, τὰ ἀπεσταλμένα εἰς πᾶσαν τὴν γῆν; the eyes consequently indicate the spiritual effects which proceed from the Lamb over the entire earth in a manner analogous to His seven horns, which are the symbols of the completeness of His power. The eye, then, is the picture and mirror of the Spirit; and the ornamentation of the cherubim and wheels with eyes, shows that the power of the divine Spirit dwells within them, and determines and guides their movements.

The remaining objects of the vision are not difficult to explain. The appearance of the expanse over above the cherubim and wheels, upon which a throne is to be seen, represents the firmament or heaven as the place of God's throne. God appears upon the throne in human form, in the terrible glory of His holy majesty. The whole appearance draws nigh to the prophet in the covering of a great fiery cloud (ver. 4). This cloud points back to the "thick cloud" in which Jehovah, in the ancient time, descended upon Mount Sinai amid thunders and lightnings (Ex. xix. 16) to establish His covenant of grace, promised to the patriarchs with their seed,—the people of Israel brought forth from Egypt,—and to found His kingdom of grace upon the earth. If we observe the connection of our theophany with that manifestation of God on Sinai for the founding of the Old Testament dispensation of salvation, we shall neither confine the fire and the lightnings in our vision to the manifestation of God for the destruction of Jerusalem and the temple, nor refer the splendour which appears above the throne in the form of a rainbow to the grace which returns after the execution of judgment, or to the new dispensation of salvation which is to be established. Nor may we regard these differing attributes, by referring them specially to individual historical elements of the revelation of God in His kingdom, as in opposition; but must conceive of them, more generally and from the point of view of unity, as symbols of the righteousness, holiness, and grace which God reveals in the preservation, government, and consummation of His kingdom. It holds true also of our theophany what Düsterdieck remarks on Apoc. iv. 3 (cf. p. 219 of the second edition of his Commentary) regarding the importance of the divine appearance described in that passage: "We may not hastily apply in a general way the description before us by special reference to the judgments of God (which are seen at a later time) in their relation to the divine grace; it is enough that here, where the everlasting and personal ground of all that follows is described, the sacred glory and righteousness of God appear in the closest connection with His unchanging, friendly grace, so that the entire future development of the kingdom of God, and of the world down to the final termination, as that is determined by the marvellous unity of being which is in the holy, righteous, and gracious God, must not only according to its course, but also according to its object, correspond to this threefold glory of the living God." As this fundamental vision (of the Apocalypse) contains all that serves to alarm the enemies and to comfort the friends of Him who sits on the throne, so the vision of Ezekiel also has its fundamental significance not only for the whole of the prophet's ministry, but, generally, for the continuation and development of the kingdom of God in Israel, until its aim has been reached in its consummation in glory This, its fundamental significance, unmistakeably appears from the twofold circumstance,—firstly, that the theophany was imparted to the prophet at his call, and was then repeated at the principal points in his prophetic ministry, at the announcement both of the dissolution of the old kingdom of God by the destruction of Jerusalem and the temple, ch. ix.-xi., and also at the erection of the new temple and a new arrangement of the kingdom (ch. xl.-xlviii.). Since, as was formerly already remarked (p. 35), a theophany was not required either for the calling of Ezekiel to the office of a prophet, or for the announcement which was entrusted to him of the annihilation of the old and the foundation of the new kingdom of God, so the revelation of God, which pointed in its phenomenal shape to the dwelling of the Lord among His people in the Holy of Holies in the temple (and which was imparted in this place to Ezekiel, living among the exiles in the land of Chaldea by the banks of the Chebar), could only be intended, in view of the dissolution of the theocracy, which had already begun, and was shortly to be completed, to give to the prophet and those of his contemporaries who were living with him in exile, a real pledge that the essential element of the theocracy was not to be removed by the penal judgment which was passing over the sinful people and kingdom; but that God the Lord would still continue to attest Himself to His people as the living God, and preserve His kingdom, and one day bring it again to a glorious consummation.—In correspondence with this aim, God appears in the temple in the symbolical forms of His gracious presence as He who is throned above the cherubim; but cherubim and throne are furnished with attributes, which represent the movement of the throne in all directions, not merely to indicate the spreading of the kingdom of God over all the earth, but to reveal Himself as Lord and King, whose might extends over the whole world, and who possesses the power to judge all the heathen, and to liberate from their bondage His people, who have been given into their hands, if they repent and turn unto Him; and who will again gather them together, and raise them in the place of their inheritance to the glory which had been promised.

Such is the significance of the theophany at the inauguration of Ezekiel to the prophetic office. The significance, however, which its repetition possesses is clearly contained in the facts which the prophet was herewith permitted by God to behold. From the temple and city, polluted by sinful abominations, the gracious presence of God departs, in order that temple and city may be given over to the judgment of destruction; into the new and glorious temple there enters again the glory of God, to dwell for ever among the children of Israel.

Chap. ii. 1–iii. 3. CALL OF EZEKIEL TO THE PROPHETIC OFFICE.—Vers. 1 and 2. Upon the manifestation of the Lord follows the word of vocation. Having, in the feeling of his weakness and sinfulness, fallen to the ground before the terrible revelation of Jehovah's glory, Ezekiel is first of all raised up again by the voice of God, to hear the word which calls him to the prophetic function.—Ver. 1. *And He said to me, Son of man, stand upon thy feet, I will speak with thee.* Ver. 2. *Then came spirit unto me as He spake unto me, and it placed me on my feet, and I heard Him speaking unto me.*—The address בֶּן־אָדָם occurs so frequently in Ezekiel, that it must be regarded as one of the peculiarities of his prophecies. Elsewhere it occurs only once, Dan. viii. 17. That it is significant, is generally recognised, although its meaning is variously given. Most expositors take it as a reminder of the weakness and frailness of human nature; Coccejus and Kliefoth, on the contrary, connect it with the circumstance that God appears to Ezekiel in human form, and find in it a τεκμήριον amicitiæ, that God speaks in him as man to man, converses with him as a man with his friend. This last interpretation, however, has against it the *usus loquendi*. As בֶּן־אָדָם denotes man according to his natural condition, it is used throughout as a synonym with אֱנוֹשׁ, denoting the weakness and fragility of man in opposition to God; cf. Ps. viii. 5; Job xxv. 6; Isa. li. 12, lvi. 2; and Num. xxiii. 19. This is the meaning also of בֶּן־אָדָם in the address, as may be distinctly seen from the various addresses in Daniel. Daniel is addressed, where comfort is to be imparted to him, as אִישׁ חֲמֻדוֹת, "man greatly beloved," Dan. x. 11, 19, cf. ix. 23; but, on the contrary, in ch. viii. 17, where he has fallen on his face in terror before the appearance of Gabriel, with the words, "Understand, O son of man," in order to remind him of his human weakness. This is also the case in our verse, where Ezekiel, too, had fallen upon his face, and by God's word spoken to him, is again raised to his feet. It is only in Ezekiel that this address is constantly employed to mark the distance between the human weakness of his nature and the divine power which gives him the capacity and the impulse to speak. Not, however, with the design, mentioned by Jerome on Dan. viii. 17, "that he may not be elated on account of his high calling," because, as Hävernick subjoins, Ezekiel's extremely powerful and forcible nature may have needed to be perpetually reminded of what it is in reality before God. If this were the meaning and object of this address, it would also probably occur in the writings of several of the other prophets, as the supposition that the nature of Ezekiel was more powerful and forcible than that of the other prophets is altogether without foundation. The constant use of this form of address in Ezekiel is connected rather with the manner and fashion in which most of the revelations were imparted to him, that is, with the prevalence of "vision," in which the distinction between God and man comes out more prominently than in ordinary inspiration or revelation, effected by means of an impression upon the inner faculties of man. The bringing prominently forward, however, of the distance between God and men is to remind the prophet, as well as the people to whom he communicated his revelations, not merely of the weakness of humanity, but to show them, at the same time, how powerfully the word of God operates in feeble man, and also that God, who has selected the prophet as the organ of His will, possesses also the power to redeem the people, that were lying powerless under the oppression of the heathen, from their misery, and to raise them up again.—At the word of the Lord, "*Stand upon thy feet*," came רוּחַ into the prophet, which raised him to his feet. רוּחַ here is not "life, consciousness" (Hitzig), but the spirit-power which proceeds from God, and which is conveyed through the word which imparted to him the strength to stand before the face of God, and to undertake His command. מְדַבֵּר, *partic. Hithpa.*, properly "*collocutor*," occurs here and in ch. xliii. 6, and in Num. vii. 89; elsewhere, only in 2 Sam. xiv. 13.

Vers. 3–7. The calling of the prophet begins with the Lord describing to Ezekiel the people to whom He is sending him, in order to make him acquainted with the difficulties of his vocation, and to encourage him for the discharge of the same.

Ver. 3. *And He said to me, Son of man, I send thee to the children of Israel, to the rebels who have rebelled against me: they and their fathers have fallen away from me, even until this very day.* Ver. 4. *And the children are of hard face, and hardened heart. To them I send thee; and to them shalt thou speak: Thus says the Lord Jehovah.* Ver. 5. *And they,—they may hear thee or fail (to do so); for they are a stiff-necked race,—they shall experience that a prophet has been in their midst.* Ver. 6. *But thou, son of man, fear not before them, and be not afraid of their words, if thistles and thorns are round about thee, and thou sittest upon scorpions; fear not before their words, and tremble not before their faces; for they are a stiff-necked race.* Ver. 7. *And speak my words to them, whether they may hear or fail (to do so); for they are stiff-necked.*

The children of Israel have become heathen, no longer a people of God, not even a heathen nation (גוֹי, Isa. i. 4), but גּוֹיִם, "heathens," that is, as being rebels against God. הַמּוֹרְדִים (with the article) is not to be joined as an adjective to גּוֹיִם, which is without the article, but is employed substantively in the form of an apposition. They have rebelled against God in this, that they, like their fathers, have separated themselves from Jehovah down to this day (as regards פָּשַׁע בְּ, see on Isa. i. 2; and עֶצֶם הַיּוֹם הַזֶּה, as in the Pentateuch; cf. Lev. xxiii. 14; Gen. vii. 13, xvii. 23, etc.). Like their fathers, the sons are rebellious, and, in addition, they are קְשֵׁי פָנִים, of hard countenance" = חִזְקֵי מֵצַח, "of hard brow" (iii. 7), *i.e.* impudent, without hiding the face, or lowering the look for shame. This shamelessness springs from hardness of heart. To these hardened sinners Ezekiel is to announce the word of the Lord. Whether they hear it or not (וְאִם—אִם, *sive—sive*, as in Josh. xxiv. 15; Eccles. xi. 3, xii. 14), they shall in any case experience that a prophet has been amongst them. That they will neglect to hear is very probable, because they are a stiff-necked race (בַּיִת, "house" = family). The *Vau* before יָדְעוּ (ver. 5) introduces the *apodosis.* הָיָה is perfect, not present. This is demanded by the *usus loquendi* and the connection of the thought. The meaning is not: they shall know from his testimony that a prophet is there; but they shall experience from the result, viz. when the word announced by him will have been fulfilled, that a prophet has been amongst them. Ezekiel, therefore, is not to be prevented by fear of them and their words from delivering a testimony against their sins. The ἅπαξ λεγόμενα, סָרָבִים and סַלּוֹנִים, are not, with the older expositors, to be explained adjectively: "*rebelles et renuentes*," but are substantives. As regards סַלּוֹן, the signification "thorn" is placed beyond doubt by סִלּוֹן in xxviii. 24, and סָרָב in Aramaic does indeed denote "*refractarius;*" but this signification is a derived one, and inappropriate here. סָרָב is related to צָרַב, "to burn, to singe," and means "*urtica*," "stinging-nettle, thistle," as Donasch in *Raschi* has already explained it. אוֹתְךָ is, according to the later usage, for אִתָּךְ, expressing the "by and with of association," and occurs frequently in Ezekiel. Thistles and thorns are emblems of dangerous, hostile men. The thought is strengthened by the words "to sit on (אֶל for עַל) scorpions," as these animals inflict a painful and dangerous wound. For the similitude of dangerous men to scorpions, cf. Sir. xxvi. 10, and other proof passages in Bochart, *Hierozoic.* III. p. 551 sq., ed. Rosenmüll.

Ver. 8 *ad fin.* and ch. iii. 3.—After the Lord had pointed out to the prophet the difficulties of the call laid upon him, He prepares him for the performance of his office, by inspiring him with the divine word which he is to announce.—Ver. 8. *And thou, son of man, hear what I say to thee, Be not stiff-necked like the stiff-necked race; open thy mouth, and eat what I give unto thee.* Ver. 9. *Then I saw, and, lo, a hand outstretched towards me; and, lo, in the same a roll of a book.* Ver. 10. *And He spread it out before me; the same was written upon the front and back: and there were written upon it lamentations, and sighing, and woe.* Ch. iii. 1. *And He said to me: Son of man, what thou findest eat; eat the roll, and go and speak to the house of Israel.* Ver. 2. *Then opened I my mouth, and He gave me this roll to eat.* Ver. 3. *And said to me: Son of man, feed thy belly, and fill thy body with this roll which I give thee. And I ate it, and it was in my mouth as honey and sweetness.*—The prophet is to announce to the people of Israel only that which the Lord inspires him to announce. This thought is embodied in symbol, in such a way that an outstretched hand reaches to him a book, which he is to swallow, and which also, at God's command, he does swallow; cf. Apoc. x. 9 sqq. This roll was inscribed on both sides with lamentations, sighing, and woe (הִי is either abbreviated from נְהִי, not = אִי, or as Ewald, § 101c, thinks, is only a more distinct form of הוֹי or הֹה). The meaning is not, that upon the roll was inscribed a multitude of mournful expressions of every kind, but that there was written upon it all that the prophet was to announce, and what we now read in his book. These contents were of a mournful nature, for they related to the destruction of the kingdom, the destruction of Jerusalem and of the temple. That Ezekiel may look over the contents, the roll is spread out before his eyes, and then handed to him to be eaten, with the words, " Go and speak to the children of Israel," *i.e.* announce to the children of Israel what you have received into yourself, or as it is termed in ver. 5, דְּבָרַי, " my words." The words in iii. 3a were spoken by God while handing to the prophet the roll to be eaten. He is not merely to eat, *i.e.* take it into his mouth, but he is to fill his body and belly therewith, *i.e.* he is to receive into his innermost being the word of God presented to him, to change it, as it were, into sap and blood. Whilst eating it, it was sweet in his mouth. The sweet taste must not, with Kliefoth, be explained away into a sweet " after-taste," and made to bear this reference, that the destruction of Jerusalem would be followed by a more glorious restoration. The roll, inscribed with lamentation, sorrow, and woe, tasted to him sweetly, because its contents was God's word, which sufficed for the joy and gladness of his heart (Jer. xv. 16); for it is "infinitely sweet and lovely to be the organ and spokesman of the Omnipotent," and even the most painful of divine truths possess to a spiritually-minded man a joyful and quickening side (Hengstenberg on the Apoc. x. 9). To this it is added, that the divine penal judgments reveal not only the holiness and righteousness of God, but also prepare the way for the revelation of salvation, and minister to the saving of the soul.

Chap. iii. 4–21. THE SENDING OF THE PROPHET.—This consists in God's promise to give him power to overcome the difficulties of his vocation (vers. 4–9); in next transporting him to the place where he is to labour (vers. 10–15); and lastly, in laying upon him the responsibility of the souls entrusted to his charge (vers. 16–21). After Ezekiel had testified, by eating the roll which had been given him, his willingness to announce the word of the Lord, the Lord acquaints him with the peculiar difficulties of his vocation, and promises to bestow upon him strength to overcome them.— *Ver. 4. And He said to me, Son of man, go away to the house of Israel, and speak with my words to them. Ver. 5. For not to a people of hollow lips and heavy tongue art thou sent, (but) to the house of Israel. Ver. 6. Not to many nations of hollow lips and heavy tongue, whose words thou dost not understand; but to them have I sent thee, they can understand thee. Ver. 7. But the house of Israel will not hear thee, because they will not hear me; for the whole house of Israel, of hard brow and hardened heart are they. Ver. 8. Lo, I make thy countenance hard like their countenances, and thy brow hard like their brow. Ver. 9. Like to adamant, harder than rock, do I make thy brow: fear not, and tremble not before them, for they are a stiff-necked race.*—The contents of this section present a great similarity to those in ch. ii. 3–7, inasmuch as here as well as there the obduracy and stiff-neckedness of Israel is stated as a hindrance which opposes the success of Ezekiel's work. This is done here, however, in a different relation than there, so that there is no tautology.

Here, where the Lord is sending the prophet, He first brings prominently forward what lightens the performance of his mission; and next, the obduracy of Israel, which surrounds it with difficulty for him, in order at the same time to promise him strength for the vanquishing of these difficulties. Ezekiel is to speak, in the words communicated to him by God, to the house (people) of Israel. This he can do, because Israel is not a foreign nation with an unintelligible language, but possesses the capacity of understanding the words of the prophet (vers. 5–7), עַם עִמְקֵי שָׂפָה, " a people of deep lips," *i.e.* of a style of speech hollow, and hard to be understood; cf. Isa. xxxiii. 19. עִמְקֵי שׂ' is not genitive, and עַם is not the *status constructus*, but an adjective belonging to עַם, and used in the plural, because עַם contains a collective conception. "And of heavy tongue," *i.e.* with a language the understanding of which is attended with great difficulty. Both epithets denote a barbarously sounding, unintelligible, foreign tongue. The unintelligibility of a language, however, does not alone consist in unacquaintance with the meaning of its words and sounds, but also in the peculiarities of each nation's style of thought, of which language is only the expression in sounds. In this respect we may, with Coccejus and Kliefoth, refer the prophet's inability to understand the language of the heathen to this, that their manner of thinking and speaking was not formed according to the word of God, but was developed out of purely earthly, and even God-resisting factors. Only the exclusive prominence given by Kliefoth to this side of the subject is incorrect, because irreconcilable with the words, "many nations, whose words (discourse) thou dost not understand" (ver. 6). These words show that the unintelligibility of the language lies in not understanding the sounds of its words. Before אֶל־בֵּית יִשׂ', in ver. 5, the adversative particle *sed* is omitted (cf. Ewald, § 354*a*); the omission here is perhaps caused by this, that אַתָּה שָׁלוּחַ, in consequence of its position between both sentences, can be referred to both. In ver. 6 the thought of ver. 5 is expanded by the addition of עַמִּים רַבִּים, "*many nations*" with different languages, in order to show that it is not in the ability, but in the willingness, to hear the word of the Lord that the Israelites are wanting. It is not to many nations with unintelligible languages that God is sending the prophet, but to such men as are able to hear him, *i.e.* can understand his language. The second hemistich of ver. 6 is rendered by the old translators as if they had not read לֹא after אִם, "*if I sent thee to them* (the heathen), *they would hear thee.*" Modern expositors have endeavoured to extract this meaning, either by taking אִם לֹא as a particle of adjuration, *profecto*, "verily" (Rosenmüller, Hävernick, and others), or reading אִם לֹא, as Ewald does, after Gen. xxiii. 13. But the one is as untenable as the other: against אִם לֹא stands the fact that לוֹ is written with ו, not with א; against the view that it is a particle of adjuration, stands partly the position of the words before אֲלֵיהֶם שֶׁל, which, according to the sense, must belong to הֵמָּה יִשְׁמְ, partly the impossibility of taking שְׁלַחְתִּיךָ conditionally after the preceding אִם לֹא. "If such were the case, Ezekiel would have really done all he could to conceal his meaning" (Hitzig), for אִם לֹא, after a negative sentence preceding, signifies "but;" cf. Gen. xxiv. 38. Consequently neither the one view nor the other yields an appropriate sense. "If I had sent thee to the heathen," involves a repenting of the act, which is not beseeming in God. Against the meaning "*profecto*" is the consideration that the idea, "Had I sent thee to the heathen, verily they would hear thee," is in contradiction with the designation of the heathen as those whose language the prophet does not understand. If the heathen spoke a language unintelligible to the prophet, they consequently did not understand his speech, and could not therefore comprehend his preaching. It only remains, then, to apply the sentence simply to the Israelites, "not to heathen nations, but to the Israelites have I sent thee," and to take יִשְׁמְעוּ as potential, "they are able to fear thee," "they can understand thy words." This in ver. 7 is closed by the *antithesis*,

" But the house of Israel will not hear thee, because they will not hear me (Jehovah), as they are morally hardened." With 7*b*, cf. ii. 4. The Lord, however, will provide His prophet with power to resist this obduracy; will lend him unbending courage and unshaken firmness, ver. 8; cf. Jer. xv. 20. He will make his brow hard as adamant (cf. Zech. vii. 12), which is harder than rock; therefore he shall not fear before the obduracy of Israel. צר, as in Ex. iv. 25, = צור. As parallel passages in regard of the subject-matter, cf. Isa. l. 7 and Jer. i. 18.

Vers. 10-15. Prepared then for his vocation, Ezekiel is now transported to the sphere of his activity.—Ver. 10. *And He said to me, Son of man, all my words which I shall speak to thee, take into thy heart, and hear with thine ears.* Ver. 11. *And go to the exiles, to the children of thy people, and speak to them, and say to them, " Thus saith the Lord Jehovah," whether they may hear thee or fail (to hear thee).* Ver. 12. *And a wind raised me up, and I heard behind me the voice of a great tumult, " Praised be the glory of Jehovah," from their place hitherward.* Ver. 13. *And the noise of the wings of the creatures touching each other, and the noise of the wheels beside them, the noise of a great tumult.* Ver. 14. *And a wind raised me up, and took me, and I went thither embittered in the warmth of my spirit; and the hand of Jehovah was strong upon me.* Ver. 15. *And I came to Tel-Abib to the exiles, who dwelled by the river Chebar, and where they sat there sat I down seven days, motionless and dumb, in their midst.*—The apparent *hysteron proteron,* "take into thy heart, and hear with thine ears" (ver. 10), disappears so soon as it is observed that the clause " hear with thine ears" is connected with the following " go to the exiles," etc. The meaning is not, "*postquam auribus tuis percepisses mea mandata, ea ne oblivioni tradas, sed corde suscipe et animo infige*" (Rosenmüller), but this, " All my words which I shall speak to thee lay to heart, that thou mayest obey them. When thou hast heard my words with thine ears, then go to the exiles and announce them to them." With ver. 11 cf. ii. 4, 5. Observe that it is still בְּנֵי עַמֶּךָ, "the children of thy" (not "my") "people." Stiff-necked Israel is no longer Jehovah's people. The command "to go to the people" is, in ver. 12 sqq., immediately executed by the prophet, the wind raising him up and transporting him to Tel-Abib, among the exiles. רוּחַ, phenomenally considered, is a wind of which God makes use to conduct the prophet to the scene of his labour; but the wind is only the sensible substratum of the spirit which transports him thither. The representation is, that "he was borne thither through the air by the wind" (Kliefoth); but not as Jerome and Kliefoth suppose, *in ipso corpore*, *i.e.* so that an actual bodily removal through the air took place, but the raising up and taking away by the wind was effected in spirit in the condition of ecstasy. Not a syllable indicates that the theophany was at an end before this removal; the contrary rather is clearly indicated by the remark that Ezekiel heard behind him the noise of the wings of the cherubim and of the wheels. And that the words תִּשָּׂאֵנִי רוּחַ do not necessitate us to suppose a bodily removal is shown by the comparison with viii. 3, xi. 1, 24, where Kliefoth also understands the same words in a spiritual sense of a merely internal—*i.e.* experienced in a state of ecstasy—removal of the prophet to Jerusalem and back again to Chaldea. The great noise which Ezekiel hears behind him proceeds, at least in part, from the appearance of the כְּבוֹד יְהֹוָה being set in motion, but (according to ver. 13) not in order to remove itself from the raptured prophet, but by changing its present position, to attend the prophet to the sphere of his labour. It tells decidedly in favour of this supposition, that the prophet, according to ver. 23, again sees around him the same theophany in the valley where he begins his work. This reappearance, indeed, presupposes that it had previously disappeared from his sight, but the disappearance is to be supposed as taking place only after his call has been completed, *i.e.* after ver. 21. While being removed in a condition of ecstasy, Ezekiel heard the rushing sound, "Praised be the glory of Jehovah." מִמְּקוֹמוֹ

belongs not to בָּרוּךְ וגו׳, which would yield no appropriate sense, but to אֶשְׁמַע, where it makes no difference of importance in the meaning whether the suffix is referred to יהוה or to כבוד. Ezekiel heard the voice of the praise of God's glory issuing forth from the place where Jehovah or His glory were to be found, *i.e.* where they had appeared to the prophet, not at all from the temple. Who sounded this song of praise is not mentioned. Close by Ezekiel heard the sound, the rustling of the wings of the cherubim setting themselves in motion, and how the wings came into contact with the tips of each other, touched each other (מַשִּׁיקוֹת, from נָשַׁק, "to join," "to touch one another"). Ver. 14 describes the prophet's mood of mind as he is carried away. Raised by the wind, and carried on, he went, *i.e.* drove thither, מַר בַּחֲמַת רוּחַ, "bitter in the heat of his spirit." Although מַר is used as well of grief and mourning as of wrath and displeasure, yet mourning and sorrow are not appropriate to חֵמָה, "warmth of spirit," "anger." The supposition, however, that sorrow as well as anger were in him, or that he was melancholy while displeased (Kliefoth), is incompatible with the fundamental idea of מַר as "sharp," "bitter." Ezekiel feels himself deeply roused, even to the bitterness of anger, partly by the obduracy of Israel, partly by the commission to announce to this obdurate people, without any prospect of success, the word of the Lord. To so heavy a task he feels himself unequal, therefore his natural man rebels against the Spirit of God, which, seizing him with a strong and powerful grasp, tears him away to the place of his work; and he would seek to withdraw himself from the divine call, as Moses and Jonah once did. The hand of the Lord, however, was strong upon him, *i.e.* "held him up in this inner struggle with unyielding power" (Kliefoth); cf. Isa. viii. 11. חָזַק, "firm," "strong," differs from כָּבֵד, "heavy," Ps. xxxii. 4. תֵּל אָבִיב, *i.e.* "the hill of ears," is the name of the place where resided a colony of the exiles. The place was situated on the river Chebar (see on ch. i. 3), and derived its name, no doubt, from the fertility of the valley, rich in grain (הַבִּקְעָה, ver. 23), by which it was surrounded; nothing further, however, is known of it; cf. Gesen. *Thesaur.* p. 1505. The *Chetib* וָאֵשֵׁר, at which the Masoretes and many expositors have unnecessarily taken offence, is to be read וַאֲשֶׁר, and to be joined with the following שָׁם, "where they sat" (so rightly the Chaldee, Syriac, and Vulgate). That this signification would be expressed differently, as Hitzig thinks, cannot be established by means of Job xxxix. 30. The *Keri* וָאֵשֵׁב is not only unnecessary, but also inappropriate, which holds true also of other conjectures of modern expositors. Ezekiel sat there seven days, מַשְׁמִים, *i.e.* neither "deprived of sensation," nor "being silent," but as the *partic. Hiphil* from שָׁמֵם, as מְשׁוֹמֵם in Ezra ix. 3, 4, " rigidly without moving," therefore "motionless and dumb." The seven days are not regarded as a period of mourning, in support of which Job ii. 13 is referred to; but as both the purification and the dedication and preparation for a holy service is measured by the number seven, as being the number of God's works (cf. Ex. xxix. 29 sqq.; Lev. viii. 33 sqq.; 2 Chron. xxix. 17), so Ezekiel sits for a week "motionless and dumb," to master the impression which the word of God, conveyed to him in ecstatic vision, had made upon his mind, and to prepare and sanctify himself for his vocation (Kliefoth).

Vers. 16–21. When these seven days are completed, there comes to him the final word, which appoints him watchman over Israel, and places before him the task and responsibility of his vocation.—Ver. 16. *And it came to pass after the lapse of seven days, that the word of Jehovah came to me as follows:* Ver. 17. *Son of man, I have set thee to be a watchman over the house of Israel; thou shalt hear the word from my mouth, and thou shalt warn them from me* Ver. 18. *If I say to the sinner, Thou shalt surely die, and thou warnest him not, and speakest not to warn the sinner from his evil way that he may live, then shall he, the sinner, die because of his evil deeds, but his blood will I require at thy hand.* Ver. 19. *But if thou warnest the sinner, and he turn not from his wickedness and his evil way, then shall he die because of his evil deeds, but thou hast saved thy soul.* Ver. 20. *And if a righteous man turn from his righteousness, and do unrighteousness, and I lay a stumblingblock before him, then shall he die; if thou hast not warned him, he shall die because of his sin, and his righteousness which he has done shall not be remembered, but his blood will I require at thy hand.* Ver. 21. *But if thou warnest him—the righteous man—so that the righteous man sin not, and he do not sin, then will he live, because he has been warned, and thou hast saved thy soul.*—As a prophet for Israel, Ezekiel is like one standing upon a watchtower (Hab. ii. 1), to watch over the condition of the people, and warn them of the dangers that threaten them (Jer. vi. 17; Isa. lvi. 10). As such, he is responsible for the souls entrusted to his charge. From the mouth of Jehovah, *i.e.* according to God's word, he is to admonish the wicked to turn from their evil ways, that they die not in their sins. מִמֶּנִּי, "from me," *i.e.* in my name, and with my commission. "If I say to the sinner," *i.e.* if I commission thee to say to him (Kimchi). As מוֹת תָּמוּת reminds us of Gen. ii. 17, so is the threatening, "his blood will I require at thy hand," an allusion to Gen. ix. 5. If the prophet does not warn the wicked man, as God has commanded him, he renders himself guilty of a deadly sin, for which God will take vengeance on him as on the murderer for the shedding of blood. An awfully solemn statement for all ministers of the word. הָרִשְׁעָה, in vers. 18 and 19, at which the LXX. have stumbled, so that they have twice omitted it, is not a substantive, and to be changed, with Hitzig, into רִשְׁעָה, but is an adjective, *foemin. gen.*, and belongs to דַּרְכּוֹ, which is construed as feminine. The righteous man who backslides is, before God, regarded as equal with the sinner who persists in his sin, if the former, notwithstanding the warning, perseveres in his backsliding (ver. 20 sqq.). שׁוּב מִצִּדְקוֹ, "to turn oneself from his righteousness," denotes the formal falling away from the path of righteousness, not mere "stumbling or sinning from weakness." עָשָׂה עָוֶל, "to do unrighteousness," "to act perversely," is "*se prorsus dedere impietati*" (Calvin). וְנָתַתִּי מִכְשׁוֹל belongs still to the *protasis*, הוּא יָמוּת forming the *apodosis*, not a relative sentence, — as Ewald and Hitzig suppose,—" so that he, or, in consequence of which, he die." מִכְשׁוֹל, "object of offence," by which any one comes to fall, is not destruction, considered as punishment deserved (Calvin, Hävernick), but everything that God puts in the way of the sinner, in order that the sin, which is germinating in his soul, may come forth to the light, and ripen to maturity. God, indeed, neither causes sin, nor desires the death of the sinner; and in this sense He does not tempt to evil (Jas. i. 13), but He guides and places the sinner in relations in life in which he must come to a decision for or against what is good and divine, and either suppress the sinful lusts of his heart, or burst the barriers which are opposed to their satisfaction. If he does not do the former, but the latter, evil gains within him more and more strength, so that he becomes the servant of sin, and finally reaches a point where conversion is impossible. In this consists the מִכְשׁוֹל, which God places before him, who turns away from righteousness to unrighteousness or evil, but not in this, that God lets man run on in order that he may die or perish. For יָמוּת does not stand for וָמֵת, and there is therefore no ground for a change of punctuation to carry forward *Athnach* to הִזְהַרְתּוֹ (Hitzig). For the subject spoken of is not that the backsliding righteous man " in general only dies if he is not warned" (Hitzig),—that meaning is not in ver. 21, " that he, in contrast to the רָשָׁע, gives sure obedience to the warning," —but only the possibility is supposed that a צַדִּיק, who has transgressed upon the way of evil, will yield obedience to the warning, but not that he will of a certainty do this. As with the רָשָׁע in ver. 19, only the case of his resisting the warning is expressly mentioned; while the opposite case—that he may, in consequence of the warning, be converted—is not excluded; so in ver. 21, with the צַדִּיק, who has entered upon the path of unrighteousness, only the case of conversion in consequence of the warning is expressly mentioned, without the possibility of his hardening himself against the prophet's word being thereby excluded. For the instruction of the prophet it was sufficient to bring forward the two cases mentioned, as it appears from them that in the one case as well as in the other he has done his duty, and saved his soul.

CHAP. III. 22–V. 17. THE DESTINY OF JERUSALEM AND ITS INHABITANTS.

Vers. 22–27 in ch. iii. no longer belong to the prophet's inauguration and introduction into office, nor do they form the conclusion of his call, but the introduction to his first prophetic act and prediction, as has been rightly recognised by Ewald and Kliefoth. This appears already from the introductory formula, "The hand of Jehovah came upon me" (ver. 22), and, more distinctly still, from the glory of Jehovah appearing anew to the prophet (when, in obedience to a divine impulse, he had gone down into the valley), in the form in which he had seen it by the river Chebar, and giving him a commission to announce by word and symbol the siege of Jerusalem, and the fate of its inhabitants. For, that the divine commission did not consist merely in the general directions, ch. iii. 25–27, but is first given in its principal parts in ch. iv. and v., is indisputably evident from the repetition of the words וְאַתָּה בֶן־אָדָם in ch. iii. 25, iv. 1, and v. 1. With וְאַתָּה neither can the first nor, in general, a new prophecy begin. This has been recognised by Hitzig himself in ch. iv. 1, where he remarks that the first of the three oracles which follow down to viii. 1, and which he makes begin with iv. 1, "attaches itself to ch. iii. 25–27 as a continuation of the same." But what holds true of iv. 1 must hold true also of iii. 25, viz. that no new oracle can begin with this verse, but that it is connected with iii. 22–24. The commencement, then, we have to seek in the formula, "and the hand of Jehovah came upon me" (iii. 22), with which also viii. 1 (where only וַתְּהִי stands instead of וַיְהִי) and xl. 1—new oracles—are introduced. No doubt these passages are preceded by chronological notices, while in iii. 22 every note of time is wanting. But nothing further can be inferred from this, than that the divine word contained in iii. 25–v. 17 was imparted to the prophet immediately after his consecration and call, so that it still falls under the date of ch. i. 2; which may also be discovered from this, that the שָׁם in ver. 22 points to the locality named in ver. 15.

Immediately after his call, then, and still in the same place where the last word of calling (iii. 16-21) was addressed to him, namely, at Tel-Abib, in the midst of the exiles, Ezekiel received the first divine revelation which, as prophet, he was to announce to the people. This revelation is introduced by the words in ch. iii. 22-24; and divided into three sections by the thrice-occurring, similar address, "And thou, son of man" (iii. 25, iv. 1, v. 1). In the first section, ch. iii. 25-27, God gives him general injunctions as to his conduct while carrying out the divine commission; in the second, ch. iv., He commands him to represent symbolically the siege of Jerusalem with its miseries; and in the third, ch. v., the destiny of the inhabitants after the capture of the city.

Chap. iii. 22-27. Introduction to the first prophetic announcement.—Ver. 22. *And there came upon me there the hand of Jehovah, and He said to me, Up! go into the valley, there will I speak to thee.* Ver. 23. *And I arose, and went into the valley: and, lo, there stood the glory of Jehovah, like the glory which I had seen at the river Chebar: and I fell upon my face.* Ver. 24. *And spirit came into me, and placed me on my feet, and He spake with me, and said to me, Go, and shut thyself in thy house.*—הַבִּקְעָה is, without doubt, the valley situated near Tel-Abib. Ezekiel is to go out from the midst of the exiles—where, according to ver. 15, he had found himself—into the valley, because God will reveal Himself to him only in solitude.

When he had complied with this command, there appears to him there the glory of Jehovah, in the same form in which it had appeared to him at the Chaboras (i. 4–28); before it he falls, a second time, on his face; but is also, as on the first occasion, again raised to his feet, cf. i. 28–ii. 2. Hereupon the Lord commands him to shut himself up in his house,— which doubtless he inhabited in Tel-Abib,—not probably " as a sign of his future destiny," as a realistic explanation of the words, " Thou canst not walk in their midst (ver. 25); they will prevent thee by force from freely exercising thy vocation in the midst of the people." For in that case the " shutting of himself up in the house" would be an arbitrary identification with the " binding with fetters" (ver. 25); and besides, the significance of the address וְאַתָּה בֶן־אָדָם, and its repetition in iv. 1 and v. 1, would be misconceived. For as in iv. 1 and v. 1 there are introduced with this address the principal parts of the duty which Ezekiel was to perform, so the proper divine instruction may also first begin with the same in iii. 25; consequently the command " to shut himself up in his house" can only have the significance of a preliminary divine injunction, without possessing any significancy in itself; but only " serve as a means for carrying out what the prophet is commissioned to do in the following chapters" (Kliefoth), *i.e.* can only mean that he is to perform in his own house what is commanded him in ch. iv. and v., or that he is not to leave his house during their performance. More can hardly be sought in this injunction, nor can it at all be taken to mean that, having shut himself up from others in his house, he is to allow no one to approach him; but only that he is not to leave his dwelling. For, according to iv. 3, the symbolical representation of the siege of Jerusalem is to be a sign for the house of Israel; and according to iv. 12, Ezekiel is, during this symbolical action, to bake his bread before their eyes. From this it is seen that his contemporaries might come to him and observe his proceedings.

Vers. 25-27. The general divine instructions.—Ver. 25. *And thou, son of man, lo, they will lay cords upon thee, and bind thee therewith, so that thou canst not go out into their midst.* Ver. 26. *And I shall make thy tongue cleave to thy palate, that thou mayest be dumb, and mayest not serve them as a reprover: for they are a stiff-necked generation.* Ver. 27. *But when I speak to thee, I will open thy mouth, that thou mayest say to them, Thus sayeth the Lord Jehovah, Let him who wishes to hear, hear, and let him who neglects, neglect (to hear): for they are a stiff necked generation.*—The meaning of this general injunction depends upon the determination of the subject in נָתְנוּ, ver. 25. Most expositors think of the prophet's countrymen, who are to bind him with cords so that he shall not be able to leave his house. The words וְלֹא תֵצֵא בְּתוֹכָם appear to support this, as the suffix in בְּתוֹכָם indisputably refers to his countrymen. But this circumstance is by no means decisive; while against this view is the twofold difficulty,—firstly, that a binding of the prophet with cords by his countrymen is scarcely reconcilable with what he performs in ch. iv. and v.; secondly, of hostile attacks by the exiles upon the prophet there is not a trace to be discovered in the entire remainder of the book. The house of Israel is indeed repeatedly described as a stiff-necked race, as hardened and obdurate towards God's word; but any embitterment of feeling against the prophet, which should have risen so far as to bind him, or even to make direct attempts to prevent him from exercising his prophetic calling, can, after what is related in xxxiii. 30-33 regarding the position of the people towards him, hardly be imagined. Further, the binding and fettering of the prophet is to be regarded as of the same kind with the cleaving of his tongue to his jaws, so that he should be silent and not speak (ver. 26). It is God, however, who suspends this dumbness over him; and according to iv. 8, it is also God who binds him with cords, so that he cannot stir from one side to the other. The demonstrative power of the latter passage is not to be weakened by the objection that it is a passage of an altogether different kind, and the connection altogether different (Hävernick). For the complete difference between the two passages would first have to be proved. The object, indeed, of the binding of the prophet in iv. 8 is different from that in our verse. Here it is to render it impossible for the prophet to go out of the house; in iv. 8, it is to prevent him from moving from one side to the other. But the one object does not exclude the other; both statements coincide, rather, in the general thought that the prophet must adapt himself entirely to the divine will,—not only not leave the house, but lie also for 390 days upon one side without turning.—We might rather, with Kliefoth, understand iv. 8 to mean that God accomplished the binding of the prophet by human instruments—viz. that He caused him to be bound by foreigners (iii. 25). But this supposition also would only be justified, if either the sense of the words in iii. 25, or other good reasons, pronounced in favour of the view that it was the exiles who had bound the prophet. But as this is not the case, so we are not at liberty to explain the definite נָתַתִּי, "I lay on" (iv. 8), according to the indefinite נָתְנוּ, "they lay on," or "one lays on" (iii. 25); but must, on the contrary, understand our verse in accordance with iv. 8, and (with Hitzig) think of heavenly powers as the subject to נָתְנוּ,—as in Job vii. 3; Dan. iv. 28; Luke xii. 20,—without, in so doing, completely identifying the declaration in our verse with that in iv. 8, as if in the latter passage only that was brought to completion which had been here (iii. 25) predicted. If, however, the binding of the prophet proceeds from invisible powers, the expression is not to be understood literally,—of a binding with material cords;—but God binds him by a spiritual power, so that he can neither leave his house nor go forth to his countrymen, nor, at a later time (iv. 8), change the position prescribed to him. This is done, however, not to prevent the exercise of his vocation, but, on the contrary, to make him fitted for the successful performance of the work commanded him. He is not to quit his house, nor enter into fellowship and intercourse with his exiled countrymen, that he may show himself, by separation from them, to be a prophet and organ of the Lord. On the same grounds he is also (vers. 26, 27) to keep silence, and not even correct them with words, but only to speak when God opens his mouth for that purpose; to remain, moreover, unconcerned whether they listen to his words or not (cf. ii. 4, 7). He is to do both of these things, because his contemporaries are a stiff-necked race; cf. ver. 9 and ii. 5, 7. That he may not speak from any impulse of his own, God will cause his tongue to cleave to his jaws, so that he cannot speak; cf. Ps. cxxxvii. 6. "That the prophet is to refrain from all speech—even from the utterance of the words given him by God—will, on the one hand, make the divine words which he utters appear the more distinctly as such; while, on the other, be an evidence to his hearers of the silent sorrow with which he is filled by the contents of the divine word, and with which they also ought justly to be filled" (Kliefoth).

This state of silence, according to which he is only then to speak when God opened his mouth for the utterance of words which were to be given him, is, indeed, at first imposed upon the prophet—as follows from the relation of vers. 25–27 to ch. iv. and v.—only for the duration of the period ch. iii. 25 to v. 17, or rather vii. 27. But the divine injunction extends, as Kliefoth has rightly recognised, still further on — over the whole period up to the fulfilment of his prophecies of threatening by the destruction of Jerusalem. This appears especially from this, that in xxiv. 27 and xxxiii. 22 there is an undeniable reference to the silence imposed upon him in our verse, and with reference to which it is said, that when the messenger should bring back the news of the fall of Jerusalem, his mouth should be opened and he should be no longer dumb. The reference in xxiv. 27 and in xxxiii. 22 to the verse before us has been observed by most expositors; but several of them would limit the silence of the prophet merely to the time which lies between ch. xxiv. and xxxiii. 21 sqq. This is quite arbitrary, as neither in ch. xxiv. nor in ch. xxxiii. is silence imposed upon him; but in both chapters it is only stated that he should no longer be dumb after the receipt of the intelligence that Jerusalem had been destroyed by the Chaldeans. The supposition of Schmieder, moreover, is untenable, that the injunction of ver. 25 refers to the turning-point in the prophet's office, which commenced on the day when the siege of Jerusalem actually began. For although this day forms a turning-point in the prophetic activity of Ezekiel, in so far as he on it announced to the people for the last time the destruction of Jerusalem, and then spake no more to Israel until the occurrence of this event, yet it is not said in xxiv. 27 that he was then to be dumb from that day onwards. The hypothesis then only remains, that what was imposed and enjoined on the prophet, in vers. 26 and 27, should remain in force for the whole period from the commencement of his prophetic activity to the receipt of the news of the fall of Jerusalem, by the arrival of a messenger on the banks of the Chaboras. Therewith is also connected the position of this injunction at the head of the first prophecy delivered to him (not at his call), if only the contents and importance of this oracle be understood and recognised, that it embraces not merely the siege of Jerusalem, but also the capture and destruction of the city, and the dispersion of the people among the heathen,—consequently contains *in nuce* all that Ezekiel had to announce to the people down to the occurrence of this calamity, and which, in all the divine words from ch. vi. to ch. xxiv., he had again and again, though only in different ways, actually announced. If all the discourses down to ch. xxiv. are only further expositions and attestations of the revelation of God in ch. iv. and v., then the behaviour which was enjoined on him at the time of this announcement was to be maintained during all following discourses of similar contents. Besides, for a correct appreciation of the divine precept in vers. 26 and 27, it is also to be noticed that the prophet is not to keep entire silence, except when God inspires him to speak; but that his keeping silence is explained to mean, that he is to be to his contemporaries no אִישׁ מוֹכִיחַ, "no reprover," and consequently will place their sins before them to no greater extent, and in no other way, than God expressly directs him. Understood in this way, the silence is in contradiction neither with the words of God communicated in ch. vi. to xxiv., nor with the predictions directed against foreign nations in ch. xxv.–xxxiii., several of which fall within the time of the siege of Jerusalem. Cf. with this the remark upon xxiv. 27 and xxxiii. 22.

Chap. iv. THE SIGN OF THE SIEGE OF JERUSALEM.—This sign, which Ezekiel is to perform in his own house before the eyes of the exiles who visit him, consists in three inter-connected and mutually-supplementary symbolical acts, the first of which is described in vers. 1–3, the second in vers. 4–8, and the third in vers. 9–17. In the first place, he is symbolically to represent the impending siege of Jerusalem (vers. 1-3); in the second place, by lying upon one side, he is to announce the punishment of Israel's sin (vers. 4-8); in the third place, by the nature of his food, he is, while lying upon one side, to hold forth to view the terrible consequences of the siege to Israel. The close connection as to their subject-matter of these three actions appears clearly from this, that the prophet, according to ver. 7, while lying upon one side, is to direct his look and his arm upon the picture of the besieged city before him; and, according to ver. 8, is to lie upon his side as long as the siege lasts, and during that time is to nourish himself in the manner prescribed in ver. 9 sqq. In harmony with this is the formal division of the chapter, inasmuch as the three acts, which the prophet is to perform for the purpose of portraying the impending siege of Jerusalem, are co-ordinated to each other by the repetition of the address וְאַתָּה in vers. 3, 4, and 8, and subordinated to the general injunction—to portray Jerusalem as a besieged city—introduced in ver. 1 with the words וְאַתָּה בֶן אָדָם.

Vers. 1–3. The first symbolical action.—Ver. 1. *And thou, son of man, take to thyself a brick, and lay it before thee, and draw thereon a city, Jerusalem:* Ver. 2. *And direct a siege against it; build against it siege-towers, raise up a mound against it, erect camps against it, and place battering-rams against it round about.* Ver. 3. *And thou, take to thyself an iron pan, and place it as an iron wall between thee and the city, and direct thy face towards it; thus let it be in a state of siege, and besiege it. Let it be a sign to the house of Israel.*

The directions in vers. 1 and 2 contain the general basis for the symbolical siege of Jerusalem, which the prophet is to lay before Israel as a sign. Upon a brick he is to sketch a city (חָקַק, to engrave with a writing instrument) which is to represent Jerusalem: around the city he is to erect siege-works—towers, walls, camps, and battering-rams; *i.e.* he is to inscribe the representation of them, and place before himself the picture of the besieged city. The selection of a brick, *i.e.* of a tile-stone, not burnt in a kiln, but merely dried in the sun, is not, as Hävernick supposes, a reminiscence of Babylon and monumental inscriptions; in Palestine, also, such bricks were a common building material (Isa. ix. 9), in consequence of which the selection of such a soft mass of clay, on which a picture might be easily inscribed, was readily suggested. נָתַן מָצוֹר = שׂוּם מָצוֹר, Mic. iv. 14, " to make a siege," *i.e.* " to bring forward siege-works." מָצוֹר is therefore the general expression which is specialized in the following clauses by דָּיֵק, " siege-towers " (see on 2 Kings xxv. 1); by סֹלְלָה, " mound " (see on 2 Sam. xx. 15); מַחֲנוֹת, " camps " in the plural, because the hostile army raises several camps around the city; כָּרִים, " battering-rams," " wall-breakers," *arietes;* according to Joseph Kimchi, " iron rams," to break in the walls (and gates, xxi. 27). They consisted of strong beams of hard wood, furnished at the end with a ram's head made of iron, which were suspended by a chain, and driven forcibly against the wall by the soldiers. Compare the description of them by Josephus, *de bello Judaico* iii. 7. 19. The suffix in עָלֶיהָ, in ver. 2, refers to עִיר. The siege-works which are named were not probably to be placed by Ezekiel as little figures around the brick, so that the latter would represent the city, but to be engraved upon the brick around the city thereon portrayed. The expressions, "to *make* a siege," "to *build* towers," "to erect a mound," etc., are selected because the drawing was to represent what is done when a city is besieged. In ver. 3, in reference to this, the inscribed picture of the city is at once termed "city," and in ver. 7 the picture of the besieged Jerusalem, "the siege of Jerusalem." The meaning of the picture is clear. Every one who saw it was to recognise that Jerusalem will be besieged. But the prophet is to do still more; he is to take in hand the siege itself, and to carry it out. To that end, he is to place an iron pan as an iron wall between himself and the city sketched on the brick, and direct his countenance stedfastly towards the city (הֲכִין), and so besiege it. The iron pan, erected as a wall, is to represent neither the wall of the city (Ewald) nor the enemies' rampart, for this was already depicted on the brick; while to represent it, *i.e.* the city wall, as "iron," *i.e.* immoveably fast, would be contrary to the meaning of the prophecy. The iron wall represents, as Rosenmüller, after the hints of Theodoret, Cornelius a Lapide, and others, has already observed, a firm, impregnable wall of partition, which the prophet as messenger and representative of God is to raise between himself and the beleaguered city, *ut significaret, quasi ferreum murum interjectum esse cives inter et se*, i.e. *Deum Deique decretum et sententiam contra illos latam esse irrevocabilem, nec Deum civium preces et querimonias auditurum aut iis ad misericordiam flectendum*. Cf. Isa lix. 2; Lam. iii. 44. מַחֲבַת, "pan," *i.e.* an iron plate for baking their loaves and slices of cakes; see on Lev. ii. 5. The selection of such an iron plate for the purpose mentioned is not to be explained, as Kliefoth thinks, from the circumstance that the pan is primarily to serve the prophet for preparing his food while he is occupied in completing his sketch. The text says nothing of that. If he were to have employed the pan for such a purpose, he could not, at the same time, have placed it as a wall between himself and the city. The choice is to be explained simply from this, that such a plate was to be found in every household, and was quite fitted for the object intended. If any other symbolical element is contained in it, the hard ignoble metal might, perhaps, with Grotius, be taken to typify the hard, wicked heart of the inhabitants of Jerusalem; cf. xxii. 18; Jer. xv. 12. The symbolical siege of Jerusalem is to be a sign for the house of Israel, *i.e.* a pre-announcement of its impending destiny. The house of Israel is the whole covenant people, not merely the ten tribes as in ver. 5, in contradistinction to the house of Judah (ver. 6).

Vers. 4–8. The second symbolical act.—Ver. 4. *And do thou lay thyself upon thy left side, and lay upon it the evil deeds of the house of Israel; for the number of the days during which thou liest thereon shalt thou bear their evil deeds.* Ver. 5. *And I reckon to thee the years of their evil deeds as a number of days; three hundred and ninety days shalt thou bear the evil deeds of the house of Israel.* Ver. 6. *And (when) thou hast completed these, thou shalt then lay thyself a second time upon thy right side, and bear the evil deeds of the house of Judah forty days; each day I reckon to thee as a year.* Ver. 7. *And upon the siege of Jerusalem shalt thou stedfastly direct thy countenance, and thy naked arm, and shalt prophesy against it.* Ver. 8. *And, lo, I lay cords upon thee, that thou stir not from one side to the other until thou hast ended the days of thy siege.*—Whilst Ezekiel, as as God's representative, carries out in a symbolical manner the siege of Jerusalem, he is in this situation to portray at the same time the destiny of the people of Israel beleaguered in their metropolis. Lying upon his left side for 390 days without turning, he is to bear the guilt of Israel's sin; then, lying 40 days more upon his right side, he is to bear the guilt of Judah's sin. In so doing, the number of the *days* during which he reclines upon his sides shall be accounted as exactly equal to the same number of *years* of their sinning. נְשׂא עָוֹן, "to bear the evil deeds," *i.e.* to take upon himself the consequence of sin, and to atone for them, to suffer the punishment of sin; cf. Num. xiv. 34, etc. Sin, which produces guilt and punishment, is regarded as a burden or weight, which Ezekiel is to lay upon the side upon which he reclines, and in this way bear it. This bearing, however, of the guilt of sin is not to be viewed as vicarious and mediatorial, as in the sacrifice of atonement, but is intended as purely epideictic and symbolical; that is to say, Ezekiel, by his lying so long bound under the burden of Israel and Judah which was laid upon his side, is to show to the people how they are to be cast down by the siege of Jerusalem, and how, while lying on the ground, without the possibility of turning or rising, they are to bear the punishment of their sins. The full understanding of this symbolical act, however, depends upon the explanation of the specified periods of time, with regard to which the various views exhibit great discrepancy.

In the first place, the separation of the guilt into that of the house of Israel and that of the house of Judah is closely connected with the division of the covenant people into the two kingdoms of Israel and Judah. That Ezekiel now is to bear the sin of Israel upon the left, that of Judah on the right side, is not fully explained by the circumstance that the kingdom of the ten tribes lay to the left, *i.e.* to the north, the kingdom of Judah to the right, *i.e.* to the south of Jerusalem, but must undoubtedly point at the same time to the pre-eminence of Judah over Israel; cf. Eccles. x. 2. This pre-eminence of Judah is manifestly exhibited in its period of punishment extending only to 40 days = 40 years; that of Israel, on the contrary, 390 days = 390 years. These numbers, however, cannot be satisfactorily explained from a chronological point of view, whether they be referred to the time during which Israel and Judah sinned, and heaped upon themselves guilt which was to be punished, or to the time during which they were to atone, or suffer punishment for their sins. Of themselves, both references are possible; the first, viz. in so far as the days in which Ezekiel is to bear the guilt of Israel, might be proportioned to the number of the years of their guilt, as many Rabbins, Vatablus, Calvin, Lightfoot, Vitringa, J. D. Michaelis, and others suppose, while in so doing the years are calculated very differently; cf. des Vignoles, *Chronol.* I. p. 479 sqq., and Rosenmüller, *Scholia, Excurs.* to ch. iv. All these hypotheses, however, are shattered by the impossibility of pointing out the specified periods of time, so as to harmonize with the chronology. If the days, reckoned as years, correspond to the duration of their sinning, then, in the case of the house of Israel, only the duration of this kingdom could come into consideration, as the period of punishment began with the captivity of the ten tribes. But this kingdom lasted only 253 years. The remaining 137 years the Rabbins have attempted to supply from the period of the Judges; others, from the time of the destruction of the ten tribes down to that of Ezekiel, or even to that of the destruction of Jerusalem. Both are altogether arbitrary. Still less can the 40 years of Judah be calculated, as all the determinations of the beginning and the end are mere phantoms of the air. The fortieth year before our prophecy would nearly coincide with the eighteenth year of Josiah's reign, and therefore with the year in which this pious king effected the reformation of religion. Ezekiel, however, could not represent this year as marking the commencement of Judah's sin. We must therefore, as the literal meaning of the words primarily indicates, regard the specified periods of time as periods of punishment for Israel and Judah. Since Ezekiel, then, had to maintain during the symbolical siege of Jerusalem this attitude of reclining for Israel and Judah, and after the completion of the 390 days for Israel must lie a second time (יִשְׂרָאֵל, ver. 6) 40 days for Judah, he had to recline in all 430 (390 + 40) days. To include the *forty* days in the *three hundred and ninety* is contrary to the statements in the text. But to reckon the two periods *together* has not only no argument against it, but is even suggested by the circumstance that the prophet, while reclining on his left and right sides, is to represent the siege of Jerusalem. Regarded, however, as periods of punishment, both the numbers cannot be explained consistently with the chronology, but must be understood as having a symbolical signification. The space of 430 years, which is announced to both kingdoms together as the duration of their chastisement, recalls the 430 years which in the far past Israel had spent in Egypt in bondage (Ex. xii. 40). It had been already intimated to Abraham (Gen. xv. 13) that the sojourn in Egypt would be a period of servitude and humiliation for his seed; and at a later time, in consequence of the oppression which the Israelites then experienced on account of the rapid increase of their number, it was—upon the basis of the threat in Deut. xxviii. 68, that God would punish Israel for their persistent declension, by bringing them back into ignominious bondage in Egypt—taken by the prophet as a type of the banishment of rebellious Israel among the *heathen*. In this sense Hosea already threatens (viii. 13, ix. 3, 6) the ten tribes with being carried back to Egypt; see on Hos. ix. 3. Still more frequently, upon the basis of this conception, is the redemption from Assyrian and Babylonian exile announced as a new and miraculous exodus of Israel from the bondage of Egypt, *e.g.* Hos. ii. 2; Isa. xi. 15, 16.—This typical meaning lies also at the foundation of the passage before us, as, in accordance with the statement of Jerome,[1] it was already accepted by the Jews of his time, and has been again recognised in

---

[1] *Alii vero et maxime Judaei a secundo anno Vespasiani, quando Hierusalem a Romanis capta templumque subversum est, supputari volunt in tribulatione et angustia et captivitatis jugo populi constitui annos quadringentos*

modern times by Hävernick and Hitzig. That Ezekiel looked upon the period during which Israel had been subject to the heathen in the past as " typical of the future, is to be assumed, because only then does the number of 430 cease to be arbitrary and meaningless, and at the same time its division into 390 + 40 become explicable."—Hitzig. This latter view is not, of course, to be understood as Hitzig and Hävernick take it, *i.e.* as if the 40 years of Judah's chastisement were to be viewed apart from the 40 years' sojourn of the Israelites in the wilderness, upon which the look of the prophet would have been turned by the sojourn in Egypt. For the 40 years in the wilderness are not included in the 430 years of the Egyptian sojourn, so that Ezekiel could have reduced these 430 years to 390, and yet have added to them the 40 years of the desert wanderings. For the coming period of punishment, which is to commence for Israel with the siege of Jerusalem, is fixed at 430 years with reference to the Egyptian bondage of the Israelites, and this period is divided into 390 and 40; and this division therefore must also have, if not its point of commencement, at least a point of connection, in the 430 years of the Egyptian sojourn. The division of the period of chastisement into two parts is to be explained probably from the sending of the covenant people into the kingdom of Israel and Judah, and the appointment of a longer period of chastisement for Israel than for Judah, from the greater guilt of the ten tribes in comparison with Judah, but not the incommensurable relation of the divisions into 390 and 40 years. The foundation of this division can, first of all, only lie in this, that the number *forty* already possessed the symbolical significance of a measured period of divine visitation. This significance it had already received, not through the 40 years of the desert wandering, but through the 40 days of rain at the time of the deluge (Gen. vii. 17), so that, in conformity

triginta, et sic redire populum ad pristinum statum ut quomodo filii Israel 430 *annis fuerunt in Aegypto, sic in eodem numero finiatur: scriptumque esse in* Ex. xii. 40.—HIERONYMUS.

with this, the punishment of dying in the wilderness, suspended over the rebellious race of Israel at Kadesh, is already stated at 40 years, although it included in reality only 38 years; see on Num. xiv. 32 sqq. If now, however, it should be supposed that this penal sentence had contributed to the fixing of the number 40 as a symbolical number to denote a longer period of punishment, the 40 years of punishment for Judah could not yet have been viewed apart from this event. The fixing of the chastisement for Israel and Judah at 390 + 40 years could only in that case be measured by the sojourn of the Israelites in Egypt, if the relations of this sojourn presented a point of connection for a division of the 430 years into 390 and 40, *i.e.* if the 40 last years of the Egyptian servitude could somehow be distinguished from the preceding 390. A point of contact for this is offered by an event in the life of Moses which falls within that period, and was fertile in results for him as well as for the whole of Israel, viz. his flight from Egypt in consequence of the slaughter of an Egyptian who had ill-treated an Israelite. As the Israelites, his brethren, did not recognise the meaning of this act, and did not perceive that God would save them by his hand, Moses was necessitated to flee into the land of Midian, and to tarry there 40 years as a stranger, until the Lord called him to be the saviour of his nation, and sent him as His messenger to Pharaoh (Ex. ii. 11–iii. 10; Acts vii. 23–30). These 40 years were for Moses not only a time of trial and purification for his future vocation, but undoubtedly also the period of severest Egyptian oppression for the Israelites, and in this respect quite fitted to be a type of the coming time of punishment for Judah, in which was to be repeated what Israel had experienced in Egypt, that, as Israel had lost their helper and protector with the flight of Moses, so now Judah was to lose her king, and be given over to the tyranny of the heathen world-power.[1]

---

[1] Another ingenious explanation of the numbers in question has been attempted by Kliefoth, *Comment.* p. 123. Proceeding from the symbolical

While Ezekiel thus reclines upon one side, he is to direct his look unchangingly upon the siege of Jerusalem, *i.e.* upon the picture of the besieged city, and keep his arm bare, *i.e.* ready for action (Isa. lii. 10), and outstretched, and prophesy against the city, especially through the menacing attitude which he had taken up against it. To be able to carry this out, God will bind him with cords, *i.e.* fetter him to his couch (see on iii. 25), so that he cannot stir from one side to another until he has completed the time enjoined upon him for the siege. In this is contained the thought that the siege of Jeru-

signification of the number 40 as a measure of time for divine visitation and trial, he supposes that the prescription in Deut. xxv. 3—that if an Israelite were to be subjected to corporal punishment, he was not to receive more than 40 stripes—is founded upon this symbolical signification,—a prescription which, according to 2 Cor. xi. 24, was in practice so carried out that only 39 were actually inflicted. From the application and bearing thus given to the number 40, the symbolical numbers in the passage before us are to be explained. Every year of punishment is equivalent to a stripe of chastisement. To the house of Israel 10×39 years = stripes, were adjudged, *i.e.* to each of the ten tribes 39 years = stripes; the individual tribes are treated as so many single individuals, and each receives the amount of chastisement usual in the case of one individual. Judah, on the contrary, is regarded as the one complete historical national tribe, because in the two faithful tribes of Judah and Benjamin the people collectively were represented. Judah, then, may receive, not the number of stripes falling to individuals, but that only which fell upon one, although, as a fair compensation, not the usual number of 40, but the higher number— compatible with the Torah—of 40 stripes = years. To this explanation we would give our assent, if only the transformation into stripes or blows of the days of the prophet's reclining, or of the years of Israel's punishment, could be shown to be probable through any analogous *Biblical* example, and were not merely a deduction from the modern law of punishment, in which corporal punishment and imprisonment hold the same importance. The assumption, then, is altogether arbitrary irrespective of this, that in the case of the house of Israel the measure of punishment is fixed differently from that of Judah; in the former case, according to the number of the tribes; in the latter, according to the unity of the kingdom: in the former at 39, in the latter at 40 stripes. Finally, the presupposition that the later Jewish practice of inflicting only 39 instead of 40 stripes—in order not to transgress the letter of the law in the enumeration which probably was made at the infliction of the punishment—goes back to the time of the exile, is extremely improbable, as it altogether breathes the spirit of Pharisaic micrology.

salem is to be mentally carried on until its capture; but no new symbol of the state of prostration of the besieged Jerusalem is implied. For such a purpose the food of the prophet (ver. 9 sqq.) during this time is employed.

Vers. 9–17. The third symbolical act.—Ver. 9. *And do thou take to thyself wheat, and barley, and beans, and lentiles, and millet, and spelt, and put them in a vessel, and prepare them as bread for thyself, according to the number of the days on which thou liest on thy side; three hundred and ninety days shalt thou eat it.* Ver. 10. *And thy food, which thou eatest, shall be according to weight, twenty shekels for a day; from time to time shalt thou eat it.* Ver. 11. *And water shalt thou drink according to measure, a sixth part of the hin, from time to time shalt thou drink it.* Ver. 12. *And as barley cakes shalt thou eat it, and shalt bake it before their eyes with human excrement.* Ver. 13. *And Jehovah spake; then shall the children of Israel eat their bread polluted amongst the heathen, whither I shall drive them.* Ver. 14. *Then said I: Ah! Lord, Jehovah, my soul has never been polluted; and of a carcase, and of that which is torn, have I never eaten from my youth up until now, and abominable flesh has not come into my mouth.* Ver. 15. *Then said He unto me: Lo, I allow thee the dung of animals instead of that of man; therewith mayest thou prepare thy bread.* Ver. 16. *And He said to me, Son of man, lo, I will break the staff of bread in Jerusalem, so that they will eat bread according to weight, and in affliction, and drink water by measure, and in amazement.* Ver. 17. *Because bread and water shall fail, and they shall pine away one with another, and disappear in their guilt.*—For the whole duration of the symbolical siege of Jerusalem, Ezekiel is to furnish himself with a store of grain corn and leguminous fruits, to place this store in a vessel beside him, and daily to prepare in the form of bread a measured portion of the same, 20 shekels in weight (about 9 ounces), and to bake this as barley cakes upon a fire, prepared with dried dung, and then to partake of it at the different hours for meals throughout the day. In addition to this, he is, at the hours appointed for eating, to drink water, in like manner according to measure, a sixth part of the hin daily, *i.e.* a quantity less than a pint (cf. *Biblisch. Archäol.* II. p. 141). The Israelites, probably, *generally* prepared the עֻגָּה from wheat flour, and not merely when they had guests (Gen. xviii. 6). Ezekiel, however, is to take, in addition, other kinds of grain with leguminous fruits, which were employed in the preparation of bread when wheat was deficient; barley—baked into bread by the poor (Judg. vii. 13; 2 Kings iv. 42; John vi. 9; see on 1 Kings v. 8); פּוֹל, "beans," a common food of the Hebrews (2 Sam. xvii. 28), which appears to have been mixed with other kinds of grain for the purpose of being baked into bread.[1] This especially holds true of the lentiles, a favourite food of the Hebrews (Gen. xxv. 29 sq.), from which, in Egypt at the present day, the poor still bake bread in times of severe famine (Sonnini, *R.* II. 390; ἄρτος φάκινος, *Athenaeus,* IV. 158). דֹּחַן, "millet," termed by the Arabs "*Dochn*" (دخن), *panicum*, a fruit cultivated in Egypt, and still more frequently in Arabia (see Wellsted, *Arab.* I. 295), consisting of longish round brown grain, resembling rice, from which, in the absence of better fruits, a sort of bad bread is baked. Cf. Celsius, *Hierobotan,* i. 453 sqq.; and Gesen. *Thesaur.* p. 333. כֻּסְּמִים, "spelt or German corn" (cf. Ex. ix. 32), a kind of grain which produces a finer and whiter flour than wheat flour; the bread, however, which is baked from it is somewhat dry, and is said to be less nutritive than wheat bread; cf. Celsius, *Hierobotan,* ii. 98 sq. Of all these fruits Ezekiel is to place certain quantities in a vessel—to indicate that all kinds of grain and leguminous fruits capable of being converted into bread will be collected, in order to bake bread for the appeasing of hunger. In the intermixture of various kinds of flour we are not, with Hitzig, to seek a transgression of the

---

[1] Cf. Plinii *Histor. Natur.* xviii. 30: "*Inter legumina maximus honos fabae, quippe ex qua tentatus sit etiam panis ... Frumento etiam miscetur apud plerasque gentes et maxime panico solida ac delicatius fracta.*"

law in Lev. xix. 19; Deut. xxii. 9. מִסְפָּר is the accusative of measure or duration. The quantity is to be fixed according to the number of the days. In ver. 9 only the 390 days of the house of Israel's period of punishment are mentioned—*quod plures essent et fere universa summa* (Prado); and because this was sufficient to make prominent the hardship and oppression of the situation, the 40 days of Judah were omitted for the sake of brevity.[1] כְּמַאֲכָלְךָ וגו׳, "thy food which thou shalt eat," *i.e.* the definite portion which thou shalt have to eat, shall be according to weight (between subject and predicate the substantive verb is to be supplied). Twenty shekels = 8 or 9 ounces of flour, yield 11 or 12 ounces of bread, *i.e.* at most the half of what a man needs in southern countries for his daily support.[2] The same is the case with the water. A sixth part of a hin, *i.e.* a quantity less than a pint, is a very niggardly allowance for a day. Both, however,—eating the

---

[1] Kliefoth's supposition is untenable, that what is required in vers. 9–17 refers in reality only to the 390 days of Israel, and not also to the 40 days of Judah, so that so long as Ezekiel lay and bore the sins of Israel, he was to eat his food by measure, and unclean. For this is in contradiction with the distinct announcement that during the whole time that he lay upon the one side and the other, he was besieging Jerusalem; and by the scanty and unclean food, was to portray both the deficiency of bread and water which occurred in the besieged city (ver. 17), as well as the eating of unclean bread, which impended over the Israelites when among the heathen nations. The famine which took place in Jerusalem during the siege did not affect the ten tribes, but that of Judah; while unclean bread had to be eaten among the heathen not only by the Israelites, but also by the Jews transported to Babylon. By the limitation of what is prescribed to the prophet in vers. 9–15 to the time during which the sin of Israel was to be borne, the significance of this symbolical act for Jerusalem and Judah is taken away.

[2] In our climate (Germany) we count 2 lbs. of bread for the daily supply of a man; but in warm countries the demand for food is less, so that scarcely 1½ lbs. are required. Wellsted (*Travels in Arabia*, II. p. 200) relates that "the Bedoweens will undertake a journey of 10 to 12 days without carrying with them any nutriment, save a bottle full of small cakes, baked of white flour and camel or goat's milk, and a leather bag of water. Such a cake weighs about 5 ounces. Two of them, and a mouthful of water, the latter twice within 24 hours, is all which they then partake of."

bread and drinking the water,—he shall do from time to time, *i.e.* "not throughout the entire fixed period of 390 days" (Hävernick); but he shall not eat the daily ration at once, but divided into portions according to the daily hours of meals, so that he will never be completely satisfied. In addition to this is the pollution (ver. 12 sqq.) of the scanty allowance of food by the manner in which it is prepared. עֻגַת שְׂעֹרִים is predicate: "as barley cakes," "prepared in the form of barley cakes," shalt thou eat them. The suffix in תֹּאכֲלֶנָּה is neuter, and refers to לֶחֶם in ver. 9, or rather to the kinds of grain there enumerated, which are ground and baked before them: לֶחֶם, *i.e.* "food." The addition שְׂעֹרִים is not to be explained from this, that the principal part of these consisted of barley, nor does it prove that in general no other than barley cakes were known (Hitzig), but only that the cakes of barley meal, baked in the ashes, were an extremely frugal kind of bread, which that prepared by Ezekiel was to resemble. The עֻגָה was probably always baked on hot ashes, or on hot stones (1 Kings xix. 6), not on pans, as Kliefoth here supposes. The prophet, however, is to bake them in (with) human ordure. This is by no means to be understood as if he were to mix the ordure with the food, for which view Isa. xxxvi. 12 has been erroneously appealed to; but —as עֲלֵיהֶם in ver. 15 clearly shows—he is to bake it *over* the dung, *i.e.* so that dung forms the material of the fire. That the bread must be polluted by this is conceivable, although it cannot be proved from the passages in Lev. v. 3, vii. 21, and Deut. xxiii. 13 that the use of fire composed of dung made the food prepared thereon levitically unclean. The use of fire with human ordure must have communicated to the bread a loathsome smell and taste, by which it was rendered unclean, even if it had not been immediately baked in the hot ashes. That the pollution of the bread is the object of this injunction, we see from the explanation which God gives in ver. 13: "Thus shall the children of Israel eat their defiled bread among the heathen." The heart of the prophet, however, rebels against such food.

He says he has never in his life polluted himself by eating food forbidden in the law; from his youth up he has eaten no unclean flesh, neither of a carcase, nor of that which was torn by wild beasts (cf. Ex. xxii. 30; Deut. xiv. 21), nor flesh of sacrifices decayed or putrefying (פִּגּוּל, see on Lev. vii. 18; Isa. lxv. 4). On this God omits the requirement in ver. 12, and permits him to take for firing the dung of oxen instead of that of men.[1] In ver. 16 sq., finally, is given the explanation of the scanty allowance of food meted out to the prophet, namely, that the Lord, at the impending siege of Jerusalem, is to take away from the people the staff of bread, and leave them to languish in hunger and distress. The explanation is in literal adherence to the threatenings of the law (Lev. xxvi. 26 and 39), which are now to pass into fulfilment. Bread is called " staff of bread" as being indispensable for the preservation of life. To בְּמִשְׁקָל, Lev. xxvi. 26, בִּדְאָגָה, "in sorrow," is added; and to the water, בְּשִׁמָּמוֹן, " in astonishment," *i.e.* in fixed, silent pain at the miserable death, by hunger and thirst, which they see before them. נְמַקּוּ בַּעֲוֹנָם as Lev. xxvi. 39. If we, finally, cast a look over the contents of this first sign, it says that Jerusalem is soon to be besieged, and during the siege is to suffer hunger and terror as a punishment for the sins of Israel

---

[1] The use of dung as a material for burning is so common in the East, that it cannot be supposed that Ezekiel first became acquainted with it in a foreign country, and therefore regarded it with peculiar loathing. Human ordure, of course, so far as our knowledge goes, is never so employed, although the objection raised by Hitzig, on the other hand, that it would not yield so much heat as would be necessary for roasting without immediate contact, *i.e.* through the medium of a brick, rests upon an erroneous representation of the matter. But the employment of cattle-dung for firing could not be unknown to the Israelites, as it forms in the Hauran (the ancient Bashan) the customary firing material; cf. Wetzstein's remarks on Delitzsch's *Job*, vol. I. pp. 377, 8 (Eng. tran.), where the preparation of the *ǵelle*—this prevalent material for burning in the Hauran—from cow-dung mixed with chopped straw is minutely described; and this remark is made among others, that the flame of the *ǵelle*, prepared and dried from the dung of oxen that feed at large, is entirely without smoke, and that the ashes, which retain their heat for a lengthened time, are as clean as those of wood.

and Judah; that upon the capture of the city of Israel (Judah) they are to be dispersed among the heathen, and will there be obliged to eat unclean bread. To this in ch. v. is joined a second sign, which shows further how it shall fare with the people at and after the capture of Jerusalem (vers. 1–4); and after that a longer oracle, which developes the significance of these signs, and establishes the necessity of the penal judgment (vers. 5–17).

Chap. v. 1–4.—THE SIGN WHICH IS TO PORTRAY ISRAEL'S IMPENDING DESTINY.—Ver. 1. *And thou, son of man, take to thyself a sharp sword, as a razor shalt thou take it to thyself, and go with it over thy head, and over thy chin, and take to thee scales, and divide it (the hair).* Ver. 2. *A third part burn with fire in the midst of the city, when the days of the siege are accomplished: and take the (other) third, smite with the sword round about it: and the (remaining) third scatter to the winds; and the sword will I draw out after them.* Ver. 3. *Yet take a few of them by number, and bind them in the skirt of thy garment.* Ver. 4. *And of these again take a few, and cast them into the fire, and burn them with fire; from thence a fire shall go forth over the whole house of Israel.*—The description of this sign is easily understood. תַּעַר הַגַּלָּבִים, "razor of the barbers," is the predicate, which is to be understood to the suffix in תִּקָּחֶנָּה; and the clause states the purpose for which Ezekiel is to use the sharp sword—viz. as a razor, in order to cut off therewith the hair of his head and beard. The hair, when cut off, he is to divide into three parts with a pair of scales (the suffix in חִלַּקְתָּם refers *ad sensum* to the hair). The one third he is to burn in the city, *i.e.* not in the actual Jerusalem, but in the city, sketched on the brick, which he is symbolically besieging (iv. 3). To the city also is to be referred the suffix in סְבִיבוֹתֶיהָ, ver. 2, as is placed beyond doubt by ver. 12. In the last clause of ver. 2, which is taken from Lev. xxvi. 33, the description of the sign passes over into its exposition, for אַחֲרֵיהֶם does not refer to the hair, but to the inhabitants of Jerusalem. The significance also of this symbolical act is easily recognised, and is, moreover, stated in ver. 12. Ezekiel, in this act, represents the besieged Jerusalem. What he does to his hair, that will God do to the inhabitants of Jerusalem. As the hair of the prophet falls under the sword, used as a razor, so will the inhabitants of Jerusalem fall, when the city is captured, into destruction, and that verily an ignominious destruction. This idea is contained in the picture of the hair-cutting, which was a dishonour done to what forms the ornament of a man. See on 2 Sam. x. 4 sqq. A third of the same is to perish in the city. As the fire destroys the hair, so will pestilence and hunger consume the inhabitants of the beleaguered city (ver. 12). The second third will, on the capture of the city, fall by the sword in the environs (ver. 12); the last third will God scatter to the winds, and—as Moses has already threatened the people—will draw forth the sword after them, still to persecute and smite them (ver. 12). This sign is continued (vers. 3 and 4) in a second symbolical act, which shadows forth what is further to happen to the people when dispersed among the heathen. Of the third scattered to the winds, Ezekiel is to bind a small portion in the skirt of his garment. מִשָּׁם, "from thence," refers not to הַשְּׁלִישִׁית, but, *ad sensum*, to תִּזְרֶה לָרוּחַ: "from the place where the third that is scattered to the winds is found"—*i.e.*, as regards the subject-matter, of those who are to be found among the dispersion. The binding up into the כְּנָפַיִם, "the corners or ends of the garment" (cf. Jer. ii. 34), denotes the preservation of the few, who are gathered together out of the whole of those who are dispersed among the heathen; cf. 1 Sam. xxv. 29; Ezek. xvi. 8. But even of these few He shall still cast some into the fire, and consume them. Consequently those who are gathered together out of exile are not all to be preserved, but are still to be sifted by fire, in which process a part is consumed. This image does not refer to those who remain behind in the land, when the nation is led away captive to Babylon (Theodoret, Grotius, and others), but, as Ephrem the Syrian and Jerome saw, to those who were saved from Babylon, and to their further destiny, as is already clear from the מִשָּׁם, rightly understood. The meaning of the last clause of ver. 4 is disputed; in it, as in the final clause of ver. 2, the symbolical representation passes over into the announcement of the thing itself. מֵהֶם, which Ewald would arbitrarily alter into מִפְּנֵי, cannot, with Hävernick, be referred to אֶל־תּוֹךְ הָאֵשׁ, because this yields a very forced sense, but relates to the whole act described in vers. 3 and 4: that a portion thereof is rescued and preserved, and yet of this portion many are consumed by fire,—from that a fire shall go forth over the whole house of Israel. This fire is explained by almost all expositors, from Theodoret and Jerome onwards, of the penal judgments which were inflicted after the exile upon the Jews, which reached their culminating point in the siege and destruction of Jerusalem by the Romans, and which still continue in their dispersion throughout the whole world. But this view, as Kliefoth has already remarked, is not only in decided antagonism to the intention of the text, but it is, moreover, altogether impossible to see how a judgment of extermination for all Israel can be deduced from the fact that a small number of the Israelites, who are scattered to the winds, is saved, and that of those who are saved a part is still consumed with fire. From thence there can only come forth a fire of purification for the whole of Israel, through which the remnant, as Isaiah had already predicted (vi. 12 sqq.), is converted into a holy seed. In the last clause, consuming by fire is not referred to. The fire, however, has not merely a destructive, but also a cleansing, purifying, and quickening power. To kindle such a fire on earth did Christ come (Luke xii. 49), and from Him the same goes out over the whole house of Israel. This view, for which Kliefoth has already rightly decided, receives a confirmation through ch. vi. 8–10, where is announced the conversion of the remnant of those Israelites who had been dispersed among the nations.

So far the symbolical acts. Before, however, we pass on to the explanation of the following oracle, we must still briefly touch the question, whether these acts were undertaken and performed by the prophet in the world of external reality, or whether they were occurrences only *internally* real, which Ezekiel experienced in spirit—*i.e.* in an ecstatic condition—and afterwards communicated to the people. Amongst modern expositors, Kliefoth has defended the former view, and has adduced the following considerations in support: A significant act, and yet also a silent, leisurely one, must be performed, that it may show something to those who behold it. Nor is the case such, as Hitzig supposes, that it would have been impossible to carry out what had been required of the prophet in ch. iv. 1–17. It had, indeed, its difficulty; but God sometimes requires from His servants what is difficult, although He also helps them to the performance of it. So here He will make it easy for the prophet to recline, by binding him (iv. 8). "In the sign, this certainly was kept in view, that it should be performed; and it, moreover, *was* performed, although the text, in a manner quite intelligible with reference to an act commanded by God, does not expressly state it." For these latter assertions, however, there is anything but convincing proof. The matter is not so simple as Kliefoth supposes, although we are at one with him in this, that neither the difficulty of carrying out what was commanded in the world of external reality, nor the non-mention of the actual performance, furnishes sufficient grounds for the supposition of merely internal, spiritual occurrences. We also are of opinion that very many of the symbolical acts of the prophets were undertaken and performed in the external world, and that this supposition, as that which corresponds most fully with the literal meaning of the words, is on each occasion the most obvious, and is to be firmly adhered to, unless there can be good grounds for the opposite view. In the case now before us, we have first to take into consideration that the oracle which enjoins these symbolical acts on Ezekiel stands in close connection, both as to time and place, with the inauguration of Ezekiel to the prophetic office. The hand of the Lord comes upon him at the same place, where the concluding word at his call was addressed to him (the שָׁם, iii. 22, points back to שָׁם in iii. 15); and the circumstance that Ezekiel found himself still on the same spot to which he had been transported by the Spirit of God (iii. 14), shows that the new revelation, which he here still received, followed very *soon*, if not *immediately*, after his consecration to the office of prophet. Then, upon the occasion of this divine revelation, he is again, as at his consecration, transported into an ecstatic condition, as is clear not only from the formula, "the hand of the Lord came upon me," which in our book always has this signification, but also most undoubtedly from this, that he again sees the glory of Jehovah in the same manner as he had seen it in ch. i. —viz. when in an ecstatic condition. But if this were an ecstatic vision, it is obvious that the acts also which the divine appearance imposed upon him must be regarded as ecstatic occurrences; since the assertion that every significant act must be *performed*, in order that something may be *shown* to those who witness it, is fundamentally insufficient for the proof that this act must fall within the domain of the earthly world of sense, because the occurrences related in ch. viii.–xi. are viewed even by Kliefoth himself as purely *internal* events. As decisive, however, for the purely internal character of the symbolical acts under consideration (ch. iv. and v.), is the circumstance that the supposition of Ezekiel having, in his own house, actually lain 390 days upon his left, and then, again, 40 days upon his right side without turning, stands in irreconcilable contradiction with the fact that he, according to ch. viii. 1 sqq., was carried away in ecstasy to Jerusalem, there to behold in the temple the monstrosities of Israel's idolatry and the destruction of Jerusalem. For the proof of this, see the introduction to ch. viii.

Vers. 5–17. THE DIVINE WORD WHICH EXPLAINS THE SYMBOLICAL SIGNS, in which the judgment that is announced is laid down as to its cause (5–9) and as to its nature (10–17). —Ver. 5. *Thus says the Lord Jehovah: This Jerusalem have I placed in the midst of the nations, and raised about her the countries.* Ver. 6. *But in wickedness she resisted my laws more than the nations, and my statutes more than the countries which are round about her; for they rejected my laws, and did not walk in my statutes.* Ver. 7. *Therefore thus says the Lord Jehovah: Because ye have raged more than the nations round about you, and have not walked in my statutes, and have not obeyed my laws, and have not done even according to the laws of the nations which are round about you;* Ver. 8. *Therefore thus saith the Lord Jehovah: Lo, I, even I, shall be against thee, and will perform judgments in thy midst before the eyes of the nations.* Ver. 9. *And I will do unto thee what I have never done, nor will again do in like manner, on account of all thine abominations.*

זֹאת יְרוּשָׁ׳, not "this is Jerusalem," *i.e.* this is the *destiny* of Jerusalem (Hävernick), but "this Jerusalem" (Hitzig); זֹאת is placed before the noun in the sense of *iste*, as in Ex. xxxii. 1; cf. Ewald, § 293*b*. To place the culpability of Jerusalem in its proper prominence, the censure of her sinful conduct opens with the mention of the exalted position which God had assigned her upon earth. Jerusalem is described in ver. 5 as forming the central point of the earth: this is done, however, neither in an external, geographical (Hitzig), nor in a purely typical sense, as the city that is blessed more than any other (Calvin, Hävernick), but in a historical sense, in so far as " God's people and city actually stand in the central point of the God-directed world-development and its movements" (Kliefoth); or, in relation to the history of salvation, as the city in which God hath set up His throne of grace, from which shall go forth the law and the statutes for all nations, in order that the salvation of the whole world may be accomplished (Isa. ii. 2 sqq.; Mic. iv. 1 sqq.). But instead of keeping the laws and statutes of the Lord, Jerusalem has, on the contrary, turned to do wickedness more than the heathen nations in all the lands round about (הִמְרָה, *cum accusat. object.*, "to act rebelliously towards"). Here we may not quote Rom. ii. 12, 14 against this, as if the heathen, who did not know the law of God, did not also transgress the same, but sinned ἀνόμως; for the sinning ἀνόμως, of which the apostle speaks, is really a transgression of the law written on the heart of the heathen. With לָכֵן, in ver. 7, the penal threatening is introduced; but before the punishment is laid down, the correspondence between guilt and punishment is brought forward more prominently by repeatedly placing in juxtaposition the godless conduct of the rebellious city. הֲמָנְכֶם is infinitive, from הָמַן, a secondary form הָמוֹן, in the sense of הָמָה, "to rage," *i.e.* to rebel against God; cf. Ps. ii. 1. The last clause of ver. 7 contains a climax: "And ye have not even acted according to the laws of the heathen." This is not in any real contradiction to ch. xi. 12 (where it is made a subject of reproach to the Israelites that they have acted according to the laws of the heathen), so that we would be obliged, with Ewald and Hitzig, to expunge the לֹא in the verse before us, because wanting in the Peshito and several Hebrew manuscripts. Even in these latter, it has only been omitted to avoid the supposed contradiction with xi. 12. The solution of the apparent contradiction lies in the double meaning of the מִשְׁפְּטֵי הַגּוֹיִם. The heathen had laws which were opposed to those of God, but also such as were rooted in the law of God written upon their hearts. Obedience to the latter was good and praiseworthy; to the former, wicked and objectionable. Israel, which hated the law of God, followed the wicked and sinful laws of the heathen, and neglected to observe their *good* laws. The passage before us is to be judged by Jer. ii. 10, 11, to which Raschi had already made reference.[1] In ver. 8 the announcement of

---

[1] Coccejus had already well remarked on ch. xi. 12: "*Haec probe concordant. Imitabantur Judaei gentiles vel fovendo opiniones gentiles, vel etiam assumendo ritus et sacra gentilium. Sed non faciebant ut gentes, quae integre*

the punishment, interrupted by the repeated mention of the cause, is again resumed with the words לָכֵן כֹּה וגו׳. Since Jerusalem has acted worse than the heathen, God will execute His judgments upon her before the eyes of the heathen. עָשָׂה שְׁפָטִים or עָשָׂה כְּישְׁפָּטִים (vers. 10, 15, ch. xi. 9, xvi. 41, etc.), "to accomplish or execute judgments," is used in Ex. xii. 12 and Num. xxxiii. 4 of the judgments which God suspended over Egypt. The punishment to be suspended shall be so great and heavy, that the like has never happened before, nor will ever happen again. These words do not require us either to refer the threatening, with Cocccjus, to the last destruction of Jerusalem, which was marked by greater severity than the earlier one, or to suppose, with Hävernick, that the prophet's look is directed to both the periods of Israel's punishment—the times of the Babylonian and Roman calamity together. Both suppositions are irreconcilable with the words, as these can only be referred to the first impending penal judgment of the destruction of Jerusalem. This was, so far, more severe than any previous or subsequent one, inasmuch as by it the existence of the people of God was for a time suspended, while that Jerusalem and Israel, which were destroyed and annihilated by the Romans, were no longer the people of God, inasmuch as the latter consisted at that time of the Christian community, which was not affected by that catastrophe (Kliefoth).

Vers. 10-17. *Further execution of this threat.*—Ver. 10. *Therefore shall fathers devour their children in thy midst, and children shall devour their fathers: and I will exercise judgments upon thee, and disperse all thy remnant to the winds.* Ver. 11. *Therefore, as I live, is the declaration of the Lord Jehovah, Verily, because thou hast polluted my sanctuary with all thine abominations and all thy crimes, so shall I take away mine eye without mercy, and will not spare.* Ver. 12. *A third of thee shall die by the pestilence, and perish by hunger in thy*

diis suis serviebant. Nam Israelitae nomine Dei abutebantur et ipsius populus videri volebant."

midst; and the third part shall fall by the sword about thee; and the third part will I scatter to all the winds; and will draw out the sword after them. Ver. 13. *And my anger shall be fulfilled, and I will cool my wrath against them, and will take vengeance. And they shall experience that I, Jehovah, have spoken in my zeal, when I accomplish my wrath upon them.* Ver. 14. *And I will make thee a desolation and a mockery among the nations which are round about thee, before the eyes of every passer-by.* Ver. 15. *And it shall be a mockery and a scorn, a warning and a terror for the nations round about thee, when I exercise my judgments upon thee in anger and wrath and in grievous visitations. I, Jehovah, have said it.* Ver. 16. *When I send against thee the evil arrows of hunger, which minister to destruction, which I shall send to destroy you; for hunger shall I heap upon you, and shall break to you the staff of bread:* Ver. 17. *And I shall send hunger upon you, and evil beasts, which shall make thee childless; and pestilence and blood shall pass over thee; and the sword will I bring upon thee. I, Jehovah, have spoken it.*—As a proof of the unheard-of severity of the judgment, there is immediately mentioned in ver. 10 a most horrible circumstance, which had been already predicted by Moses (Lev. xxvi. 29; Deut. xxviii. 53) as that which should happen to the people when hard pressed by the enemy, viz. a famine so dreadful, during the siege of Jerusalem, that parents would eat their children, and children their parents; and after the capture of the city, the dispersion of those who remained " to all the winds, *i.e.* to all quarters of the world." This is described more minutely, as an appendix to the symbolical act in vers. 1 and 2, in vers. 11 and 12, with a solemn oath, and with repeated and prominent mention of the sins which have drawn down such chastisements. As sin, is mentioned the pollution of the temple by idolatrous abominations, which are described in detail in ch. viii. The אֶנְרַע, which is variously understood by the old translators (for which some *Codices* offer the explanatory correction אגרע), is to be explained, after Job xxxvi. 7, of the " turning away of the eye," and the עֵינִי following as the object; while וְלֹא־תָחוֹס, " that it feel no compassion," is interjected between the verb and its object with the adverbial signification of " mercilessly." For that the words ולא תחום are adverbially subordinate to אֶגְרַע, distinctly appears from the correspondence—indicated by וְגַם אֲנִי —between אֶגְרַע and לֹא אֶחְמוֹל. Moreover, the thought, " Jehovah will mercilessly withdraw His care for the people," is not to be termed "feeble" in connection with what follows; nor is the contrast, which is indicated in the clause וְגַם־אֲנִי, lost, as Hävernick supposes. וְגַם־אֲנִי does not require גָּרַע to be understood of a positive act, which would correspond to the desecration of the sanctuary. This is shown by the last clause of the verse. The withdrawal without mercy of the divine providence is, besides, in reality, equivalent to complete devotion to destruction, as it is particularized in ver. 12. For ver. 12 see on vers. 1 and 2. By carrying out the threatened division of the people into three parts, the wrath of God is to be fulfilled, *i.e.* the full measure of the divine wrath upon the people is to be exhausted (cf. 7, 8), and God is to appear and "cool" His anger. הֵנִיחַ חֵמָה, "*sedavit iram*," occurs again in xvi. 42, xxi. 22, xxiv. 13. הִנֶּחָמְתִּי, *Hithpael*, pausal form for הִנֶּחַמְתִּי, "*se consolari*," "to procure satisfaction by revenge;" cf. Isa. i. 24, and for the thing, Deut. xxviii. 63. In ver. 14 sqq. the discourse turns again from the people to the city of Jerusalem. It is to become a wilderness, as was already threatened in Lev. xxvi. 31 and 33 to the cities of Israel, and thereby a " mockery " to all nations, in the manner described in Deut. xxix. 23 sq. וְהָיְתָה, in ver. 15, is not to be changed, after the LXX., Vulgate, and some MSS., into the second person; but Jerusalem is to be regarded as the subject which is to become the object of scorn and hatred, etc., when God accomplishes His judgments. מוּסָר is a warning-example. Among the judgments which are to overtake it, in ver. 16, hunger is again made specially prominent (cf. iv. 16); and first in ver. 17 are wild beasts, pestilence, blood, and sword added, and a quartette of judgments announced as in

xiv. 21. For pestilence and blood are comprehended together as a unity by means of the predicate. Their connection is to be understood according to xiv. 19, and the number four is significant, as in xiv. 21; Jer. xv. 3 sqq. For more minute details as to the meaning, see on xiv. 21. The evil arrows point back to Deut. xxxii. 23; the evil beasts, to Lev. xxiv. 22 and Deut. xxxii. 24 sqq. To produce an impression, the prophet heaps his words together. *Unum ejus consilium fuit penetrare in animos populi quasi lapideos et ferreos. Hæc igitur est ratio, cur hic tanta varietate utatur et exornet suam doctrinam variis figuris* (Calvin).

CHAP. VI. THE JUDGMENT UPON THE IDOLATROUS PLACES, AND ON THE IDOL-WORSHIPPERS.

To God's address in vers. 5-17, explaining the signs in ch. iv. 1-5, are appended in ch. vi. and vii. two additional oracles, which present a further development of the contents of these signs, the judgment portrayed by them in its extent and greatness. In ch. vi. there is announced, in the first section, to the idolatrous places, and on their account to the land, desolation, and to the idolaters, destruction (vers. 3-7); and to this is added the prospect of a remnant of the people, who are dispersed among the heathen, coming to be converted to the Lord (vers. 8-10). In the second section the necessity and terrible character of the impending judgment is repeatedly described at length as an appendix to vers. 12, 14 (vers. 11-14).

Vers. 1-7. The desolation of the land, and destruction of the idolaters.—Ver. 1. *And the word of the Lord came to me, saying:* Ver. 2. *Son of man, turn thy face towards the mountains of Israel, and prophesy against them.* Ver. 3. *And say, Ye mountains of Israel, hear the word of the Lord Jehovah: Thus saith the Lord Jehovah to the mountains, and to the hills, to the valleys, and to the low grounds, Behold, I bring the sword upon you, and destroy your high places.* Ver. 4. *Your altars shall be made desolate, and your sun-pillars shall be broken; and I shall make your slain fall in the presence of your idols.* Ver. 5. *And I will lay the corpses of the children of Israel before their idols, and will scatter your bones round about your altars.* Ver. 6. *In all your dwellings shall the cities be made desolate, and the high places waste; that your altars may be desolate and waste, and your idols broken and destroyed, and your sun-pillars hewn down, and the works of your hands exterminated.* Ver. 7. *And the slain will fall in your midst; that you may know that I am Jehovah.*—With ver. 1 cf. iii. 16. The prophet is to prophesy against the mountains of Israel. That the mountains are mentioned (ver. 2) as *pars pro toto,* is seen from ver. 3, when to the mountains and hills are added also the valleys and low grounds, as the places where idolatry was specially practised; cf. Hos. iv. 13; Jer. ii. 20, iii. 6; see on Hos. *l.c.* and Deut. xii. 2. אֲפִיקִים, in the older writings, denotes the "river channels," "the beds of the stream;" but Ezekiel uses the word as equivalent to valley, *i.e.* נַחַל, a valley with a brook or stream, like the Arabic *wady.* גַּיְא, properly "deepening," "the deep ground," "the deep valley;" on the form גֵּאָיוֹת, cf. Ewald, § 186*da.* The juxtaposition of mountains and hills, of valleys and low grounds, occurs again in xxxvi. 4, 6, and xxxv. 8; the opposition between mountains and valleys also, in xxxii. 5, 6, and xxxiv. 13. The valleys are to be conceived of as furnished with trees and groves, under the shadow of which the worship of Astarte especially was practised; see on ver. 15. On the mountains and in the valleys were sanctuaries erected to Baal and Astarte. The announcement of their destruction is appended to the threatening in Lev. xxvi. 30, which Ezekiel takes up and describes at greater length. Beside the בָּמוֹת, the places of sacrifice and worship, and the חַמָּנִים, pillars or statues of Baal, dedicated to him as the sun-god, he names also the altars, which, in Lev. *l.c.* and other places, are comprehended along with the בָּמוֹת; see on Lev. xxvi. 30 and 1 Kings iii. 3. With the destruction of the idol temples, altars, and statues, the idol-worshippers are also to be smitten, so as to fall down in the presence of their idols. The fundamental meaning of the word גִּלּוּלִים, "idols," borrowed from Lev. l.c., and frequently employed by Ezekiel, is uncertain; signifying either "logs of wood," from גָּלַל, "to roll" (Gesen.), or *stercorei*, from גֵּל, "dung;" not "monuments of stone" (Hävernick). Ver. 5a is taken quite literally from Lev. xxvi. 30b. The ignominy of the destruction is heightened by the bones of the slain idolaters being scattered round about the idol altars. In order that the idolatry may be entirely rooted out, the cities throughout the whole land, and all the high places, are to be devastated, ver. 6. The forms תִּישַׁמְנָה and יֵאשְׁמוּ are probably not to be derived from שָׁמֵם (Ewald, § 138b), but to be referred back to a stem-form יָשֵׁם, with the signification of שָׁמֵם, the existence of which appears certain from the old name יְשִׁימוֹן in Ps. lxviii. and elsewhere. The א in יֵאשְׁמוּ is certainly only *mater lectionis*. In ver. 7, the singular חָלָל stands as indefinitely general. The thought, "slain will fall *in your midst*," involves the idea that not all the people will fall, but that there will survive some who are saved, and prepares for what follows. The falling of the slain—the idolaters with their idols—leads to the recognition of Jehovah as the omnipotent God, and to conversion to Him.

Vers. 8-10. The survivors shall go away into banishment amongst the heathen, and shall remember the word of the Lord that will have been fulfilled.—Ver. 8. *But I shall preserve a remnant, in that there shall be to you some who have escaped the sword among the nations, when ye shall be dispersed among the lands.* Ver. 9. *And those of you who have escaped, will make mention of me among the nations whither they are led captive, when I have broken to me their whorish heart, which had departed from me, and their eyes, which went a whoring after their idols: and they shall loathe themselves because of the evil which they have done in reference to all their abominations.* Ver. 10. *And ye shall know that I am Jehovah. Not in vain have I spoken this evil to you.*— הוֹתִיר, *superstites facere*, "to make or preserve survivors." The connection with בִּהְיוֹת וגו׳. is analogous to the construction of

הוֹתִיר, in the sense of "giving a superabundance," with בְּ *rei*, Deut. xxviii. 11 and xxx. 9, and is not to be rejected, with Ewald and Hitzig, as inadmissible. For בִּהְיוֹת is supported by the old versions, and the change of וְהוֹתַרְתִּי into וְדִבַּרְתִּי, which would have to be referred to ver. 7, is in opposition to the two-fold repetition of the (וְיָדְעוּ) וִידַעְתֶּם כִּי אֲנִי יהוה, vers. 10 and 14, as this repetition shows that the thought in ver. 7 is different from that in 17, 21, not "they shall know that Jehovah has spoken," but "they shall know that He who has done this is Jehovah, the God of Israel." The preservation of a remnant will be shown in this, that they shall have some who have escaped the sword. הִוָּרוֹתֵיכֶם is *infin. Niph.* with a plural form of the suffix, as occurs elsewhere only with the plural ending וֹת of nouns, while Ezekiel has extended it to the וֹת of the infinitive of לה verbs; cf. xvi. 31, and Ewald, § 259b. The remembrance of Jehovah (ver. 9) is the commencement of conversion to Him. אֲשֶׁר before נִשְׁבַּרְתִּי is not to be connected as relative pronoun with לִבָּם, but is a conjunction, though not used conditionally, "if," as in Lev. iv. 22, Deut. xi. 27, and elsewhere, but of time, ὅτε, "when," as Deut. xi. 6 and 2 Chron. xxxv. 20, and נִשְׁבַּרְתִּי in the signification of the *futur. exact*. The *Niphal* נִשְׁבַּר here is not to be taken as passive, but middle, *sibi frangere, i.e.* לִבָּם, *poenitentiâ conterere animum eorum ut ad ipsum (Deum) redeant* (Maurer, Hävernick). Besides the heart, the eyes also are mentioned, which God is to smite, as the external senses which allure the heart to whoredom. וְנָקֹטּוּ corresponds to וְזָכְרוּ at the beginning of the verse. קוֹט, the later form for קוּץ, "to feel a loathing," *Hiphil*, "to be filled with loathing;" cf. Job x. 1 with בְּ *object.*, "in (on) their פָּנִים, faces," *i.e.* their persons or themselves: so also in xx. 43, xxxvi. 31. אֶל הָרָעוֹת, in allusion to the evil things; לְכָל־תוֹעֵב, in reference to all their abominations. This fruit, which is produced by chastisement, namely, that the idolaters are inspired with loathing for themselves, and led to the knowledge of Jehovah, will furnish the proof that God has not spoken in vain.

Vers. 11–14. The punishment is just and well deserved.—
Ver. 11. *Thus saith the Lord Jehovah, Smite with thy hand, and stamp with thy foot, and say, Woe on all the wicked abominations of the house of Israel! that they must perish by sword, hunger, and pestilence.* Ver. 12. *He that is afar off will die by the pestilence; and he that is near at hand shall fall by the sword; and he who survives and is preserved will die of hunger: and I shall accomplish my wrath upon them.* Ver. 13. *And ye shall know that I am Jehovah, when your slain lie in the midst of your idols round about your altars, on every high hill, upon all the summits of the mountains, and under every green tree, and under every thick-leaved terebinth, on the places where they brought their pleasant incense to all their idols.* Ver. 14. *And I will stretch out my hand against them, and make the land waste and desolate more than the wilderness of Diblath, in all their dwellings: so shall ye know that I am Jehovah.*—Through clapping of the hands and stamping of the feet—the gestures which indicate violent excitement—the prophet is to make known the displeasure of Jehovah at the horrible idolatry of the people, and thereby make manifest that the penal judgment is well deserved. הַכֵּה בְכַפְּךָ is in xxi. 19 expressed more distinctly by הַךְ כַּף אֶל כַּף, "to strike one hand against the other," *i.e.* "to clap the hands;" cf. Num. xxiv. 10. אָח, an exclamation of lamentation, occurring only here and in xxi. 20. אֲשֶׁר, ver. 11, is a conjunction, "at." Their abominations are so wicked, that they must be exterminated on account of them. This is specially mentioned in ver. 12. No one will escape the judgment: he who is far removed from its scene as little as he who is close at hand; while he who escapes the pestilence and the sword is to perish of hunger. נָצוּר, *servatus*, preserved, as in Isa. xlix. 6. The signification "besieged" (LXX., Vulgate, Targum, etc.), Hitzig can only maintain by arbitrarily expunging הַנִּשְׁאָר as a gloss. On ver. 12*b*, cf. v. 13; on 13*a*, cf. ver. 5; and on 13*b*, cf. ver. 3, and Hos. iv. 13; Jer. ii. 20, iii. 6; Deut. xii. 2. אֶל כָּל־גֵּב, according to later usage, for עַל כָּל־גֵּב. רֵיחַ נִיחֹחַ, used

in the Pentateuch of sacrifices pleasing to God, is here transferred to idol sacrifices; see on Lev. i. 9 and Gen. viii. 21. On account of the prevalence of idolatry in all parts, God will make the land entirely desolate. The union of שְׁמָמָה וּמְשַׁמָּה serves to strengthen the idea; cf. xxxiii. 8 sqq., xxxv. 3. The words מִמִּדְבָּר דִּבְלָתָה are obscure, either "in the wilderness towards Diblath" (even to Diblath), or "more than the wilderness of Diblath" (כְּ of comparison). There is no doubt that דִּבְלָתָה is a *nom. prop.*; cf. the name of the city דִּבְלָתַיִם in Jer. xlviii. 22; Num. xxxiii. 46. The second acceptation of the words is more probable than the first. For, if מִמִּדְבָּר is the *terminus a quo*, and דִּבְלָתָה the *terminus ad quem* of the extent of the land, then must מִמִּדְבָּר be punctuated not only as *status absolut.*, but it must also have the article; because a definite wilderness—that, namely, of Arabia—is meant. The omission of the article cannot be justified by reference to xxi. 3 or to Ps. lxxv. 7 (Hitzig, Ewald), because both passages contain general designations of the quarters of the world, with which the article is always omitted. In the next place, no *Dibla* can be pointed out in the north; and the change of *Diblatha* into *Ribla*, already proposed by Jerome, and more recently brought forward again by J. D. Michaelis, has not only against it the authority of all the old versions, but also the circumstance that the *Ribla* mentioned in 2 Kings xxiii. 33 did not form the northern boundary of Palestine, but lay on the other side of it, in the land of *Hamath;* while the הָרִבְלָה, named in Num. xxxiv. 11, is a place on the eastern boundary to the north of the Sea of Gennesareth, which would, moreover, be inappropriate as a designation of the northern boundary. Finally, the extent of the land from the south to the north is constantly expressed in a different way; cf. Num. xiii. 21 (xxxiv. 8); Josh. xiii. 5; 1 Kings viii. 65; 2 Kings xiv. 65; Amos vi. 14; 1 Chron. xiii. 5; 2 Chron. vii. 8; and even by Ezekiel himself (xlviii. 1) לְבוֹא חֲמָת is named as the boundary on the north. The form דִּבְלָתָה is similar to תִּמְנָתָה for תִּמְנָה, although the name is hardly to be explained, with Hävernick, as an appellation, after the Arabic بَلْ, *calamitas, exitium*. The wilderness of *Diblah* is unknown. With וַיֵּדְעוּ כִּי וגו׳ the discourse is rounded of in returning to the beginning of ver. 13, while the thoughts in vers. 13 and 14 are only a variation of vers. 4–7.

CHAP. VII. THE OVERTHROW OF ISRAEL.

The second " word of God," contained in this chapter, completes the announcement of judgment upon Jerusalem and Judah, by expanding the thought, that the end will come both quickly and inevitably upon the land and people. This word is divided into two unequal sections, by the repetition of the phrase, " Thus saith Adonai Jehovah " (vers. 2 and 5). In the first of these sections the theme is given in short, expressive, and monotonous clauses; namely, the end is drawing nigh, for God will judge Israel without mercy according to its abominations. The second section (vers. 5–27) is arranged in four strophes, and contains, in a form resembling the lamentation in chap. xix., a more minute description of the end predicted.

Vers. 1–4. The end cometh.—Ver. 1. *And the word of Jehovah came to me thus:* Ver. 2. *And thou, son of man, thus saith the Lord Jehovah: An end to the land of Israel! the end cometh upon the four borders of the land.* Ver. 3. *Now (cometh) the end upon thee, and I shall send my wrath upon thee, and judge thee according to thy ways, and bring upon thee all thine abominations.* Ver. 4. *And my eye shall not look with pity upon thee, and I shall not spare, but bring thy ways upon thee; and thy abominations shall be in the midst of thee, that ye may know that I am Jehovah.*—וְאַתָּה, with the copula, connects this word of God with the preceding one, and shows it to be a continuation. It commences with an emphatic utterance of the thought, that the end is coming to the land of Israel, *i.e.* to the kingdom of Judah, with its capital Jerusalem. Desecrated as it has been by the abominations of its inhabitants, it will cease to be the land of God's people Israel. לְאַדְמַת יִשׂ׳ (to the land of Israel) is not to be taken with כֹּה אָמַר (thus saith the Lord) in opposition to the accents, but is connected with קֵץ (an end), as in the Targ. and Vulgate, and is placed first for the sake of greater emphasis. In the construction, compare Job vi. 14. אַרְבַּעַת כַּנְפוֹת הָאָרֶץ is limited by the parallelism to the four extremities of the land of Israel. It is used elsewhere for the whole earth (Isa. xi. 12). The *Chetib* אַרְבַּעַת is placed, in opposition to the ordinary rule, before a noun in the feminine gender. The *Keri* gives the regular construction (*vid.* Ewald, § 267*c*). In ver. 3 the end is explained to be a wrathful judgment. "Give (נָתַן) thine abominations upon thee;" *i.e.* send the consequences, inflict punishment for them. The same thought is expressed in the phrase, "thine abominations shall be in the midst of thee;" in other words, they would discern them in the punishments which the abominations would bring in their train. For ver. 4*a* compare ch. v. 11.

Vers. 5-27. The execution of the judgment announced in vers. 2-4, arranged in four strophes: vers. 5-9, 10-14, 15-22, 23-27.—The *first* strophe depicts the end as a terrible calamity, and as near at hand. Vers. 3 and 4 are repeated as a refrain in vers. 8 and 9, with slight modifications. Ver. 5. *Thus saith the Lord Jehovah: Misfortune, a singular misfortune, behold, it cometh.* Ver. 6. *End cometh: there cometh the end; it waketh upon thee; behold, it cometh.* Ver. 7. *The fate cometh upon thee, inhabitants of the land: the time cometh, the day is near; tumult and not joy upon the mountains.* Ver. 8. *Now speedily will I pour out my fury upon thee, and accomplish mine anger on thee; and judge thee according to thy ways, and bring upon thee all thine abominations.* Ver. 9. *My eye shall not look with pity upon thee, and I shall not spare; according to thy ways will I bring it upon thee, and thy abominations shall be in the midst of thee, that ye may know that I, Jehovah, am smiting.*—Misfortune of a singular kind shall come. רָעָה is made more emphatic by אַחַת רָעָה, in which אַחַת is placed first for the sake of emphasis, in the sense of *unicus, singularis;* a calamity singular (unique) of its kind, such as never had occurred before (cf. ch. v. 9). In ver. 6 the poetical הֵקִיץ, it (the end) waketh upon thee, is suggested by the paronomasia with הַקֵּץ. The force of the words is weakened by supplying Jehovah as the subject to הֵקִיץ, in opposition to the context. And it will not do to supply רָעָה (evil) from ver. 5 as the subject to הִנֵּה בָאָה (behold, it cometh). בָּאָה is construed impersonally: It cometh, namely, every dreadful thing which the end brings with it. The meaning of *tzʻphirâh* is doubtful. The only other passage in which it occurs is Isa. xxviii. 5, where it is used in the sense of diadem or crown, which is altogether unsuitable here. Raschi has therefore had recourse to the Syriac and Chaldee צַפְרָא, *aurora, tempus matutinum,* and Hävernick has explained it accordingly, "the dawn of an evil day." But the dawn is never used as a symbol or omen of misfortune, not even in Joel ii. 2, but solely as the sign of the bursting forth of light or of salvation. Abarbanel was on the right track when he started from the radical meaning of צָפַר, to twist, and taking *tzʻphirâh* in the sense of *orbis, ordo,* or periodical return, understood it as probably denoting *rerum fatique vicissitudinem in orbem redeuntem* (Ges. *Thes.* p. 1188). But it has been justly observed, that the rendering succession, or periodical return, can only give a forced sense in ver. 10. Winer has given a better rendering, viz. *fatum, malum fatale,* fate or destiny, for which he refers to the Arabic صَبَرَ, *intortum,* then *fatum haud mutandum inevitabile.* Different explanations have also been given of הֵד הָרִים. But the opinion that it is synonymous with הֵידָד, the joyous vintage cry (Jer. xxv. 30; Isa. xvi. 10), is a more probable one than that it is an unusual form of הוֹד, *splendor, gloria.* So much at any rate is obvious from the context, that the *hapax legomenon* הֵד is the antithesis of מְהוּמָה, tumult, or the noise of war. The shouting of the mountains, is shouting, a rejoicing upon the mountains. מִקָּרוֹב, from the immediate vicinity, in a temporal not a local sense, as in Deut. xxxii. 17 (=immediately). For בְּכָה אָף, see ch. vi. 12. The remainder of the strophe (vers. 8*b* and 9) is a repetition of vers. 3 and 4; but מַכֶּה is added in the last clause. They shall learn that it is Jehovah who smites. This thought is expanded in the following strophe.

Vers. 10–14. *Second* strophe.—Ver. 10. *Behold the day, behold, it cometh; the fate springeth up; the rod sprouteth; the pride blossometh.* Ver. 11. *The violence riseth up as the rod of evil: nothing of them, nothing of their multitude, nothing of their crowd, and nothing glorious upon them.* Ver. 12. *The time cometh, the day approacheth: let not the buyer rejoice, and let not the seller trouble himself; for wrath cometh upon the whole multitude thereof.* Ver. 13. *For the seller will not return to that which was sold, even though his life were still among the living: for the prophecy against its whole multitude will not turn back; and no one will strengthen himself as to his life through his iniquity.* Ver. 14. *They blow the trumpet and make everything ready; but no one goeth into the battle: for my wrath cometh upon all their multitude.*—The rod is already prepared; nothing will be left of the ungodly. This is the leading thought of the strophe. The three clauses of ver. 10*b* are synonymous; but there is a gradation in the thought. The approaching fate springs up out of the earth (יָצָא, applied to the springing up of plants, as in 1 Kings v. 13; Isa. xi. 1, etc.); it sprouts as a rod, and flowers as pride. *Matteh,* the rod as an instrument of chastisement (Isa. x. 5). This rod is then called *zâdhōn,* pride, inasmuch as God makes use of a proud and violent people, namely the Chaldeans (Hab. i. 6 sqq.; Jer. l. 31 *seq.*), to inflict the punishment. Sprouting and blossoming, which are generally used as figurative representations of fresh and joyous prosperity, denote here the vigorous growth of that power which is destined to inflict the punishment. Both *châmâs* (violence) and *zâdhōn* (pride) refer to the enemy who is to chastise Israel. The violence which he employs rises up into the chastening rod of "evil," *i.e.* of ungodly Israel. In ver. 11*b* the effect of the blow is described in short, broken sentences. The emotion apparent in the frequent repetition of לֹא is intensified by the omission of the verb, which gives to the several clauses the character of exclamations. So far as the meaning is concerned, we have to insert יִהְיֶה in thought, and to take מִ in a partitive sense: there will not be anything of them, *i.e.* nothing will be left of them (the Israelites, or the inhabitants of the land). מֵהֶם (of them) is explained by the nouns which follow. הָמוֹן and the ἅπ. λεγ. הֶמֵהֶם, plural of הָם or הָמֵה, both derivatives of הָמָה, are so combined that הָמוֹן signifies the tumultuous multitude of people, הָמֵה the multitude of possessions (like הָמוֹן, Isa. lx. 2; Ps. xxxvii. 16, etc.). The meaning which Hävernick assigns to *hâmeh*, viz. anxiety or trouble, is unsupported and inappropriate. The ἅπ. λεγ. נֹהַּ is not to be derived from נָהָה, to lament, as the Rabbins affirm; or interpreted, as Kimchi—who adopts this derivation—maintains, on the ground of Jer. xvi. 4 sqq., as signifying that, on account of the multitude of the dying, there will be no more lamentation for the dead. This leaves the *Mappik* in ה unexplained. נֹהַּ is a derivative of a root נָוָה; in Arabic, نَابَ, *elata fuit res, eminuit, magnificus fuit;* hence נֹהַּ, *res magnifica.* When everything disappears in such a way as this, the joy occasioned by the acquisition of property, and the sorrow caused by its loss, will also pass away (ver. 12). The buyer will not rejoice in the property he has bought, for he will not be able to enjoy it; and the seller will not mourn that he has been obliged to part with his possession, for he would have lost it in any case.[1] The wrath of God is kindled against their whole multitude; that is to say, the judgment falls equally upon them all. The suffix in הֲמוֹנָהּ refers, as

---

[1] "It is a natural thing to rejoice in the purchase of property, and to mourn over its sale. But when slavery and captivity stare you in the face, rejoicing and mourning are equally absurd."—JEROME.

Jerome has correctly shown, to the "land of Israel" (*admath, Yisrâêl*) in ver. 2, *i.e.* to the inhabitants of the land. The words, "the seller will not return to what he has sold," are to be explained from the legal regulations concerning the year of jubilee in Lev. xxv., according to which all landed property that had been sold was to revert to its original owner (or his heir), without compensation, in the year of jubilee; so that he would then return to his *mimkâr* (Lev. xxv. 14, 27, 28). Henceforth, however, this will take place no more, even if הַיָּתָם, their (the sellers') life, should be still alive (*sc.* at the time when the return to his property would take place, according to the regulations of the year of jubilee), because Israel will be banished from the land. The clause וְעוֹד בַּחַיִּים ה׳ is a conditional circumstantial clause. The seller will not return (לֹא יָשׁוּב) to his possession, because the prophecy concerning the whole multitude of the people will not return (לֹא יָשׁוּב), *i.e.* will not turn back (for this meaning of שׁוּב, compare Isa. xlv. 23, lv. 11). As לֹא יָשׁוּב corresponds to the previous לֹא יָשׁוּב, so does חָזוֹן אֶל־כָּל־הֲמוֹנָהּ to חֲזוֹן אֶת־כָּל־הֲמוֹנָהּ in ver. 12. In the last clause of ver. 13, חַיָּתוֹ is not to be taken with בַּעֲוֹנוֹ in the sense of "in the iniquity of his life," which makes the suffix in בַּעֲוֹנוֹ superfluous, but with יִתְחַזָּק, the *Hithpael* being construed with the accusative, "strengthen himself in his life." Whether these words also refer to the year of jubilee, as Hävernick supposes, inasmuch as the regulation that every one was to recover his property was founded upon the idea of the restitution and re-creation of the theocracy, we may leave undecided; since the thought is evidently simply this: ungodly Israel shall be deprived of its possession, because the wicked shall not obtain the strengthening of his life through his sin. This thought leads on to ver. 14, in which we have a description of the utter inability to offer any successful resistance to the enemy employed in executing the judgment. There is some difficulty connected with the word בִּתְקוֹעַ, since the *infin. absolute*, which the form תָּקוֹעַ seems to indicate, cannot be construed with either a preposition or the article. Even if the expression בְּתָקוֹעַ תִּקְעוּ in Jer. vi. 1 was floating before the mind of Ezekiel, and led to his employing the bold phrase בַּתָּקוֹעַ, this would not justify the use of the infinitive absolute with a preposition and the article. תָּקוֹעַ must be a substantive form, and denote not *clangour*, but the instrument used to sound an alarm, viz. the *shôphâr* (ch. xxxiii. 3). הָכִין, an unusual form of the *inf. abs.* (see Josh. vii. 7), used in the place of the finite tense, and signifying to equip for war, as in Nah. ii. 4. הַכֹּל, everything requisite for waging war. And no one goes into the battle, because the wrath of God turns against them (Lev. xxvi. 17), and smites them with despair (Deut. xxxii. 30).

Vers. 15–22. *Third* strophe. Thus will they fall into irresistible destruction; even their silver and gold they will not rescue, but will cast it away as useless, and leave it for the enemy.—Ver. 15. *The sword without, and pestilence and famine within: he who is in the field will die by the sword; and famine and pestilence will devour him that is in the city.* Ver. 16. *And if their escaped ones escape, they will be upon the mountains like the doves of the valleys, all moaning, every one for his iniquity.* Ver. 17. *All hands will become feeble, and all knees flow with water.* Ver. 18. *They will gird themselves with sackcloth, and terrors will cover them; on all faces there will be shame, and baldness on all their heads.* Ver. 19. *They will throw their silver into the streets, and their gold will be as filth to them. Their silver and their gold will not be able to rescue them in the day of Jehovah's wrath; they will not satisfy their souls therewith, nor fill their stomachs thereby, for it was to them a stumbling-block to guilt.* Ver. 20. *And His beautiful ornament, they used it for pride; and their abominable images, their abominations they made thereof: therefore I make it filth to them.* Ver. 21. *And I shall give it into the hand of foreigners for prey, and to the wicked of the earth for spoil, that they may defile it.* Ver. 22. *I shall turn my face from them, that they defile my treasure;*

and oppressors shall come upon it and defile it.—The chastisement of God penetrates everywhere (ver. 15 compare with ch. v. 12); even flight to the mountains, that are inaccessible to the foe (compare 1 Macc. ii. 28; Matt. xxiv. 16), will only bring misery. Those who have fled to the mountains will coo —*i.e.* mourn, moan—like the doves of the valleys, which (as Bochart has correctly interpreted the simile in his *Hieroz.* II. p. 546, ed. Ros.), "when alarmed by the bird-catcher or the hawk, are obliged to forsake their natural abode, and fly elsewhere to save their lives. The mountain doves are contrasted with those of the valleys, as wild with tame." In כְּיוֹנֵי הֹמוֹת the figure and the fact are fused together. The words actually relate to the men who have fled; whereas the gender of הֹמוֹת is made to agree with that of כְּיוֹנֵי. The cooing of doves was regarded by the ancients as a moan (*hâgâh*), a mournful note (for proofs, see Gesen. on Isa. xxxviii. 14); for which Ezekiel uses the still stronger expression *hâmâh fremere*, to howl or growl (cf. Isa. lix. 11). The low moaning has reference to their iniquity, the punishment of which they are enduring. When the judgment bursts upon them, they will all (not merely those who have escaped, but the whole nation) be overwhelmed with terror, shame, and suffering. The words, "all knees flow with water" (for *hâlak* in this sense, compare Joel iv. 18), are a hyperbolical expression used to denote the entire loss of the strength of the knees (here, ver. 17 and ch. xxi. 12), like the heart melting and turning to water in Josh. vii. 5. With this utter despair there are associated grief and horror at the calamity that has fallen upon them, and shame and pain at the thought of the sins that have plunged them into such distress. For בְּפֻתָה בֻּלְצוּת, compare Ps. lv. 6; for אֶל־כָּל־פָּנִים בּוּשָׁה, Mic. vii. 10, Jer. li. 51; and for בְּכָל־רֹאשׁ קָרְחָה, Isa. xv. 2, Amos viii. 10. On the custom of shaving the head bald on account of great suffering or deep sorrow, see the comm. on Mic. i. 16.—In this state of anguish they will throw all their treasures away as sinful trash (ver. 19 sqq.). By the silver and gold which they will throw away (ver. 19), we are not to understand idolatrous images particularly,— these are first spoken of in ver. 20,—but the treasures of precious metals on which they had hitherto set their hearts. They will not merely throw these away as worthless, but look upon them as *niddâh*, filth, an object of disgust, inasmuch as they have been the servants of their evil lust. The next clause, "silver and gold cannot rescue them," are a reminiscence from Zeph. i. 18. But Ezekiel gives greater force to the thought by adding, "they will not appease their hunger therewith,"—that is to say, they will not be able to protect their lives thereby, either from the sword of the enemy (see the comm. on Zeph. i. 18) or from death by starvation, because there will be no more food to purchase within the besieged city. The clause כִּי מִכְשׁוֹל וגו׳ assigns the reason for that which forms the leading thought of the verse, namely, the throwing away of the silver and gold as filth; מִכְשׁוֹל עֲוֹנָם, a stumbling-block through which one falls into guilt and punishment; צְבִי עֶדְיוֹ, the beauty of his ornament, *i.e.* his beautiful ornament. The allusion is to the silver and gold; and the singular suffix is to be explained from the fact that the prophet fixed his mind upon the people as a whole, and used the singular in a general and indefinite sense. The words are written absolutely at the commencement of the sentence; hence the suffix attached to שָׂמָהוּ. Jerome has given the true meaning of the words: "what I (God) gave for an ornament of the possessors and for their wealth, they turned into pride." And not merely to ostentatious show (in the manner depicted in Isa. iii. 16 sqq.), but to abominable images, *i.e.* idols, did they apply the costly gifts of God (cf. Hos. viii. 4, xiii. 2). עָשָׂה בְ, to make of (gold and silver); בְ denoting the material with which one works and of which anything is made (as in Ex. xxxi. 4, xxxviii. 8). God punishes this abuse by making it (gold and silver) into *niddâh* to them, *i.e.*, according to ver. 19, by placing them in such circumstances that they cast it away as filth, and (ver. 21) by giving it as booty to the foe. The enemy is described as "the wicked of the earth" (cf. Ps. lxxv. 9), *i.e.* godless men, who not only seize upon the possession of Israel, but in the most wicked manner lay hands upon all that is holy, and defile it. The *Chetib* חִלְּלוּהָ is to be retained, notwithstanding the fact that it was preceded by a masculine suffix. What is threatened will take place, because the Lord will turn away His face from His people (מֵהֶם, from the Israelites), *i.e.* will withdraw His gracious protection from them, so that the enemy will be able to defile His treasure. *Tsáphŭn*, that which is hidden, the treasure (Job xx. 26; Obad. ver. 6). *Ts^ephŭnī* is generally supposed to refer to the temple, or the Most Holy Place in the temple. Jerome renders it *arcanum meum*, and gives this explanation: "signifying the Holy of Holies, which no one except the priests and the high priest dared to enter." This interpretation was so commonly adopted by the Fathers, that even Theodoret explains the rendering given in the Septuagint, τὴν ἐπισκοπήν μου, as signifying the Most Holy Place in the temple. On the other hand, the Chaldee has אַרְעָא בֵית שְׁכִינְתִּי, "the land of the house of my majesty;" and Calvin understands it as signifying "the land which was safe under His (*i.e.* God's) protection." But it is difficult to reconcile either explanation with the use of the word *tsáphŭn*. The verb *tsáphan* signifies to hide, shelter, lay up in safety. These meanings do not befit either the Holy of Holies in the temple or the land of Israel. It is true that the Holy of Holies was unapproachable by the laity, and even by the ordinary priests, but it was not a secret, a hidden place; and still less was this the case with the land of Canaan. We therefore adhere to the meaning, which is so thoroughly sustained by Job xx. 26 and Obad. ver. 6,—namely, "treasure," by which, no doubt, the temple-treasure is primarily intended. This rendering suits the context, as only treasures have been referred to before; and it may be made to harmonize with בָּאוּ בָהּ which follows. בּוֹא בְ signifies not merely *intrare in locum*, but also *venire in* (*e.g.* 2 Kings vi. 23; possibly Ezek.

xxx. 4), and may therefore be very properly rendered, "to get possession of," since it is only possible to obtain possession of a treasure by penetrating into the place where it is laid up or concealed. There is nothing at variance with this in the word חָלַל, *profunare*, since it has already occurred in ver. 21 in connection with the defiling of treasures and jewels. Moreover, as Calvin has correctly observed, the word is employed here to denote " an indiscriminate abuse, when, instead of considering to what purpose things have been entrusted to us, we squander them rashly and without selection, in contempt and even in scorn."

Vers. 23-27. *Fourth* strophe. Still worse is coming, namely, the captivity of the people, and overthrow of the kingdom.— Ver. 23. *Make the chain, for the land is full of capital crime, and the city full of outrage.* Ver. 24. *I shall bring evil ones of the nations, that they may take possession of their houses; and I shall put an end to the pride of the strong, that their sanctuaries may be defiled.* Ver. 25. *Ruin has come; they seek salvation, but there is none.* Ver. 26. *Destruction upon destruction cometh, and report upon report ariseth; they seek visions from prophets, but the law will vanish away from the priest, and counsel from the elders.* Ver. 27. *The king will mourn, and the prince will clothe himself in horror, and the hands of the common people will tremble. I will deal with them according to their way, and according to their judgments will I judge them, that they may learn that I am Jehovah.*—Those who have escaped death by sword or famine at the conquest of Jerusalem have captivity and exile awaiting them. This is the meaning of the command to make the chain, *i.e.* the fetters needed to lead the people into exile. This punishment is necessary, because the land is full of *mishpat dâmim*, judgment of blood. This cannot mean, there is a judgment upon the shedding of blood, *i.e.* upon murder, which is conducted by Jehovah, as Hävernick supposes. Such a thought is irreconcilable with מָלְאָה, and with the parallel מָלְאָה חָמָס. מִשְׁפַּט דָּמִים is to be explained after the same manner as מִשְׁפַּט מָוֶת (a matter for sentence of death, a capital crime) in Deut. xix. 6, 21, 22, as signifying a matter for sentence of bloodshed, *i.e.* a crime of blood, or capital crime, as the Chaldee has already rendered it. Because the land is filled with capital crime, and the city (Jerusalem) with violence, the Lord will bring רָעֵי גּוֹיִם, evil ones of the heathen, *i.e.* the worst of the heathen, to put an end to the pride of the Israelites. גְּאוֹן עַזִּים is not "pride of the insolents;" for עַזִּים does not stand for עַזֵּי פָנִים (Deut. xxviii. 50, etc.). The expression is rather to be explained from גְּאוֹן עֹז, pride of strength, in ch. xxiv. 21, xxx. 6, 18 (cf. Lev. xxvi. 19), and embraces everything on which a man (or a nation) bases his power and rests his confidence. The Israelites are called עַזִּים, because they thought themselves strong, or, according to ch. xxiv. 21, based their strength upon the possession of the temple and the holy land. This is indicated by וְנִחֲלוּ מִקְדְּשֵׁיהֶם which follows. נִחַל, *Niphal* of חָלַל and מִקְדְּשֵׁיהֶם, not a participle *Piel*, from מְקַדֵּשׁ, with the Dagesh dropped, but an unusual form, from מִקְדָּשׁ for מִקְדְּשֵׁיהֶם (*vid.* Ew. § 215*a*).—The ἅπ. λεγ. קְפָדָה, with the tone drawn back on account of the tone-syllable which follows (cf. Ges. § 29. 3. 6), signifies *excidium*, destruction (according to the Rabbins), from קָפַד, to shrink or roll up (Isa. xxxviii. 12). בָּא is a prophetic perfect. In ver. 25 the ruin of the kingdom is declared to be certain, and in vers. 26 and 27 the occurrence of it is more minutely depicted. Stroke upon stroke does the ruin come; and it is intensified by reports, alarming accounts, which crowd together and increase the terror, and also by the desperation of the spiritual and temporal leaders of the nation, —the prophets, priests, and elders,—whom God deprives of revelation, knowledge, and counsel; so that all ranks (king and princes and the common people) sink into mourning, alarm, and horror. That it is to no purpose that visions or prophecies are sought from the prophets (ver. 26), is evident from the antithetical statement concerning the priests and elders which immediately follows. The three statements serve as complements of one another. They seek for predictions from prophets, but the prophets receive no vision, no revelation. They seek instruction from priests, but instruction is withdrawn from the priests; and so forth. *Tōrāh* signifies instruction out of the law, which the priests were to give to the people (Mal. ii. 7). In ver. 27, the three classes into which the people were divided are mentioned—viz. king, prince (*i.e.* tribe-princes and heads of families), and, in contradistinction to both, עַם הָאָרֶץ, the common people, the people of the land, in distinction from the civil rulers, as in 2 Kings xxi. 24, xxiii. 30. מִדַּרְכָּם, literally from their way, their mode of action, will I do to them: *i.e.* my action will be derived from theirs, and regulated accordingly. אוֹתָם for אִתָּם, as in ch. iii. 22, etc. (See the comm. on ch. xvi. 59.)

CHAP. VIII.–XI. VISION OF THE DESTRUCTION OF JERUSALEM.

A year and two months after his call, the glory of the Lord appeared to the prophet a second time, as he had seen it by the Chebar. He is transported in spirit to Jerusalem into the court of the temple (ch. viii. 1–4), where the Lord causes him to see, first the idolatry of Israel (ch. viii. 5–18), and secondly, the judgment why, on account of this idolatry, all the inhabitants of Jerusalem are smitten (chap. ix.), the city is burned with fire, and the sanctuary forsaken by God (ch. x.). Lastly, after he has been charged to foretell to the representatives of the people more especially the coming judgment, and to those who are sent into exile a future salvation (ch. xi. 1–21), he describes how the gracious presence of God forsakes the city before his own eyes (ch. xi. 22, 23). After this has taken place, Ezekiel is carried back in the vision to Chaldea once more; and there, after the vision has come to an end, he announces to the exiles what he has seen and heard (ch. xi. 24, 25).

Chap. viii. ABOMINATIONS OF THE IDOLATRY OF THE HOUSE OF ISRAEL.—Vers. 1-4. Time and place of the divine revelation.—Ver. 1. *And it came to pass in the sixth year, in the sixth (month), on the fifth (day) of the month, I was sitting in my house, and the elders of Judah were sitting before me; there fell upon me the hand of the Lord Jehovah there.* Ver. 2. *And I saw, and behold a figure like the look of fire, from the look of its loins downwards fire, and from its loins upwards like a look of brilliance, like the sight of red-hot brass.* Ver. 3. *And he stretched out the form of a hand, and took me by the locks of my head, and wind carried me away between earth and heaven, and brought me to Jerusalem in visions of God, to the entrance of the gate of the inner court, which faces towards the north, where the image of jealousy exciting jealousy had its stand.* Ver. 4. *And, behold, the glory of the God of Israel was there, like the vision which I have seen in the valley.*—The place where Ezekiel received this new theophany agrees with the statements in ch. iii. 24 and iv. 4, 6, that he was to shut himself up in his house, and lie 390 days upon the left side, and 40 days upon the right side—in all, 430 days. The use of the word יֹשֵׁב, "I sat," is not at variance with this, as יָשַׁב does not of necessity signify sitting as contrasted with lying, but may also be used in the more general sense of staying, or living, in the house. Nor is the presence of the elders of Judah opposed to the command, in ch. iii. 24, to shut himself up in the house, as we have already observed in the notes on that passage. The new revelation is made to him in the presence of these elders, because it is of the greatest importance to them. They are to be witnesses of his ecstasy; and after this has left the prophet, are to hear from his lips the substance of the divine revelation (ch. xi. 25). It is otherwise with the time of the revelation. If we compare the date given in ch. viii. 1 with those mentioned before, this new vision apparently falls within the period required for carrying out the symbolical actions of the previous vision. Between ch. i. 1, 2 (the fifth day of the fourth month in the fifth year) and ch. viii. 1 (the fifth day of the sixth month in the sixth year) we have one year and two months, that is to say (reckoning the year as a lunar year at 354 days, and the two months at 59 days), 413 days; whereas the two events recorded in ch. i. 1–vii. 27 require at least 437 days, namely 7 days for ch. iii. 15, and $390 + 40 = 430$ days for ch. iv. 5, 6. Consequently the new theophany would fall within the 40 days, during which Ezekiel was to lie upon the right side for Judah. To get rid of this difficulty, Hitzig conjectures that the fifth year of Jehoiachin (ch. i. 2) was a leap year of 13 months or 385 days, by which he obtains an interval of 444 days after adding 59 for the two months,—a period sufficient not only to include the 7 days (ch. iii. 15) and $390 + 40$ days (ch. iv. 5, 6), but to leave 7 days for the time that elapsed between ch. vii. and viii. But however attractive this reckoning may appear, the assumption that the fifth year of the captivity of Jehoiachin was a leap year is purely conjectural; and there is nothing whatever to give it probability. Consequently the only thing that could lead us to adopt such a solution, would be the impossibility of reconciling the conclusion to be drawn from the chronological data, as to the time of the two theophanies, with the substance of these divine revelations. If we assume that Ezekiel carried out the symbolical acts mentioned in ch. iv. and v. in all their entirety, we can hardly imagine that the vision described in the chapters before us, by which he was transported in spirit to Jerusalem, occurred within the period of forty days, during which he was to typify the siege of Jerusalem by lying upon his right side. Nevertheless, Kliefoth has decided in favour of this view, and argues in support of it, that the vision described in ch. viii. 1 sqq. took place in the prophet's own house, that it is identical in substance with what is contained in ch. iii. 22–vii. 27, and that there is no discrepancy, because all that occurred here was purely internal, and the prophet himself was to address the words contained in ch. xi. 4–12 and xi. 14–21 to the inhabitants of Jerusalem in his state of ecstasy.

Moreover, when it is stated in ch. xi. 25 that Ezekiel related to the exiles all that he had seen in the vision, it is perfectly open to us to assume that this took place at the same time as his report to them of the words of God in ch. vi. and vii., and those which follow in ch. xii. But, on the other hand, it may be replied that the impression produced by ch. xi. 25 is not that the prophet waited several weeks after his visionary transport to Jerusalem before communicating to the elders what he saw in the vision. And even if the possibility of this cannot be disputed, we cannot imagine any reason why the vision should be shown to the prophet four weeks before it was to be related to the exiles. Again, there is not sufficient identity between the substance of the vision in ch. viii.-xi. and the revelation in ch. iv.-vii., to suggest any motive for the two to coincide. It is true that the burning of Jerusalem, which Ezekiel sees in ch. viii.-xi., is consequent upon the siege and conquest of that city, which he has already predicted in ch. iv.-vii. both in figure and word; but they are not so closely connected, that it was necessary on account of this connection for it to be shown to him before the completion of the symbolical siege of Jerusalem. And, lastly, although the ecstasy as a purely internal process is so far reconcilable with the prophet's lying upon his right side, that this posture did not preclude a state of ecstasy or render it impossible, yet this collision would ensue, that while the prophet was engaged in carrying out the former word of God, a new theophany would be received by him, which must necessarily abstract his mind from the execution of the previous command of God, and place him in a condition in which it would be impossible for him to set his face firmly upon the siege of Jerusalem, as he had been commanded to do in ch. iv. 7. On account of this collision, we cannot subscribe to the assumption, that it was during the time that Ezekiel was lying bound by God upon his right side to bear the sin of Jerusalem, that he was transported in spirit to the temple at Jerusalem. On the contrary, the fact that this transport occurred, according to ch. viii. 1, at a time when he could not have ended the symbolical acts of ch. iv., if he had been required to carry them out in all their external reality, furnishes us with conclusive evidence of the correctness of the view we have already expressed, that the symbolical acts of ch. iv. and v. did not lie within the sphere of outward reality (see comm. on ch. v. 4).—And if Ezekiel did not really lie for 430 days, there was nothing to hinder his having a fresh vision 14 months after the theophany in ch. i. and ch. iii. 22 sqq. For תִּפֹּל עָלַי יָד יְיָ, see at ch. iii. 22 and i. 3.

The figure which Ezekiel sees in the vision is described in ver. 2 in precisely the same terms as the appearance of God in ch. i. 27. The sameness of the two passages is a sufficient defence of the reading כְּמַרְאֵה־אֵשׁ against the arbitrary emendation כמ' אִישׁ, after the Sept. rendering ὁμοίωμα ἀνδρός, in support of which Ewald and Hitzig appeal to ch. i. 26, though without any reason, as the reading there is not אִישׁ, but אָדָם. It is not expressly stated here that the apparition was in human form—the fiery appearance is all that is mentioned; but this is taken for granted in the allusion to the מָתְנַיִם (the loins), either as self-evident, or as well known from ch. i. זֹהַר is synonymous with נֹגַהּ in ch. i. 4, 27. What is new in the present theophany is the stretching out of the hand, which grasps the prophet by the front hair of his head, whereupon he is carried by wind between heaven and earth, *i.e.* through the air, to Jerusalem, not in the body, but in visions of God (cf. ch. i. 1), that is to say, in spiritual ecstasy, and deposited at the entrance of the inner northern door of the temple. הַפְּנִימִית is not an adjective belonging to שַׁעַר, for this is not a feminine noun, but is used as a substantive, as in ch. xliii. 5 (= הֶחָצֵר הַפְּנִימִית: cf. ch. xl. 40): gate of the inner court, *i.e.* the gate on the north side of the inner court which led into the outer court. We are not informed whether Ezekiel was placed on the inner or outer side of this gate, *i.e.* in the inner or outer court; but it is evident from ver. 5 that he was placed in the inner court, as his position commanded a view of the image which stood at the entrance of the gate towards the north. The further statement, "where the standing place of the image of jealousy was," anticipates what follows, and points out the reason why the prophet was placed just there. The expression "image of jealousy" is explained by הַמַּקְנֶה, which excites the jealousy of Jehovah (see the comm. on Ex. xx. 5). Consequently, we have not to think of any image of Jehovah, but of an image of a heathen idol (cf. Deut. xxxii. 21); probably of Baal or Asherah, whose image had already been placed in the temple by Manasseh (2 Kings xxi. 7); certainly not the image of the corpse of Adonis moulded in wax or clay. This opinion, which Hävernick advances, is connected with the erroneous assumption that all the idolatrous abominations mentioned in this chapter relate to the celebration of an Adonis-festival in the temple. There (ver. 4) in the court of the temple Ezekiel saw once more the glory of the God of Israel, as he had seen it in the valley (ch. iii. 22) by the Chaboras, *i.e.* the appearance of God upon the throne with the cherubim and wheels; whereas the divine figure, whose hand grasped him in his house, and transported him to the temple (ver. 2), showed neither throne nor cherubim. The expression "God of Israel," instead of Jehovah (ch. iii. 23), is chosen as an antithesis to the strange god, the heathen idol, whose image stood in the temple. As the God of Israel, Jehovah cannot tolerate the image and worship of another god in *His* temple. To set up such an image in the temple of Jehovah was a practical renunciation of the covenant, a rejection of Jehovah on the part of Israel as its covenant God.

Here, in the temple, Jehovah shows to the prophet the various kinds of idolatry which Israel is practising both publicly and privately, not merely in the temple, but throughout the whole land. The arrangement of these different forms of idolatry in four groups or abomination scenes (vers. 5, 6, 7–12, 13–15, and 16–18), which the prophet sees both in and from the court of the temple, belong to the visionary drapery of this divine revelation. It is altogether erroneous to interpret the vision as signifying that all these forms of idolatry were practised in the temple itself; an assumption which cannot be carried out without doing violence to the description, more especially of the second abomination in vers. 7-12. Still more untenable is Hävernick's view, that the four pictures of idolatrous practices shown to the prophet are only intended to represent different scenes of a festival of Adonis held in the temple. The selection of the courts of the temple for depicting the idolatrous worship, arises from the fact that the temple was the place where Israel was called to worship the Lord its God. Consequently the apostasy of Israel from the Lord could not be depicted more clearly and strikingly than by the following series of pictures of idolatrous abominations practised in the temple under the eyes of God.

Vers. 5 and 6. *First* abomination-picture.—Ver. 5. *And He said to me, Son of man, lift up thine eyes now towards the north. And I lifted up my eyes towards the north, and, behold, to the north of the gate of the altar was this image of jealousy at the entrance.* Ver. 6. *And He said to me, Son of man, seest thou what they do? great abominations, which the house of Israel doeth here, that I may go far away from my sanctuary; and thou shalt yet again see greater abominations still.*—As Ezekiel had taken his stand in the inner court at the entrance of the north gate, and when looking thence towards the north saw the image of jealousy to the north of the altar gate, the image must have stood on the outer side of the entrance, so that the prophet saw it as he looked through the open doorway. The altar gate is the same as the northern gate of the inner court mentioned in ver. 3. But it is impossible to state with certainty how it came to be called the altar gate. Possibly from the circumstance that the sacrificial animals were taken through this gate to the altar, to be slaughtered on the northern side of the altar, according to Lev. i. 4, v. 11, etc. מֵהֵם, contracted from מֵהֵיהֶם, like

מַזֶּה from מַה זֶּה in Ex. iv. 2. The words "what they are doing here" do not force us to assume that at that very time they were worshipping the idol. They simply describe what was generally practised there. The setting up of the image involved the worship of it. The subject to לְרָחֳקָה is not the house of Israel, but Jehovah. They perform great abominations, so that Jehovah is compelled to go to a distance from His sanctuary, *i.e.* to forsake it (cf. ch. xi. 23), because they make it an idol-temple.

Vers. 7–12. *Second* abomination : Worship of beasts.—Ver. 7. *And He brought me to the entrance of the court, and I saw, and behold there was a hole in the wall.* Ver. 8. *And He said to me, Son of man, break through the wall: and I broke through the wall, and behold there was a door.* Ver. 9. *And He said to me, Come and see the wicked abominations which they are doing here.* Ver. 10. *And I came and saw, and behold there were all kinds of figures of reptiles, and beasts, abominations, and all kinds of idols of the house of Israel, drawn on the wall round about.* Ver. 11. *And seventy men of the elders of the house of Israel, with Jaazaniah the son of Shaphan standing among them, stood in front, every man with his censer in his hand; and the smell of a cloud of incense arose.* Ver. 12. *And He said to me, Seest thou, son of man, what the elders of the house of Israel do in the dark, every one in his image-chambers? For they say: Jehovah doth not see us; Jehovah hath forsaken the land.*—The entrance of the court to which Ezekiel was now transported cannot be the principal entrance to the outer court towards the east (Ewald). This would be at variance with the context, as we not only find the prophet at the northern entrance in vers. 3 and 5, but at ver. 14 we find him there still. If he had been taken to the eastern gate in the meantime, this would certainly have been mentioned. As that is not the case, the reference must be to that entrance to the court which lay between the entrance-gate of the inner court (ver. 3) and the northern entrance-gate to the house of Jehovah (ver. 14), or northern gate of the outer court, in other words, the northern entrance into the outer court. Thus the prophet was conducted out of the inner court through its northern gate into the outer court, and placed in front of the northern gate, which led out into the open air. There he saw a hole in the wall, and on breaking through the wall, by the command of God, he saw a door, and having entered it, he saw all kinds of figures of animals engraved on the wall round about, in front of which seventy of the elders of Israel were standing and paying reverence to the images of beasts with burning incense. According to ver. 12, the prophet was thereby shown what the elders of Israel did in the dark, every one in his image-chamber. From this explanation on the part of God concerning the picture shown to the prophet, it is very evident that it had no reference to any idolatrous worship practised by the elders in one or more of the cells of the outer court of the temple. For even though the objection raised by Kliefoth to this view, namely, that it cannot be proved that there were halls with recesses in the outer court, is neither valid nor correct, since the existence of such halls is placed beyond the reach of doubt by Jer. xxxv. 4, 2 Kings xxiii. 11, and 1 Chron. xxviii. 12; such a supposition is decidedly precluded by the fact, that the cells and recesses at the gates cannot have been large enough to allow of seventy-one men taking part in a festive idolatrous service. The supposition that the seventy-one men were distributed in different chambers is at variance with the distinct words of the text. The prophet not only sees the seventy elders standing along with Jaazaniah, but he could not look through one door into a number of chambers at once, and see the pictures drawn all round upon their walls. The assembling of the seventy elders in a secret cell by the northern gate of the outer temple to worship the idolatrous images engraved on the walls of the cell, is one feature in the visionary form given to the revelation of what the elders of the people were doing secretly throughout the whole land. To bring out more strikingly the secrecy of this idolatrous worship, the cell is so completely hidden in the wall, that the prophet is obliged to enlarge the hole by breaking through the wall before he can see the door which leads to the cell and gain a view of them and of the things it contains, and the things that are done therein.[1] And the number of the persons assembled there suggests the idea of a symbolical representation, as well as the secrecy of the cell. The seventy elders represent the whole nation; and the number is taken from Ex. xxiv. 1 sqq. and Num. xi. 16, xxiv. 25, where Moses, by the command of God, chooses seventy of the elders to represent the whole congregation at the making of the covenant, and afterwards to support his authority. This representation of the congregation was not a permanent institution, as we may see from the fact that in Num. xi. seventy other men are said to have been chosen for the purpose named. The high council, consisting of seventy members, the so-called Sanhedrim, was formed after the captivity on the basis of these Mosaic types. In the midst of the seventy was Jaazaniah the son of Shaphan, a different man therefore from the Jaazaniah mentioned in ch. xi. 1. Shaphan is probably the person mentioned as a man of distinction in 2 Kings xxii. 3 sqq.; Jer. xxix. 3, xxxvi. 10, xxxix. 14. It is impossible to decide on what ground Jaazaniah is specially mentioned by name; but it can hardly be on account of the meaning of the name he bore, "Jehovah hears," as Hävernick supposes. It is probable that he held a prominent position among the elders of the nation, so that he is mentioned here by name as the leader of this national representation. —On the wall of the chamber round about there were drawn all kinds of figures of רֶמֶשׂ וּבְהֵמָה, reptiles and quadrupeds (see Gen. i. 24). שֶׁקֶץ is in apposition not only to בְּהֵמָה, but also to רֶמֶשׂ, and therefore, as belonging to both, is not to be connected with בְּהֵמָה in the construct state. The drawing of

---

[1] "Because the whole is exhibited pictorially and figuratively, he says that he saw one hole in a wall, and was directed to dig through and make it larger, that he might enter as if through an open door, and see the things which he could not possibly have seen while stationed outside."— JEROME.

reptiles and quadrupeds became a *sheqetz*, or abomination, from the fact that the pictures had been drawn for the purpose of religious worship. The following clause, "and all the idols of the house of Israel," is co-ordinate with כָּל־תַּבְנִית וגו׳. Besides the animals drawn on the walls, there were idols of other kinds in the chamber. The drawing of reptiles and quadrupeds naturally suggests the thought of the animal-worship of Egypt. We must not limit the words to this, however, since the worship of animals is met with in the nature-worship of other heathen nations, and the expression כָּל־תַּבְנִית, "all kinds of figures," as well as the clause, "all kinds of idols of the house of Israel," points to every possible form of idol-worship as spread abroad in Israel. עָתָר, according to the Aramaean usage, signifies *suffimentum*, perfume, בַּחֹשֶׁךְ, in the dark, *i.e.* in secret, like בַּסֵּתֶר in 2 Sam. xii. 12; not in the sacred darkness of the cloud of incense (Hävernick). חַדְרֵי מַשְׂכִּית, image-chambers, is the term applied to the rooms or closets in the dwelling-houses of the people in which idolatrous images were set up and secretly worshipped. מַשְׂכִּית signifies idolatrous figures, as in Lev. xxvi. 1 and Num. xxxiii. 52. This idolatry was justified by the elders, under the delusion that "Jehovah seeth us not;" that is to say, not: "He does not trouble Himself about us," but He does not see what we do, because He is not omniscient (cf. Isa. xxix. 15); and He has forsaken the land, withdrawn His presence and His help. Thus they deny both the omniscience and omnipresence of God (cf. ch. ix. 9).

Vers. 13–15. *Third* abomination: Worship of Thammuz.— Ver. 13. *And He said to me, Thou shalt yet again see still greater abominations which they do.* Ver. 14. *And He brought me to the entrance of the gate of the house of Jehovah, which is towards the north, and behold there sat the women, weeping for Thammuz.* Ver. 15. *And He said to me, Dost thou see it, O son of man? Thou shalt yet again see still greater abominations than these.*— The prophet is taken from the entrance into the court to the entrance of the gate of the temple, to see the women sitting there weeping for Thammuz. The article in הַנָּשִׁים is used generically. Whilst the men of the nation, represented by the seventy elders, were secretly carrying on their idolatrous worship, the women were sitting at the temple gate, and indulging in public lamentation for Thammuz. Under the weeping for Thammuz, Jerome (with Melito of Sardis and all the Greek Fathers) has correctly recognised the worship of Adonis. "תמוז, Θαμμούζ or Θαμμούς," says Jerome, " whom we have interpreted as Adonis, is called *Thamuz* both in Hebrew and Syriac; and because, according to the heathen legend, this lover of Venus and most beautiful youth is said to have been slain in the month of June and then restored to life again, they call this month of June by the same name, and keep an annual festival in his honour, at which he is lamented by women as though he were dead, and then afterwards celebrated in songs as having come to life again." This view has not been shaken even by the objections raised by Chwolson in his *Ssaabins* (II. 27. 202 sqq.), his relics of early Babylonian literature (p. 101), and his Tammuz and human-worship among the ancient Babylonians. For the myth of Thammuz, mentioned in the Nabataean writings as a man who was put to death by the king of Babylon, whom he had commanded to introduce the worship of the seven planets and the twelve signs of the zodiac, and who was exalted to a god after his death, and honoured with a mourning festival, is nothing more than a refined interpretation of the very ancient nature-worship which spread over the whole of Hither Asia, and in which the power of the sun over the vegetation of the year was celebrated. The etymology of the word *Tammuz* is doubtful. It is probably a contraction of תמוזה, from מזה = מסס, so that it denotes the decay of the force of nature, and corresponds to the Greek ἀφανισμὸς Ἀδώνιδος (see Hävernick *in loc.*).

Vers. 16-18. *Fourth* abomination: Worship of the sun by the priests.—Ver. 16. *And He took me into the inner court of the house of Jehovah, and behold, at the entrance into the temple of*

Jehovah, between the porch and the altar, as it were five and twenty men, with their backs towards the temple of Jehovah and their faces towards the east; they were worshipping the sun towards the east. Ver. 17. *And He said to me, Seest thou this, son of man? Is it too little for the house of Judah to perform the abominations which they are performing here, that they also fill the land with violence, and provoke me to anger again and again? For behold they stretch out the vine-branch to their nose.* Ver. 18. *But I also will act in fury; my eye shall not look compassionately, and I will not spare; and if they cry with a loud voice in my ears, I will not hear them.*—After Ezekiel has seen the idolatrous abominations in the outer court, or place for the people, he is taken back into the inner court, or court of the priests, to see still greater abominations there. Between the porch of the temple and the altar of burnt-offering, the most sacred spot therefore in the inner court, which the priests alone were permitted to tread (Joel ii. 17), he sees as if twenty-five men, with their backs toward the temple, were worshipping the sun in the east. כְּ before עֶשְׂרִים is not a preposition, *circa*, about, but a particle of comparison (an appearance): as if twenty-five men; after the analogy of כְּ before an accusative (*vid*. Ewald, § 282*e*). For the number here is not an approximative one; but twenty-five is the exact number, namely, the twenty-four leaders of the classes of priests (1 Chron. xxiv. 5 sqq.; 2 Chron. xxxvi. 14; Ezra x. 5), with the high priest at the head (see Lightfoot's *Chronol. of O. T.*, Opp. I. 124). As the whole nation was seen in the seventy elders, so is the entire priesthood represented here in the twenty-five leaders as deeply sunk in disgraceful idolatry. Their apostasy from the Lord is shown in the fact that they turn their back upon the temple, and therefore upon Jehovah, who was enthroned in the temple, and worship the sun, with their faces turned towards the east. The worship of the sun does not refer to the worship of Adonis, as Hävernick supposes, although Adonis was a sun-god; but generally to the worship of the heavenly bodies, against which

Moses had warned the people (Deut. iv. 19, xvii. 3), and which found its way in the time of Manasseh into the courts of the temple, whence it was afterwards expelled by Josiah (2 Kings xxiii. 5, 11). The form מִשְׁתַּחֲוִיתֶם must be a copyist's error for מִשְׁתַּחֲוִים; as the supposition that it is an unusual form, with a play upon הִשְׁחִית,[1] is precluded by the fact that it would in that case be a 2d per. plur. perf., and such a construction is rendered impossible by the הֵמָּה which immediately precedes it (cf. Ewald, § 118a).—To these idolatrous abominations Judah has added other sins, as if these abominations were not bad enough in themselves. This is the meaning of the question in ver. 17, הֲנָקֵל וגו׳: is it too little for the house of Judah, etc.? נָקֵל with מִן, as in Isa. xlix. 6. To indicate the fulness of the measure of guilt, reference is again briefly made to the moral corruption of Judah. חָמָס embraces all the injuries inflicted upon men; תּוֹעֵבוֹת, impiety towards God, i.e. idolatry. By violent deeds they provoke God repeatedly to anger (שׁוּב, followed by an infinitive, expresses the repetition of an action). The last clause of ver. 17 (וְהִנָּם שֹׁלְחִים וגו׳) is very obscure. The usual explanation, which has been adopted by J. D. Michaelis and Gesenius: "they hold the twig to their nose," namely, the sacred twig Barsom, which the Parsees held in their hands when praying (vid. Hyde, de relig. vet. Pars. p. 350, ed. 2; and Kleuker, Zend-Avesta, III. p. 204), suits neither the context nor the words. According to the position of the clause in the context, we do not expect an allusion to a new idolatrous rite, but an explanation of the way in which Judah had excited the wrath of God by its violent deeds. Moreover, זְמוֹרָה is not a suitable word to apply to the Barsom,—Z'môrâh is a shoot or tendril of the vine (cf. ch. xv. 2; Isa. xvii. 10; Num. xiii. 23). The Barsom, on the other hand, consisted of bunches of twigs of the tree Gez or Hom, or of branches of the pomegranate, the tamarisk, or the date (cf. Kleuker l.c., and Strabo, XV. 733),

---

[1] "An extraordinary form, invented for the purpose of more effectually expressing their extraordinary abomination."—LIGHTFOOT.

and was not held to the nose, but kept in front of the mouth as a magical mode of driving demons away (*vid.* Hyde, *l.c.*). Lastly, שָׁלַח אֶל does not mean to hold anything, but to stretch out towards, to prepare to strike, to use violence. Of the other explanations given, only two deserve any consideration,— namely, first, the supposition that it is a proverbial expression, "to apply the twig to anger," in the sense of adding fuel to the fire, which Doederlein (*ad Grotii adnott.*) applies in this way, "by these things they supply food, as it were, to my wrath, which burns against themselves," *i.e.* they bring fuel to the fire of my wrath. Lightfoot gives a similar explanation in his *Hor. hebr. ad* John xv. 6. The second is that of Hitzig: "they apply the sickle to their nose," *i.e.* by seeking to injure me, they injure themselves. In this case זְמוֹרָה must be taken in the sense of מַזְמֵרָה, a sickle or pruning-knife, and pointed זְמוֹרָה. The saying does appear to be a proverbial one, but the origin and meaning of the proverb have not yet been satisfactorily explained.—Ver. 18. Therefore will the Lord punish unsparingly (cf. ch. vii. 4, 9, v. 11). This judgment he shows to the prophet in the two following chapters.

Chap. ix. THE ANGELS WHICH SMITE JERUSALEM.— Vers. 1–3. At the call of Jehovah, His servants appear to execute the judgment.—Ver. 1. *And He called in my ears with a loud voice, saying, Come hither, ye watchmen of the city, and every one his instrument of destruction in his hand.* Ver. 2. *And behold six men came by the way of the upper gate, which is directed toward the north, every one with his smashing-tool in his hand; and a man in the midst of them, clothed in white linen, and writing materials by his hip; and they came and stood near the brazen altar.* Ver. 3. *And the glory of the God of Israel rose up from the cherub, upon which it was, to the threshold of the house, and called to the man clothed in white linen, by whose hip the writing materials were.*—פְּקֻדּוֹת הָעִיר does not mean the punishments of the city. This rendering does not suit the context, since it is not the punishments that are introduced, but the men who execute them; and it is not established by the usage of the language. פְּקֻדָּה is frequently used, no doubt, in the sense of visitation or chastisement (*e.g.* Isa. x. 3; Hos. ix. 7); but it is not met with in the plural in this sense. In the plural it only occurs in the sense of supervision or protectorate, in which sense it occurs not only in Jer. lii. 11 and Ezek. xliv. 11, but also (in the singular) in Isa. lx. 17, and as early as Num. iii. 38, where it relates to the presidency of the priests, and very frequently in the Chronicles. Consequently פְּקֻדּוֹת are those whom God has appointed to watch over the city, the city-guard (2 Kings xi. 18),—not earthly, but heavenly watchmen,—who are now to inflict punishment upon the ungodly, as the authorities appointed by God. קִרְבוּ is an imperative *Piel*, as in Isa. xli. 21, and must not be altered into קָרְבוּ (*Kal*), as Hitzig proposes. The *Piel* is used in an intransitive sense, *festinanter appropinquavit*, as in ch. xxxvi. 8. The persons called come by the way of the upper northern gate of the temple, to take their stand before Jehovah, whose glory had appeared in the inner court. The upper gate is the gate leading from the outer court to the inner, or upper court, which stood on higher ground,—the gate mentioned in ch. viii. 3 and 5. In the midst of the six men furnished with smashing-tools there was one clothed in white byssus, with writing materials at his side. The dress and equipment, as well as the instructions which he afterwards receives and executes, show him to be the prince or leader of the others. Kliefoth calls in question the opinion that these seven men are angels; but without any reason. Angels appearing in human form are frequently called אֲנָשִׁים or אִישׁ, according to their external *habitus*. But the number seven neither presupposes the dogma of the seven archangels, nor is copied from the seven Parsic *amschaspands*. The dress worn by the high priest, when presenting the sin-offering on the great day of atonement (Lev. xvi. 4, 23), was made of בַּד, *i.e.* of white material woven from byssus thread (see the comm. on Ex. xxviii. 42). It has been inferred from this, that the figure clothed in white linen was the angel of Jehovah, who appears as the heavenly high priest, to protect and care for his own. In support of this, the circumstance may be also adduced, that the man whom Daniel saw above the water of the Tigris, and whose appearance is described, in Dan. x. 5, 6, in the same manner as that of Jehovah in Ezek. i. 4, 26, 27, and that of the risen Christ in Rev. i. 13–15, appears clothed in בַּדִּים (Dan. x. 5, xii. 6, 7).[1] Nevertheless, we cannot regard this view as established. The shining white talar, which is evidently meant by the plural בַּדִּים, occurring only here and in Daniel (*ut. sup.*), is not a dress peculiar to the angel of Jehovah or to Christ. The seven angels, with the vials of wrath, also appear in garments of shining white linen (ἐνδεδυμένοι λίνον καθαρὸν λαμπρόν, Rev. xv. 6); and the shining white colour, as a symbolical representation of divine holiness and glory (see comm. on Lev. xvi. 4 and Rev. xix. 8), is the colour generally chosen for the clothing both of the heavenly spirits and of "just men made perfect" (Rev. xix. 8). Moveover, the angel with the writing materials here is described in a totally different manner from the appearance of Jehovah in Ezek. i. and Dan. x., or that of Christ in Rev. i.; and there is nothing whatever to indicate a being equal with God. Again, the distinction between him and the other six men leads to no other conclusion, than that he stood in the same relation to them as the high priest to the Levites, or the chancellor to the other officials. This position is indicated by the writing materials on his hips, *i.e.* in the girdle on

---

[1] לְבֻשׁ בַּדִּים is rendered by the LXX., in the passage before us, ἐνδεδυκὼς ποδήρη. It is in accordance with this that Christ is described in Rev. i. 13 as clothed with a ποδήρης, and not after Dan. x. 5, as Hengstenberg supposes. In Dan. x. 5, the Septuagint has ἐνδεδυμένος βαδδίν or τὰ βαδδίν. In other places, the Sept. rendering of בַּד is λίνον (thus Lev. xvi. 4, 23, vi. 3; Ex. xxviii. 42, etc.); and hence the λίνον λαμπρόν of Rev. xv. 6 answers to the בַּד made of שֵׁשׁ, βύσσος, and is really the same as the βύσσινον λαμπρόν of Rev. xix. 8.

his hips, in which scribes in the East are accustomed to carry their writing materials (*vid.* Rosenmüller, *A. u. N. Morgenland,* IV. p. 323). He is provided with these for the execution of the commission given to him in ver. 4. In this way the description can be very simply explained, without the slightest necessity for our resorting to Babylonian representations of the god Nebo, *i.e.* Mercury, as the scribe of heaven. The seven men take their station by the altar of burnt-offering, because the glory of God, whose commands they were about to receive, had taken up its position there for the moment (Kliefoth); not because the apostate priesthood was stationed there (Hävernick). The glory of Jehovah, however, rose up from the cherub to the threshold of the house. The meaning of this is not that it removed from the interior of the sanctuary to the outer threshold of the temple-building (Hävernick), for it was already stationed, according to ch. viii. 16, above the cherub, between the porch and the altar. It went back from thence to the threshold of the temple-porch, through which one entered the Holy Place, to give its orders there. The reason for leaving its place above the cherubim (the singular כְּרוּב is used collectively) to do this, was not that " God would have had to turn round in order to address the seven from the throne, since, according to ch. viii. 4 and 16, He had gone from the north gate of the outer court into the inner court, and His servants had followed Him" (Hitzig); for the cherubim moved in all four directions, and therefore God, even from the throne, could turn without difficulty to every side. God left His throne, that He might issue His command for the judgment upon Israel from the threshold of the temple, and show Himself to be the judge who would forsake the throne which He had assumed in Israel. This command He issues from the temple court, because the temple was the place whence God attested Himself to His people, both by mercy and judgment.

Vers. 4–7. The divine command.—Ver. 4. *And Jehovah said to him, Go through the midst of the city, through the midst of*

Jerusalem, and mark a cross upon the foreheads of the men who sigh and groan over all the abominations which take place in their midst. Ver. 5. *And to those he said in my ears: Go through the city behind him, and smite. Let not your eye look compassionately, and do not spare.* Ver. 6. *Old men, young men, and maidens, and children, and women, slay to destruction: but ye shall not touch any one who has the cross upon him; and begin at my sanctuary. And they began with the old men, who were before the house.* Ver. 7. *And He said to them, Defile the house, and fill the courts with slain; go ye out. And they went out, and smote in the city.*—God commands the man provided with the writing materials to mark on the forehead with a cross all the persons in Jerusalem who mourn over the abominations of the nation, in order that they may be spared in the time of the judgment. תָו, the last letter of the Hebrew alphabet, had the form of a cross in the earlier writing. הִתְוָה תָו, to mark a ת, is therefore the same as to make a mark in the form of a cross; although there was at first no other purpose in this sign than to enable the servants employed in inflicting the judgment of God to distinguish those who were so marked, so that they might do them no harm. Ver. 6. And this was the reason why the תָו was to be marked upon the forehead, the most visible portion of the body; the early Christians, according to a statement in Origen, looked upon the sign itself as significant, and saw therein a prophetic allusion to the sign of the cross as the distinctive mark of Christians. A direct prophecy of the cross of Christ is certainly not to be found here, since the form of the letter *Tāv* was the one generally adopted as a sign, and, according to Job xxxi. 35, might supply the place of a signature. Nevertheless, as Schmieder has correctly observed, there is something remarkable in this coincidence to the thoughtful observer of the ways of God, whose counsel has carefully considered all beforehand, especially when we bear in mind that in the counterpart to this passage (Rev. vii. 3) the seal of the living God is stamped upon the foreheads of the servants of

God, who are to be exempted from the judgment, and that according to Rev. xiv. 1 they had the name of God written upon their foreheads. So much, at any rate, is perfectly obvious from this, namely, that the sign was not arbitrarily chosen, but was inwardly connected with the fact which it indicated; just as in the event upon which our vision is based (Ex. xii. 13, 22 sqq.) the distinctive mark placed upon the houses of the Israelites in Egypt, in order that the destroying angel might pass them by, namely, the smearing of the doorposts with the blood of the paschal lamb that had been slain, was selected on account of its significance and its corresponding to the thing signified. The execution of this command is passed over as being self-evident; and it is not till ver. 11 that it is even indirectly referred to again.—In vers. 5, 6 there follows, first of all, the command given to the other six men. They are to go through the city, behind the man clothed in white linen, and to smite without mercy all the inhabitants of whatever age or sex, with this exception, that they are not to touch those who are marked with the cross. The עַל for אֶל before תָּהוֹם is either a slip of the pen, or, as the continued transmission of so striking an error is very improbable, is to be accounted for from the change of א into ע, which is so common in Aramaean. The *Chetib* עֵינֵיכֶם is the unusual form grammatically considered, and the singular, which is more correct, has been substituted as *Keri*. תַּהֲרְגוּ is followed by לְמַשְׁחִית, to increase the force of the words and show the impossibility of any life being saved. They are to make a commencement at the sanctuary, because it has been desecrated by the worship of idols, and therefore has ceased to be the house of the Lord. To this command the execution is immediately appended; they began with the old men who were before the house, *i.e.* they began to slay them. הָאֲנָשִׁים הַזְּקֵנִים are neither the twenty-five priests (ch. viii. 16) nor the seventy elders (ch. viii. 11). The latter were not לִפְנֵי הַבַּיִת, but in a chamber by the outer temple gate; whereas לִפְנֵי הַבַּיִת, in front of the temple house, points to the inner court. This locality makes it natural to think of priests, and consequently the LXX. rendered מִמִּקְדָּשִׁי by ἀπὸ τῶν ἁγίων μου. But the expression אֲנָשִׁים זְקֵנִים is an unsuitable one for the priests. We have therefore no doubt to think of men advanced in years, who had come into the court possibly to offer sacrifice, and thereby had become liable to the judgment. In ver. 7 the command, which was interrupted in ver. 6b, is once more resumed. They are to defile the house, *i.e.* the temple, namely, by filling the courts with slain. It is in this way that we are to connect together, so far as the sense is concerned, the two clauses, "defile . . . and fill." This is required by the facts of the case. For those slain "before the house" could only have been slain in the courts, as there was no space between the temple house and the courts in which men could have been found and slain. But לִפְנֵי הַבַּיִת cannot be understood as signifying "in the neighbourhood of the temple," as Kliefoth supposes, for the simple reason that the progressive order of events would thereby be completely destroyed. The angels who were standing before the altar of burnt-offering could not begin their work by going out of the court to smite the sinners who happened to be in the neighbourhood of the temple, and then returning to the court to do the same there, and then again going out into the city to finish their work there. They could only begin by slaying the sinners who happened to be in the courts, and after having defiled the temple by their corpses, by going out into the city to slay all the ungodly there, as is related in the second clause of the verse (ver. 7b).

Vers. 8–11. *Intercession of the prophet, and the answer of the Lord.*—Ver. 8. *And it came to pass when they smote and I remained, I fell upon my face, and cried, and said: Alas! Lord Jehovah, wilt Thou destroy all the remnant of Israel, by pouring out Thy wrath upon Jerusalem?* Ver. 9. *And He said to me: The iniquity of the house of Israel and Judah is immeasurably great, and the land is full of blood-guiltiness, and the city full of perversion; for they say Jehovah hath forsaken the land, and Jehovah seeth not.* Ver. 10. *So also shall my eye not look with pity, and I will not spare; I will give their way upon their head.* Ver. 11. *And, behold, the man clothed in white linen, who had the writing materials on his hip, brought answer, and said: I have done as thou hast commanded me.*—The *Chetib* נאשׁאר is an incongruous form, composed of participle and imperfect fused into one, and is evidently a copyist's error. It is not to be altered into אֶשָּׁאֵר, however (the 1st pers. imperf. *Niph.*), but to be read as a participle נִשְׁאָר, and taken with בְּהַכּוֹתָם as a continuation of the circumstantial clause. For the words do not mean that Ezekiel alone was left, but that when the angels smote and he was left, *i.e.* was spared, was not smitten with the rest, he fell on his face, to entreat the Lord for mercy. These words and the prophet's intercession both apparently presuppose that among the inhabitants of Jerusalem there was no one found who was marked with the sign of the cross, and therefore could be spared. But this is by no means to be regarded as established. For, in the first place, it is not stated that *all* had been smitten by the angels; and, secondly, the intercession of the prophet simply assumes that, in comparison with the multitude of the slain, the number of those who were marked with the sign of the cross and spared was so small that it escaped the prophet's eye, and he was afraid that they might all be slain without exception, and the whole of the remnant of the covenant nation be destroyed. The שְׁאֵרִית of Israel and Judah is the covenant nation in its existing state, when it had been so reduced by the previous judgments of God, that out of the whole of what was once so numerous a people, only a small portion remained in the land. Although God has previously promised that a remnant shall be preserved (ch. v. 3, 4), He does not renew this promise to the prophet, but begins by holding up the greatness of the iniquity of Israel, which admits of no sparing, but calls for the most merciless punishment, to show him that, according to the strict demand of justice, the whole nation has deserved destruction. כָּמָּה (ver. 9) is not equivalent to מוּהָט, oppression (Isa. lviii. 9), but signifies perversion of justice; although מִשְׁפָּט is not mentioned, since this is also omitted in Ex. xxiii. 2, where הִטָּה occurs in the same sense. For ver. 9*b*, *vid.* ch. viii. 12. For דַּרְכָּם בְּרֹ׳ נָתַתִּי (ver. 10 and ch. xi. 21, 22, 31), *vid.* 1 Kings viii. 32. While God is conversing with the prophet, the seven angels have performed their work; and in ver. 11 their leader returns to Jehovah with the announcement that His orders have been executed. He does this, not in his own name only, but in that of all the rest. The first act of the judgment is thus shown to the prophet in a figurative representation. The second act follows in the next chapter.

Chap. x. BURNING OF JERUSALEM, AND WITHDRAWAL OF THE GLORY OF JEHOVAH FROM THE SANCTUARY.—This chapter divides itself into two sections. In vers. 1-8 the prophet is shown how Jerusalem is to be burned with fire. In vers. 9-22 he is shown how Jehovah will forsake His temple.

Vers. 1-8. The angel scatters coals of fire over Jerusalem.— Ver. 1. *And I saw, and behold upon the firmament, which was above the cherubim, it was like sapphire-stone, to look at as the likeness of a throne; He appeared above them.* Ver. 2. *And He spake to the man clothed in white linen, and said: Come between the wheels below the cherubim, and fill thy hollow hands with fire-coals from between the cherubim, and scatter them over the city: and he came before my eyes.* Ver. 3. *And the cherubim stood to the right of the house when the man came, and the cloud filled the inner court.* Ver. 4. *And the glory of Jehovah had lifted itself up from the cherubim to the threshold of the house; and the house was filled with the cloud, and the court was full of the splendour of the glory of Jehovah.* Ver. 5. *And the noise of the wings of the cherubim was heard to the outer court, as the voice of the Almighty God when He speaketh.* Ver. 6. *And it came to pass, when He commanded the man clothed in white linen, and said, Take fire from between the wheels, from between the cherubim, and he came and stood by the side of the wheel,* Ver. 7. *That the cherub stretched out his hand between the cherubim to the fire, which was between the cherubim, and lifted (some) off and gave it into the hands of the man clothed in white linen. And he took it, and went out.* Ver. 8. *And there appeared by the cherubim the likeness of a man's hand under their wings.*—Ver. 1 introduces the description of the second act of the judgment. According to ch. ix. 3, Jehovah had come down from His throne above the cherubim to the threshold of the temple to issue His orders thence for the judgment upon the inhabitants of Jerusalem, and according to ch. x. 4 He goes thither once more. Consequently He had resumed His seat above the cherubim in the meantime. This is expressed in ver. 1, not indeed in so many words, but indirectly or by implication. Ezekiel sees the theophany; and on the firmament above the cherubim, like sapphire-stone to look at, he beholds the likeness of a throne on which Jehovah appeared. To avoid giving too great prominence in this appearance of Jehovah to the bodily or human form, Ezekiel does not speak even here of the form of Jehovah, but simply of His throne, which he describes in the same manner as in ch. i. 26. אֶל stands for עַל according to the later usage of the language. It will never do to take אֶל in its literal sense, as Kliefoth does, and render the words: "Ezekiel saw it move away to the firmament;" for the object to וָאֶרְאֶה וְהִנֵּה is not יְהוָֹה or כְּבוֹד יְהוָֹה, but the form of the throne sparkling in sapphire-stone; and this throne had not separated itself from the firmament above the cherubim, but Jehovah, or the glory of Jehovah, according to ch. ix. 3, had risen up from the cherubim, and moved away to the temple threshold. The כְּ before מַרְאֵה is not to be erased, as Hitzig proposes after the LXX., on the ground that it is not found in ch. i. 26; it is quite appropriate here. For the words do not affirm that Ezekiel saw the likeness of a throne like sapphire-stone; but that he saw something like sapphire-stone, like the appearance of the form of a throne. Ezekiel does not see Jehovah, or the glory of Jehovah, move away to the firmament, and then return to the throne. He simply sees once more the resemblance of a throne upon the firmament, and the Lord appearing thereon. The latter is indicated in נִרְאָה עֲלֵיהֶם. These words are not to be taken in connection with כְּמַרְאֵה וגו׳, so as to form one sentence; but have been very properly separated by the *athnach* under כִּפֵּא, and treated as an independent assertion. The subject to נִרְאָה might, indeed, be דְּמוּת כִּסֵּא, "the likeness of a throne appeared above the cherubim;" but in that case the words would form a pure tautology, as the fact of the throne becoming visible has already been mentioned in the preceding clause. The subject must therefore be Jehovah, as in the case of וַיֹּאמֶר in ver. 2, where there can be no doubt on the matter. Jehovah has resumed His throne, not "for the purpose of removing to a distance, because the courts of the temple have been defiled by dead bodies" (Hitzig), but because the object for which He left it has been attained. He now commands the man clothed in white linen to go in between the wheels under the cherubim, and fill his hands with fire-coals from thence, and scatter them over the city (Jerusalem). This he did, so that Ezekiel could see it. According to this, it appears as if Jehovah had issued the command from His throne; but if we compare what follows, it is evident from ver. 4 that the glory of Jehovah had risen up again from the throne, and removed to the threshold of the temple, and that it was not till after the man in white linen had scattered the coals over the city that it left the threshold of the temple, and ascended once more up to the throne above the cherubim, so as to forsake the temple (ver. 18 sqq.). Consequently we can only understand vers. 2–7 as implying that Jehovah issued the command in ver. 2, not from His throne, but from the threshold of the temple, and that He had therefore returned to the threshold of the temple for this purpose, and for the very same reason as in ch. ix. 3. The possibility of interpreting the verses in this way is apparent from the fact that ver. 2 contains a summary of the whole of the contents of this section, and that vers. 3-7 simply furnish more minute explanations, or contain circumstantial clauses, which throw light upon the whole affair. This is obvious in the case of ver. 3, from the form of the clause; and in vers. 4 and 5, from the fact that in vers. 6 and 7 the command (ver. 2) is resumed, and the execution of it, which was already indicated in וַיָּבֹא לְעֵינַי (ver. 2), more minutely described and carried forward in the closing words of the seventh verse, וַיִּקַּח וַיֵּצֵא. הַגַּלְגַּל in ver. 2 signifies the whirl or rotatory motion, *i.e.* the wheel-work, or the four *ōphannim* under the cherubim regarded as moving. The angel was to go in between these, and take coals out of the fire there, and scatter them over the city. "In the fire of God, the fire of His wrath, will kindle the fire for consuming the city" (Kliefoth). To depict the scene more clearly, Ezekiel observes in ver. 3, that at this moment the cherubim were standing to the right of the house, *i.e.* on the south or rather south-east of the temple house, on the south of the altar of burnt-offering. According to the Hebrew usage the right side was the southern side, and the prophet was in the inner court, whither, according to ch. viii. 16, the divine glory had taken him; and, according to ch. ix. 2, the seven angels had gone to the front of the altar, to receive the commands of the Lord. Consequently we have to picture to ourselves the cherubim as appearing in the neighbourhood of the altar, and then taking up their position to the south thereof, when the Lord returned to the threshold of the temple. The reason for stating this is not to be sought, as Calvin supposes, in the desire to show "that the way was opened for the angel to go straight to God, and that the cherubim were standing there ready, as it were, to contribute their labour." The position in which the cherubim appeared is more probably given with prospective reference to the account which follows in vers. 9-22 of the departure of the glory of the Lord from the temple. As an indication of the significance of this act to Israel, the glory which issued from this manifestation of the divine *doxa* is described in vers. 3b–5. The cloud, as the earthly vehicle of the divine *doxa*, filled the inner court; and when the glory of the Lord stood upon the threshold, it filled the temple also, while the court became full of the splendour of the divine glory. That is to say, the brilliancy of the divine nature shone through the cloud, so that the court and the temple were lighted by the shining of the light-cloud. The brilliant splendour is a symbol of the light of the divine grace. The wings of the cherubim rustled, and at the movement of God (i. 24) were audible even in the outer court.

After this picture of the glorious manifestation of the divine *doxa*, the fetching of the fire-coals from the space between the wheels under the cherubim is more closely described in vers. 6 and 7. One of the cherub's hands took the coals out of the fire, and put them into the hands of the man clothed in white linen. To this a supplementary remark is added in ver. 8, to the effect that the figure of a hand was visible by the side of the cherubim under their wings. The word יֵצֵא, " and he went out," indicates that the man clothed in white linen scattered the coals over the city, to set it on fire and consume it.

Vers. 9–22. The glory of the Lord forsakes the temple.—
Ver. 9. *And I saw, and behold four wheels by the side of the cherubim, one wheel by the side of every cherub, and the appearance of the wheels was like the look of a chrysolith stone.* Ver. 10. *And as for their appearance, they had all four one form, as if one wheel were in the midst of the other.* Ver. 11. *When they went, they went to their four sides; they did not turn in going; for to the place to which the head was directed, to that they went; they did not turn in their going.* Ver. 12. *And their whole body, and their back, and their hands, and their wings, and the wheels, were full of eyes round about: by all four their wheels.* Ver. 13. *To the wheels, to them was called, " whirl!" in my hearing.*
Ver. 14. *And every one had four faces; the face of the first was the face of the cherub, the face of the second a man's face, and the third a lion's face, and the fourth an eagle's face.*

Ver. 15. *And the cherubim ascended. This was the being which I saw by the river Chebar.* Ver. 16. *And when the cherubim went, the wheels went by them; and when the cherubim raised their wings to ascend from the earth, the wheels also did not turn from their side.* Ver. 17. *When those stood, they stood; and when those ascended, they ascended with them; for the spirit of the being was in them.* Ver. 18. *And the glory of Jehovah went out from the threshold of the house, and stood above the cherubim.* Ver. 19. *And the cherubim raised their wings, and ascended from the earth before my eyes on their going out, and the wheels beside them; and they stopped at the entrance of the eastern gate of the house of Jehovah; and the glory of the God of Israel was above them.* Ver. 20. *This was the being which I saw under the God of Israel by the river Chebar, and I perceived that they were cherubim.* Ver. 21. *Every one had four faces, each and every one four wings, and something like a man's hands under their wings.* Ver. 22. *And as for the likeness of their faces, they were the faces which I had seen by the river Chebar, their appearance and they themselves. They went every one according to its face.*—With the words "I saw, and behold," a new feature in the vision is introduced. The description of the appearance of the cherubim in these verses coincides for the most part *verbatim* with the account of the theophany in ch. i. It differs from this, however, not only in the altered arrangement of the several features, and in the introduction of certain points which serve to complete the former account; but still more in the insertion of a number of narrative sentences, which show that we have not merely a repetition of the first chapter here. On the contrary, Ezekiel is now describing the moving of the appearance of the glory of Jehovah from the inner court or porch of the temple to the outer entrance of the eastern gate of the outer court; in other words, the departure of the gracious presence of the Lord from the temple: and in order to point out more distinctly the importance and meaning of this event, he depicts once more the leading features of the theophany itself. The narrative sentences are found in vers. 13, 15, 18, and 19. In ver. 13 we have the exclamation addressed to the wheels by the side of the cherubim to set themselves in motion; in ver. 15, the statement that the cherubim ascended; and in vers. 18 and 19, the account of the departure of the glory of the Lord from the inner portion of the temple. To this we may add the repeated remark, that the appearance was the same as that which the prophet had seen by the river Chebar (vers. 15, 20, 22). To bring clearly out to view both the independence of these divine manifestations and their significance to Israel, Ezekiel repeats the leading features of the former description; but while doing this, he either makes them subordinate to the thoughts expressed in the narrative sentences, or places them first as introductory to these, or lets them follow as explanatory. Thus, for example, the description of the wheels, and of the manner in which they moved (vers. 9–12), serves both to introduce and explain the call to the wheels to set themselves in motion. The description of the wheels in vers. 9–11 harmonizes with ch. i. 16 and 17, with this exception, however, that certain points are given with greater exactness here; such, for example, as the statement that the movements of the wheels were so regulated, that in whichever direction the front one turned, the others did the same. הָרֹאשׁ, the head, is not the head-wheel, or the wheel which was always the first to move, but the front one, which originated the motion, drawing the others after it and determining their direction. For ver. 12*b* and the fact that the wheels were covered with eyes, see ch. i. 18. In ver. 12*a* we have the important addition, that the whole of the body and back, as well as the hands and wings, of the cherubim were full of eyes. There is all the less reason to question this addition, or remove it (as Hitzig does) by an arbitrary erasure, inasmuch as the statement itself is apparently in perfect harmony with the whole procedure; and the significance possessed by the eyes in relation to the wheels was not only appropriate in the case of the cherubim, but necessarily to be assumed in such a connection. The fact that the suffixes in בְּעֵינָ֑י, גַּבֵּהֶ֔ם, etc., refer to the cherubim, is obvious enough, if we consider that the wheels to which immediate reference is made were by the side of the cherubim (ver. 9), and that the cherubim formed the principal feature in the whole of the vision.—Ver. 13 does not point back to ver. 2, and bring the description of the wheel-work to a close, as Hitzig supposes. This assumption, by which the meaning of the whole description has been obscured, is based upon the untenable rendering, "and the wheels they named before my ears whirl" (J. D. Mich., Ros., etc.). Hävernick has already pointed out the objection to this, namely, that with such a rendering בְּאָזְנַ֖י forms an unmeaning addition; whereas it is precisely this addition which shows that קָרָא is used here in the sense of addressing, calling, and not of naming. One called to the wheels הַגַּלְגַּ֑ל, whirl; *i.e.* they were to verify their name *galgal*, viz. to revolve or whirl, to set themselves in motion by revolving. This is the explanation given by Theodoret: ἀνακυκλεῖσθαι καὶ ἀνακινεῖσθαι προσετάχθησαν. These words therefore gave the signal for their departure, and accordingly the rising up of the cherubim is related in ver. 15. Ver. 14 prepares the way for their ascent by mentioning the four faces of each cherub; and this is still further expanded in vers. 16 and 17, by the statement that the wheels moved according to the movements of the cherubim. לְאֶחָ֔ד without an article is used distributively (every one), as in ch. i. 6 and 10. The fact that in the description which follows only one face of each of the four cherubs is given, is not at variance with ch. i. 10, according to which every one of the cherubs had the four faces named. It was not Ezekiel's intention to mention all the faces of each cherub here, as he had done before; but he regarded it as sufficient in the case of each cherub to mention simply the one face, which was turned toward him. The only striking feature which still remains is the statement that the face of the one, *i.e.* of the first, was the face of the cherub instead of the face of an ox (cf. ch. i. 10), since the faces of the man, the lion, and the eagle were also cherubs' faces. We may, no doubt, get rid of the difficulty by altering the text, but this will not solve it; for it would still remain inexplicable how הַכְּרוּב could have grown out of שׁוֹר by a copyist's error; and still more, how such an error, which might have been so easily seen and corrected, could have been not only perpetuated, but generally adopted. Moreover, we have the article in הַכְּרוּב, which would also be inexplicable if the word had originated in an oversight, and which gives us precisely the index required to the correct solution of the difficulty, showing as it does that it was not merely *a* cherub's face, but the face of *the* cherub, so that the allusion is to one particular cherub, who was either well known from what had gone before, or occupied a more prominent position than the rest. Such a cherub is the one mentioned in ver. 7, who had taken the coals from the fire between the wheels, and stood nearest to Ezekiel. There did not appear to be any necessity to describe his face more exactly, as it could be easily seen from a comparison with ch. i. 10.—In ver. 15, the fact that the cherubim arose to depart from their place is followed by the remark that the cherubic figure was the being (הַחַיָּה, singular, as in ch. i. 22) which Ezekiel saw by the Chaboras, because it was a matter of importance that the identity of the two theophanies should be established as a help to the correct understanding of their real signification. But before the departure of the theophany from the temple is related, there follows in vers. 16 and 17 a repetition of the circumstantial description of the harmonious movements of the wheels and the cherubim (cf. ch. i. 19–21); and then, in ver. 18, the statement which had such practical significance, that the glory of the Lord departed from the threshold of the temple, and resumed the throne above the cherubim; and lastly, the account in ver. 19, that the glory of the God of Israel, seated upon this throne, took up its position at the entrance of the eastern gate of the temple. The entrance of this gate is not the gate of the temple, but the outer side of the eastern gate of the outer court, which formed the principal entrance to the whole of the temple-space. The expression "God of Israel" instead of "Jehovah" is significant, and is used to intimate that God, as the covenant God, withdrew His gracious presence from the people of Israel by this departure from the temple; not, indeed, from the whole of the covenant nation, but from the rebellious Israel which dwelt in Jerusalem and Judah; for the same glory of God which left the temple in the vision before the eyes of Ezekiel had appeared to the prophet by the river Chebar, and by calling him to be the prophet for Israel, had shown Himself to be the God who kept His covenant, and proved that, by the judgment upon the corrupt generation, He simply desired to exterminate its ungodly nature, and create for Himself a new and holy people. This is the meaning of the remark which is repeated in vers. 20-22, that the apparition which left the temple was the same being as Ezekiel had seen by the Chaboras, and that he recognised the beings under the throne as cherubim.

Chap. xi. THREATENING OF JUDGMENT AND PROMISE OF MERCY. CONCLUSION OF THE VISION.—This chapter contains the concluding portion of the vision; namely, *first*, the prediction of the destruction of the ungodly rulers (vers. 1-13); *secondly*, the consolatory and closing promise, that the Lord would gather to Himself a people out of those who had been carried away into exile, and would sanctify them by His Holy Spirit (vers. 14-21); and, *thirdly*, the withdrawal of the gracious presence of God from the city of Jerusalem, and the transportation of the prophet back to Chaldea with the termination of his ecstasy (vers. 22-25).

Vers. 1-13. Judgment upon the rulers of the nation.—Ver. 1. *And a wind lifted me up, and took me to the eastern gate of the house of Jehovah, which faces towards the east; and behold, at the entrance of the gate were five and twenty men, and I saw among them Jaazaniah the son of Azzur, and Pelatiah the son of*

Benaiah, the chiefs of the nation. Ver. 2. *And he said to me: Son of man, these are the men who devise iniquity, and counsel evil counsel in this city;* Ver. 3. *Who say, It is not near to build houses; it is the pot, and we are the flesh.* Ver. 4. *Therefore prophesy against them; prophesy, son of man.*—Ezekiel is once more transported from the inner court (ch. viii. 16) to the outer entrance of the eastern gate of the temple (תִּשָּׂא רוּחַ, as in ch. viii. 3), to which, according to ch. x. 19, the vision of God had removed. There he sees twenty-five men, and among them two of the princes of the nation, whose names are given. These twenty-five men are not identical with the twenty-five priests mentioned in ch. viii. 16, as Hävernick supposes. This is evident, not only from the difference in the locality, the priests standing between the porch and the altar, whereas the men referred to here stood at the outer eastern entrance to the court of the temple, but from the fact that the two who are mentioned by name are called שָׂרֵי הָעָם (princes of the people), so that we may probably infer from this that all the twenty-five were secular chiefs. Hävernick's opinion, that שָׂרֵי הָעָם is a term that may also be applied to princes among the priests, is as erroneous as his assertion that the priest-princes are called "princes" in Ezra viii. 20, Neh. x. 1, and Jer. xxxv. 4, whereas it is only to national princes that these passages refer. Hävernick is equally incorrect in supposing that these twenty-five men take the place of the seventy mentioned in ch. viii. 11; for those seventy represented the whole of the nation, whereas these twenty-five (according to ver. 2) were simply the counsellors of the city—not, however, the twenty-four *duces* of twenty-four divisions of the city, with a prince of the house of Judah, as Prado maintains, on the strength of certain Rabbinical assertions; or twenty-four members of a Sanhedrim, with their president (Rosenmüller); but the twelve tribe-princes (princes of the nation) and the twelve royal officers, or military commanders (1 Chron. xxvii.), with the king himself, or possibly with the commander-in-chief of the army; so that these twenty-five men represent the civil government of Israel, just as the twenty-four priest-princes, together with the high priest, represent the spiritual authorities of the covenant nation. The reason why two are specially mentioned by name is involved in obscurity, as nothing further is known of either of these persons. The words of God to the prophet in ver. 2 concerning them are perfectly applicable to representatives of the civil authorities or temporal rulers, namely, that they devise and give unwholesome and evil counsel. This counsel is described in ver. 3 by the words placed in their mouths: "house-building is not near; it (the city) is the caldron, we are the flesh." These words are difficult, and different interpretations have consequently been given. The rendering, "it (the judgment) is not near, let us build houses," is incorrect; for the infinitive construct בִּנוֹת cannot stand for the imperative or the infinitive absolute, but must be the subject of the sentence. It is inadmissible also to take the sentence as a question, "Is not house-building near?" in the sense of "it is certainly near," as Ewald does, after some of the ancient versions. For even if an interrogation is sometimes indicated simply by the tone in an energetic address, as, for example, in 2 Sam. xxiii. 5, this cannot be extended to cases in which the words of another are quoted. Still less can לֹא בְקָרוֹב mean *non est tempus*, it is not yet time, as Maurer supposes. The only way in which the words can be made to yield a sense in harmony with the context, is by taking them as a tacit allusion to Jer. xxix. 5. Jeremiah had called upon those in exile to build themselves houses in their banishment, and prepare for a lengthened stay in Babylon, and not to allow themselves to be deceived by the words of false prophets, who predicted a speedy return; for severe judgments had yet to fall upon those who had remained behind in the land. This word of Jeremiah the authorities in Jerusalem ridiculed, saying "house-building is not near," *i.e.* the house-building in exile is still a long way off; it will not come to this, that Jerusalem should fall either permanently or entirely into the hands of the king of Babylon. On the contrary, Jerusalem is the pot, and we, its inhabitants, are the flesh. The point of comparison is this: as the pot protects the flesh from burning, so does the city of Jerusalem protect us from destruction.[1] On the other hand, there is no foundation for the assumption that the words also contain an allusion to other sayings of Jeremiah, namely, to Jer. i. 13, where the judgment about to burst in from the north is represented under the figure of a smoking pot; or to Jer. xix., where Jerusalem is depicted as a pot about to be broken in pieces by God; for the reference in Jer. xix. is simply to an earthen pitcher, not to a meat-caldron; and the words in the verse before us have nothing at all in common with the figure in Jer. i. 13. The correctness of our explanation is evident both from ch. xxiv. 3, 6, where the figure of pot and flesh is met with again, though differently applied, and from the reply which Ezekiel makes to the saying of these men in the verses that follow (vers. 7–11). This saying expresses not only false confidence in the strength of Jerusalem, but also contempt and scorn of the predictions of the prophets sent by God. Ezekiel is therefore to prophesy, as he does in vers. 5–12, against this pernicious counsel, which is confirming the people in their sins.

Ver. 5. *And the Spirit of Jehovah fell upon me, and said to me: Say, Thus saith Jehovah, So ye say, O house of Israel, and what riseth up in your spirit, that I know.* Ver. 6. *Ye have increased your slain in this city, and filled its streets with slain.* Ver. 7. *Therefore, thus saith the Lord Jehovah, Your slain, whom ye have laid in the midst of it, they are the flesh, and it is the pot; but men will lead you out of it.* Ver. 8. *The sword you fear; but the sword shall I bring upon you, is the saying of the Lord Jehovah.* Ver. 9. *I shall lead you out of it and give you into*

---

[1] "This city is a pot, our receptacle and defence, and we are the flesh enclosed therein; as flesh is preserved in its caldron till it is perfectly boiled, so shall we continue here till an extreme old age."—Hülsemann in *Calov. Bibl. Illustr.*

the hand of foreigners, and shall execute judgments upon you. Ver. 10. *By the sword shall ye fall: on the frontier of Israel shall I judge you; and ye shall learn that I am Jehovah.* Ver. 11. *It shall not be as a pot to you, so that you should be flesh therein: on the frontier of Israel shall I judge.* Ver. 12. *And ye shall learn that I am Jehovah, in whose statutes ye have not walked, and my judgments ye have not done, but have acted according to the judgments of the heathen who are round about you.*—For תִּפֹּל עָלַי רוּחַ יְיָ, compare ch. viii. 1. Instead of the "hand" (ch. viii. 1), the Spirit of Jehovah is mentioned here; because what follows is simply a divine inspiration, and there is no action connected with it. The words of God are directed against the "house of Israel," whose words and thoughts are discerned by God, because the twenty-five men are the leaders and counsellors of the nation. מַעֲלוֹת רוּחַ, thoughts, suggestions of the mind, may be explained from the phrase עָלָה עַל לֵב, to come into the mind. Their actions furnish the proof of the evil suggestions of their heart. They have filled the city with slain; not "turned the streets of the city into a battle-field," however, by bringing about the capture of Jerusalem in the time of Jeconiah, as Hitzig would explain it. The words are to be understood in a much more general sense, as signifying murder, in both the coarser and the more refined signification of the word.[1] מִלֵּאתֶם is a copyist's error for מִלְאתָם. Those who have been murdered by you are the flesh in the caldron (ver. 7). Ezekiel gives them back their own words, as words which contain an undoubted truth, but in a different sense from that in which they have used them. By their bloodshed they have made the city into a pot in which the flesh of the slain is pickled. Only in this sense is Jerusalem a pot for them; not a pot to protect the flesh from burning while cooking, but a

---

[1] Calvin has given the correct explanation, thus: "He does not mean that men had been openly assassinated in the streets of Jerusalem; but under this form of speech he embraces all kinds of injustice. For we know that all who oppressed the poor, deprived men of their possessions, or shed innocent blood, were regarded as murderers in the sight of God."

pot into which the flesh of the slaughtered is thrown. Yet even in this sense will Jerusalem not serve as a pot to these worthless counsellors (ver. 11). They will lead you out of the city (הוֹצִיא, in ver. 7, is the 3d pers. sing. with an indefinite subject). The sword which ye fear, and from which this city is to protect you, will come upon you, and cut you down—not in Jerusalem, but on the frontier of Israel. עַל־גְּבוּל, in ver. 10, cannot be taken in the sense of "away over the frontier," as Kliefoth proposes; if only because of the synonym אֶל־גְּבוּל in ver. 11. This threat was literally fulfilled in the bloody scenes at Riblah (Jer. lii. 24–27). It is not therefore a *vaticinium ex eventu*, but contains the general thought, that the wicked who boasted of security in Jerusalem would not find protection either in Jerusalem or in the land of Israel as a whole, but were to be led out of the land, and judged outside. This threat intensifies the punishment, as Calvin has already shown.[1] In ver. 11 the negation (לֹא) of the first clause is to be supplied in the second, as, for example, in Deut. xxxiii. 6. For ver. 12, compare the remarks on ch. v. 7. The truth and the power of this word are demonstrated at once by what is related in the following verse.

Ver. 13. *And it came to pass, as I was prophesying, that Pelatiah the son of Benaiah died: then I fell upon my face, and cried with a loud voice, and said: Alas! Lord Jehovah, dost Thou make an end of the remnant of Israel?*—The sudden death of one of the princes of the nation, while Ezekiel was prophesying, was intended to assure the house of Israel of the certain fulfilment of this word of God. So far, however, as

[1] "He threatens a double punishment; *first*, that God will cast them out of Jerusalem, in which they delight, and where they say that they will still make their abode for a long time to come, so that exile may be the first punishment. He then adds, *secondly*, that He will not be content with exile, but will send a severer punishment, after they have been cast out, and both home and land have spued them out as a stench which they could not bear. *I will judge you at the frontier of Israel*, i.e. outside the holy land, so that when one curse shall have become manifest in exile, a severer and more formidable punishment shall still await you."

the fact itself is concerned, we must bear in mind, that as it was only in spirit that Ezekiel was at Jerusalem, and prophesied to the men whom he saw in spirit there, so the death of Pelatiah was simply a part of the vision, and in all probability was actually realized by the sudden death of this prince during or immediately after the publication of the vision. But the occurrence, even when the prophet saw it in spirit, made such an impression upon his mind, that with trembling and despair he once more made an importunate appeal to God, as in ch. ix. 8, and inquired whether He meant to destroy the whole of the remnant of Israel. עֹשֶׂה כָלָה, to put an end to a thing, with אֵת before the object, as in Zeph. i. 18 (see the comm. on Nah. i. 8). The Lord then gives him the comforting assurance in vers. 14–21, that He will preserve a remnant among the exiles, and make them His people once more.

Vers. 14–21. Promise of the gathering of Israel out of the nations.—Ver. 14. *And the word of Jehovah came to me, saying,* Ver. 15. *Son of man, thy brethren, thy brethren are the people of thy proxy, and the whole house of Israel, the whole of it, to whom the inhabitants of Jerusalem say, Remain far away from Jehovah; to us the land is given for a possession.* Ver. 16. *Therefore say, Thus saith the Lord Jehovah, Yea, I have sent them far away, and have scattered them in the lands, but I have become to them a sanctuary for a little while in the lands whither they have come.* Ver. 17. *Therefore say, Thus saith the Lord Jehovah, And I will gather you from the nations, and will collect you together from the lands in which ye are scattered, and will give you the land of Israel.* Ver. 18. *And they will come thither, and remove from it all its detestable things, and all its abominations.* Ver. 19. *And I will give them one heart, and give a new spirit within you; and will take the heart of stone out of their flesh, and give them a heart of flesh;* Ver. 20. *That they may walk in my statutes, and preserve my rights, and do them: and they will be my people, and I will be their God.* Ver. 21. *But those whose heart goeth to the heart of their detestable things and their abominations, I will give their way upon their head, is the saying of the Lord Jehovah.*—The prophet had interceded, first of all for the inhabitants of Jerusalem (ch. ix. 8), and then for the rulers of the nation, and had asked God whether He would entirely destroy the remnant of Israel. To this God replies that his brethren, in whom he is to interest himself, are not these inhabitants of Jerusalem and these rulers of the nation, but the Israelites carried into exile, who are regarded by these inhabitants at Jerusalem as cut off from the people of God. The nouns in ver. 15a are not "accusatives, which are resumed in the suffix to הִרְחַקְתִּים in ver. 16," as Hitzig imagines, but form an independent clause, in which אַחֶיךָ is the subject, and אַנְשֵׁי גְאֻלָּתֶךָ as well as כָּל־בֵּית יִשְׂרָאֵל the predicates. The repetition of "thy brethren" serves to increase the force of the expression: thy true, real brethren; not in contrast to the priests, who were lineal relations (Hävernick), but in contrast to the Israelites, who had only the name of Israel, and denied its nature. These brethren are to be the people of his proxy; and toward these he is to exercise גְּאֻלָּה. גְּאֻלָּה is the business, or the duty and right, of the *Goël*. According to the law, the *Goël* was the brother, or the nearest relation, whose duty it was to come to the help of his impoverished brother, not only by redeeming (buying back) his possession, which poverty had compelled him to sell, but to redeem the man himself, if he had been sold to pay his debts (*vid.* Lev. xxv. 25, 48). The *Goël* therefore became the possessor of the property of which his brother had been unjustly deprived, if it were not restored till after his death (Num. v. 8). Consequently he was not only the avenger of blood, but the natural supporter and agent of his brother; and גְּאֻלָּה signifies not merely redemption or kindred, but *proxy, i.e.* both the right and obligation to act as the legal representative, the avenger of blood, the heir, etc., of the brother. The words "and the whole of the house of Israel" are a second predicate to "thy brethren," and affirm that the brethren, for whom Ezekiel can and is to intercede, form the whole of the house of Israel, the term "whole" being rendered more emphatic by the repetition of כֹּל in כֻּלֹּה. A contrast is drawn between this "whole house of Israel" and the inhabitants of Jerusalem, who say to those brethren, "Remain far away from Jehovah, to us is the land given for a possession." It follows from this, first of all, that the brethren of Ezekiel, towards whom he was to act as *Goël*, were those who had been taken away from the land, his companions in exile; and, secondly, that the exiles formed the whole of the house of Israel, that is to say, that they alone would be regarded by God as His people, and not the inhabitants of Jerusalem or those left in the land, who regarded the exiles as no longer a portion of the nation: simply because, in their estrangement from God, they looked upon the mere possession of Jerusalem as a pledge of participation in the grace of God. This shows the prophet where the remnant of the people of God is to be found. To this there is appended in ver. 16 sqq. a promise of the way in which the Lord will make this remnant His true people. לָכֵן, therefore, viz. because the inhabitants of Jerusalem regard the exiles as rejected by the Lord, Ezekiel is to declare to them that Jehovah is their sanctuary even in their dispersion (ver. 16); and because the others deny that they have any share in the possession of the land, the Lord will gather them together again, and give them the land of Israel (ver. 17). The two לָכֵן are co-ordinate, and introduce the antithesis to the disparaging sentence pronounced by the inhabitants of Jerusalem upon those who have been carried into exile. The כִּי before the two leading clauses in ver. 16 does not mean "because," serving to introduce a protasis, to which ver. 17 would form the apodosis, as Ewald affirms; but it stands before the direct address in the sense of an assurance, which indicates that there is some truth at the bottom of the judgment pronounced by their opponents, the inhabitants of Jerusalem. The thought is this: the present position of affairs is unquestionably that Jehovah has scattered them (the house of Israel) among the Gentiles; but He has not therefore cast them off. He has become a sanctuary to them in the lands of their dispersion. *Migdásh* does not mean either asylum or an object kept sacred (Hitzig), but a sanctuary, more especially the temple. They had, indeed, lost the outward temple (at Jerusalem); but the Lord Himself had become their temple. What made the temple into a sanctuary' was the presence of Jehovah, the covenant God, therein. This even the exiles were to enjoy in their banishment, and in this they would possess a substitute for the outward temple. This thought is rendered still more precise by the word מְעַט, which may refer either to time or measure, and signify "for a short time," or "in some measure." It is difficult to decide between these two renderings. In support of the latter, which Kliefoth prefers (after the LXX. and Vulgate), it may be argued that the manifestation of the Lord, both by the mission of prophets and by the outward deliverances and inward consolations which He bestowed upon the faithful, was but a partial substitute to the exile for His gracious presence in the temple and in the holy land. Nevertheless, the context, especially the promise in ver. 17, that He will gather them again and lead them back into the land of Israel, appears to favour the former signification, namely, that this substitution was only a provisional one, and was only to last for a short time, although it also implies that this could not and was not meant to be a perfect substitute for the gracious presence of the Lord. For Israel, as the people of God, could not remain scattered abroad; it must possess the inheritance bestowed upon it by the Lord, and have its God in the midst of it in its own land, and that in a manner more real than could possibly be the case in captivity among the Gentiles. This will be fully realized in the heavenly Jerusalem, where the Lord God Almighty and the Lamb will be a temple to the redeemed (Rev. xxi. 22). Therefore will Jehovah gather together the dispersed once more, and lead them back into the land of Israel, *i.e.* into the land which He designed for Israel; whereas the inhabitants of

Jerusalem, who boast of their possession of Canaan (ver. 15), will lose what they now possess. Those who are restored will then remove all idolatrous abominations (ver. 17), and receive from God a new and feeling heart (ver. 19), so that they will walk in the ways of God, and be in truth the people of God (ver. 20).

The fulfilment of this promise did, indeed, begin with the return of a portion of the exiles under Zerubbabel; but it was not completed under either Zerubbabel or Ezra, or even in the Maccabean times. Although Israel may have entirely relinquished the practice of gross idolatry after the captivity, it did not then attain to that newness of heart which is predicted in vers. 19, 20. This only commenced with the Baptist's preaching of repentance, and with the coming of Christ; and it was realized in the children of Israel, who accepted Jesus in faith, and suffered Him to make them children of God. Yet even by Christ this prophecy has not yet been perfectly fulfilled in Israel, but only in part, since the greater portion of Israel has still in its hardness that stony heart which must be removed out of its flesh before it can attain to salvation. The promise in ver. 19 has for its basis the prediction in Deut. xxx. 6. " What the circumcision of the heart is there, viz. the removal of all uncleanliness, of which outward circumcision was both the type and pledge, is represented here as the giving of a heart of flesh instead of one of stone" (Hengstenberg). I give them *one* heart. לֵב אֶחָד, which Hitzig is wrong in proposing to alter into לֵב אַחֵר, *another* heart, after the LXX., is supported and explained by Jer. xxxii. 39, " I give them *one* heart and *one* way to fear me continually" (cf. Zeph. iii. 9 and Acts iv. 32). *One* heart is not an upright, undivided heart (לֵב שָׁלֵם), but a harmonious, united heart, in contrast to the division or plurality of hearts which prevails in the natural state, in which every one follows his own heart and his own mind, turning " every one to his own way" (Isa. liii. 6). God gives *one* heart, when He causes all hearts and minds to become one. This can only be effected by His giving a "new spirit," taking away the stone-heart, and giving a heart of flesh instead. For the old spirit fosters nothing but egotism and discord. The heart of stone has no susceptibility to the impressions of the word of God and the drawing of divine grace. In the natural condition, the heart of man is as hard as stone. "The word of God, the external leadings of God, pass by and leave no trace behind. The latter may crush it, and yet not break it. Even the fragments continue hard; yea, the hardness goes on increasing" (Hengstenberg). The heart of flesh is a tender heart, susceptible to the drawing of divine grace (compare ch. xxxvi. 26, where these figures, which are peculiar to Ezekiel, recur; and for the substance of the prophecy, Jer. xxxi. 33). The fruit of this renewal of heart is walking in the commandments of the Lord; and the consequence of the latter is the perfect realization of the covenant relation, true fellowship with the Lord God. But judgment goes side by side with this renewal. Those who will not forsake their idols become victims to the judgment (ver. 21). The first hemistich of ver. 21 is a relative clause, in which אֲשֶׁר is to be supplied and connected with לִבָּם: "Whose heart walketh after the heart of their abominations." The heart, which is attributed to the abominations and detestations, i.e. to the idols, is the inclination to idolatry, the disposition and spirit which manifest themselves in the worship of idols. Walking after the heart of the idols forms the antithesis to walking after the heart of God (1 Sam. xiii. 14). For דַּרְכָּם וגו׳, "I will give their way," see ch. ix. 10.

Vers. 22–25. The promise that the Lord would preserve to Himself a holy seed among those who had been carried away captive, brought to a close the announcement of the judgment that would fall upon the ancient Israel and apostate Jerusalem. All that is now wanting, as a conclusion to the whole vision, is the practical confirmation of the announcement of judgment. This is given in the two following verses.—Ver. 22. *And the cherubim raised their wings, and the wheels beside them; and the glory of the God of Israel was up above them.* Ver. 23. *And the glory of Jehovah ascended from the midst of the city, and took its stand upon the mountain which is to the east of the city.* Ver. 24. *And wind lifted me up, and brought me to Chaldea to the exiles, in the vision, in the Spirit of God; and the vision ascended away from me, which I had seen.* Ver. 25. *And I spoke to the exiles all the words of Jehovah, which He had shown to me.*—The manifestation of the glory of the Lord had already left the temple, after the announcement of the burning of Jerusalem, and had taken its stand before the entrance of the eastern gate of the outer court, that is to say, in the city itself (ch. x. 19, xi. 1). But now, after the announcement had been made to the representatives of the authorities of their removal from the city, the glory of the God of Israel forsook the devoted city also, as a sign that both temple and city had ceased to be the seats of the gracious presence of the Lord. The mountain on the east of the city is the Mount of Olives, which affords a lofty outlook over the city. There the glory of God remained, to execute the judgment upon Jerusalem. Thus, according to Zech. xiv. 4, will Jehovah also appear at the last judgment on the Mount of Olives above Jerusalem, to fight thence against His foes, and prepare a way of escape for those who are to be saved. It was from the Mount of Olives also that the Son of God proclaimed to the degenerate city the second destruction (Luke xix. 21; Matt. xxiv. 3); and from the same mountain He made His visible ascension to heaven after His resurrection (Luke xxiv. 50; cf. Acts i. 12); and, as Grotius has observed, "thus did Christ ascend from this mountain into His kingdom, to execute judgment upon the Jews."

After this vision of the judgments of God upon the ancient people of the covenant and the kingdom of God, Ezekiel was carried back in the spirit into Chaldea, to the river Chaboras. The vision then vanished; and he related to the exiles all that he had seen.

CHAP. XII. DEPARTURE OF THE KING AND PEOPLE;
AND BREAD OF TEARS.

The words of God which follow in ch. xii.-xix. do not contain any chronological data defining the exact period at which they were communicated to the prophet and reported by him. But so far as their contents are concerned, they are closely connected with the foregoing announcements of judgment; and this renders the assumption a very probable one, that they were not far removed from them in time, but fell within the space of eleven months intervening between ch. viii. 1 and xx. 1, and were designed to carry out still further the announcement of judgment in ch. viii.-xi. This is done more especially in the light thrown upon all the circumstances, on which the impenitent people rested their hope of the preservation of the kingdom and Jerusalem, and of their speedy liberation from the Babylonian yoke. The purpose of the whole is to show the worthlessness of this false confidence, and to affirm the certainty and irresistibility of the predicted destruction of Judah and Jerusalem, in the hope of awakening the rebellious and hardened generation to that thorough repentance, without which it was impossible that peace and prosperity could ever be enjoyed. This definite purpose in the prophecies which follow is clearly indicated in the introductory remarks in ch. xii. 2, xiv. 1, and xx. 1. In the first of these passages the hardness of Israel is mentioned as the motive for the ensuing prophecy; whilst in the other two, the visit of certain elders of Israel to the prophet, to seek the Lord and to inquire through him, is given as the circumstance which occasioned the further prophetic declarations. It is evident from this that the previous words of God had already made some impression upon the hearers, but that their hard heart had not yet been broken by them.

In ch. xii., Ezekiel receives instructions to depict, by means of a symbolical action, the departure of the king and people from Jerusalem (vers. 3-7), and to explain the action to the refractory generation (vers. 8-16). After this he is to exhibit, by another symbolical sign, the want and distress to which the people will be reduced (vers. 17-20). And lastly, he is to rebut the frivolous sayings of the people, to the effect that what is predicted will either never take place at all, or not till a very distant time (vers. 21-28).

Vers. 1-7. SYMBOL OF THE EMIGRATION.—Ver. 1. *And the word of Jehovah came to me, saying,* Ver. 2. *Son of man, thou dwellest amidst the refractory generation, who have eyes to see, and see not; and have ears to hear, and hear not; for they are a refractory generation.* Ver. 3. *And thou, son of man, make thyself an outfit for exile, and depart by day before their eyes; and depart from thy place to another place before their eyes: perhaps they might see, for they are a refractory generation.* Ver. 4. *And carry out thy things like an outfit for exile by day before their eyes; but do thou go out in the evening before their eyes, as when going out to exile.* Ver. 5. *Before their eyes break through the wall, and carry it out there.* Ver. 6. *Before their eyes take it upon thy shoulder, carry it out in the darkness: cover thy face, and look not upon the land; for I have set thee as a sign to the house of Israel.* Ver. 7. *And I did so as I was commanded: I carried out my things like an outfit for exile by day, and in the evening I broke through the wall with my hand; I carried it out in the darkness; I took it upon my shoulder before their eyes.*— In ver. 2 the reason is assigned for the command to perform the symbolical action, namely, the hard-heartedness of the people. Because the generation in the midst of which Ezekiel dwelt was blind, with seeing eyes, and deaf, with hearing ears, the prophet was to depict before its eyes, by means of the sign that followed, the judgment which was approaching; in the hope, as is added in ver. 3, that they might possibly observe and lay the sign to heart. The refractoriness (בֵּית מְרִי, as in ch. ii. 5, 6, iii. 26, etc.) is described as obduracy, viz. having eyes, and not seeing; having ears, and not hearing, after Deut. xxix. 3 (cf. Jer. v. 21; Isa. vi. 9; Matt. xiii. 14, 15). The root of this mental blindness and deafness was to be found in obstinacy, *i.e.* in not willing; "in that presumptuous insolence," as Michaelis says, "through which divine light can obtain no admission." כְּלֵי גוֹלָה, the goods (or outfit) of exile, were a pilgrim's staff and traveller's wallet, with the provisions and utensils necessary for a journey. Ezekiel was to carry these out of the house into the street in the day-time, that the people might see them and have their attention called to them. Then in the evening, after dark, he was to go out himself, not by the door of the house, but through a hole which he had broken in the wall. He was also to take the travelling outfit upon his shoulder and carry it through the hole and out of the place, covering his face all the while, that he might not see the land to which he was going. "Thy place" is thy dwelling-place. כְּמוֹצָאֵי גוֹלָה: as the departures of exiles generally take place, *i.e.* as exiles are accustomed to depart, not "at the usual time of departure into exile," as Hävernick proposes. For מוֹצָא, see the comm. on Mic. v. 1. בָּעֲלָטָה differs from בָּעֶרֶב, and signifies the darkness of the depth of night (cf. Gen. xv. 17); not, however, "darkness artificially produced, equivalent to, with the eyes shut, or the face covered; so that the words which follow are simply explanatory of בָּעֲלָטָה," as Schmieder imagines. Such an assumption would be at variance not only with ver. 7, but also with ver. 12, where the covering or concealing of the face is expressly distinguished from the carrying out "in the dark." The order was to be as follows: In the day-time Ezekiel was to take the travelling outfit and carry it out into the road; then in the evening he was to go out himself, having first of all broken a hole through the wall as evening was coming on; and in the darkness of night he was to place upon his shoulders whatever he was about to carry with him, and take his departure. This he was to do, because God had made him a *mōphēth* for Israel: in other words, by doing this he was to show himself to be a marvellous sign to Israel. For *mŏphēth*, see the comm. on Ex. iv. 21. In ver. 7, the execution of the command, which evidently took place in the strictness of the letter, is fully described. There was nothing impracticable in the action, for breaking through the wall did not preclude the use of a hammer or some other tool.

Vers. 8–16. Explanation of the symbolical action.—Ver. 8. *And the word of Jehovah came to me in the morning, saying*, Ver. 9. *Son of man, have they not said to thee, the house of Israel, the refractory generation, What art thou doing?* Ver. 10. *Say to them, Thus saith the Lord Jehovah, This burden applies to the prince in Jerusalem, and to all the house of Israel to whom they belong.* Ver. 11. *Say, I am your sign: as I have done, so shall it happen to them; into exile, into captivity, will they go.* Ver. 12. *And the prince who is in the midst of them he will lift it upon his shoulder in the dark, and will go out: they will break through the wall, and carry it out thereby: he will cover his face, that he may not see the land with eyes.* Ver. 13. *And I will spread my net over him, so that he will be caught in my snare: and I will take him to Babel, into the land of the Chaldeans; but he will not see it, and will die there.* Ver. 14. *And all that is about him, his help and all his troops, I will scatter into all winds, and draw out the sword behind them.* Ver. 15. *And they shall learn that I am Jehovah, when I scatter them among the nations, and winnow them in the lands.* Ver. 16. *Yet I will leave of them a small number of men from the sword, from the famine, and from the pestilence; that they may relate all their abominations among the nations whither they have come; and learn that I am Jehovah.*—As queries introduced with הֲלֹא have, as a rule, an affirmative sense, the words "have they not asked," etc., imply that the Israelites had asked the prophet what he was doing, though not in a proper state of mind, not in a penitential manner, as the epithet בֵּית הַמְּרִי plainly shows. The prophet is therefore to interpret the action which he had just been performing, and all its different stages. The words הַנָּשִׂיא הַמַּשָּׂא הַזֶּה, to which very different renderings have been given, are to be translated simply "the prince is this burden," *i.e.* the object of this burden. *Hammassâ* does not mean the carrying, but the burden, *i.e.* the threatening prophecy, the prophetic action of the prophet, as in the headings to the oracles (see the comm. on Nah. i. 1). The "prince" is the king, as in ch. xxi. 30, though not Jehoiachin, who had been carried into exile, but Zedekiah. This is stated in the apposition "in Jerusalem," which belongs to "the prince," though it is not introduced till after the predicate, as in Gen. xxiv. 24. To this there is appended the further definition, "the whole house of Israel," which, being co-ordinated with הַנָּשִׂיא, affirms that all Israel (the covenant nation) will share the fate of the prince. In the last clause of ver. 10 בְּתוֹכָם does not stand for בְּתוֹכָהּ, so that the suffix would refer to Jerusalem, "in the midst of which they (the house of Israel) are." אֲשֶׁר cannot be a nominative, because in that case הֵמָּה would be superfluous; it is rather to be taken with בְּתוֹכָם, and הֵמָּה to be understood as referring to the persons addressed, *i.e.* to the Israelites in exile (Hitzig, Kliefoth): in the midst of whom they are, *i.e.* to whom they belong. The sentence explains the reason why the prophet was to announce to those in exile the fate of the prince and people in Jerusalem; namely, because the exiles formed a portion of the nation, and would be affected by the judgment which was about to burst upon the king and people in Jerusalem. In this sense Ezekiel was also able to say to the exiles (in ver. 11), "I am *your* sign;" inasmuch as his sign was also of importance for them, as those who were already banished would be so far affected by the departure of the king and people which Ezekiel depicted, that it would deprive them of all hope of a speedy return to their native land. לָהֶם, in ver. 11, refers to the king and the house of Israel in Jerusalem. בַּגּוֹלָה is rendered more forcible by the addition of בַּשְּׁבִי. The announcement that both king and people must go into exile, is carried out still further in vers. 12 and 13 with reference to the king, and in ver. 14 with regard to the people. The king will experience all that Ezekiel has described. The literal occurrence of what is predicted here is related in Jer. xxxix. 1 sqq., lii. 4 sqq.; 2 Kings xxv. 4 sqq. When the Chaldeans forced their way into the city after a two years' siege, Zedekiah and his men of war fled by night out of the city through the gate between the two walls. It is not expressly stated, indeed, in the historical accounts that a breach was made in the wall; but the expression " through the gate between the two walls" (Jer. xxxix. 4, lii. 7; 2 Kings xxv. 4) renders this very probable, whether the gate had been walled up during the siege, or it was necessary to break through the wall at one particular spot in order to reach the gate. The king's attendants would naturally take care that a breach was made in the wall, to secure for him a way of escape; hence the expression, " *they will break through.*" The covering of the face, also, is not mentioned in the historical accounts; but in itself it is by no means improbable, as a sign of the shame and grief with which Zedekiah left the city. The words, " that he may not see the land with eyes," do not appear to indicate anything more than the necessary consequence of covering the face, and refer primarily to the simple fact that the king fled in the deepest sorrow, and did not want to see the land; but, as ver. 13 clearly intimates, they were fulfilled in another way, namely, by the fact that Zedekiah did not see with his eyes the land of the Chaldeans into which he was led, because he had been blinded at Riblah (Jer. xxxix. 5, lii. 11; 2 Kings xxv. 7). לְעַיִן, by eye = with his eyes, is added to give prominence to the idea of seeing. For the same purpose, the subject, which is already implied in the verb, is rendered more emphatic by הוּא; and this הוּא is placed after the verb, so that it stands in contrast with הָאָרֶץ. The capture of the king was not depicted by Ezekiel; so that in this respect the announcement (ver. 13) goes further than the symbolical action, and removes all doubt as to the credibility of the prophet's word, by a distinct prediction of the fate awaiting him. At the same time, his not seeing the land of Babylon is left so indefinite, that it cannot be regarded as a *vaticinium post eventum*. Zedekiah died in prison at Babylon (Jer. lii. 11). Along with the king, the whole of his military force will be scattered in all directions (ver. 14). עֶזְרֹה, his help, *i.e.* the troops that break through with him. כָּל־אֲגַפָּיו, all his wings (the wings of his army), *i.e.* all the rest of his forces. The word is peculiar to Ezekiel, and is rendered "wings" by Jos. Kimchi, like *k'náphaim* in Isa. viii. 8. For the rest of the verse compare ch. v. 2; and for the fulfilment, Jer. lii. 8, xl. 7, 12. The greater part of the people will perish, and only a small number remain, that they may relate among the heathen, wherever they are led, all the abominations of Israel, in order that the heathen may learn that it is not from weakness, but simply to punish idolatry, that God has given up His people to them (cf. Jer. xxii. 8).

Vers. 17–20. Sign depicting the Terrors and Consequences of the Conquest of Jerusalem.—Ver. 17. *And the word of Jehovah came to me, saying*, Ver. 18. *Son of man, thou shalt eat thy bread with quaking, and drink thy water with trembling and trouble;* Ver. 19. *And say to the people of the land, Thus saith the Lord Jehovah to the inhabitants of Jerusalem, in the land of Israel, They will eat their bread in trouble, and drink their water in amazement, because her land is laid waste of all its fulness for the wickedness of all who dwell therein.* Ver. 20. *And the inhabited cities become desolate, and the land will be laid waste; that ye may learn that I am Jehovah.*— The carrying out of this sign is not mentioned; not that there is any doubt as to its having been done, but that it is simply taken for granted. The trouble and trembling could only be expressed by means of gesture. רַעַשׁ, generally an earthquake or violent convulsion; here, simply shaking, synonymous with רִמָּה, trembling. "Bread and water" is the standing expression for food; so that even here the idea of scanty provisions is not to be sought therein. This idea is found merely in the signs of anxiety and trouble with which Ezekiel was to eat his food. עַל־אד׳ = אֶל־אֲדָמַת, "upon the land," equivalent to "in the land." This is appended to show that the prophecy does not refer to those who had already been carried into exile, but to the inhabitants of Jerusalem who were still in the land. For the subject-matter, compare ch. iv. 16, 17. לְמַעַן indicates not the intention, "in order that," but the motive, "because."

Vers. 21-28. DECLARATIONS TO REMOVE ALL DOUBT AS TO THE TRUTH OF THE THREAT. — The scepticism of the people as to the fulfilment of these threatening prophecies, which had been made still more emphatic by signs, manifested itself in two different ways. Some altogether denied that the prophecies would ever be fulfilled (ver. 22); others, who did not go so far as this, thought that it would be a long time before they came to pass (ver. 27). These doubts were fed by the lying statements of false prophets. For this reason the refutation of these sceptical opinions (vers. 21-28) is followed in the next chapter by a stern reproof of the false prophets and prophetesses who led the people astray. — Ver. 21. *And the word of Jehovah came to me, saying,* Ver. 22. *Son of man, what kind of proverb have ye in the land of Israel, that ye say, The days become long, and every prophecy comes to nothing?* Ver. 23. *Therefore say to them, Thus saith the Lord Jehovah, I will put an end to this saying, and they shall say it no more in Israel; but say to them, The days are near, and the word of every prophecy.* Ver. 24. *For henceforth there shall be no vain prophecy and flattering soothsaying in the midst of the house of Israel.* Ver. 25. *For I am Jehovah; I speak; the word which I speak will come to pass, and no longer be postponed; for in your days, O refractory generation, I speak a word and do it, is the saying of the Lord Jehovah.*—*Mâshâl,* a proverb, a saying current among the people, and constantly repeated as a truth. "The days become long," etc., *i.e.* the time is lengthening out, and yet the prophecy is not being fulfilled. אָבַד, *perire,* to come to nothing, to fail of fulfilment, is the opposite of בּוֹא, to come, to be fulfilled. God will put an end to these sayings, by causing a very speedy fulfilment of the prophecy. The days are near, and every word of the prophecy, *i.e.* the days in which every word predicted shall come to pass. The reason for this is given in vers. 24 and 25, in two co-ordinate sentences, both of which are introduced with כִּי. First, every false prophecy shall henceforth cease in Israel (ver. 24); secondly, God will bring about the fulfilment of His own word, and that without delay (ver. 25). Different explanations have been given of the meaning of ver. 24. Kliefoth proposes to take שָׁוְא and מִקְסַם חָלָק as the predicate to חָזוֹן: no prophecy in Israel shall be vain and flattering soothsaying, but all prophecy shall become true, *i.e.* be fulfilled. Such an explanation, however, is not only artificial and unnatural, since מִקְסָם would be inserted as a predicate in a most unsuitable manner, but it contains this incongruity, that God would apply the term מִקְסָם, soothsaying, to the predictions of prophets inspired by Himself. On the other hand, there is no force in the objection raised by Kliefoth to the ordinary rendering of the words, namely, that the statement that God was about to put an end to false prophecy in Israel would anticipate the substance of the sixth word of God (*i.e.* ch. xiii.). It is impossible to see why a thought should not be expressed here, and then still further expanded in ch. xiii. חָלָק, smooth, *i.e.* flattering (compare Hos. x. 2; and for the prediction, Zech. xiii. 4, 5). The same reply serves also to overthrow the sceptical objection raised by the frivolous despisers of the prophet's words. Hence there is only a brief allusion made to them in vers. 26-28.—Ver. 26. *And the word of Jehovah came to me, saying,* Ver. 27. *Son of man, behold, the house of Israel saith, The vision that he seeth is for many days off, and he prophesies for distant times.* Ver. 28. *Therefore say to them, Thus saith the Lord Jehovah, All my words shall be no longer postponed: the word which I shall speak shall come to pass, saith the Lord Jehovah.*—The words are plain; and after what has already been said, they need no special explanation. Ver. 20 compare with ver. 25.

CHAP. XIII. AGAINST THE FALSE PROPHETS AND PROPHETESSES.

The way was already prepared for the address in this chapter by the announcement in ch. xii. 24. It divides itself into two parts, viz. vers. 1–16, directed against the false prophets; and vers. 17–23, against the false prophetesses. In both parts their conduct is first described, and then the punishment foretold. Jeremiah, like Ezekiel, and sometimes still more strongly, denounces the conduct of the false prophets, who are therefore to be sought for not merely among the exiles, but principally among those who were left behind in the land (*vid.* Jer. xxiii. 9 sqq.). A lively intercourse was kept up between the two, so that the false prophets extended their operations from Canaan to the Chaboras, and *vice versa.*

Vers. 1–16. AGAINST THE FALSE PROPHETS.—Vers. 1–7. Their conduct.—Ver. 1. *And the word of Jehovah came to me, saying,* Ver. 2. *Son of man, prophesy against the prophets of Israel who prophesy, and say to the prophets out of their heart, Hear ye the word of Jehovah.* Ver. 3. *Thus saith the Lord Jehovah, Woe upon the foolish prophets, who go after their spirit, and that which they have not seen!* Ver. 4. *Like foxes in ruins have thy prophets become, O Israel.* Ver. 5. *Ye do not stand before the breaches, nor wall up the wall around the house of Israel to stand firm in the battle on the day of Jehovah.* Ver. 6. *They see vanity and lying soothsaying, who say, "Oracle of Jehovah;" and Jehovah hath not sent them; so that they might hope for the fulfilment of the word.* Ver. 7. *Do ye not see vain visions, and speak lying soothsaying, and say, Oracle of Jehovah; and I have not spoken?*—The addition הַנִּבְּאִים, "who prophesy," is not superfluous. Ezekiel is not to direct his words against the prophets as a body, but against those who follow the vocation of prophet in Israel without being called to it by God on receiving a divine revelation, but simply prophesying out of their own heart, or according to their own subjective imagination. In the name of the Lord he is to threaten them with woes, as fools who follow their own spirit; in connection with which we must bear in mind that folly, according to the Hebrew idea, was not merely a moral failing, but actual godlessness (cf. Ps. xiv. 1). The phrase "going after their spirit" is interpreted and rendered more emphatic by לְבִלְתִּי רָאוּ, which is to be taken as a relative clause, "that which they have not seen," *i.e.* whose prophesying does not rest upon intuition inspired by God. Consequently they cannot promote the welfare of the nation, but (ver. 4) are like foxes in ruins or desolate places. The point of comparison is to be found in the undermining of the ground by foxes, *qui per cuniculos subjectam terram excavant et suffodiunt* (Bochart). For the thought is not exhausted by the circumstance that they withdraw to their holes instead of standing in front of the breach (Hitzig); and there is no force in the objection that, with this explanation, בֶּחֳרָבוֹת is passed over and becomes in fact tautological (Hävernick). The expression "in ruins" points to the fall of the theocracy, which the false prophets cannot prevent, but, on the contrary, accelerate by undermining the moral foundations of the state. For (ver. 5) they do not stand in the breaches, and do not build up the wall around the house of Israel (לֹא belongs to both clauses). He who desires to keep off the enemy, and prevent his entering the fortress, will stand in the breach. For the same purpose are gaps and breaches in the fortifications carefully built up. The sins of the people had made gaps and breaches in the walls of Jerusalem; in other words, had caused the moral decay of the city. But they had not stood in the way of this decay and its causes, as the calling and duty of prophets demanded, by reproving the sins of the people, that they might rescue the people and kingdom from destruction by restoring its moral and religious life. לַעֲמֹד בַּמִּלְחָמָה, to stand, or keep ground, *i.e.* so that ye might have kept your ground in the war. The subject is the false prophets, not Israel, as Hävernick supposes. " In the day of Jehovah," *i.e.* in the judgment which Jehovah has decreed. Not to stand, does not mean merely to avert the threatening judgment, but not to survive the judgment itself, to be overthrown by it. This arises from the fact that their prophesying is a lie; because Jehovah, whose name they have in their mouths, has not sent them (ver. 6). וְיִחֲלוּ is dependent upon שְׁלָחָם: God has not sent them, so that they could hope for the fulfilment of the word which they speak. The rendering adopted by others, " and they cause to hope," is untenable; for יָחַל with לְ does not mean " to cause to hope," or give hope, but simply to hope for anything. This was really the case; and it is affirmed in the declaration, which is repeated in the form of a direct appeal in ver. 7, to the effect that their visions were vain and lying soothsaying. For this they are threatened with the judgment described in the verses which follow.

Vers. 8–16. Punishment of the false prophets.—Ver. 8. *Therefore thus saith the Lord Jehovah, Because ye speak vanity and prophesy lying, therefore, behold, I will deal with you, is the saying of the Lord Jehovah.* Ver. 9. *And my hand shall be against the prophets who see vanity and divine lies: in the council of my people they shall not be, and in the register of the house of Israel they shall not be registered, and into the land of Israel shall they not come; and ye shall learn that I am the Lord Jehovah.* Ver. 10. *Because, yea because they lead my people astray, and say, " Peace," though there is no peace; and when it (my people) build a wall, behold, they plaster it with cement:* Ver. 11. *Say to the plasterers, that it will fall: there cometh a pouring rain; and ye hailstones fall, and thou stormy wind break loose!* Ver. 12. *And, behold, the wall falleth; will men not say to you, Where is the plaster with which ye have plastered it?* Ver. 13. *Therefore thus saith the Lord Jehovah, I cause a stormy wind to break forth in my wrath, and a pouring rain will come in my anger, and hailstones in wrath, for destruction.* Ver. 14. *And I demolish the wall which ye have plastered, and cast it to the ground, that its foundation may be exposed, and it shall fall, and ye shall perish in the midst of it; and shall learn that I am Jehovah.* Ver. 15. *And I will exhaust my wrath upon the wall, and upon those who plaster it; and will say to you, It is all over with the wall, and all over with those who plastered it;* Ver. 16. *With the prophets of Israel who prophesied to Jerusalem, and saw visions of peace for her, though there is no peace, is the saying of the Lord Jehovah.*—In ver. 8 the punishment which is to fall upon the false prophets is threatened in general terms; and in ver. 9 it is more specifically described in the form of a climax, rising higher and higher in the severity of its announcements. (1) They are no longer to form part of the council of the people of God; that is to say, they will lose their influential position among the people. (סוֹד is the sphere of counsellors, not the social sphere.) (2) Their names shall not be registered in the book of the house of Israel. The book of the house of Israel is the register in which the citizens of the kingdom of God are entered. Any one whose name was not admitted into this book, or was struck out of it, was separated thereby from the citizenship of Israel, and lost all the privileges which citizenship conferred. The figure of the book of life is a similar one (cf. Ex. xxxii. 32). For Israel is not referred to here with regard to its outward nationality, but as the people of God; so that exclusion from Israel was also exclusion from fellowship with God. The circumstance that it is not the erasure of their names from the book that is mentioned here, but their not being entered in the book at all, may be accounted for from the reference contained in the words to the founding of the new kingdom of God. The old theocracy was abolished, although Jerusalem was not yet destroyed. The covenant nation had fallen under the judgment; but out of that portion of Israel which was dispersed among the heathen, a remnant would be gathered together again, and having been brought back to its own land, would be made anew into a holy people of God (cf. ch. xi. 17 sqq.). But the false prophets are not to be received into the citizenship of the new kingdom. (3) They are not even to come into the land of Israel; *i.e.* they are not merely to remain in exile, but to lose all share in the privileges and blessings of the kingdom of God. This judgment will come upon them because they lead astray the people of God, by proclaiming peace where there is no peace; *i.e.* by raising and cherishing false hopes of prosperity and peace, by which they encourage the people in their sinful lives, and lead them to imagine that all is well, and there is no judgment to be feared (cf. Jer. xxiii. 17 and Mic. iii. 5). The exposure of this offence is introduced by the solemn יַעַן וּבְיַעַן, because and because (cf. Lev. xxvi. 43); and the offence itself is exhibited by means of a figure. When the people build a wall, the false prophets plaster the wall with lime. וְהוּא (ver. 10) refers to עַמִּי, and the clause is a circumstantial one. תָּפֵל signifies the plaster coating or cement of a wall, probably from the primary meaning of תָּפַל, to stick or plaster over (= טָפַל, *conglutinare*, to glue, or fasten together), from which the secondary meaning of weak, insipid, has sprung. The proper word for plaster or cement is טִיחַ (ver. 12), and תָּפֵל is probably chosen with an allusion to the tropical signification of that which is silly or absurd (Jer. xxiii. 13; Lam. ii. 14). The meaning of the figure is intelligible enough. The people build up foolish hopes, and the prophets not only paint these hopes for them in splendid colours, but even predict their fulfilment, instead of denouncing their folly, pointing out to the people the perversity of their ways, and showing them that such sinful conduct must inevitably be followed by punishment and ruin. The plastering is therefore a figurative description of deceitful flattery or hypocrisy, *i.e.* the covering up of inward corruption by means of outward appearance (as in Matt. xxiii. 27 and Acts xxiii. 3). This figure leads the prophet to describe the judgment which they are bringing upon the nation and themselves, as a tempest accompanied with hail and pouring rain, which throws down the wall that has been erected and plastered over; and in connection with this figure he opens out this double thought: (1) the conduct of the people, which is encouraged by the false prophets, cannot last (vers. 11 and 12); and (2) when this work of theirs is overthrown, the false prophets themselves will also meet with the fate they deserve (vers. 13-16). The threat of judgment commences with the short, energetic וְיִפֹּל, let it (the wall) fall, or it shall fall, with *Vav* to indicate the train of thought (Ewald, § 347*a*). The subject is חֵל, to which יִפֹּל suggests a resemblance in sound. In ver. 12 this is predicted as the fate awaiting the plastered wall. In the description of the bursting storm the account passes with וְאַתֵּנָה (and ye) into a direct address; in other words, the description assumes the form of an appeal to the destructive forces of nature to burst forth with all their violence against the work plastered over by the prophets, and to destroy it. גֶּשֶׁם שׁוֹטֵף, pouring rain; cf. ch. xxxviii. 22. אַבְנֵי אֶלְגָּבִישׁ here and ch. xxxviii. 22 are hail-stones. The word אֶלְגָּבִישׁ, which is peculiar to Ezekiel, is probably גָּבִישׁ (Job xxviii. 18), with the Arabic article אל; ice, then crystal. רוּחַ סְעָרוֹת, wind of storms, a hurricane or tempest. תִּבָּקַע (ver. 11) is used intransitively, to break loose; but in ver. 13 it is transitive, to cause to break loose. The active rendering adopted by Kliefoth, "the storm will rend," *sc.* the plaster of the wall, is inappropriate in ver. 11; for a tempest does not rend either the plaster or the wall, but throws the wall down. The translation which Kliefoth gives in ver. 13, " I will rend by tempest," is at variance with both the language and the sense. Jehovah will cause this tempest to burst forth in His wrath and destroy the wall, and lay it level with the ground. The suffix in בְּתוֹכָהּ refers (*ad sensum*) to Jerusalem, not to קִיר (the wall), which is masculine, and has no תָּוֶךְ (midst). The words pass from the figure to the reality here; for the plastered wall is a symbol of Jerusalem, as the centre of the theocracy, which is to be destroyed, and to bury the lying prophets in its ruins. וְכִלֵּיתִי (ver. 15) contains a play upon the word לְכָלָה in ver. 13. By a new turn given to כלה, Ezekiel repeats the thought that the wrath of God is to destroy the wall and its plasterers; and through this repetition he rounds off the threat with the express declaration, that the false prophets who are ever preaching peace are the plasterers to whom he refers.

Vers. 17-23. AGAINST THE FALSE PROPHETESSES.—As the Lord had not endowed men only with the gifts of prophecy, but sometimes women also, *e.g.* Miriam, Deborah, and Huldah; so women also rose up along with the false prophets, and prophesied out of their own hearts without being impelled by the Spirit of God. Vers. 17-19. Their conduct.—Ver. 17. *And thou, son of man, direct thy face towards the daughters of thy people, who prophesy out of their heart and prophesy against them,* Ver. 18. *And say, Thus saith the Lord Jehovah, Woe to those who sew coverings together over all the joints of my hands, and make caps for the head of every size, to catch souls! Ye catch the souls of my people, and keep your souls alive.* Ver. 19. *And ye profane me with my people for handfuls of barley and for pieces of bread, to slay souls which should not die, and to keep alive which should not live, by your lying to my people who hearken to lying.*—Like the prophets in ver. 2, the prophetesses are here described as prophesying out of their own heart (ver. 17); and in vers. 18 and 19 their offences are more particularly described. The meaning of these verses is entirely dependent upon the view to be taken of יָדַי, which the majority of expositors, following the lead of the LXX., the Syriac, and the Vulgate, have regarded as identical with יָדַיִם or יָד, and understood as referring to the hands of the women or prophetesses. But there is nothing to justify the assumption that יָדַי is an unusual form for יָדַיִם, which even Ewald takes it to be (*Lehrbuch,* § 177*a*). Still less can it stand for the singular יָד. And we have not sufficient ground for altering the text, as the expression וּרְעֹתֵיכֶם in ver. 20 (I will tear the כְּסָתוֹת from your arms) does not require the assumption that the prophetesses had hidden their arms in כסתות; and such a supposition is by no means obviously in harmony with the facts. The word כְּסָתוֹת, from כֶּסֶת, with ת fem. treated as a radical letter (cf. Ewald, § 186e), means a covering or concealment = כְּסוּת. The meaning "cushion" or "pillow" (LXX. προσκεφάλαια, Vulg. *pulvilli*) is merely an inference drawn from this passage, and is decidedly erroneous; for the word תָּפַר (to sew together) is inapplicable to cushions, as well as the phrase עַל כָּל־אַצִּילֵי יָדַי, inasmuch as cushions are not placed upon the joints of the hands, and still less are they sewed together upon them. The latter is also a decisive reason for rejecting the explanation given by Hävernick, namely, that the *kᵉsâthôth* were carpets, which were used as couches, and upon which these voluptuous women are represented as reclining. For cushions or couches are not placed upon, but under, the arm-joints (or elbows) and the shoulders, which Hävernick understands by אַצִּילֵי יָד. This also overthrows another explanation given of the words, namely, that they refer to carpets, which the prophetesses had sewed together for all their arm-joints, so as to form comfortable beds upon splendid carpets, that they may indulge in licentiousness thereon. The explanation given by Ephraem Syrus, and adopted by Hitzig, namely, that the *kᵉsâthôth* were amulets or straps, which they wound round their arm-joints when they received or delivered their oracles, is equally untenable. For, as Kliefoth has observed, "it is evident that there is not a word in the text about adultery, or amulets, or straps used in prayer." And again, when we proceed to the next clause, the traditional rendering of מִסְפָּחוֹת, as signifying either pillows (ὑπαυχένια, Symm.; *cervicalia*, Vulg.) or broad cloaks = מִטְפָּחוֹת (Hitzig, Hävernick, etc.), is neither supported by the usage of the language, nor in harmony with עַל רֹאשׁ. *Mispáchōth*, from *sáphach*, to join, cannot have any other meaning in the present context than a cap fitting close to the head; and עַל must denote the pattern which was followed, as in Ps. cx. 4, Esth. ix. 26: they make the caps after (answering to) the head of every stature. The words of both clauses are figurative, and have been correctly explained by Kliefoth as follows: "A double charge is brought against the prophetesses. In the first place, they sew coverings together to wrap round all the joints of the hand of God, so that He cannot touch them; *i.e.* they cover up and conceal the word of God by their prophesying, more especially its rebuking and threatening force, so that the threatening and judicial arm of God, which ought above all to become both manifest and effective through His prophetic word, does not become either one or the other. In the second place, they make coverings upon the heads of men, and construct them in such a form that they exactly fit the stature or size of every individual, so that the men neither hear nor see; *i.e.*, by means of their flattering lies, which adapt themselves to the subjective inclinations of their hearers at the time, they cover up the senses of the men, so that they retain neither ear nor eye for the truth." They do both of these to catch souls. The inevitable consequence of their act is represented as having been intended by them; and this intention is then still further defined as being to catch the souls of the people of God; *i.e.* to allure them to destruction, and take care of their own souls. The clause הַנְּפָשׁוֹת תְּצוֹדֵדְנָה is not to be taken as a question, "Will ye catch the souls?" implying a doubt whether they really thought that they could carry on such conduct as theirs with perfect impunity (Hävernick). It contains a simple statement of what really took place in their catching of souls, namely, "they catch the souls of the people of God, and preserve their own souls;" *i.e.* they rob the people of God of their lives, and take care of their own (Kliefoth). לְעַמִּי is used instead of the genitive (*stat. constr.*) to show that the accent rests upon עַמִּי. And in the same way we have לְכֶנָה instead of the suffix. The construction is the same as in 1 Sam xiv. 16. Ver. 19 shows how great their sin had been. They profane God among His people; namely, by delivering the suggestions of their own heart to the people as divine revelations, for the purpose of getting their daily bread thereby (cf. Mic. iii. 5); by hurling into destruction, through their lies, those who are only too glad to listen to lying; by slaying the souls of the people which ought to live, and by preserving those which ought not to live, *i.e.* their own souls (Deut. xviii. 20). The punishment for this will not fail to come.

Vers. 20-23. Punishment of the false prophetesses.—Ver. 20. *Therefore thus saith the Lord Jehovah, Behold, I will deal with your coverings with which ye catch, I will let the souls fly; and I will tear them away from your arms, and set the souls free, which ye catch, the souls to fly.* Ver. 21. *And I will tear your caps in pieces, and deliver my people out of your hand, and they shall no more become a prey in your hand; and ye shall learn that I am Jehovah.* Ver. 22. *Because ye grieve the heart of the righteous with lying, when I have not pained him; and strengthen the hands of the wicked, so that he does not turn from his evil way, to preserve his life.* Ver. 23. *Therefore ye shall no more see vanity, and no longer practise soothsaying: and I will deliver my people out of your hand; and ye shall learn that I am Jehovah.*—The threat of judgment is closely connected with the reproof of their sins. Vers. 20 and 21 correspond to the reproof in ver. 18, and vers. 22 and 23 to that in ver. 19. In the first place, the Lord will tear in pieces the coverings and caps, *i.e.* the tissue of lies woven by the false prophetesses, and rescue the people from their snares (vers. 20 and 21); and, secondly, He will entirely put an end to the pernicious conduct of the persons addressed (vers. 22 and 23). The words from אֲשֶׁר אַתֵּנָה to לְפֹרְחוֹת (ver. 20*a*), when taken as one clause, as they generally are, offer insuperable difficulties, since it is impossible to get any satisfactory meaning from שָׁם, and לְפֹרְחוֹת will not fit in. Whether we understand by *keṣâthôth* coverings or cushions, the connection of שָׁם with אֲשֶׁר (*where* ye catch the souls), which the majority of commentators prefer, is untenable; for coverings and cushions were not the places where the souls were caught, but could only be the means employed for catching them. Instead of שָׁם we should expect בָּם or בָּהֶם; and Hitzig proposes to amend it in this way. Still less admissible is the proposal to take שָׁם as referring to Jerusalem ("wherewith ye catch souls *there*"); as שָׁם would not only contain a perfectly superfluous definition of locality, but would introduce a limitation altogether at variance with the context. It is not affirmed either of the prophets or of the prophetesses that they lived and prophesied in Jerusalem alone. In vers. 2 and 17 reference is made in the most general terms to the prophets of Israel and the daughters of thy people; and in ver. 16 it is simply stated that the false prophets prophesied peace to Jerusalem when there was no peace at all. Consequently we must regard the attempt to find in שָׁם an allusion to Jerusalem (cf. ver. 16) as a mere loophole, which betrays an utter inability to get any satisfactory sense from the word. Moreover, if we construe the words in this manner, לְפֹרְחוֹת is also incomprehensible. Commentators have for the most part admitted that פָּרַח is used here in the Aramaean sense of *volare*, to fly. In the second half of the verse there is no doubt about its having this meaning. For שִׁלַּח is used in Deut. xxii. 7 for liberating a bird, or letting it fly; and the combination שַׁלֵּחַ אֶת־הנפ׳ לְפֹרְחוֹת is supported by the expression שַׁלֵּחַ לַחָפְשִׁי in Ex. xxi. 26, while the comparison of souls to birds is sustained by Ps. xi. 1 and cxxiv. 7. Hence the true meaning of the whole passage שִׁלַּחְתִּי אֶת־הַנְּפָשׁוֹת . . . לְפֹרְחוֹת is, I send away (set free) the souls, which ye have caught, as flying ones, *i.e.* so that they shall be able to fly away at liberty. And in the first half also we must not adopt a different rendering for לְפֹרְחוֹת, since אֶת־הַנְּפָשׁוֹת is also connected with it there. But if the words in question are combined into one clause in the first hemistich, they will give us a sense which is obviously wrong, viz. "wherewith ye catch the souls to let them fly." As the impossibility of adopting this rendering has been clearly seen, the attempt has been made to cloak over the difficulty by means of paraphrases. Ewald, for example, renders לְפֹרְחוֹת in both cases "as if they were birds of passage;" but in the first instance he applies it to birds of passage, for which nets are spread for the purpose of catching them; and in the second, to birds of passage which are set at liberty. Thus, strictly speaking, he understands the first לְפֹרְחוֹת as signifying the catching of birds; and the second, letting them fly : an explanation which refutes itself, as *parach*, to fly, cannot mean " to catch " as well. The rendering adopted by Kimchi, Rosenmüller, and others, who translate לְפֹרְחוֹת *ut advolent ad vos* in the first hemistich, and *ut avolent* in the second, is no better. And the difficulty is not removed by resorting to the dialects, as Hävernick, for the purpose of forcing upon פֹּרְחוֹת the meaning dissoluteness or licentiousness, for which there is no authority in the Hebrew language itself. If, therefore, it is impossible to obtain any satisfactory meaning from the existing text, it cannot be correct; and no other course is open to us than to alter the unsuitable שָׁם into שָׂם, and divide the words from אֲשֶׁר אַתֵּנָה to לְפֹרְחוֹת into two clauses, as we have done in our translation above. There is no necessity to supply anything to the relative אֲשֶׁר, as צוּד is construed with a double accusative (*e.g.* Mic. vii. 2, צוּד חֵרֶם, to catch with a net), and the object to מִצֹּדְדוֹת, viz. the souls, can easily be supplied from the next clause. שָׂם, as a particiole, can either be connected with הִנְנִי, "behold, I make," or taken as introducing an explanatory clause: "making the souls into flying ones," *i.e.* so that they are able to fly (שׂוּם לְ, Gen. xii. 2, etc.). The two clauses of the first hemistich would then exactly correspond to the two clauses of the second half of the verse. וְקָרַעְתִּי אֹתָם is explanatory of הִנְנִי אֶל כסת׳, I will tear off the coverings from their arms. These words do not require the assumption that the prophetesses wore the לסתות on their arms, but may be fully explained from the supposition that the persons in question prepared them with their own hands. וְשִׁלַּחְתִּי וגו׳ corresponds to עַם אֶת־הַנְּפָשׁוֹת וגו׳; and לְפֹרְחוֹת is governed by שִׁלַּחְתִּי. The insertion of אֶת־הַנְּפָשִׁים is to be accounted for from the copious nature of Ezekiel's style; at the same time, it is not merely a repetition of אֶת־הַנְּפָשׁוֹת, which is separated from לְפֹרְחוֹת by the relative clause אֲשֶׁר אַתֶּם מצ׳, but as the unusual plural form נְפָשִׁים shows, is intended as a practical explanation of the fact, that the souls, while compared to birds, are regarded as living beings, which is the meaning borne by נֶפֶשׁ in other passages. The omission of the article after אֶת may be explained, however, from the fact that the souls had been more precisely defined just before; just as, for example, in 1 Sam. xxiv. 6, 2 Sam. xviii. 18, where the more precise definition follows immediately afterwards (cf. Ewald, § 277a, p. 683).—The same thing is said in ver. 21, with regard to the caps, as has already been said of the coverings in ver. 20. God will tear these in pieces also, to deliver His people from the power of the lying prophetesses. In what way God will do this is explained in vers. 22 and 23, namely, not only by putting their lying prophecies to shame through His judgments, but by putting an end to soothsaying altogether, and exterminating the false prophetesses by making them an object of ridicule and shame. The reason for this threat is given in ver. 22, where a further description is given of the disgraceful conduct of these persons; and here the disgracefulness of their conduct is exhibited in literal terms and without any figure. They do harm to the righteous and good, and strengthen the hands of the wicked. הַכְאוֹת, *Hiphil* of כָּאָה, in Syriac, to use harshly or depress; so here in the *Hiphil*, connected with לֵב, to afflict the heart. שֶׁקֶר is used adverbially: with lying, or in a lying manner; namely, by predicting misfortune and divine punishments, with which they threatened the godly, who would not acquiesce in their conduct; whereas, on the contrary, they predicted prosperity and peace to the ungodly, who were willing to be ensnared by them, and thus strengthened them in their evil ways. For this God would put them to shame through His judgments, which would make their deceptions manifest, and their soothsaying loathsome.

CHAP. XIV. ATTITUDE OF GOD TOWARDS THE WORSHIPPERS OF IDOLS, AND CERTAINTY OF THE JUDGMENTS.

This chapter contains two words of God, which have obviously an internal connection with each other. The first (vers. 1-11) announces to the elders, who have come to the prophet to inquire of God, that the Lord will not allow idolaters to inquire of Him, but will answer all who do not turn from idolatry with severe judgments, and will even destroy the prophets who venture to give an answer to such inquirers. The second (vers. 12-23) denounces the false hope that God will avert the judgment and spare Jerusalem because of the righteousness of the godly men therein.

Vers. 1-11. THE LORD GIVES NO ANSWER TO THE IDOLATERS.—Ver. 1 narrates the occasion for this and the following words of God: *There came to me men of the elders of Israel, and sat down before me.* These men were not deputies from the Israelites in Palestine, as Grotius and others suppose, but elders of the exiles among whom Ezekiel had been labouring. They came to visit the prophet (ver. 3), evidently with the intention of obtaining, through him, a word of God concerning the future of Jerusalem, or the fate of the kingdom of Judah. But Hävernick is wrong in supposing that we may infer, from either the first or second word of God in this chapter, that they had addressed to the prophet a distinct inquiry of this nature, to which the answer is given in vers. 12-23. For although their coming to the prophet showed that his prophecies had made an impression upon them, it is not stated in ver. 1 that they had come to inquire of God, like the elders in ch. xx. 1, and there is no allusion to any definite questions in the words of

God themselves. The first (vers. 2–11) simply assumes that they have come with the intention of asking, and discloses the state of heart which keeps them from coming to inquire; and the second (vers. 12–23) points out the worthlessness of their false confidence in the righteousness of certain godly men.

Ver. 2. *And the word of Jehovah came to me, saying*, Ver. 3. *Son of man, these men have let their idols rise up in their heart, and have set the stumbling-block to guilt before their face: shall I allow myself to be inquired of by them?* Ver. 4. *Therefore speak to them, and say to them, Thus saith the Lord Jehovah, Every man of the house of Israel who lifteth up his idols in his heart, and setteth the stumbling-block to his sin before his face, and cometh to the prophet, to him do I, Jehovah, show myself, answering according thereto, according to the multitude of his idols;* Ver. 5. *To grasp the house of Israel by their heart, because they have turned away from me, all of them through their idols.*—We have not to picture these elders to ourselves as given up to gross idolatry. הֶעֱלָה עַל לֵב means, to allow anything to come into the mind, to permit it to rise up in the heart, to be mentally busy therewith. "To set before one's face" is also to be understood, in a spiritual sense, as relating to a thing which a man will not put out of his mind. מִכְשׁוֹל עֲוֹנָם, stumbling-block to sin and guilt (cf. ch. vii. 19), *i.e.* the idols. Thus the two phrases simply denote the leaning of the heart and spirit towards false gods. God does not suffer those whose heart is attached to idols to seek and find Him. The interrogative clause הַאִדָּרֹשׁ וגו' contains a strong negation. The emphasis lies in the infinitive absolute אִדְּרֹשׁ placed before the verb, in which the ה is softened into א, to avoid writing ה twice. נִדְרָשׁ, to allow oneself to be sought, involves the finding of God; hence in Isa. lxv. 1 we have נִדְרָשׁ as parallel to נִמְצָא. In vers. 4, 5, there follows a positive declaration of the attitude of God towards those who are devoted to idolatry in their heart. Every such Israelite will be answered by God according to the measure of the multitude of his idols. The *Niphal* נַעֲנָה has not the signification of the *Kal*, and does not mean "to be answerable," as Ewald supposes, or to converse; but is generally used in a passive sense, "to be answered," *i.e.* to find or obtain a hearing (Job xi. 2, xix. 7). It is employed here in a reflective sense, to hold or show oneself answering. בָּה, according to the *Chetib* בָּה, for which the *Keri* suggests the softer gloss בָא, refers to בְּרֹב גִּל׳ which follows; the nominative being anticipated, according to an idiom very common in Aramaean, by a previous pronoun. It is written here for the sake of emphasis, to bring the following object into more striking prominence. ב is used here in the sense of *secundum*, according to, not because, since this meaning is quite unsuitable for the ב in ver. 7, where it occurs in the same connection (בִּי). The manner in which God will show Himself answering the idolatry according to their idols, is reserved till ver. 8. Here, in ver. 5, the design of this procedure on the part of God is given: viz. to grasp Israel by the heart; *i.e.* not merely to touch and to improve them, but to bring down their heart by judgments (cf. Lev. xxvi. 41), and thus move them to give up idolatry and return to the living God. נָזֹרוּ, as in Isa. i. 4, to recede, to draw away from God. כֻּלָּם is an emphatic repetition of the subject belonging to נָזֹרוּ.

Vers. 6–8. In these verses the divine threat, and the summons to repent, are repeated, expanded, and uttered in the clearest words.—Ver. 6. *Therefore say to the house of Israel, Thus saith the Lord Jehovah, Repent, and turn away from your idols; and turn away your face from all your abominations.* Ver. 7. *For every one of the house of Israel, and of the foreigners who sojourn in Israel, if he estrange himself from me, and let his idols rise up in his heart, and set the stumbling-block to his sin before his face, and come to the prophet to seek me for himself; I will show myself to him, answering in my own way.* Ver. 8. *I will direct my face against that man, and will destroy him, for a sign and for proverbs, and will cut him off out of my people; and ye shall learn that I am Jehovah.*—לָכֵן in ver. 6 is co-ordinate with the

לָכֵן in ver. 4, so far as the thought is concerned, but it is directly attached to ver. 5b: because they have estranged themselves from God, therefore God requires them to repent and turn. For God will answer with severe judgments every one who would seek God with idols in his heart, whether he be an Israelite, or a foreigner living in the midst of Israel. שׁוּבוּ, turn, be converted, is rendered still more emphatic by the addition of הָשִׁיבוּ ... פְּנֵיכֶם. This double call to repentance corresponds to the double reproof of their idolatry in ver. 3, viz. שׁוּבוּ, to הֶעֱלָה גִּל׳ עַל לֵב; and פְּנֵיכֶם הָשִׁיב, to their setting the idols נֹכַח פְּנֵיהֶם. הָשִׁיבוּ is not used intransitively, as it apparently is in ch. xviii. 30, but is to be taken in connection with the object פְּנֵיכֶם, which follows at the end of the verse; and it is simply repeated before פניכם for the sake of clearness and emphasis. The reason for the summons to repent and give up idolatry is explained in ver. 7, in the threat that God will destroy every Israelite, and every foreigner in Israel, who draws away from God and attaches himself to idols. The phraseology of ver. 7a is adopted almost *verbatim* from Lev. xvii. 8, 10, 13. On the obligation of foreigners to avoid idolatry and all moral abominations, *vid.* Lev. xx. 2, xviii. 26, xvii. 10; Ex. xii. 19, etc. The ו before יִנָּזֵר and יַעַל does not stand for the *Vav relat.*, but simply supposes a case: "should he separate himself from my followers, and let his idols rise up, etc." לִדְרָשׁ־לוֹ בִי does not mean, "to seek counsel of him (the prophet) from me," for לוֹ cannot be taken as referring to the prophet, although דָּרַשׁ with לְ does sometimes mean to seek any one, and לְ may therefore indicate the person to whom one goes to make inquiry (cf. 2 Chron. xv. 13, xvii. 4, xxxi. 21), because it is Jehovah who is sought in this case; and Hävernick's remark, that "דָּרַשׁ with לְ merely indicates the external object sought by a man, and therefore in this instance the medium or organ through whom God speaks," is proved to be erroneous by the passages just cited. לוֹ is reflective, or to be taken as a *dat. commodi*, denoting the inquirer or seeker. The person approached for the purpose of inquiring or seeking, *i.e.* God, is indicated by the preposition בְּ, as in 1 Chron. x. 14 (דָּרַשׁ בַּיהוָֹה); and also frequently, in the case of idols, when either an oracle or help is sought from them (1 Sam. xxviii. 7; 2 Kings i. 2 sqq.). It is only in this way that לֹ and בְּ can be made to correspond to the same words in the apodosis: Whosoever seeks counsel of God, to him will God show Himself answering בְּ, in Him, *i.e.* in accordance with His nature, in His own way,— namely, in the manner described in ver. 8. The threat is composed of passages in the law: 'נָתַתִּי פָנַי וגו and 'הִכְרַתִּי וגו, after Lev. xx. 3, 5, 6; and 'וַהֲשִׁמּוֹתִיהוּ וגו, though somewhat freely, after Deut. xxviii. 37 ('הָיָה לְשַׁמָּה לְמָשָׁל וגו). There is no doubt, therefore, that הֲשִׁמוֹתִי is to be derived from שָׁמֵם, and stands for הֲשִׁמּוֹתִי, in accordance with the custom in later writings of resolving the *Dagesh forte* into a long vowel. The allusion to Deut. xxviii. 37, compared with הָיָה לְאוֹת in ver. 46 of the same chapter, is sufficient to set aside the assumption that הׁשמותי is to be derived from שִׂים, and pointed accordingly; although the LXX., Targ., Syr., and Vulg. have all renderings of שִׂים (cf. Ps. xliv. 16). Moreover, שִׂים in the perfect never takes the *Hiphil* form; and in ch. xx. 26 we have אֲשִׁמֵּם in a similar connection. The expression is a pregnant one: I make him desolate, so that he becomes a sign and proverbs.

Vers. 9–11. No prophet is to give any other answer.—Ver. 9. *But if a prophet allow himself to be persuaded, and give a word, I have persuaded this prophet, and will stretch out my hand against him, and cut him off out of my people Israel.* Ver. 10. *They shall bear their guilt: as the guilt of the inquirer, so shall the guilt of the prophet be;* Ver. 11. *In order that the house of Israel may no more stray from me, and may no more defile itself with all its transgressions; but they may be my people, and I their God, is the saying of the Lord Jehovah.*—The prophet who allows himself to be persuaded is not a prophet מִלִּבּוֹ (ch. xiii. 2), but one who really thinks that he has a word of God. פָּתָה, to persuade, to entice by friendly words (in a good sense,

Hos. ii. 16); but generally *sensu malo,* to lead astray, or seduce to that which is unallowable or evil. "If he allow himself to be persuaded:" not necessarily "with the hope of payment from the hypocrites who consult him" (Michaelis). This weakens the thought. It might sometimes be done from unselfish good-nature. And "the word" itself need not have been a divine oracle of his own invention, or a false prophecy. The allusion is simply to a word of a different character from that contained in vers. 6–8, which either demands repentance or denounces judgment upon the impenitent: every word, therefore, which could by any possibility confirm the sinner in his security.—By אֲנִי יְהוָה (ver. 9) the apodosis is introduced in an emphatic manner, as in vers. 4 and 7; but פִּתֵּיתִי cannot be taken in a future sense ("I will persuade"). It must be a perfect; since the persuading of the prophet would necessarily precede his allowing himself to be persuaded. The Fathers and earlier Lutheran theologians are wrong in their interpretation of פִּתֵּיתִי, which they understand in a permissive sense, meaning simply that God allowed it, and did not prevent their being seduced. Still more wrong are Storr and Schmieder, the former of whom regards it as simply declaratory, "I will declare him to have gone astray from the worship of Jehovah;" the latter, "I will show him to be a fool, by punishing him for his disobedience." The words are rather to be understood in accordance with 1 Kings xxii. 20 sqq., where the persuading (*pittâh*) is done by a lying spirit, which inspires the prophets of Ahab to predict success to the king, in order that he may fall. As Jehovah sent the spirit in that case, and put it into the mouth of the prophets, so is the persuasion in this instance also effected by God: not merely divine permission, but divine ordination and arrangement; though this does not destroy human freedom, but, like all "persuading," presupposes the possibility of not allowing himself to be persuaded. See the discussion of this question in the commentary on 1 Kings xxii. 20 sqq. The remark of Calvin on the verse before us is correct: "it teaches that neither impostures nor frauds take place apart from the will of God" (*nisi Deo volente*). But this willing on the part of God, or the persuading of the prophets to the utterance of self-willed words, which have not been inspired by God, only takes place in persons who admit evil into themselves, and is designed to tempt them and lead them to decide whether they will endeavour to resist and conquer the sinful inclinations of their hearts, or will allow them to shape themselves into outward deeds, in which case they will become ripe for judgment. It is in this sense that God persuades such a prophet, in order that He may then cut him off out of His people. But this punishment will not fall upon the prophet only. It will reach the seeker or inquirer also, in order if possible to bring Israel back from its wandering astray, and make it into a people of God purified from sin (vers. 10 and 11). It was to this end that, in the last times of the kingdom of Judah, God allowed false prophecy to prevail so mightily,— namely, that it might accelerate the process of distinguishing between the righteous and the wicked; and then, by means of the judgment which destroyed the wicked, purify His nation and lead it on to the great end of its calling.

Vers. 12–23. THE RIGHTEOUSNESS OF THE GODLY WILL NOT AVERT THE JUDGMENT.—The threat contained in the preceding word of God, that if the idolaters did not repent, God would not answer them in any other way than with an exterminating judgment, left the possibility still open, that He would avert the destruction of Judah and Jerusalem for the sake of the righteous therein, as He had promised the patriarch Abraham that He would do in the case of Sodom and Gomorrah (Gen. xviii. 23 sqq.). This hope, which might be cherished by the people and by the elders who had come to the prophet, is now to be taken from the people by the word of God which follows, containing as it does the announcement, that if any land should sin so grievously against God by its apostasy, He would be driven to inflict upon it the punishments threatened by Moses against apostate Israel (Lev. xxvi. 22, 25, 26, and elsewhere), namely, to destroy both man and beast, and make the land a desert; it would be of no advantage to such a land to have certain righteous men, such as Noah, Daniel, and Job, living therein. For although these righteous men would be saved themselves, their righteousness could not possibly secure salvation for the sinners. The manner in which this thought is carried out in vers. 13-20 is, that four exterminating punishments are successively supposed to come upon the land and lay it waste; and in the case of every one, the words are repeated, that even righteous men, such as Noah, Daniel, and Job, would only save their own souls, and not one of the sinners. And thus, according to vers. 21-23, will the Lord act when He sends His judgments against Jerusalem; and He will execute them in such a manner that the necessity and righteousness of His acts shall be made manifest therein.—This word of God forms a supplementary side-piece to Jer. xv. 1-4, where the Lord replies to the intercession of the prophet, that even the intercession of a Moses and a Samuel on behalf of the people would not avert the judgments which were suspended over them.

Ver. 12. *And the word of Jehovah came to me, saying,* Ver. 13. *Son of man, if a land sin against me to act treacherously, and I stretch out my hand against it, and break in pieces for it the support of bread, and send famine into it, and cut off from it man and beast:* Ver. 14. *And there should be these three men therein, Noah, Daniel, and Job, they would through their righteousness deliver their soul, is the saying of the Lord Jehovah.* Ver. 15. *If I bring evil beasts into the land, so that they make it childless, and it become a desert, so that no one passeth through it because of the beasts:* Ver. 16. *These three men therein, as I live, is the saying of the Lord Jehovah, would not deliver sons and daughters; they only would be delivered, but the land would become a desert.* Ver. 17. *Or I bring the sword into that land, and say, Let the sword go through the land; and I cut off from it man and beast:* Ver. 18. *These three men therein, as I live, is the saying of the Lord Jehovah, would not deliver sons and daughters, but they only would be delivered.* Ver. 19. *Or I send pestilence into that land, and pour out my fury upon it in blood, to cut off from it man and beast:* Ver. 20. *Verily, Noah, Daniel, and Job, in the midst of it, as I live, is the saying of the Lord Jehovah, would deliver neither son nor daughter; they would only deliver their own soul through their righteousness.*—אֶרֶץ in ver. 13 is intentionally left indefinite, that the thought may be expressed in the most general manner. On the other hand, the sin is very plainly defined as לִמְעָל־מָעַל. מָעַל, literally, to cover, signifies to act in a secret or treacherous manner, especially towards Jehovah, either by apostasy from Him, in other words, by idolatry, or by withholding what is due to Him (see comm. on Lev. v. 15). In the passage before us it is the treachery of apostasy from Him by idolatry that is intended. As the epithet used to denote the sin is taken from Lev. xxvi. 40 and Deut. xxxii. 51, so the four punishments mentioned in the following verses, as well as in ch. v. 17, are also taken from Lev. xxvi.,—viz. the breaking up of the staff of bread, from ver. 26; the evil beasts, from ver. 22; and the sword and pestilence, from ver. 25. The three men, Noah, Daniel, and Job, are named as examples of true righteousness of life, or צְדָקָה (vers. 14, 20); *i.e.*, according to Calvin's correct explanation, *quicquid pertinet ad regulam sancte et juste vivendi*. Noah is so described in Gen. vi. 9; and Job, in the Book of Job i. 1, xii. 4, etc.; and Daniel, in like manner, is mentioned in Dan. i. 8 sqq., vi. 11 sqq., as faithfully confessing his faith in his life. The fact that Daniel is named before Job does not warrant the conjecture that some other older Daniel is meant, of whom nothing is said in the history, and whose existence is merely postulated. For the enumeration is not intended to be chronological, but is arranged according to the subject-matter; the order being determined by the nature of the deliverance experienced by these men for their righteousness in the midst of great judgments. Consequently, as Hävernick and Kliefoth have shown, we have a climax here: Noah saved his family along with himself; Daniel was able to save his friends (Dan. ii. 17, 18); but Job, with his righteousness, was not even able to save his children.—The second judgment (ver. 15) is introduced with לֹא, which, as a rule, supposes a case that is not expected to occur, or even regarded as possible; here, however, לֹא is used as perfectly synonymous with אִם. שִׁכְּלָתָה has no *Mappik*, because the tone is drawn back upon the penultima (see comm. on Amos i. 11). In ver. 19, the expression "to pour out my wrath in blood" is a pregnant one, for to pour out my wrath in such a manner that it is manifested in the shedding of blood or the destruction of life, for the life is in the blood. In this sense pestilence and blood were also associated in ch. v. 17.—If we look closely at the four cases enumerated, we find the following difference in the statements concerning the deliverance of the righteous: that, in the first instance, it is simply stated that Noah, Daniel, and Job would save their soul, *i.e.* their life, by their righteousness; whereas, in the three others, it is declared that as truly as the Lord liveth they would not save either sons or daughters, but they alone would be delivered. The difference is not merely a rhetorical climax or progress in the address by means of asseveration and antithesis, but indicates a distinction in the thought. The first case is only intended to teach that in the approaching judgment the righteous would save their lives, *i.e.* that God would not sweep away the righteous with the ungodly. The three cases which follow are intended, on the other hand, to exemplify the truth that the righteousness of the righteous will be of no avail to the idolaters and apostates; since even such patterns of righteousness as Noah, Daniel, and Job would only save their own lives, and would not be able to save the lives of others also. This tallies with the omission of the asseveration in ver. 14. The first declaration, that God would deliver the righteous in the coming judgments, needed no asseveration, inasmuch as this truth was not called in question; but it was required in the case of the declaration that the righteousness of the righteous would bring no deliverance to the sinful nation, since this was the hope which the ungodly cherished, and it was this hope which was to be taken from them. The other differences which we find in the description given of the several cases are merely formal in their nature, and do not in any way affect the sense; e.g. the use of לֹא, in ver. 18, instead of the particle אִם, which is commonly employed in oaths, and which we find in vers. 16 and 20; the choice of the singular בֵּן and בַּת, in ver. 20, in the place of the plural בָּנִים וּבָנוֹת, used in vers. 16 and 18; and the variation in the expressions, יְנַצְּלוּ נַפְשָׁם (ver. 14), יַצִּילוּ נַפְשָׁם (ver. 20), and הֵמָּה לְבַדָּם יִנָּצֵלוּ (vers. 16 and 18), which Hitzig proposes to remove by altering the first two forms into the third, though without the slightest reason. For although the *Piel* occurs in Ex. xii. 36 in the sense of taking away or spoiling, and is not met with anywhere else in the sense of delivering, it may just as well be used in this sense, as the *Hiphil* has both significations.

Vers. 21–23. The rule expounded in vers. 13–20 is here applied to Jerusalem. — Ver. 21. *For thus saith the Lord Jehovah, How much more when I send my four evil judgments, sword, and famine, and evil beasts, and pestilence, against Jerusalem, to cut off from it man and beast?* Ver. 22. *And, behold, there remain escaped ones in her who will be brought out, sons and daughters; behold, they will go out to you, that ye may see their walk and their works; and console yourselves concerning the evil which I have brought upon Jerusalem.* Ver. 23. *And they will console you, when ye see their walk and their works: and ye will see that I have not done without cause all that I have done to her, is the saying of the Lord Jehovah.* — By כִּי in ver. 21 the application of the general rule to Jerusalem is made in the form of a reason. The meaning, however, is not, that the reason why Jehovah was obliged to act in this unsparing manner was to be found in the corrupt condition of the nation, as Hävernick supposes,—a thought quite foreign to the context; but כִּי indicates that the judgments upon Jerusalem will furnish a practical proof of the general truth expressed in vers. 13–20, and so confirm it. This כִּי is no more an emphatic yea than the following "אַף is a forcible introduction to the antithesis formed by the coming fact, to the merely imaginary cases mentioned above" (Hitzig). אַף has undoubtedly the force of a climax, but not of an asseveration, "verily" (Häv.); a meaning which this particle never has. It is used here, as in Job iv. 19, in the sense of אַף כִּי; and the כִּי which follows אַף in this case is a conditional particle of time, "when." Consequently כִּי ought properly to be written twice; but it is only used once, as in ch. xv. 5; Job ix. 14, etc. The thought is this: how much more will this be the case, namely, that even a Noah, Daniel, and Job will not deliver either sons or daughters when I send my judgments upon Jerusalem. The perfect שִׁלַּחְתִּי is used, and not the imperfect, as in ver. 13, because God has actually resolved upon sending it, and does not merely mention it as a possible case. The number four is significant, symbolizing the universality of the judgment, or the thought that it will fall on all sides, or upon the whole of Jerusalem; whereby it must also be borne in mind that Jerusalem as the capital represents the kingdom of Judah, or the whole of Israel, so far as it was still in Canaan. At the same time, by the fact that the Lord allows sons and daughters to escape death, and to be led away to Babylon, He forces the acknowledgment of the necessity and righteousness of His judgments among those who are in exile. This is in general terms the thought contained in vers. 22 and 23, to which very different meanings have been assigned by the latest expositors. Hävernick, for example, imagines that, in addition to the four ordinary judgments laid down in the law, ver. 22 announces a new and extraordinary one; whereas Hitzig and Kliefoth have found in these two verses the consolatory assurance, that in the time of the judgments a few of the younger generation will be rescued and taken to those already in exile in Babylon, there to excite pity as well as to express it, and to give a visible proof of the magnitude of the judgment which has fallen upon Israel. They differ so far from each other, however, that Hitzig regards those of the younger generation who are saved as צַדִּיקִים, who have saved themselves through their innocence, but not their guilty parents, and who will excite the commiseration of those already in exile through their blameless conduct; whilst Kliefoth imagines that those who are rescued are simply less criminal than the rest, and when they come to Babylon will be pitied by those who have been longer in exile, and will pity them in return.—Neither of these views does justice to the words themselves or to the context. The meaning of ver. 22a is clear enough; and in the main there has been no difference of opinion concerning it. When man and beast are cut off out of Jerusalem by the four judgments, all will not perish; but פְּלֵיטָה, i.e. persons who have escaped destruction, will be left, and will be led out of the city. These are called sons and daughters, with an allusion to vers. 16, 18, and 20; and consequently we must not take these words as referring to the younger generation in contrast to the older. They will be led out of Jerusalem, not to remain in the land, but to come to "you," i.e. those already in exile, that is to say, to go into exile to Babylon. This does not imply either a modification or a sharpening of the punishment; for the cutting off of man and beast from a town may be effected not only by slaying, but by leading away. The design of God in leaving some to escape, and carrying them to Babylon, is explained in the clauses which follow from וּרְאִיתֶם onwards, the meaning of which depends partly upon the more precise definition of דַּרְכָּם and עֲלִילוֹתָה, and partly upon the explanation to be given of נִחַמְתֶּם עַל־הָרָעָה and וְנִחֲמוּ אֶתְכֶם. The ways and works are not to be taken without reserve as good and righteous works, as Kliefoth has correctly shown in his reply to Hitzig. Still less can ways and works denote their experience or fate, which is the explanation given by Kliefoth of the words, when expounding the meaning and connection of vers. 21-23. The context certainly points to wicked ways and evil works. And it is only the sight of such works that could lead to the conviction that it was not חִנָּם, in vain, *i.e.* without cause, that God had inflicted such severe judgments upon Jerusalem. And in addition to this effect, which is mentioned in ver. 23 as produced upon those who were already in exile, by the sight of the conduct of the פְּלֵיטָה that came to Babylon, the immediate design of God is described in ver. 22*b* as וְנִחַמְתֶּם עַל־הָרָעָה וגו׳. The verb נָחַם with עַל cannot be used here in the sense of to repent of anything, or to grieve over it (Hitzig); still less can it mean to pity any one (Kliefoth). For a man cannot repent of, or be sorry for, a judgment which God has inflicted upon him, but only of evil which he himself has done; and נָחַם does not mean to pity a person, either when construed in the *Piel* with an accusative of the person, or in the *Niphal* c. עַל, *rei*. נִחַמְתֶּם is *Niphal*, and signifies here to console oneself, as in Gen. xxxviii. 12 with עַל, concerning anything, as in 2 Sam. xiii. 39, Jer. xxxi. 15, etc.; and נִחֲמוּ (ver. 23), with the accusative of the person, to comfort any one, as in Gen. li. 21; Job ii. 11, etc. But the works and doings of those who came to Babylon could only produce this effect upon those who were already there, from the fact that they were of such a character as to demonstrate the necessity for the judgments which had fallen upon Jerusalem. A conviction of the necessity for the divine judgments would cause them to comfort themselves with regard to the evil inflicted by God; inasmuch as they would see, not only that the punishment endured was a chastisement well deserved, but that God in His righteousness would stay the punishment when it had fulfilled His purpose, and restore the penitent sinner to favour once more. But the consolation which those who were in exile would derive from a sight of the works of the sons and daughters who had escaped from death and come to Babylon, is attributed in ver. 23 (נִחֲמוּ אֶתְכֶם) to the persons themselves. It is in this sense that it is stated that "they will comfort you;" not by expressions of pity, but by the sight of their conduct. This is directly affirmed in the words, " when ye shall see their conduct and their works." Consequently ver. 23a does not contain a new thought, but simply the thought already expressed in ver. 22b, which is repeated in a new form to make it the more emphatic. And the expression אֵת כָּל־אֲשֶׁר הֵבֵאתִי עָלֶיהָ, in ver. 22, serves to increase the force; whilst אֵת, in the sense of *quoad*, serves to place the thought to be repeated in subordination to the whole clause (cf. Ewald, § 277a, p. 683).

CHAP. XV. JERUSALEM, THE USELESS WOOD OF A WILD VINE.

As certainly as God will not spare Jerusalem for the sake of the righteousness of the few righteous men therein, so certain is it that Israel has no superiority over other nations, which could secure Jerusalem against destruction. As the previous word of God overthrows false confidence in the righteousness of the godly, what follows in this chapter is directed against the fancy that Israel cannot be rejected and punished by the overthrow of the kingdom, because of its election to be the people of God.

Ver. 1. *And the word of Jehovah came to me, saying,* Ver. 2. *Son of man, what advantage has the wood of the vine over every wood, the vine-branch, which was among the trees of the forest?* Ver. 3. *Is wood taken from it to use for any work? or do men take a peg from it to hang all kinds of vessels upon?* Ver. 4. *Behold, it is given to the fire to consume. If the fire has consumed its two ends, and the middle of it is scorched, will it then be fit for any work?* Ver. 5. *Behold, when it is uninjured, it is not used for any work: how much less when the fire has consumed it and scorched it can it be still used for work!* Ver. 6. *Therefore thus saith the Lord Jehovah, As the wood of the vine among the wood of the forest, which I give to the fire to consume,*

so do I give up the inhabitants of Jerusalem, Ver. 7. *And direct my face against them. They have gone out of the fire, and the fire will consume them; that ye may learn that I am Jehovah, when I set my face against them.* Ver. 8. *And I make the land a desert, because they committed treachery, is the saying of the Lord Jehovah.*
—Israel is like the wood of the wild vine, which is put into the fire to burn, because it is good for nothing. From Deut. xxxii. 32, 33 onwards, Israel is frequently compared to a vine or a vineyard (cf. Ps. lxxx. 9 sqq.; Isa. v.; Hos. x. 1; Jer. ii. 21), and always, with the exception of Ps. lxxx., to point out its degeneracy. This comparison lies at the foundation of the figure employed, in vers. 2–5, of the wood of the wild vine. This wood has no superiority over any other kind of wood. It cannot be used, like other timber, for any useful purposes; but is only fit to be burned, so that it is really inferior to all other wood (vers. 2 and 3*a*). And if, in its perfect state, it cannot be used for anything, how much less when it is partially scorched and consumed (vers. 4 and 5)! מַה־יִּהְיֶה, followed by מִן, means, what is it above (מִן, comparative)?—*i.e.* what superiority has it to כָּל־עֵץ, all kinds of wood? *i.e.* any other wood. הַזְּמוֹרָה אֲשֶׁר וגו׳ is in apposition to עֵץ הַגֶּפֶן, and is not to be connected with מִכָּל־עֵץ, as it has been by the LXX. and Vulgate,—notwithstanding the Masoretic accentuation,—so as to mean every kind of fagot; for זְמוֹרָה does not mean a fagot, but the tendril or branch of the vine (cf. ch. viii. 17), which is still further defined by the following relative clause: to be a wood-vine, *i.e.* a wild vine, which bears only sour, uneatable grapes. The preterite הָיָה (which *was*; not, "*is*") may be explained from the idea that the vine had been fetched from the forest in order that its wood might be used. The answer given in ver. 3 is, that this vine-wood cannot be used for any purpose whatever, not even as a peg for hanging any kind of domestic utensils upon (see comm. on Zech. x. 4). It is too weak even for this. The object has to be supplied to לַעֲשׂוֹת לִמְלָאכָה: to make, or apply *it*, for any work. Because it cannot

be used as timber, it is burned. A fresh thought is introduced in ver. 4b by the words אֶת שְׁנֵי ק'. The two clauses in ver. 4b are to be connected together. The first supposes a case, from which the second is deduced as a conclusion. The question, "Is it fit for any work?" is determined in ver. 5 in the negative. אַף כִּי: as in ch. xiv. 21. נָחָר: perfect; and יֵחָר: imperfect, *Niphal*, of חָרַר, in the sense of, to be burned or scorched. The subject to וַיֵּחָר is no doubt the wood, to which the suffix in אֲכָלַתְהוּ refers. At the same time, the two clauses are to be understood, in accordance with ver. 4b, as relating to the burning of the ends and the scorching of the middle.— Vers. 6-8. In the application of the parable, the only thing to which prominence is given, is the fact that God will deal with the inhabitants of Jerusalem in the same manner as with the vine-wood, which cannot be used for any kind of work. This implies that Israel resembles the wood of a forest-vine. As this possesses no superiority to other wood, but, on the contrary, is utterly useless, so Israel has no superiority to other nations, but is even worse than they, and therefore is given up to the fire. This is accounted for in ver. 7 : " They have come out of the fire, and the fire will consume them " (the inhabitants of Jerusalem). These words are not to be interpreted proverbially, as meaning, " he who escapes one judgment falls into another" (Hävernick), but show the application of vers. 4b and 5 to the inhabitants of Jerusalem. Out of a fire one must come either burned or scorched. Israel has been in the fire already. It resembles a wild vine which has been consumed at both ends by the fire, while the middle has been scorched, and which is now about to be given up altogether to the fire. We must not restrict the fire, however, out of which it has come half consumed, to the capture of Jerusalem in the time of Jehoiachin, as Hitzig does, but must extend it to all the judgments which fell upon the covenant nation, from the destruction of the kingdom of the ten tribes to the catastrophe in the reign of Jehoiachin, and in consequence of which Israel now resembled a vine burned at both ends and scorched in the middle. The threat closes in the same manner as the previous one. Compare ver. 7*b* with ch. xiv. 8*b*, and ver. 8 with ch. xiv. 15 and 13.

CHAP. XVI. INGRATITUDE AND UNFAITHFULNESS OF JERUSALEM. ITS PUNISHMENT AND SHAME.

The previous word of God represented Israel as a wild and useless vine, which had to be consumed. But as God had planted this vine in His vineyard, as He had adopted Israel as His own people, the rebellious nation, though met by these threatenings of divine judgment, might still plead that God would not reject Israel, on account of its election as the covenant nation. This proof of false confidence in the divine covenant of grace is removed by the word of God in the present chapter, which shows that by nature Israel is no better than other nations; and that, in consequence of its shameful ingratitude towards the Lord, who saved it from destruction in the days of its youth, it has sinned so grievously against Him, and has sunk so low among the heathen through its excessive idolatry, that God is obliged to punish and judge it in the same manner as the others. At the same time, the Lord will continue mindful of His covenant; and on the restoration of Sodom and Samaria, He will also turn the captivity of Jerusalem,—to the deep humiliation and shame of Israel,—and will establish an everlasting covenant with it.—The contents of this word of God divide themselves, therefore, into three parts. In the *first*, we have the description of the nation's sin, through its falling away from its God into idolatry (vers. 2–34); in the *second*, the announcement of the punishment (vers. 35–52); and in the *third*, the restoration of Israel to favour (vers. 53–63). The past, present, and future of Israel are all embraced, from its first commencement to its ultimate consummation.— These copious contents are draped in an allegory, which is carried out on a magnificent scale. Starting from the representation of the covenant relation existing between the Lord and His people, under the figure of a marriage covenant,—which runs through the whole of the Scriptures,—Jerusalem, the capital of the kingdom of God, as the representative of Israel, the covenant nation, is addressed as a wife; and the attitude of God to Israel, as well of that of Israel to its God, is depicted under this figure.

Vers. 1–14. Israel, by nature unclean, miserable, and near to destruction (vers. 3–5), is adopted by the Lord and clothed in splendour (vers. 6–14). Vers. 1 and 2 form the introduction.—Ver. 1. *And the word of Jehovah came to me, saying*, Ver. 2. *Son of man, show Jerusalem her abominations.*—The " abominations" of Jerusalem are the sins of the covenant nation, which were worse than the sinful abominations of Canaan and Sodom. The theme of this word of God is the declaration of these abominations. To this end the nation is first of all shown what it was by nature.—Ver. 3. *And say, Thus saith the Lord Jehovah to Jerusalem, Thine origin and thy birth are from the land of the Canaanites; thy father was the Amorite, and thy mother a Hittite.* Ver. 4. *And as for thy birth, in the day of thy birth thy navel was not cut, and thou wast not bathed in water for cleansing; and not rubbed with salt, and not wrapped in bandages.* Ver. 5. *No eye looked upon thee with pity, to do one of these to thee in compassion; but thou wast cast into the field, in disgust at thy life, on the day of thy birth.*—According to the allegory, which runs through the whole chapter, the figure adopted to depict the origin of the Israelitish nation is that Jerusalem, the existing representative of the nation, is described as a child, born of Canaanitish parents, mercilessly exposed after its birth, and on the point of perishing. Hitzig and Kliefoth show that they have completely misunderstood the allegory, when they not only explain the statement concerning the descent of Jerusalem, in ver. 3, as relating to the city of that name, but restrict it to the city alone, on the ground that " Israel as a whole was not of

Canaanitish origin, whereas the city of Jerusalem was radically a Canaanitish, Amoritish, and Hittite city." But were not all the cities of Israel radically Canaanaean? Or was Israel not altogether, but only half, of Aramaean descent? Regarded merely as a city, Jerusalem was neither of Amoritish nor Hittite origin, but simply a Jebusite city. And it is too obvious to need any proof, that the prophetic word does not refer to the city as a city, or to the mass of houses; but that Jerusalem, as the capital of the kingdom of Judah at that time, so far as its inhabitants were concerned, represents the people of Israel, or the covenant nation. It was not the mass of houses, but the population,—which was the foundling,—that excited Jehovah's compassion, and which He multiplied into myriads (ver. 7), clothed in splendour, and chose as the bride with whom He concluded a marriage covenant. The descent and birth referred to are not physical, but spiritual descent. Spiritually, Israel sprang from the land of the Canaanites; and its father was the Amorite and its mother a Hittite, in the same sense in which Jesus said to the Jews, " Ye are of your father the devil " (John viii. 44). The land of the Canaanites is mentioned as the land of the worst heathen abominations; and from among the Canaanitish tribes, the Amorites and Hittites are mentioned as father and mother, not because the Jebusites are placed between the two, in Num. xiii. 29, as Hitzig supposes, but because they were recognised as the leaders in Canaanitish ungodliness. The iniquity of the Amorites (הָאֱמֹרִי) was great even in Abraham's time, though not yet full or ripe for destruction (Gen. xv. 16); and the daughters of Heth, whom Esau married, caused Rebekah great bitterness of spirit (Gen. xxvii. 46). These facts furnish the substratum for our description. And they also help to explain the occurrence of הָאֱמֹרִי with the article, and חִתִּית without it. The plurals מְכֹרֹתַיִךְ and מֹלְדֹתַיִךְ also point to spiritual descent; for physical generation and birth are both acts that take place once for all. מְכֻרָה or מְכוֹרָה (ch. xxi. 35, xxix. 14) is not the place of begetting, but generation itself, from כּוּר=פָּרָה, to dig = to beget (cf. Isa. li. 1). It is not equivalent to מָקוֹר, or a plural corresponding to the Latin *natales, origines.* מוֹלֶדֶת: birth. Vers. 4 and 5 describe the circumstances connected with the birth. וּמֹלְדוֹתַיִךְ (ver. 4) stands at the head as an absolute noun. At the birth of the child it did not receive the cleansing and care which were necessary for the preservation and strengthening of its life, but was exposed without pity. The construction הֻלֶּדֶת אוֹתָךְ (the passive, with an accusative of the object) is the same as in Gen. xl. 20, and many other passages of the earlier writings. כָּרַּת: for כֹּרַת (Judg. vi. 28), *Pual* of כָּרַת; and שָׁרֻּךְ: from שׁר, with the reduplication of the ר, which is very rare in Hebrew (*vid.* Ewald, § 71). By cutting the navel-string, the child is liberated after birth from the blood of the mother, with which it was nourished in the womb. If the cutting be neglected, as well as the tying of the navel-string, which takes place at the same time, the child must perish when the decomposition of the *placenta* begins. The new-born child is then bathed, to cleanse it from the impurities attaching to it. מִשְׁעִי cannot be derived from שָׁעָה = יָשַׁע; because neither the meaning to see, to look (שעה), nor the other meaning to smear (שעע), yields a suitable sense. Jos. Kimchi is evidently right in deriving it from מָשַׁע, in Arabic مسح, ii. and iv., to wipe off, cleanse. The termination י is the Aramaean form of the absolute state, for the Hebrew מִשְׁעִית, cleansing (cf. Ewald, § 165*a*). After the washing, the body was rubbed with salt, according to a custom very widely spread in ancient times, and still met with here and there in the East (*vid. Hieron. ad h. l. Galen, de Sanit.* i. 7; *Troilo Reisebeschr.* p. 721); and that not merely for the purpose of making the skin drier and firmer, or of cleansing it more thoroughly, but probably from a regard to the virtue of salt as a protection from putrefaction, "to express in a symbolical manner a hope and desire for the vigorous health of the child" (Hitzig and Hävernick). And, finally, it was bound round with swaddling-clothes. Not one of these things, so indispensable to the preservation and strengthening of the child, was performed in the case of Israel at the time of its birth from any feeling of compassionate love (לְחֻמְלָה, infinitive, to show pity or compassion towards it); but it was cast into the field, *i.e.* exposed, in order that it might perish בְּגֹעַל נַפְשֵׁךְ in disgust at thy life (compare גָּעַל, to thrust away, reject, despise, Lev. xxvi. 11, xv. 30). The day of the birth of Jerusalem, *i.e.* of Israel, was the period of its sojourn in Egypt, where Israel as a nation was born,—the sons of Jacob who went down to Egypt having multiplied into a nation. The different traits in this picture are not to be interpreted as referring to historical peculiarities, but have their explanation in the totality of the figure. At the same time, they express much more than " that Israel not only stood upon a level with all other nations, so far as its origin and its nature were concerned, but was more helpless and neglected as to both its nature and its natural advantages, possessing a less gifted nature than other nations, and therefore inferior to the rest " (Kliefoth). The smaller gifts, or humbler natural advantages, are thoughts quite foreign to the words of the figure as well as to the context. Both the Canaanitish descent and the merciless exposure of the child point to a totally different point of view, as indicated by the allegory. The Canaanitish descent points to the moral depravity of the nature of Israel; and the neglected condition of the child is intended to show how little there was in the heathen surroundings of the youthful Israel in Canaan and Egypt that was adapted to foster its life and health, or to educate Israel and fit it for its future destination. To the Egyptians the Israelites were an abomination, as a race of shepherds; and not long after the death of Joseph, the Pharaohs began to oppress the growing nation.

Vers. 6-14. Israel therefore owes its preservation and exaltation to honour and glory to the Lord its God alone.—Ver. 6. *Then I passed by thee, and saw thee stamping in thy blood, and said to thee, In thy blood live! and said to thee, In thy blood live!* Ver. 7. *I made thee into myriads as the growth of the field, and thou grewest and becamest tall, and camest to ornament of cheeks. The breasts expanded, and thy hair grew, whereas thou wast naked and bare.* Ver. 8. *And I passed by thee, and saw thee, and, behold, it was thy time, the time of love; and I spread my wing over thee, and covered thy nakedness; and I swore to thee, and entered into covenant with thee, is the saying of the Lord Jehovah, and thou becamest mine.* Ver. 9. *And I bathed thee in water, and rinsed thy blood from thee, and anointed thee with oil.* Ver. 10. *And I clothed thee with embroidered work, and shod thee with morocco, and wrapped thee round with byssus, and covered thee with silk.* Ver. 11. *I adorned thee with ornaments, and put bracelets upon thy hands, and a chain around thy neck.* Ver. 12. *And I gave thee a ring in thy nose, and earrings in thine ears, and a splendid crown upon thy head.* Ver. 13. *And thou didst adorn thyself with gold and silver; and thy clothing was byssus, and silk, and embroidery. Wheaten-flour, and honey, and oil thou didst eat; and thou wast very beautiful; and didst thrive to regal dignity.* Ver. 14. *Thy name went forth among the nations on account of thy beauty; for it was perfect through my glory, which I put upon thee, is the saying of the Lord Jehovah.*—The description of what the Lord did for Israel in His compassionate love is divided into two sections by the repetition of the phrase "I passed by thee" (vers. 6 and 8). The first embraces what God had done for the preservation and increase of the nation; the second, what He had done for the glorification of Israel, by adopting it as the people of His possession. When Israel was lying in the field as a neglected new-born child, the Lord passed by and adopted it, promising it life, and giving it strength to live. To bring out the magnitude of the compassion of God, the fact that the child was lying in its blood is mentioned again and again. The explanation to be given of מִתְבּוֹסֶסֶת (the *Hithpolel* of בּוּס, to trample upon, tread under foot) is doubtful, arising from the difficulty of deciding whether the *Hithpolel* is to be taken in a passive or a reflective sense. The passive rendering, "trampled upon" (Umbreit), or *ad conculcandum projectus*, thrown down, to be trodden under foot (Gesenius, etc.), is open to the objection that the *Hophal* is used for this. We therefore prefer the reflective meaning, treading oneself, or stamping; as the objection offered to this, namely, that a new-born child thrown into a field would not be found stamping with the feet, has no force in an allegorical description. In the clause ver. 6*b*, which is written twice, the question arises whether בְּדָמַיִךְ is to be taken with חֲיִי or with וָאֹמַר לָךְ: I said to thee, "In thy blood live;" or, "I said to thee in thy blood, 'Live.'" We prefer the former, because it gives a more emphatic sense. בְּדָמַיִךְ is a concise expression; for although lying in thy blood, in which thou wouldst inevitably bleed to death, yet thou shalt live. Hitzig's proposal to connect בְּדָמַיִךְ in the first clause with חי, and in the second with אמר, can hardly be entertained. A double construction of this kind is not required either by the repetition of אֹמַר לָךְ, or by the uniform position of בדמיך before חיי in both clauses, as compared with 1 Kings xx. 18 and Isa. xxvii. 5.— In ver. 7*a* the description of the real fact breaks through the allegory. The word of God חֲיִי, live, was visibly fulfilled in the innumerable multiplication of Israel. But the allegory is resumed immediately. The child grew (רָבָה, as in Gen. xxi. 20; Deut. xxx. 16), and came into ornament of cheeks (בּוֹא with בְּ, to enter into a thing, as in ver. 8; not to proceed in, as Hitzig supposes). עֲדִי עֲדָיִים, not most beautiful ornament, or highest charms, for עֲדָיִים is not the plural of עֲדִי; but according to the *Chetib* and most of the editions, with the tone upon the penultima, is equivalent to עֲדָיִים, a dual form; so that עֲדִי cannot mean ornament in this case, but, as in Ps. xxxix. 9 and ciii. 5, "the cheek," which is the traditional meaning (cf. Ges. *Thes.* p. 993). Ornament of cheeks is youthful freshness and beauty of face. The clauses which follow describe the arrival of puberty. נָכֹן, when applied to the breasts, means to expand, lit. to raise oneself up. שֵׂעָר רַגְלַיִם = שֵׂעָר, *pubes*. The description given in these verses refers to the preservation and marvellous multiplication of Israel in Egypt, where the sons of Israel grew into a nation under the divine blessing. Still it was quite naked and bare (עֵרֹם and עֶרְיָה are substantives in the abstract sense of nakedness and bareness, used in the place of adjectives to give greater emphasis). Naked and bare are figurative expressions for still destitute of either clothing or ornaments. This implies something more than "the poverty of the people in the wilderness attached to Egypt" (Hitzig). Nakedness represents deprivation of all the blessings of salvation with which the Lord endowed Israel and made it glorious, after He had adopted it as the people of His possession. In Egypt, Israel was living in a state of nature, destitute of the gracious revelations of God.—Ver. 8. The Lord then went past again, and chose for His bride the virgin, who had already grown up to womanhood, and with whom He contracted marriage by the conclusion of the covenant at Sinai. עִתֵּךְ, thy time, is more precisely defined as עֵת דֹּדִים, the time of conjugal love. I spread my wing over thee, i.e. the lappet of my garment, which also served as a counterpane; in other words, I married thee (cf. Ruth iii. 9), and thereby covered thy nakedness. "I swore to thee," sc. love and fidelity (cf. Hos. ii. 21, 22), and entered into a covenant with thee, i.e. into that gracious connection formed by the adoption of Israel as the possession of Jehovah, which is represented as a marriage covenant (compare Ex. xxiv. 8 with xix. 5, 6, and Deut. v. 2: —אֹתָךְ for אִתָּךְ). Vers. 9 sqq. describe how Jehovah provided for the purification, clothing, adorning, and maintenance of His wife. As the bride prepares herself for the wedding by washing and anointing, so did the Lord cleanse Israel from the blemishes and impurities which adhered to it from its birth. The rinsing from the blood must not be understood as specially referring either to the laws of purification given to the nation (Hitzig), or as relating solely to the purification effected by the covenant sacrifice (Hävernick). It embraces all that the Lord did for the purifying of the people from the pollution of sin, *i.e.* for its sanctification. The anointing with oil indicates the powers of the Spirit of God, which flowed to Israel from the divine covenant of grace. The clothing with costly garments, and adorning with all the jewellery of a wealthy lady or princess, points to the equipment of Israel with all the gifts that promote the beauty and glory of life. The clothing is described as made of the costliest materials with which queens were accustomed to clothe themselves. רִקְמָה, embroidered cloth (Ps. xlv. 15). תַּחַשׁ, probably the sea-cow, *Manati* (see the comm. on Ex. xxv. 5). The word is used here for a fine description of leather of which ornamental sandals were made; a kind of morocco. "I bound thee round with byssus:" this refers to the headband; for חָבַשׁ is the technical expression for the binding or winding round of the turban-like headdress (cf. ch. xxiv. 17; Ex. xxix. 9; Lev. viii. 13), and is applied by the Targum to the headdress of the priests. Consequently covering with כְּסִי, as distinguished from clothing, can only refer to covering with the veil, one of the principal articles of a woman's toilet. The ἀπ. λεγ. כְּסִי (vers. 10 and 13) is explained by the Rabbins as signifying silk. The LXX. render it τρίχαπτον. According to Jerome, this is a word formed by the LXX.: *quod tantae subtilitatis fuerit vestimentum, ut pilorum et capillorum tenuitatem habere credatur.* The jewellery included not only armlets, nose-rings, and ear-rings, which the daughters of Israel were generally accustomed to wear, but also necklaces and a crown, as ornaments worn by princesses and queens. For רָבִיד, see comm. on Gen. xli. 42. Ver. 13 sums up the contents of vers. 9–12. שֵׁשִׁי is made to conform to כְּסִי; the food is referred to once more; and the result of the whole is said to have been, that Jerusalem became exceedingly beautiful, and flourished even to royal dignity. The latter cannot be taken as referring simply to the establishment of the monarchy under David, any more than merely to the spiritual sovereignty for which Israel was chosen from the very beginning (Ex. xix. 5, 6). The expression includes both, viz. the call of Israel to be a kingdom of priests, and the historical realization of this call through the Davidic sovereignty. The beauty, *i.e.* glory, of Israel became so great, that the name or fame of Israel sounded abroad in consequence among the nations. It was perfect, because the Lord had put His glory upon His Church. This, too, we must not restrict (as Hävernick does) to the far-sounding fame of Israel on its departure from Egypt (Ex. xv. 14 sqq.); it refers pre-eminently to the glory of the theocracy under David and Solomon, the fame of which spread into all lands.—Thus had Israel been glorified by its God above all the nations, but it did not continue in fellowship with its God.

Vers. 15-34. The apostasy of Israel. Its origin and nature, vers. 15-22; its magnitude and extent, vers. 23-34. In close connection with what precedes, this apostasy is described as whoredom and adultery.—Ver. 15. *But thou didst trust in thy beauty, and didst commit fornication upon thy name, and didst pour out thy fornication over every one who passed by: his it became.* Ver. 16. *Thou didst take of thy clothes, and didst make to thyself spotted heights, and didst commit fornication upon them: things which should not come, and that which should not take place.* Ver. 17. *And thou didst take jewellery of thine ornament of my gold and of my silver, which I had given thee, and didst make thyself male images, and didst commit fornication with them;* Ver. 18. *And thou didst take thy embroidered clothes, and didst cover them therewith: and my oil and my incense thou didst set before them.* Ver. 19. *And my bread, which I gave to thee, fine flour, and oil, and honey, wherewith I fed thee, thou didst set before them for a pleasant odour: this came to pass, is the saying of the Lord Jehovah.* Ver. 20. *And thou didst take thy sons and thy daughters, whom thou barest to me, and didst sacrifice them to them to devour. Was thy fornication too little?* Ver. 21. *Thou didst slay my sons, and didst give them up, devoting them to them.* Ver. 22. *And in all thine abominations and thy fornications thou didst not remember the days of thy youth, when thou wast naked and bare, and layest stamping in thy blood.*—The beauty, *i.e.* the glory, of Israel led to its fall, because it made it the ground of its confidence; that is to say, it looked upon the gifts and possessions conferred upon it as its desert; and forgetting the giver, began to traffic with the heathen nations, and allowed itself to be seduced to heathen ways. For the fact, compare Deut. xxxii. 15 and Hos. xiii. 6. "We are inflamed with pride and arrogance, and consequently profane the gifts of God, in which His glory ought to be resplendent" (Calvin). תִּזְנִי עַל שְׁמֵךְ does not mean either " thou didst commit fornication notwithstanding thy name " (Winer and Ges. *Thes.* p. 422), or "against thy name" (Hävernick); for עַל connected with זָנָה has neither of these meanings, even in Judg. xix. 2. It means, " thou didst commit fornication upon thy name, *i.e.* in reliance upon thy name " (Hitzig and Maurer); only we must not understand שֵׁם as referring to the name of the city of God, but must explain it, in accordance with ver. 14, as denoting the name, *i.e.* the renown, which Israel had acquired among the heathen on account of its beauty. In the closing words, יְהִי לוֹ, לוֹ refers to כָּל־עוֹבֵר, and יְהִי stands for וַיְהִי, the copula having been dropped from וַיְהִי because לוֹ ought to stand first, and only יְהִי remaining (compare יַךְ, Hos. vi. 1). The subject to יְהִי is יָפְיֵ; the beauty became his (cf. Ps. xlv. 12). This fornication is depicted in concrete terms in vers. 16–22; and with the marriage relation described in vers. 8–13 still in view, Israel is represented as giving up to idolatry all that it had received from its God.—Ver. 16. With the clothes it made spotted heights for itself. בָּמוֹת stands for בָּתֵּי בָמוֹת, temples of heights, small temples erected upon heights by the side of the altars (1 Kings xiii. 32; 2 Kings xvii. 29; for the fact, see the comm. on 1 Kings iii. 2), which may probably have consisted simply of tents furnished with carpets. Compare 2 Kings xxiii. 7, where the women are described as weaving tents for Astarte, also the tent-like temples of the Slavonian tribes in Germany, which consisted of variegated carpets and curtains (see Mohne on Creuzer's *Symbolik*, V. p. 176). These *bamoth* Ezekiel calls טְלֻאוֹת, not variegated, but spotted or speckled (cf. Gen. xxx. 32), possibly with the subordinate idea of patched (מְטֻלָּא, Josh. ix. 5), because they used for the carpets not merely whole garments, but pieces of cloth as well; the word being introduced here for the purpose of indicating contemptuously the worthlessness of such conduct. "Thou didst commit whoredom upon them," *i.e.* upon the carpets in the tent-temples. The words לֹא בָאוֹת וגו' are no doubt relative clauses; but the usual explanation, "which has not occurred, and will not be," after Ex. x. 14, cannot be vindicated, as it is impossible to prove either the use of בוֹא in the sense of occurring or happening (= הָיָה), or the use of the participle instead of the preterite in connection with the future. The participle בָּאוֹת in this connection can only supply one of the many senses of the imperfect (Ewald, § 168c), and, like יִהְיֶה, express that which ought to be. The participial form בָּאוֹת is evidently chosen for the sake of obtaining a *paronomasia* with בָּמוֹת: the heights which should not come (*i.e.* should not be erected); while לֹא יִהְיֶה points back to וַתִּתְּנִי עֲלֵיהֶם: "what should not happen."—Ver. 17. The jewellery of gold and silver was used by Israel for צַלְמֵי זָכָר, idols of the male sex, to commit fornication with them. Ewald thinks that the allusion is to Penates (*teraphim*), which were set up in the house, with ornaments suspended upon them, and worshipped with *lectisternia*. But there is no more allusion to *lectisternia* here than in ch. xxiii. 41. And there is still less ground for thinking, as Vatke, Movers, and Hävernick do, of Lingam- or Phallus-worship, of which it is impossible to find the slightest trace among the Israelites. The arguments used by Hävernick have been already proved by Hitzig to have no force whatever. The context does not point to idols of any particular kind, but to the many varieties of Baal-worship; whilst the worship of Moloch is specially mentioned in vers. 20 sqq. as being the greatest abomination of the whole. The fact that נָתַן לִפְנֵיהֶם, to set before them (the idols), does not refer to *lectisternia*, but to sacrifices offered as food for the gods, is indisputably evident from the words לְרֵיחַ נִיחֹחַ, the technical expression for the sacrificial odour ascending to God (cf. Lev. i. 9, 13, etc.). וַיְהִי (ver. 19), and it came to pass (*sc.* this abomination), merely serves to give emphatic expression to the disgust which it occasioned (Hitzig).—Vers. 20, 21. And not even content with this, the adulteress sacrificed the children which God had given her to idols. The revulsion of feeling produced by the abominations of the Moloch-worship is shown in the expression לֶאֱכוֹל, thou didst sacrifice thy children to idols, that they might devour them; and still more in the reproachful question הַמְעַט מִתּ, "was there too little in thy whoredom?" מִן before תַּזְנוּתֵךְ is used in a comparative sense, though not to signify "was this a smaller thing than thy whoredom?" which would mean far too little in this connection. The מִן is rather used, as in ch. viii. 17 and Isa. xlix. 6, in the sense of *too*: was thy whoredom, already described in vers. 16–19, too little, that thou didst also slaughter thy children to idols? The *Chetib* תזנותך (vers. 20 and 25) is a singular, as in vers. 25 and 29; whereas the *Keri* has treated it as a plural, as in vers. 15, 22, and 33, but without any satisfactory ground. The indignation comes out still more strongly in the description given of these abominations in ver. 21: "thou didst slay *my* sons" (whereas in ver. 20 we have simply "thy sons, whom thou hast born to me"), "and didst give them up to them, בְּהַעֲבִיר, by making them pass through," *sc.* the fire. הַעֲבִיר is used here not merely for lustration or februation by fire, but for the actual burning of the children slain as sacrifices, so that it is equivalent to הַעֲבִיר בָּאֵשׁ לַמֹּלֶךְ (2 Kings xxiii. 10). By the process of burning, the sacrifices were given to Moloch to devour. Ezekiel has the Moloch-worship in his eye in the form which it had assumed from the times of Ahaz downwards, when the people began to burn their children to Moloch (cf. 2 Kings xvi. 3, xxi. 6, xxiii. 10), whereas all that can be proved to have been practised in earlier times by the Israelites was the passing of children through fire without either slaying or burning; a februation by fire (compare the remarks on this subject in the comm. on Lev. xviii. 21).—Amidst all these abominations Israel did not remember its youth, or how the Lord had adopted it out of the deepest wretchedness to be His people, and had made it glorious through the abundance of His gifts. This base ingratitude shows the depth of its fall, and magnifies its guilt. For ver. 22*b* compare vers. 7 and 6.

Vers. 23–34. Extent and magnitude of the idolatry.—Ver. 23. *And it came to pass after all thy wickedness—Woe, woe to thee! is the saying of the Lord Jehovah*—Ver. 24. *Thou didst build thyself arches, and didst make thyself high places in all the streets.* Ver. 25. *Thou didst build thy high places at every cross road, and didst disgrace thy beauty, and stretch open thy feet for every one that passed by, and didst increase thy whoredom.* Ver. 26. *Thou didst commit fornication with the sons of Egypt thy neighbours, great in flesh, and didst increase thy whoredom to provoke me.* Ver. 27. *And, behold, I stretched out my hand against thee, and diminished thine allowance, and gave thee up to the desire of those who hate thee, the daughters of the Philistines, who are ashamed of thy lewd way.* Ver. 28. *And thou didst commit fornication with the sons of Asshur, because thou art never satisfied; and didst commit fornication with them, and wast also not satisfied.* Ver. 29. *And thou didst increase thy whoredom to Canaan's land, Chaldaea, and even thereby wast not satisfied.* Ver. 30. *How languishing is thy heart! is the saying of the Lord Jehovah, that thou doest all this, the doings of a dissolute prostitute.* Ver. 31. *When thou buildest thy arches at every cross road, and madest thy high places in every road, thou wast not like the harlot, since thou despisedst payment.* Ver. 32. *The adulterous wife taketh strangers instead of her husband.* Ver. 33. *Men give presents to all prostitutes; but thou gavest thy presents to all thy suitors, and didst reward them for coming to thee from all sides, for fornication with thee.* Ver. 34. *And there was in thee the very opposite of the women in thy whoredom, that men did not go whoring after thee. In that thou givest payment, and payment was not given to thee, thou wast the very opposite.*—By אַחֲרֵי כָּל־רָעָתֵךְ, the picture of the wide spread of idolatry, commenced in ver. 22, is placed in the relation of chronological sequence to the description already given of the idolatry itself. For all sin, all evil, must first exist before it can spread. The spreading of idolatry was at the same time an increase of apostasy from God. This is not to be sought, however, in the fact that Israel forsook the sanctuary, which God had appointed for it as the scene of His gracious presence, and built itself idol-temples (Kliefoth). It consisted rather in this, that it erected idolatrous altars and little temples at all street-corners and cross-roads (vers. 24, 25), and committed adultery with all heathen nations (vers. 26, 28, 29), and could not be induced to relinquish idolatry either by the chastisements of God (ver. 27), or by the uselessness of such conduct (vers. 32-34). כָּל־רָעָתֵךְ is the whole of the apostasy from the Lord depicted in vers. 15-22, which prevailed more and more as idolatry spread. The picture of this extension of idolatry is introduced with woe! woe! to indicate at the outset the fearful judgment which Jerusalem was bringing upon itself thereby. The exclamation of woe is inserted parenthetically; for וַתִּבְנִי (ver. 24) forms the apodosis to וַיְהִי in ver. 23. גַּב and רָמָה are to be taken as general terms; but, as the singular גַּבֵּךְ with the plural רָמֹתָיִךְ in ver. 39 plainly shows, גַּב is a collective word. Hävernick has very properly called attention to the analogy between גַּב and קֻבָּה in Num. xxv. 8, which is used there to denote an apartment furnished or used for the service of Baal-Peor. As קֻבָּה, from קָבַב, signifies literally that which is arched, a vault; so גַּב, from גָּבַב, is literally that which is curved or arched, a hump or back, and hence is used here for buildings erected for idolatrous purposes, small temples built on heights, which were probably so called to distinguish them as chapels for fornication. The ancient translations suggest this, viz.:

LXX. οἴκημα πορνικόν and ἔκθεμα, which Polychron. explains thus: προαγώγιον, ἔνθα τὰς πόρνας τρέφειν εἴωθασι; Vulg.: *lupanar* and *prostibulum*. רָמָה signifies artificial heights, *i.e.* altars built upon eminences, commonly called *bâmōth*. The word *râmâh* is probably chosen here with an allusion to the primary signification, height, as Jerome has said: *quod excelsus sit ut volentibus fornicari procul appareat fornicationis locus et non necesse sit quaeri*. The increase of the whoredom, *i.e.* of the idolatry and illicit intercourse with heathenish ways, is individualized in vers. 26–29 by a specification of historical facts. We cannot agree with Hitzig in restricting the illicit intercourse with Egypt (ver. 26), Asshur (ver. 28), and Chaldaea (ver. 29) to political apostasy, as distinguished from the religious apostasy already depicted. There is nothing to indicate any such distinction. Under the figure of whoredom, both in what precedes and what follows, the inclination of Israel to heathen ways in all its extent, both religious and political, is embraced. Egypt stands first; for the apostasy of Israel from the Lord commenced with the worship of the golden calf, and the longing in the wilderness for the fleshpots of Egypt. From time immemorial Egypt was most deeply sunken in the heathenish worship of nature. The sons of Egypt are therefore described, in accordance with the allegory, as גִּדְלֵי בָשָׂר, *magni carne* (*bâzâr*, a euphemism; cf. ch. xxiii. 20), *i.e.* according to the correct explanation of Theodoret: μεθ' ὑπερβολῆς τῇ τῶν εἰδώλων θεραπείᾳ προστετηκότας, οὗτοι γὰρ καὶ τράγους καὶ βόας καὶ πρόβατα, κύνας τε καὶ πιθήκους καὶ κροκοδείλους καὶ ἴβεις καὶ ἱέρακας προσεκύνησαν. The way in which God punished this erring conduct was, that, like a husband who endeavours by means of chastisement to induce his faithless wife to return, He diminished the supply of food, clothing, etc. (*chōg*, as in Prov. xxx. 8), intended for the wife (for the fact compare Hos. ii. 9, 10); this He did by "not allowing Israel to attain to the glory and power which would otherwise have been conferred upon it; that is to say, by not permitting it to acquire the undisturbed and undivided possession of Canaan, but giving it up to the power and scorn of the princes of the Philistines" (Kliefoth). נָתַן בְּנֶפֶשׁ, to give any one up to the desire of another. The daughters of the Philistines are the Philistian states, corresponding to the representation of Israel as an adulterous wife. The Philistines are mentioned as the principal foes, because Israel fell completely into their power at the end of the period of the Judges (cf. Judg. xiii.-xvi.; 1 Sam. iv.); and they are referred to here, for the deeper humiliation of Israel, as having been ashamed of the licentious conduct of the Israelites, because they adhered to their gods, and did not exchange them for others as Israel had done (compare Jer. ii. 10, 11). זִמָּה (ver. 27) is in apposition to דַּרְכֵּךְ: thy way, which is *zimmâh*. *Zimmâh* is applied to the sin of profligacy, as in Lev. xviii. 17.—But Israel was not improved by this chastisement. It committed adultery with Asshur also from the times of Ahaz, who sought help from the Assyrians (2 Kings xvi. 7 sqq.); and even with this it was not satisfied; that is to say, the serious consequences brought upon the kingdom of Judah by seeking the friendship of Assyria did not sober it, so as to lead it to give up seeking for help from the heathen and their gods. In ver. 28, זָנָה אֶל is distinguished from זָנָה (זָנִים, with accus.). The former denotes the immoral pursuit of a person for the purpose of procuring his favour; the latter, adulterous intercourse with him, when his favour has been secured. The thought of the verse is this: Israel sought the favour of Assyria, because it was not satisfied with illicit intercourse with Egypt, and continued to cultivate it; yet it did not find satisfaction or sufficiency even in this, but increased its adultery אֶל־אֶרֶץ כְּנַעַן כַּשְׂדִּימָה, to the Canaan's-land Chaldaea. אֶרֶץ כְּנַעַן is not the proper name of the land of Canaan here, but an appellative designation applied to Chaldaea (*Kasdim*) or Babylonia, as in ch. xvii. 4 (Raschi). The explanation of the words, as signifying the land of Canaan, is precluded by the fact that an allusion to Canaanitish idolatry and intercourse after the mention of Asshur would be out of place, and would not coincide with the historical order of things; since it cannot be shown that "a more general diffusion of the religious customs of Canaan took place after the Assyrian era." And it is still more decidedly precluded by the introduction of the word בַּשְׂדִּימָה, which cannot possibly mean as far as, or unto, Chaldaea, and can only be a more precise definition of ארץ כנען. The only thing about which a question can be raised, is the reason why the epithet כנען should have been applied to Chaldaea; whether it merely related to the commercial spirit, in which Babylon was by no means behind the Canaanitish Tyre and Sidon, or whether allusion was also made to the idolatry and immorality of Canaan. The former is by no means to be excluded, as we find that in ch. xvii. 4 "the land of Canaan" is designated "a city of merchants" (*rōkh'lim*). But we must not exclude the latter either, inasmuch as in the Belus- and Mylitta-worship of Babylon the voluptuous character of the Baal- and Astarte-worship of Canaan had degenerated into shameless unchastity (cf. Herodotus, i. 199).

In ver. 30, the contents of vers. 16–29 are summed up in the verdict which the Lord pronounces upon the harlot and adulteress: "yet how languishing is thy heart!" אֲמֻלָה (as a participle *Kal* ἅπ. λεγ.; since the verb only occurs elsewhere in the *Pual*, and that in the sense of faded or pining away) can only signify a morbid pining or languishing, or the craving of immodest desire, which has grown into a disease. The form לִבָּה is also ἅπ. λεγ.; but it is analogous to the plural לִבּוֹת.[1] שַׁלֶּטֶת, powerful, commanding; as an epithet applied to *zōnāh*, one who knows no limit to her actions, unrestrained;

---

[1] Hitzig objects to the two forms, which do not occur elsewhere; and with the help of the Sept. rendering τί διαθῶ τὴν θυγατέρα σου, which is a mere guess founded upon the false reading מה אמלה לבתך, he adopts the conjectural reading מָה אָמְלָה לְבִתֵּךְ, "what hope is there for thy daughter?" by which he enriches the Hebrew language with a new word (אָמְלָה), and the prophecy contained in this chapter with a thought which is completely foreign to it, and altogether unsuitable.

hence in Arabic, insolent, shameless. Ver. 31 contains an independent sentence, which facilitates the transition to the thought expanded in vers. 32–34, namely, that Jerusalem had surpassed all other harlots in her whoredoms. If we take ver. 31 as dependent upon the protasis in ver. 30, we not only get a very draggling style of expression, but the new thought expressed in ver. 31b is reduced to a merely secondary idea; whereas the expansion of it in vers. 32 sqq. shows that it introduces a new feature into the address. And if this is the case, וְלֹא־הָיִיתִי cannot be taken as co-ordinate with עָשִׂית, but must be construed as the apodosis: "in thy building of rooms . . . thou wast not like the (ordinary) harlot, since thou disdainest payment." For the plural suffix attached to בִּבְנוֹתַיִךְ, see the commentary on ch. vi. 8. The infinitive לְקַלֵּס answers to the Latin gerund in *ndo* (*vid.* Ewald, § 237c and 280d), indicating wherein, or in what respect, the harlot Jerusalem differed from an ordinary prostitute; namely, in the fact that she disdained to receive payment for her prostitution. That this is the meaning of the words, is rendered indisputable by vers. 32–34. But the majority of expositors have taken לְקַלֵּס אֶתְנָן as indicating the point of comparison between Israel and other harlots, *i.e.* as defining in what respect Israel resembled other prostitutes; and then, as this thought is at variance with what follows, have attempted to remove the discrepancy by various untenable explanations. Most of them resort to the explanation: thou wast not like the other prostitutes, who disdain to receive the payment offered for their prostitution, in the hope of thereby obtaining still more,[1]—an explanation which imports into the

---

[1] Jerome adopts this rendering: *non facta es quasi meretrix fastidio augens pretium*, and gives the following explanation: "thou hast not imitated the cunning prostitutes, who are accustomed to raise the price of lust by increasing the difficulties, and in this way to excite their lovers to greater frenzy." Rosenmüller and Maurer have adopted a similar explanation: "thou differest greatly from other harlots, who despise the payment offered them by their lovers, that they may get still more; for thou acceptest any reward, being content with the lowest payment; yea, thou dost even offer a price to thine own lovers."

words a thought that has no existence in them at all. Hävernick seeks to fix upon קלם, by means of the Aramaean, the meaning to cry out (crying out payment), in opposition to the ordinary meaning of קלם, to disdain, or ridicule, in which sense Ezekiel also uses the noun קְלָסָה in ch. xxii. 4. Hitzig falls back upon the handy method of altering the text; and finally, Kliefoth gives to לְ the imaginary meaning " so far as," *i.e.* " to such a degree that," which cannot be defended either through Ex. xxxix. 19 or from Deut. xxiv. 5.—With the loose way in which the infinitive construct with לְ is used, we grant that the words are ambiguous, and might have the meaning which the majority of the commentators have discovered in them; but this view is by no means necessary, inasmuch as the subordinate idea introduced by לְקַלֵּס אֶתְךָ may refer quite as well to the subject of the sentence, "*thou*," as to the *zōnáh* with whom the subject is compared. Only in the latter case the קַלֵּס אֶתְךָ would apply to other harlots as well as to Israel; whereas in the former it applies to Israel alone, and shows in what it was that Israel did not resemble ordinary prostitutes. But the explanation which followed was a sufficient safeguard against mistake. In this explanation adulteresses are mentioned first (ver. 32), and then common prostitutes (vers. 33, 34). Ver. 32 must not be taken, as it has been by the majority of commentators, as an exclamation, or a reproof addressed to the adulteress Jerusalem: O thou adulterous wife, that taketh strangers instead of her husband! Such an exclamation as this does not suit the connection at all. But the verse is not to be struck out on that account, as Hitzig proposes. It has simply to be construed in another way, and taken as a statement of what adulteresses do (Kliefoth). They take strangers instead of their husband, and seek their recompense in the simple change, and the pleasure of being with other men. תַּחַת אִישָׁהּ, lit. under her husband, *i.e.* as a wife subject to her husband, as in the connection with זָנָה in ch. xxiii. 5 and Hos. iv. 12 (see the comm. on Num. v. 19).— Vers. 33, 34. Common prostitutes give themselves up for presents; but Israel, on the contrary, gave presents to its lovers, so that it did the very opposite to all other harlots, and the practice of ordinary prostitutes was left far behind by that of Israel. The change of forms נֵדֶא and נֵדֶן (a present) is probably to be explained simply on the ground that the form נדא was lengthened into נדן with a consonant as the termination, because the suffix could be attached more easily to the other. הֵפֶּךְ, the reverse, the opposite, *i.e.* with the present context, something unheard of, which never occurred in the case of any other harlot.—Ezekiel has thus fulfilled the task appointed him in ver. 2, to charge Jerusalem with her abominations. The address now turns to an announcement of the punishment.

Vers. 35–52. As Israel has been worse than all the heathen, Jehovah will punish it notwithstanding its election, so that its shame shall be uncovered before all the nations (vers. 36–42), and the justice of the judgment to be inflicted upon it shall be made manifest (vers. 43–52). According to these points of view, the threat of punishment divides itself into two parts in the following manner:—In the first (vers. 35–42) we have, first of all (in ver. 36), a recapitulation of the guilty conduct described in vers. 16–34; and secondly, an announcement of the punishment corresponding to the guilt, as the punishment of adultery and murder (vers. 37 and 48), and a picture of its infliction, as retribution for the enormities committed (vers. 39–42). In the second part (vers. 43–52) there follows a proof of the justice of this judgment.

Vers. 35–42. The punishment will correspond to the sin. —Ver. 35. *Therefore, O harlot, hear the word of Jehovah!* Ver. 36. *Thus saith the Lord Jehovah, Because thy brass has been lavished, and thy shame exposed in thy whoredom with thy lovers, and because of all the idols of thine abominations, and according to the blood of thy sons, which thou hast given them;* Ver. 37. *Therefore, behold, I will gather together all thy lovers, whom thou hast pleased, and all whom thou hast loved, together with all whom thou hast hated, and will gather them against thee from round about, and will expose thy shame to them, that they may see all thy shame.* Ver. 38. *I will judge thee according to the judgment of adulteresses and murderesses, and make thee into blood of wrath and jealousy.* Ver. 39. *And I will give thee into their hand, that they may destroy thy arches, and pull down thy heights; that they may strip thy clothes off thee, and take thy splendid jewellery, and leave thee naked and bare.* Ver. 40. *And they shall bring up a company against thee, and stone thee, and cut thee in pieces with their swords.* Ver. 41. *And they shall burn thy houses with fire, and execute judgment upon thee before the eyes of many women. Thus do I put an end to thy whoredom; and thou wilt also give payment no more.* Ver. 42. *And I quiet my fury toward thee, and will turn away my jealousy from thee, that I may repose and vex myself no more.* —In the brief summary of the guilt of the whore, the following objects are singled out, as those for which she is to be punished: (1) the pouring out of her brass and the exposure of her shame; (2) the idols of her abominations (with עַל before the noun, corresponding to יַעַן before the infinitive); (3) the blood of her sons, with the preposition כְּ, *according to*, to indicate the measure of her punishment. Two things are mentioned as constituting the first ground of punishment. The first is, "because thy brass has been poured out." Most of the commentators have explained this correctly, as referring to the fact that Israel had squandered the possessions received from the Lord, viz. gold, silver, jewellery, clothing, and food (vers. 10–13 and 16–19), upon idolatry. The only difficulty connected with this is the use of the word *n'chosheth*, brass or copper, in the general sense of money or metal, as there are no other passages to support this use of the word. At the same time, the objection raised to this, namely, that *n'chosheth* cannot signify money, because the Hebrews had no copper coin, is an assertion without proof, since all that can be affirmed with certainty is, that the use of copper or brass as money is not mentioned anywhere in the Old Testament, with the exception of the passage before us. But we cannot infer with certainty from this that it was not then in use. As soon as the Hebrews began to stamp coins, bronze or copper coins were stamped as well as the silver shekels, and specimens of these are still in existence from the time of the Maccabees, with the inscription "Simon, prince of Israel" (cf. Cavedoni, *Bibl. Numismatik*, transl. by Werlhof, p. 20 sqq.). Judging from their size, these coins were in all probability worth a whole, a half, and a quarter gerah (Caved. pp. 50, 51). If, then, the silver shekel of the value of 21 grains contained twenty gerahs in Moses' time, and they had already silver pieces of the weight of a shekel and half shekel, whilst quarter shekels are also mentioned in the time of Samuel, there would certainly be metal coins in use of the value of a gerah for the purposes of trade and commerce, and these would in all probability be made of brass, copper, or bronze, as silver coins of the value of a penny would have been found too small. Consequently it cannot be positively denied that brass or copper may have been used as coin for the payment of a gerah, and therefore that the word *nʻchōsheth* may have been applied to money. We therefore adhere to the explanation that brass stands for money, which has been already adopted by the LXX. and Jerome; and we do so all the more, because every attempt that has been made to fasten another meaning upon *nʻchōsheth*, whether by allegorical interpretation (Rabb.), or from the Arabic, or by altering the text. is not only arbitrary, but does not even yield a meaning that suits the context. הִשָּׁפֵךְ, to be poured out = squandered or lavished. To the squandering of the possessions bestowed by the Lord upon His congregation, there was added the exposure of its shame, *i.e.* the disgraceful sacrifice of the honour and dignity of the people of God, of which Israel had made itself guilty by its whoredom with idols, *i.e.* by falling into idolatry, and adopting heathen ways. עַל־מְאַהֲבַיִךְ, to (towards), *i.e.* with thy lovers (עַל standing for אֶל, according to later usage: *vid.* Ewald, § 217*i*, p. 561), is to be explained after the analogy of

זָנָה אֶל, as signifying to commit adultery towards a person, *i.e.* with him. But it was not enough to sacrifice the gifts of the Lord, *i.e.* His possessions and His glory, to the heathen and their idols; Israel also made for itself כָּל־גִּלּוּלֵי תוֹעֵבוֹת, all kinds of logs of abominations, *i.e.* of idols, upon which it hung its ornaments, and before which it set oil and incense, meal and honey (vers. 18 and 19). And it was not even satisfied with this, but gave to its idols the blood of its sons, by slaying its children to Moloch (ver. 20). Therefore (vers. 37 sqq.) the Lord will uncover the shame of His people before all the nations. He will gather them together, both friend and foe, against Jerusalem, and let them execute the judgment. The punishment will correspond to the sin. Because Israel has cultivated friendship with the heathen, it shall now be given up altogether into their power. On the uncovering of the nakedness as a punishment, compare Hos. ii. 12. The explanation of the figure follows in ver. 38. The heathen nations shall inflict upon Jerusalem the punishment due to adultery and bloodshed. Jerusalem (*i.e.* Israel) had committed this twofold crime. It had committed adultery, by falling away from Jehovah into idolatry; and bloodshed, by the sacrifices offered to Moloch. The punishment for adultery was death by stoning (see the comm. on ver. 40); and blood demanded blood (Gen. ix. 6; Ex. xxi. 12). וּנְתַתִּיךְ דָּם וגו׳ does not mean, "I will put blood in thee" (Ros.), or "I will cause thy blood to be shed in anger" (De Wette, Maurer, etc.); but I make thee into blood; which we must not soften down, as Hitzig proposes, into cause thee to bleed. The thought is rather the following: thou shalt be turned into blood, so that nothing but blood may be left of thee, and that the blood of fury and jealousy, as the working of the wrath and jealousy of God (compare ver. 42). To this end the heathen will destroy all the objects of idolatry (גַּב and רָמוֹת, ver. 39, as in vers. 24, 25), then take from the harlot both clothes and jewellery, and leave her naked, *i.e.* plunder Jerusalem and lay it waste, and, lastly, execute upon her the punishment of death by stoning and by sword; in other words, destroy both city and kingdom. The words וְהֶעֱלוּ, they bring (up) against thee an assembly, may be explained from the ancient mode of administering justice, according to which the popular assembly (*qâhâl*, cf. Prov. v. 14) sat in judgment on cases of adultery and capital crimes, and executed the sentence, as the law for stoning expressly enjoins (Lev. xx. 2; Num. xv. 36; Deut. xxii. 21; compare my *Bibl. Archäol.* II. p. 257). But they are also applicable to the foes, who would march against Jerusalem (for *qâhâl* in this sense, compare ch. xvii. 17). The punishment of adultery (according to Lev. xx. 10) was death by stoning, as we may see from Lev. xx. 2–27 and Deut. xx. 24 compared with John viii. 5. This was the usual mode of capital punishment under the Mosaic law, when judicial sentence of death was pronounced upon individuals (see my *Archäol.* II. p. 264). The other form of punishment, slaying by the sword, was adopted when there were many criminals to be put to death, and was not decapitation, but cutting down or stabbing (*bâthaq*, to hew in pieces) with the sword (see my *Archäol. l.c.*). The punishment of death was rendered more severe by the burning of the corpse (Lev. xx. 14, xxi. 9). Consequently the burning of the houses in ver. 41 is also to be regarded as intensifying the punishment; and it is in the same light that the threat is to be regarded, that the judgment would be executed "before the eyes of many women.' The many women are the many heathen nations, according to the description of Jerusalem or Israel as an unfaithful wife. "As it is the greatest punishment to an adulterous woman to be exposed in her sin before the eyes of other women; so will the severest portion of Israel's punishment be, that it will stand exposed in its sin before the eyes of all other nations" (Kliefoth). This is the way in which God will put an end to the fornication, and appease His wrath and jealousy upon the harlot (vers. 41*b* and 42). הִשְׁבַּתִּי, with מִן, to cause a person to cease to be or do anything. For ver. 42, compare ch. v. 13.

By the execution of the judgment the jealousy (קִנְאָה) of the injured husband is appeased.

Vers. 43–52. This judgment is perfectly just; for Israel has not only forgotten the grace of its God manifested towards it in its election, but has even surpassed both Samaria and Sodom in its abominations.—Ver. 43. *Because thou hast not remembered the days of thy youth, and hast raged against me in all this; behold, I also give thy way upon thy head, is the saying of the Lord Jehovah, that I may not do that which is wrong above all thine abominations.* Ver. 44. *Behold, every one that useth proverbs will use this proverb concerning thee: as the mother, so the daughter.* Ver. 45. *Thou art the daughter of thy mother, who casteth off her husband and her children; and thou art the sister of thy sisters, who cast off their husbands and their children. Your mother is a Hittite, and your father an Amorite.* Ver. 46. *And thy great sister is Samaria with her daughters, who dwelleth at thy left; and thy sister, who is smaller than thou, who dwelleth at thy right, is Sodom with her daughters.* Ver. 47. *But thou hast not walked in their ways and done according to their abominations a little only; thou didst act more corruptly than they in all thy ways.* Ver. 48. *As I live, is the saying of the Lord Jehovah, Sodom thy sister, she with her daughters hath not done as thou hast done with thy daughters.* Ver. 49. *Behold, this was the sin of Sodom, thy sister: pride, superabundance of food, and rest undisturbed had she with her daughters, and the hand of the poor and needy she did not hold.* Ver. 50. *They were haughty, and did abominations before me; and I swept them away when I saw it.* Ver. 51. *And Samaria, she hath not sinned to the half of thy sins; thou hast increased thine abominations more than they, and hast made thy sisters righteous by all thine abominations which thou hast done.* Ver. 52. *Bear, then, also thy shame, which thou hast adjudged to thy sisters. Through thy sins, which thou hast committed more abominably than they, they become more righteous than thou. Be thou, then, also put to shame, and bear thy disgrace, as thou hast justified thy sisters.*—יַעַן אֲשֶׁר, which corresponds to יַעַן in ver. 36, introduces a new train of thought. Most of the commentators take ver. 43 in connection with what precedes, and place the pause at ver. 44. But the perfect נָתַתִּי shows that this is wrong. If ver. 43 simply contained a recapitulation, or a concluding summary, of the threat of judgment in vers. 35-42, the punishment would be announced in the future tense, as it is in ver. 37. By the perfect נָתַתִּי, on the contrary, the punishment is exhibited as a completed fact, and further reasons are then assigned in vindication of the justice of the divine procedure, which we find in vers. 44 sqq. To this end the guilt of Jerusalem is mentioned once more: "thou didst not remember the days of thy youth," *i.e.* what thou didst experience in thy youth; the misery in which thou didst find thyself, and out of which I rescued thee and exalted thee to glory (vers. 4-14). To this there was added rage against Jehovah, which manifested itself in idolatrous acts. רָגַז לְ, to be excited upon or against any person, to rage; thus in *Hithpael* with אֶל in 2 Kings xix. 27, 28. For נָתַן דֶּרֶךְ בְּרֹאשׁ, compare ch. ix. 10. The last clause of ver. 43, וְלֹא עָשִׂיתִי וגו, has been misinterpreted in many ways. According to the Masoretic pointing, עָשִׂיתִי is the second person; but this does not yield a suitable meaning. For עָשָׂה זִמָּה is not used in the sense adopted by the Targum, upon which the Masoretic pointing is undoubtedly based, and which Raschi, Kimchi, and Rosenmüller retain, viz. *cogitationem facere:* "thou hast not taken any thought concerning all thy abominations," *i.e.* hast not felt any remorse. The true meaning is to commit a crime, a wrong, and is used for the most part of unnatural offences (cf. Judg. xx. 6; Hos. vi. 9). There is all the more reason for retaining this meaning, that זִמָּה (apart from the plural זִמּוֹת = מְזִמּוֹת) only occurs *sensu malo*, and for the most part in the sense of an immoral action (*vid.* Job xxxi. 11). Consequently we should have to adopt the rendering: and thou no longer committest this immorality above all thine abominations.

But in that case not only would עוֹד have to be supplied, but a distinction would be drawn between the abominations committed by Israel and the sin of lewdness, *i.e.* adultery, which is quite foreign to the connection and to the contents of the entire chapter; for, according to these, the abominations of Israel consisted in adultery or the sin of lewdness. We must therefore take עָשִׂיתִי as the first person, as Symm. and Jerome have done, and explain the words from Lev. xix. 29, where the toleration by a father of the whoredom of a daughter is designated as *zimmâh*. If we adopt this interpretation, Jehovah says that He has punished the spiritual whoredom of Israel, in order that He may not add another act of wrong to the abominations of Israel by allowing such immorality to go on unpunished. If He did not punish, He would commit a *zimmâh* Himself,— in other words, would make Himself accessory to the sins of Israel. The concluding characteristic of the moral degradation of Israel fits in very appropriately here in vers. 44 sqq., in which Jerusalem is compared to Samaria and Sodom, both of which had been punished long ago with destruction on account of their sins. This characteristic is expressed in the form of proverbial sayings. Every one who speaks in proverbs (*môshêl*, as in Num. xxi. 27) will then say over thee: as the mother, so her daughter. Her abominable life is so conspicuous, that it strikes every one, and furnishes occasion for proverbial sayings. אִמָּה may be a feminine form of אֵם, as לִבָּה is of לֵב (ver. 30); or it may also be a *Raphe* form for אִמָּהּ: as her (the daughter's) mother, so her (the mother's) daughter (cf. Ewald, § 174*e*, note, with § 21, 22³). The daughter is of course Jerusalem, as the representative of Israel. The mother is the Canaanitish race of Hittites and Amorites, whose immoral nature had been adopted by Israel (cf. vers. 3 and 45*b*). In ver. 45 the sisterly relation is added to the maternal, to carry out the thought still further. Some difficulty arises here from the statement, that the mothers and the sisters despise their husbands and their children, or put them away. For it is unquestionable that the participle נֹעֲלַת belongs to אִמֵּךְ, and not to בַּת, from the parallel relative clause אֲשֶׁר גָּעֲלוּ, which applies to the sisters. The husband of the wife Jerusalem is Jehovah, as the matrimonial head of the covenant nation or congregation of Israel. The children of the wives, viz. the mother, her daughter, and her sisters, are the children offered in sacrifice to Moloch. The worship of Moloch was found among the early Canaanites, and is here attributed to Samaria and Sodom also, though we have no other proofs of its existence there than the references made to it in the Old Testament. The husband, whom the mother and sisters have put away, cannot therefore be any other than Jehovah; from which it is evident that Ezekiel regarded idolatry generally as apostasy from Jehovah, and Jehovah as the God not only of the Israelites, but of the heathen also.[1] אֲחוֹתֵךְ (ver. 45) is a plural noun, as the relative clause which follows and ver. 46 clearly show, and therefore is a contracted form of אֲחוֹתַיִךְ (ver. 51) or אַחְיוֹתֵךְ (ver. 52; vid. Ewald, § 212b, p. 538). Samaria and Sodom are called sisters of Jerusalem, not because both cities belonged to the same mother-land of Canaan, for the origin of the cities does not come into consideration here at all, and the cities represent the kingdoms, as the additional words "her daughters," that is to say, the cities of a land or kingdom dependent upon the capital, clearly prove. Samaria and Sodom, with the daughter cities belonging to them, are sisters of Jerusalem in a spiritual sense, as animated by the same spirit of idolatry. Samaria is called the great (greater) sister of Jerusalem, and Sodom the smaller sister. This is not equivalent to the older and the younger, for Samaria was not more deeply sunk in idolatry than Sodom, nor was her idolatry more ancient than that of Sodom (Theodoret and Grotius); and Hävernick's explanation, that "the finer form

---

[1] Theodoret has explained it correctly in this way: "He shows by this, that He is not the God of Jews only, but of Gentiles also; for God once gave oracles to them, before they chose the abomination of idolatry. Therefore he says that they also put away both the husband and the children by denying God, and slaying the children to demons."

of idolatry, the mixture of the worship of Jehovah with that of nature, as represented by Samaria, was the first to find an entrance into Judah, and this was afterwards followed by the coarser abominations of heathenism," is unsatisfactory, for the simple reason that, according to the historical books of the Old Testament, the coarser forms of idolatry forced their way into Judah at quite as early a period as the more refined. The idolatry of the time of Rehoboam and Abijam was not merely a mixture of Jehovah-worship with the worship of nature, but the introduction of heathen idols into Judah, along with which there is no doubt that the syncretistic worship of the high places was also practised. גָּדוֹל and קָטָן do not generally mean old and young, but great and small. The transferred meaning old and young can only apply to men and animals, when greatness and littleness are really signs of a difference in age; but it is altogether inapplicable to kingdoms or cities, the size of which is by no means dependent upon their age. Consequently the expressions great and small simply refer to the extent of the kingdoms or states here named, and correspond to the description given of their situation: "at the left hand," *i.e.* to the north, and "at the right hand," *i.e.* to the south of Jerusalem and Judah.

Jerusalem had not only equalled these sisters in sins and abominations, but had acted more corruptly than they (ver. 47). The first hemistich of this verse, "thou walkest not in their ways," etc., is more precisely defined by וַתַּשְׁחִתִי מֵהֵן in the second half. The link of connection between the two statements is formed by כִּמְעַט קָט. This is generally rendered, "soon was there disgust," *i.e.* thou didst soon feel disgust at walking in their ways, and didst act still worse. But apart from the fact that while disgust at the way of the sisters might very well constitute a motive for forsaking those ways, *i.e.* relinquishing their abominations, it could not furnish a motive for surpassing those abominations. This explanation is exposed to the philological difficulty, that קָט by itself cannot signify *taeduit te*, and the impersonal use of קוּם would at all events require לָהּ, which could not be omitted, even if קוּם were intended for a substantive. These difficulties fall away if we interpret קוּם from the Arabic قَمْ, *omnino, tantum*, as Alb. Schultens has done, and connect the definition "a little only" with the preceding clause. We then obtain this very appropriate thought: thou didst walk in the ways of thy sisters; and that not a little only, but thou didst act still more corruptly than they. This is proved in vers. 48 sqq. by an enumeration of the sins of Sodom. They were pride, satiety,—*i.e.* superabundance of bread (*vid.* Prov. xxx. 9),—and careless rest or security, which produce haughtiness and harshness, or uncharitableness, towards the poor and wretched. In this way Sodom and her daughters (Gomorrah, Admah, and Zeboim) became proud and haughty, and committed abominations לְפָנַי, *i.e.* before Jehovah (alluding to Gen. xviii. 21); and God destroyed them when He saw this. The sins of Samaria (ver. 51) are not specially mentioned, because the principal sin of this kingdom, namely, image-worship, was well known. It is simply stated, therefore, that she did not sin half so much as Jerusalem; and in fact, if we except the times of Ahab and his dynasty, pure heathenish idolatry did not exist in the kingdom of the ten tribes, so that Samaria seemed really a righteous city in comparison with the idolatry of Jerusalem and Judah, more especially from the time of Ahaz onward (*vid.* Jer. iii. 11). The punishment of Samaria by the destruction of the kingdom of the ten tribes is also passed over as being well known to every Israelite; and in ver. 52 the application is directly made to Jerusalem, *i.e.* to Judah: "Thou also, bear thy shame, thou who hast adjudged to thy sisters,"—*sc.* by pronouncing an uncharitable judgment upon them, thinking thyself better than they, whereas thou hast sinned more abominably, so that they appear more righteous than thou. צָדֵק, to be righteous, and צִדֵּק, to justify, are used in a comparative sense. In comparison with the abominations of Jerusalem, the sins of Sodom and Samaria appeared perfectly trivial. After אַף גַּם, the announcement of punishment is repeated for the sake of emphasis, and that in the form of a consequence resulting from the sentence with regard to the nature of the sin: therefore be thou also put to shame, and bear thy disgrace.

Vers. 53–63. But this disgrace will not be the conclusion. Because of the covenant which the Lord concluded with Israel, Jerusalem will not continue in misery, but will attain to the glory promised to the people of God;—and that in such a way that all boasting will be excluded, and Judah, with the deepest shame, will attain to a knowledge of the true compassion of God.—Yet, in order that all false confidence in the gracious promises of God may be prevented, and the sinful nation be thoroughly humbled, this last section of our word of God announces the restoration of Sodom and Samaria as well as that of Jerusalem, so that all boasting on the part of Israel is precluded.—Ver. 53. *And I will turn their captivity, the captivity of Sodom and her daughters, and the captivity of Samaria and her daughters, and the captivity of thy captivity in the midst of them:* Ver. 54. *That thou mayest bear thy shame, and be ashamed of all that thou hast done, in comforting them.* Ver. 55. *And thy sisters, Sodom and her daughters, will return to their first estate; and Samaria and her daughters will return to their first estate; and thou and thy daughters will return to your first estate.* Ver. 56. *And Sodom thy sister was not a discourse in thy mouth in the day of thy haughtinesses,* Ver. 57. *Before thy wickedness was disclosed, as at the time of the disgrace of the daughters of Aram and all its surroundings, the daughters of the Philistines, who despised thee round about.* Ver. 58. *Thy wrongdoing and all thy abominations, thou bearest them, is the saying of Jehovah.* Ver. 59. *For thus saith the Lord Jehovah, And I do with thee as thou hast done, who hast despised oath to break covenant.* Ver. 60. *And I shall remember my covenant with thee in the days of thy youth, and shall establish an everlasting covenant with thee.* Ver. 61. *And thou wilt remember thy ways, and be ashamed, when thou receivest thy sisters, those greater than thou to those smaller than thou; and I give them to thee for daughters, although they are not of thy covenant.* Ver. 62. *And I will establish my covenant with thee; and thou wilt perceive that I am Jehovah;* Ver. 63. *That thou mayest remember, and be ashamed, and there may no longer remain to thee an opening of the mouth because of thy disgrace, when I forgive thee all that thou hast done, is the saying of the Lord Jehovah.*—The promise commences with an announcement of the restoration, not of Jerusalem, but of Sodom and Samaria. The two kingdoms, or peoples, upon which judgment first fell, shall also be the first to receive mercy; and it will not be till after then that Jerusalem, with the other cities of Judah, will also be restored to favour, in order that she may bear her disgrace, and be ashamed of her sins (ver. 54); that is to say, not because Sodom and Samaria have borne their punishment for a longer time, but to the deeper shaming, the more complete humiliation of Jerusalem. שׁוּב שְׁבוּת, to turn the captivity, not "to bring back the captives" (see the comm. on Deut. xxx. 3), is here used in a figurative sense for *restitutio in statum integritatis*, according to the explanation given of the expression in ver. 55. No carrying away, or captivity, took place in the case of Sodom. The form שְׁבִית, which the *Chetib* has adopted several times here, has just the same meaning as שְׁבוּת. שְׁבִית שְׁבִיתָיךְ does not mean the captives of thy captivity, since the same word cannot be used first as a concrete and then as an abstract noun; nor does the combination serve to give greater emphasis, in the sense of a superlative,—viz. " the captivity of thy captivities, equivalent to thy severest or most fearful captivity,"—as Stark and Hävernick suppose. The genitive must be taken as explanatory, as already proposed by Hengstenberg and Kliefoth: " captivity, which is thy captivity;" and the pleonastic mode of expression is chosen to give greater prominence to the thought, " thine own captivity," than would have been given to it by a suffix attached to the simple noun. בְּתוֹכְהֵנָה, in their midst, does not imply, that just as Judah was situated now in the very midst between Sodom and Samaria, so its captives would return home occupying the centre between those two (Hitzig); the reference is rather to fellowship in captivity, to the fact that Jerusalem would share the same fate, and endure the same punishment, as Samaria and Sodom (Hengst., Klief.). The concluding words of ver. 54, "in that thou comfortest them," do not refer to the sins already committed by Israel (as Kliefoth, who adopts the rendering, "didst comfort them," imagines), but to the bearing of such disgrace as makes Jerusalem ashamed of its sins. By bearing disgrace, *i.e.* by its endurance of well-merited and disgraceful punishment, Jerusalem consoles her sisters Samaria and Sodom; and that not merely by fellowship in misfortune, — *solamen miseris, etc.* (Calvin, Hitzig, etc.),—but by the fact that from the punishment endured by Jerusalem, both Samaria and Sodom can discern the righteousness of the ways of God, and find therein a foundation for their hope, that the righteous God will bring to an end the merited punishment as soon as its object has been attained (see the comm. on ch. xiv. 22, 23). The turning of the captivity, according to ver. 55, will consist in the fact that Sodom, Samaria, and Jerusalem return לְקַדְמָתָן, to their original state. קַדְמָה does not mean the former or earlier state, but the original state (ὡς ἦσαν ἀπ' ἀρχῆς, LXX.), as in Isa. xxiii. 7. Kliefoth is wrong, however, in explaining this as meaning: "as they were, when they came in Adam from the creative hand of God." The original state is the *status integritatis*, not as a state of sinlessness or original righteousness and holiness,—for neither Jerusalem on the one hand, nor Samaria and Sodom on the other, had ever been in such a state as this, —but as an original state of glory, in which they were before they had fallen and sunk into ungodly ways.

But how could a restoration of Sodom and her daughters (Gomorrah, etc.) be predicted, when the destruction of these cities was accompanied by the sweeping away of all their inhabitants from off the face of the earth? Many of the commentators have attempted to remove the difficulty by assuming that Sodom here stands for the Moabites and Ammonites, who were descendants of Lot, who escaped from Sodom. But the untenableness of such an explanation is obvious, from the simple fact that the Ammonites and Moabites were no more Sodomites than Lot himself. And the view expressed by Origen and Jerome, and lately revived by Hävernick, that Sodom is a typical name denoting heathenism generally, is also unsatisfactory. The way in which Sodom is classed with Samaria and Jerusalem, and the special reference to the judgment that fell upon Sodom (vers. 49, 50), point undeniably to the real Sodom. The heathen world comes into consideration only so far as this, that the pardon of a heathen city, so deeply degraded as Sodom, carries with it the assurance that mercy will be extended to all heathen nations. We must therefore take the words as referring to the literal Sodom. Yet we certainly cannot for a moment think of any earthly restoration of Sodom. For even if we could conceive of a restoration of the cities that were destroyed by fire, and sunk into the depths of the Dead Sea, it is impossible to form any conception of an earthly and corporeal restoration of the inhabitants of those cities, who were destroyed at the same time; and in this connection it is chiefly to them that the words refer. This does not by any means prove that the thing itself is impossible, but simply that the realization of the prophecy must be sought for beyond the present order of things, in one that extends into the life everlasting.

As ver. 55 elucidates the contents of ver. 53, so the thought of ver. 54 is explained and still further expanded in vers. 56 and 57 The meaning of ver. 56a is a subject of dispute; but so much is indisputable, that the attempt of Kliefoth to explain vers. 56 and 57 as referring to the future, and signifying that in the coming day of its glory Israel will no longer carry

Sodom as a legend in its mouth as it does now, does violence to the grammar, and is quite a mistake. It is no more allowable to take וְלֹא הָיְתָה as a future, in the sense of "and will not be," than to render כְּמוֹ עֵת חֶרְפַּת (ver. 57), "it will be like the time of scorn." Moreover, the application of בְּיוֹם גְּאוֹנַיִךְ to the day of future glory is precluded by the fact that in ver. 49 the word גָּאוֹן is used to denote the pride which was the chief sin of Sodom; and the reference to this verse very naturally suggests itself. The meaning of ver. 56 depends upon the rendering to be given to לִשְׁמוּעָה. The explanation given by Rosenmüller and Maurer, after Jerome,—viz. *non erat in auditione*, i.e. *non audiebatur*, thou didst not think at all of Sodom, didst not take its name into thy mouth,—is by no means satisfactory. שְׁמוּעָה means proclamation, discourse, and also report. If we adopt the last, we must take the sentence as interrogatory (לֹא for הֲלֹא), as Hengstenberg and Hitzig have done. Although this is certainly admissible, there are no clear indexes here to warrant our assumption of an interrogation, which is only hinted at by the tone. We therefore prefer the meaning "discourse:" thy sister Sodom was not a discourse in thy mouth in the day of thy haughtinesses, that thou didst talk of the fate of Sodom and lay it to heart when thou wast in prosperity. The plural גְּאוֹנַיִךְ is more emphatic than the singular. The day of the haughtinesses is defined in ver. 57 as the period before the wickedness of Judah had been disclosed. This was effected by means of the judgment, which burst upon Jerusalem on the part of Babylon. Through this judgment Jerusalem is said to have been covered with disgrace, as at the time when the daughters of Aram, *i.e.* the cities of Syria, and those of the Philistines (Aram on the east, and the Philistines on the west, Isa. ix. 11), scorned and maltreated it round about. This refers primarily to the times of Ahaz, when the Syrians and Philistines pressed hard upon Judah (2 Kings xv. 37, xvi. 6; and 2 Chron. xxviii. 18, 19). It must not be restricted to this, however; but was repeated in the reign of

Jehoiachin, when Jehovah sent troops of the Chaldaeans, *Aramaeans*, Ammonites, and Moabites against him, to destroy Judah (2 Kings xxiv. 2). It is true, the Philistines are not mentioned here; but from the threat in Ezek. xxv. 15, we may infer that they also attempted at the same time to bring disgrace upon Judah. שָׁאט = שׁוּט, according to Aramaean usage, to treat contemptuously, or with repudiation (cf. ch. xxviii. 24, 26). Jerusalem will have to atone for this pride, and to bear its wrong-doing and its abominations (ver. 58). For *zimmâh*, see the comm. on ver. 43. The perfect נְשָׂאתִים indicates that the certainty of the punishment is just as great as if it had already commenced. The reason assigned for this thought in ver. 59 forms a transition to the further expansion of the promise in vers. 60 sqq. וְעָשִׂיתִי (ver. 59) has been correctly pointed by the Masoretes as the 1st person. The ו is copulative, and shows that what follows forms the concluding summary of all that precedes. אוֹתָךְ for אִתָּךְ, as in vers. 60, etc., to deal with any one. The construction of עָשָׂה, with an accusative of the person, to treat any one, cannot be sustained either from ch. xvii. 17 and xxiii. 25, or from Jer. xxxiii. 9; and Gesenius is wrong in assuming that we meet with it in Isa. xlii. 16.—Despising the oath (אָלָה) points back to Deut. xxix. 11, 12, where the renewal of the covenant concluded at Sinai is described as an entrance into the covenant and oath which the Lord then made with His people.—But even if Israel has faithlessly broken the covenant, and must bear the consequent punishment, the unfaithfulness of man can never alter the faithfulness of God. This is the link of connection between the resumption and further expansion of the promise in ver. 60 and the closing words of ver. 59. The remembrance of His covenant is mentioned in Lev. xxvi. 42 and 45 as the only motive that will induce God to restore Israel to favour again, when the humiliation effected by the endurance of punishment has brought it to a confession of its sins. The covenant which God concluded with Israel in the day of its youth, *i.e.* when He led it out of Egypt, He will establish as an everlasting covenant. Consequently it is not an entirely new covenant, but simply the perfecting of the old one for everlasting duration. For the fact itself, compare Isa. lv. 3, where the making of the everlasting covenant is described as granting the stedfast mercies of David, *i.e.* as the fulfilment of the promise given to David (2 Sam. vii.). This promise is called by David himself an everlasting covenant which God had made with him (2 Sam. xxiii. 5). And the assurance of its everlasting duration was to be found in the fact that this covenant did not rest upon the fulfilment of the law, but simply upon the forgiving grace of God (compare ver. 63 with Jer. xxxi. 31–34).—The bestowal of this grace will put Israel in remembrance of its ways, and fill it with shame. In this sense וְזָכַרְתְּ (and thou shalt remember), in ver. 61, is placed side by side with זָכַרְתִּי (I will remember) in ver. 60. This shame will seize upon Israel when the establishment of an everlasting covenant is followed by the greater and smaller nations being associated with it in glory, and incorporated into it as children, though they are not of its covenant. The greater and smaller sisters are the greater and smaller nations, as members of the universal family of man, who are to be exalted to the glory of one large family of God. The restoration, which is promised in vers. 53 and 55 to Sodom and Samaria alone, is expanded here into a prophecy of the reception of all the greater and smaller nations into fellowship in the glory of the people of God. We may see from this that Sodom and Samaria represent the heathen nations generally, as standing outside the Old Testament dispensation: Sodom representing those that were sunk in the deepest moral degradation, and Samaria those that had fallen from the state of grace. The attitude in which these nations stand towards Israel in the everlasting covenant of grace, is defined as the relation of daughters to a mother. If, therefore, Israel, which has been thrust out among the heathen on account of its deep fall, is not to return to its first estate till after the return of Sodom, which has been destroyed, and Samaria, which has been condemned, the election of Israel before all the nations of the earth to be the first-born son of Jehovah will continue unchanged, and Israel will form the stem of the new kingdom of God, into which the heathen nations will be incorporated. The words, "and not of thy covenant," have been taken by most of the commentators in the sense of, "not because thou hast kept the covenant;" but this is certainly incorrect. For even if "thy covenant" really formed an antithesis to "my covenant" (vers. 60 and 62), "thy covenant" could not possibly signify the fulfilment of thy covenant obligations. The words belong to *bânōth* (daughters), who are thereby designated as extra-testamental,—*i.e.* as not included in the covenant which God made with Israel, and consequently as having no claim by virtue of that covenant to participate in the glory of the everlasting covenant which is hereafter to be established.—When this covenant has been established, Israel will know that God is Jehovah, the unchangeably true (for the meaning of the name *Jehovah*, see the commentary on Gen. ii. 4); that it may call to mind, *sc.* both its sinful abominations and the compassionate grace of God, and be so filled with shame and penitence that it will no more venture to open its mouth, either for the purpose of finding excuses for its previous fall, or to murmur against God and His judgments,—namely, when the Lord forgives all its sins by establishing the everlasting covenant, the kernel and essence of which consists in the forgiveness of sins (cf. Jer. xxxi. 34). Thus will the experience of forgiving grace complete what judgment has already begun, viz. the transformation of proud and haughty sinners into meek and humble children of God, for whom the kingdom has been prepared from the beginning.

This thought brings the entire prophecy to a close,—a prophecy which embraces the whole of the world's history and the New Testament, the parallel to which is contained in the apostle's words, "God hath concluded them all in unbelief, that He might have mercy upon all" (Rom. xi. 32).—As the punishment threatened to the adulteress, *i.e.* to the nation of Israel that had despised its God and King, had been fulfilled upon Jerusalem and the Jews, and is in process of fulfilment still, so has the promise also been already fulfilled, so far as its commencement is concerned, though the complete and ultimate fulfilment is only to be expected in time to come. The turning of the captivity, both of Jerusalem and her daughters, and of Samaria and her daughters, commenced with the establishment of the everlasting covenant, *i.e.* of the covenant made through Christ, and with the reception of the believing portion of Israel in Judaea, Samaria, and Galilee (Acts viii. 5 sqq., 25, ix. 31). And the turning of the captivity of Sodom commenced with the spread of the gospel among the heathen, and their entrance into the kingdom of Christ, inasmuch as Sodom with her daughters represents the morally degraded heathen world. Their reception into the kingdom of heaven, founded by Christ on earth, forms the commencement of the return of the forgiven to their first estate on the " restitution of all things," *i.e.* the restoration of all moral relations to their original normal constitution (compare Acts iii. 21 and Meyer's comm. thereon with Matt. xvii. 11), which will attain its perfection in the $\pi\alpha\lambda\iota\gamma\gamma\epsilon\nu\epsilon\sigma\iota\alpha$, the general restoration of the world to its original glory (compare Matt. xix. 28 with Rom. viii. 18 sqq. and 2 Pet. iii. 13). The prophecy before us in ver. 55 clearly points to this final goal. It is true that one might understand the return of Jerusalem and Samaria to their original state, which is predicted here as simply relating to the pardon of the covenant nation, whose apostasy had led to the rejection of both its parts; and this pardon might be sought in its reception into the kingdom of Christ and its restoration as the people of God. In that case the complete fulfilment of our prophecy would take place during the present aeon in the spread of the gospel among all nations, and the conversion of that portion of Israel which still remained hardened after the entrance of the full number of the Gentiles into the kingdom of God. But this limitation would be out of harmony with the equality of position assigned to Sodom and her daughters on the one hand, and Samaria and Jerusalem on the other. Though Sodom is not merely a type of the heathen world, the restoration of Sodom and her daughters cannot consist in the reception of the descendants of the cities on which the judgment fell into the kingdom of God or the Christian Church, since the peculiar manner in which those cities were destroyed prevented the possibility of any of the inhabitants remaining alive whose descendants could be converted to Christ and blessed in Him during the present period of the world. On the other hand, the opinion expressed by C. a Lapide, that the restoration of Sodom is to be referred and restricted to the conversion of the descendants of the inhabitants of Zoar, which was spared for Lot's sake, when the other cities of the plain were destroyed, is too much at variance with the words of the passage to allow of our accepting such a solution as this. The turning of the captivity of Sodom and her daughters, *i.e.* the forgiveness of the inhabitants of Sodom and the other cities of the plain, points beyond the present aeon, and the realization can only take place on the great day of the resurrection of the dead in the persons of the former inhabitants of Sodom and the neighbouring cities. And in the same way the restoration of Samaria and Jerusalem will not be completely fulfilled till after the perfecting of the kingdom of Christ in glory at the last day.

Consequently the prophecy before us goes beyond Rom. xi. 25 sqq., inasmuch as it presents, not to the covenant nation only, but, in Samaria and Sodom, to all the larger and smaller heathen nations also, the prospect of being eventually received into the everlasting kingdom of God; although, in accordance with the main purpose of this prophetic word, namely, to bring the pride of Israel completely down, this is simply hinted at, and no precise intimation is given of the manner in which the predicted *apokatastasis* will occur. But notwithstanding this indefiniteness, we must not explain away the fact itself by arbitrary expositions, since it is placed beyond all possible doubt by other passages of the Scriptures. The words of our Lord in Matt. x. 15 and xi. 24, to the effect that it will be more tolerable in the day of judgment for Sodom than for Capernaum and every other city that shall have rejected the preaching of the gospel, teach most indisputably that the way of mercy stands open still even for Sodom itself, and that the judgment which has fallen upon it does not carry with it the final decision with regard to its inhabitants. For Sodom did not put away the perfect revelation of mercy and salvation. If the mighty works which were done in Capernaum had been done in Sodom, it would have stood to the present day (Matt. xi. 23). And from this it clearly follows that all the judgments which fell before the time of Christ, instead of carrying with them the final decision, and involving eternal damnation, leave the possibility of eventual pardon open still. The last judgment, which is decisive for eternity, does not take place till after the full revelation of grace and truth in Christ. Not only will the gospel be preached to all nations before the end comes (Matt. xxiv. 14), but even to the dead; to the spirits in prison, who did not believe at the time of Noah, it has been already preached, at the time when Christ went to them in spirit, in order that, although judged according to man's way in the flesh, they might live according to God's way in the spirit (1 Pet. iii. 19, iv. 6). What the apostle teaches in the first of these passages concerning the unbelievers before the flood, and affirms in the second concerning the dead in general, is equally applicable according to our prophecy to the Sodomites who were judged after man's way in the flesh, and indeed generally to all heathen nations who either lived before Christ or departed from this earthly life without having heard the gospel preached.—It is according to these distinct utterances of the New Testament that the prophecy before us respecting the *apokatastasis* of Sodom, Samaria, and Jerusalem is to be interpreted; and this is not to be confounded with the heretical doctrine of the restoration, *i.e.* the ultimate salvation of all the ungodly, and even of the devil himself. If the preaching of the gospel precedes the last judgment, the final sentence in the judgment will be regulated by the attitude assumed towards the gospel by both the living and the dead. All souls that obstinately reject it and harden themselves in unbelief, will be given up to everlasting damnation. The reason why the conversion of Sodom and Samaria is not expressly mentioned, is to be found in the general tendency of the promise, in which the simple fact is announced without the intermediate circumstances, for the purpose of humbling Jerusalem. The conversion of Jerusalem also is not definitely stated to be the condition of pardon, but this is assumed as well known from the words of Lev. xxvi., and is simply implied in the repeated assertion that Jerusalem will be seized with the deepest shame on account of the pardon which she receives.

CHAP. XVII. HUMILIATION AND EXALTATION OF THE DAVIDIC FAMILY.

The contents of this chapter are introduced as a riddle and a parable, and are divided into three sections. Vers. 1-10 contain the parable; vers. 11-21, the interpretation and application of it to King Zedekiah; and vers. 22-24, the promise of the Messianic kingdom.

Vers. 1-10. The Parable.—Ver. 1. *And the word of Jehovah came to me, saying,* Ver. 2. *Son of man, give a riddle, and relate a parable to the house of Israel;* Ver. 3. *And say, Thus saith the Lord Jehovah, A great eagle, with great wings and long pinions, full of feathers of variegated colours, came to Lebanon and took the top of the cedar :* Ver. 4. *He plucked off the topmost of its shoots, and brought it into Canaan's land ; in a merchant-city he set it.* Ver. 5. *And he took of the seed of the land, and put it into seed-land ; took it away to many waters, set it as a willow.*

Ver. 6. *And it grew, and became an overhanging vine of low stature, that its branches might turn towards him, and its roots might be under him; and it became a vine, and produced shoots, and sent out foliage.* Ver. 7. *There was another great eagle with great wings and many feathers; and, behold, this vine stretched its roots languishingly towards him, and extended its branches towards him, that he might water it from the beds of its planting.* Ver. 8. *It was planted in a good field by many waters, to send out roots and bear fruit, to become a glorious vine.* Ver. 9. *Say, Thus saith the Lord Jehovah, Will it thrive? will they not pull up its roots, and cut off its fruit, so that it withereth? all the fresh leaves of its sprouting will wither, and not with strong arm and with much people will it be possible to raise it up from its roots.* Ver. 10. *And, behold, although it is planted, will it thrive? will it not wither when the east wind touches it? upon the beds in which it grew it will wither.*

The parable (*mâshâl*, corresponding exactly to the New Testament παραβολή) is called *chîdhâh*, a riddle, because of the deeper meaning lying beneath the parabolic shell. The symbolism of this parable has been traced by many commentators to Babylonian influences working upon the prophet's mind; but without any tenable ground. The figure of the eagle, or bird of prey, applied to a conqueror making a rapid descent upon a country, has as little in it of a specifically Babylonian character as the comparison of the royal family to a cedar or a vine. Not only is Nebuchadnezzar compared to an eagle in Jer. xlviii. 40, xlix. 22, as Cyrus is to a bird of prey in Isa. xlvi. 11; but even Moses has described the paternal watchfulness of God over His own people as bearing them upon eagle's wings (Ex. xix. 4; Deut. xxxii. 11). The cedar of Lebanon and the vine are genuine Israelitish figures. The great eagle in ver. 3 is the great King Nebuchadnezzar (compare ver. 12) The article is simply used to indicate the species, for which *we* should use the indefinite article. In ver. 7, instead of the article, we have אֶחָד in the sense of "another." This first eagle has large wings and long pinions; he has already flown victoriously over wide-spread countries. אֲשֶׁר־לוֹ הָרִקְמָה, literally, which is to him the variegated ornament, *i.e.* which he has as such an ornament. The feathers of variegated ornamental colours point to the many peoples, differing in language, manners, and customs, which were united under the sceptre of Nebuchadnezzar (Hitzig, etc.); not to the wealth and splendour of the conqueror, as such an allusion is altogether remote from the tendency of the parable. He came to Lebanon. This is not a symbol of the Israelitish land, or of the kingdom of Judah; but, as in Jer. xxii. 23, of Jerusalem, or Mount Zion, with its royal palace so rich in cedar wood (see the comm. on Hab. ii. 17 and Zech. xi. 1), as being the place where the cedar was planted (compare the remarks on ver. 12). The cedar is the royal house of David, and the top of it is King Jehoiachin. The word *tzammereth* is only met with in Ezekiel, and there only for the top of a cedar (compare ch. xxxi. 3 sqq.). The primary meaning is doubtful. Some derive it from the curly, or, as it were, woolly top of the older cedars, in which the small twigs that constitute their foliage are only found at the top of the tree. Others suppose it to be connected with the Arabic ضم, to conceal, and understand it as an epithet applied to the foliage, as the veil or covering of the tree. In ver. 4, *tzammereth* is explained to be רֹאשׁ יְנִיקוֹתָיו, the topmost of its shoots. This the eagle plucked off and carried אֶל־אֶרֶץ כְּנַעַן, an epithet applied to Babylonia here and in ch. xvi. 29, as being a land whose trading spirit had turned it into a Canaan. This is evident from the parallel עִיר רֹכְלִים, city of traders, *i.e.* Babylon (compare ver. 12). The seed of the land, according to ver. 13, is King Zedekiah, because he was of the land, the native king, in contrast to a foreign, Babylonian governor. קָח, for לָקַח, after the analogy of קָם in Hos. xi. 3, and pointed with Kametz to distinguish it from the imperative. לָקַח אֶל is used as in Num. xxiii. 27. The ἄπ. λεγ. צַפְצָפָה signifies, in Arabic and the Talmud, the willow, probably so called because it grows in well-watered places; according to Gesenius, it is derived from צוּף, to overflow, literally, the inundated tree. This meaning is perfectly appropriate here. "He set it as a willow" means he treated it as one, inasmuch as he took it to many waters, set it in a well-watered soil, *i.e.* in a suitable place. The cutting grew into an overhanging vine, *i.e.* to a vine spreading out its branches in all directions, though not growing very high, as the following expression שִׁפְלַת קוֹמָה more clearly shows. The object of this growth was, that its branches might turn to him (the eagle), and its roots might be under him (the eagle). The suffixes attached to אֵלָיו and תַּחְתָּיו refer to נֶשֶׁר. This allusion is required not only by the explanation in ver. 14 (? vers. 14, 15), but also by ver. 7, where the roots and branches of the vine stretch to the (other) eagle. In ver. 6*b*, what has already been affirmed concerning the growth is briefly summed up again. The form פֹּארָה is peculiar to Ezekiel. Isaiah has פֻּארָה = פֹּארָה in ch. x. 33. The word signifies branch and foliage, or a branch covered with foliage, as the ornament of a tree.—The other eagle mentioned in ver. 7 is the king of Egypt, according to ver. 15. He had also large wings and many feathers, *i.e.* a widely spread and powerful kingdom; but there is nothing said about pinions and variegated colours, for Pharaoh had not spread out his kingdom over many countries and peoples, or subjugated a variegated medley of peoples and tribes. כָּפַן, as a verb ἅπ. λεγ., signifies to yearn or pine after a thing; in Chaldee, to hunger. לְהַשְׁקוֹת, that he (the eagle-Pharaoh) might give it to drink, or water it. The words מֵעֲרֻגוֹת מַטָּעָהּ are not connected with לְהַשְׁקוֹת, but with שִׁלְּחָה and כַּנָּפֶיהָ, from the beds of its planting, *i.e.* in which it was planted; it stretched out roots and branches to the other eagle, that he might give it to drink. The interpretation is given in ver. 15. The words לְהַשְׁקוֹת אוֹתָהּ, which are added by way of explanation, do not interrupt the train of thought; nor are they superfluous, as Hitzig supposes, because the vine had water enough already (vers. 5 and 8). For this is precisely what the passage is intended to show, namely, that there was no occasion for this pining and stretching out of the branches towards the other eagle, inasmuch as it could thrive very well in the place where it was planted. The latter is expressly stated once more in ver. 8, the meaning of which is perfectly clear,—namely, that if Zedekiah had remained quiet under Nebuchadnezzar, as a hanging vine, his government might have continued and prospered. But, asks Ezekiel in the name of the Lord, will it prosper? תִּצְלָח is a question, and the third person, neuter gender. This question is answered in the negative by the following question, which is introduced with an affirmative הֲלוֹא. The subject to יְנַתֵּק and יְקוֹסֵס is not the first eagle (Nebuchadnezzar), but the indefinite "one" (man, they). In the last clause of ver. 9 מַשְׂאוֹת is a substantive formation, used instead of the simple form of the infinitive, after the form מַשָּׂא in 2 Chron. xix. 7, with the termination ות, borrowed from the verb ל׳ה (compare Ewald, § 160b and 239a), and the construction is the same as in Amos vi. 10: it will not be to raise up = it will not be possible to raise it up (compare Ges. § 132, 3, Anm. 1). To raise it up from its root does not mean to tear it up by the root (Hävernick), but to rear the withered vine from its roots again, to cause it to sprout again. This rendering of the words corresponds to the interpretation given in ver. 17. —In ver. 10 the leading thought is repeated with emphasis, and rounded off. The east wind is peculiarly dangerous to plants on account of its dryness (compare Gen. xli. 6, and Wetstein on Job xxvii. 21 in Delitzsch's *Commentary*); and it is used very appropriately here, as the Chaldeans came from the east.

Vers. 11–21. Interpretation of the riddle.—Ver. 11. *And the word of Jehovah came to me, saying,* Ver. 12. *Say to the refractory race: Do ye not know what this is? Say, Behold, the king of Babel came to Jerusalem, and took its king and its princes, and brought them to himself to Babel.* Ver. 13. *And he took of the royal seed, and made a covenant with him, and caused him to enter into an oath; and he took the strong ones of the land:* Ver. 14. *That it might be a lowly kingdom, not to lift itself up, that he might keep his covenant, that it might stand.* Ver. 15. *But he rebelled against him by sending his messengers to Egypt, that it might give him horses and much people. Will he prosper? will he that hath done this escape? He has broken the covenant, and should he escape?* Ver. 16. *As I live, is the saying of the Lord Jehovah, surely in the place of the king, who made him king, whose oath he despised, and whose covenant he broke with him, in Babel he will die.* Ver. 17. *And not with great army and much people will Pharaoh act with him in the war, when they cast up a rampart and build siege-towers, to cut off many souls.* Ver. 18. *He has despised an oath to break the covenant, and, behold, he has given his hand and done all this; he will not escape.* Ver. 19. *Therefore thus saith the Lord Jehovah, As I live, surely my oath which he has despised, and my covenant which he has broken, I will give upon his head.* Ver. 20. *I will spread out my net over him, so that he will be taken in my snare, and will bring him to Babel, and contend with him there on account of his treachery which he has been guilty of towards me.* Ver. 21. *And all his fugitives in all his regiments, by the sword will they fall, and those who remain will be scattered to all winds; and ye shall see that I Jehovah have spoken it.*

In vers. 12–17 the parable in vers. 2–10 is interpreted; and in vers. 19–21 the threat contained in the parable is confirmed and still further expanded. We have an account of the carrying away of the king, *i.e.* Jehoiachin, and his princes to Babel in 2 Kings xxiv. 11 sqq., Jer. xxiv. 1, and xxix. 2. The king's seed (זֶרַע הַמְּלוּכָה, ver. 13, as in Jer. xli. 1 = זֶרַע הַמֶּלֶךְ, 1 Kings xi. 14) is Jehoiachin's uncle Mattaniah, whom Nebuchadnezzar made king under the name of Zedekiah (2 Kings xxiv. 17), and from whom he took an oath of fealty (2 Chron. xxxvi. 13). The strong of the land (אֵילֵי = אוּלֵי, 2 Kings xxiv. 15), whom Nebuchadnezzar took (לקח), *i.e.* took away to Babel, are not the heads of tribes and families (2 Kings xxiv. 15); but the expression is used in a wide sense for the several classes of men of wealth, who are grouped together in 2 Kings xxiv. 14 under the one term כָּל־גִּבּוֹרֵי חַיִל (אַנְשֵׁי חַיִל, 2 Kings xxiv. 16), including masons, smiths, and carpenters (2 Kings xxiv. 14 and 16), whereas the heads of tribes and families are classed with the court officials (סָרִיסִים, 2 Kings xxiv. 15) under the title שָׂרֶיהָ (princes) in ver. 12. The design of these measures was to make a lowly kingdom, which could not raise itself, *i.e.* could not revolt, and to deprive the vassal king of the means of breaking the covenant. The suffix attached to לְעָמְדָהּ is probably to be taken as referring to מַמְלָכָה rather than בְּרִיתִי, although both are admissible, and would yield precisely the same sense, inasmuch as the stability of the kingdom was dependent upon the stability of the covenant. But Zedekiah rebelled (2 Kings xxiv. 20). The Egyptian king who was to give Zedekiah horses and much people, in other words, to come to his assistance with a powerful army of cavalry and fighting men, was Hophrah, the Apries of the Greeks, according to Jer. xliv. 30 (see the comm. on 2 Kings xxiv. 19, 20). הֲיִצְלָח points back to תִּצְלָח in ver. 9; but here it is applied to the rebellious king, and is explained in the clause הֲיִמָּלֵט וגו׳. The answer is given in ver. 16 as a word of God confirmed by a solemn oath: he shall die in Babel, the capital of the king, who placed him on the throne, and Pharaoh will not render him any effectual help (ver. 17). עָשָׂה אוֹתוֹ, as in ch. xv. 59, to act with him, that is to say, assist him, come to his help. אוֹתוֹ refers to Zedekiah, not to Pharaoh, as Ewald assumes in an inexplicable manner. For שְׁפֹךְ סֹלְלָה וגו׳, compare ch. iv. 2; and for the fact itself, Jer. xxxiv. 21, 22, and xxxvii. 5, according to which, although an Egyptian army came to the rescue of Jerusalem at the time when it was besieged by the Chaldeans, it was repulsed by the Chaldeans who marched to meet it, without having rendered any permanent assistance to the besieged.—In ver. 18, the main thought that breach of faith can bring no deliverance is repeated for the sake of appending the further expansion contained in vers. 19-21. נָתַן יָדוֹ, he gave his hand, *i.e.* as a pledge of fidelity. The oath which Zedekiah swore to the king of Babel is designated in ver. 19 as Jehovah's oath (אָלָתִי), and the covenant made with him as Jehovah's covenant, because the oath had been sworn by Jehovah, and the covenant of fidelity towards Nebuchadnezzar had thereby been made *implicite* with Jehovah Himself; so that the breaking of the oath and covenant became a breach of faith towards Jehovah. Consequently the very same expressions are used in vers. 16, 18, and 19, to designate this breach of oath, which are applied in ch. xvi. 59 to the treacherous apostasy of Jerusalem (Israel) from Jehovah, the covenant God. And the same expressions are used to describe the punishment as in ch. xii. 13, 14. נִשְׁפַּט אִתּוֹ is construed with the accusative of the thing respecting which he was to be judged, as in 1 Sam. xii. 7. Jehovah regards the treacherous revolt from Nebuchadnezzar as treachery against Himself (מָעַל בִּי); not only because Zedekiah had sworn the oath of fidelity by Jehovah, but also from the fact that Jehovah had delivered up His people and kingdom into the power of Nebuchadnezzar, so that revolt from him really became rebellion against God. אֶת before כָּל־מִבְרָחָו is *nota accus.*, and is used in the sense of *quod adtinet ad*, as, for example, in 2 Kings vi. 5. מִבְרָחָו, his fugitives, is rendered both by the Chaldee and Syriac " his brave men," or " heroes," and is therefore identified with מִבְחָרָו (his chosen ones), which is the reading in some manuscripts. But neither these renderings nor the parallel passage in ch. xii. 14, where סְבִיבוֹתָיו apparently corresponds to it, will warrant our adopting this explanation, or making any alteration in the text. The Greek versions have πάσας φυγαδείας αὐτοῦ; Theodoret: ἐν πάσαις ταῖς φυγαδείαις αὐτοῦ; the Vulgate: *omnes profugi ejus;* and therefore they all had the reading מברחו, which also yields a very suitable meaning. The mention of some who remain, and who are to be scattered toward all the winds, is not at variance with the statement that all the fugitives in the wings of the army are to fall by the sword.

The latter threat simply declares that no one will escape death by flight. But there is no necessity to take those who remain as being simply fighting men; and the word "all" must not be taken too literally.

Vers. 22–24. *The planting of the true twig of the stem of David.*—Ver. 22. *Thus saith the Lord Jehovah, And I will take from the top of the high cedar, and will set it; from the topmost of its shoots will I pluck off a tender one, and will plant it upon a high and exalted mountain.* Ver. 23. *On the high mountain of Israel will I plant it, and it will put forth branches, and bear fruit, and become a splendid cedar, so that all the birds of every plumage will dwell under it. In the shade of its branches will they dwell.* Ver. 24. *And all the trees of the field will learn that I Jehovah have lowered the lofty tree, lifted up the low tree, made the green tree wither, and the withered tree become green. I Jehovah have said it, and have done it.*—Although the sprout of David, whom Nebuchadnezzar had made king, would lose the sovereignty because of his breach of faith, and bring about the destruction of the kingdom of Judah, the Lord would not let His kingdom be destroyed, but would fulfil the promise which He had given to the seed of David. The announcement of this fulfilment takes its form from the preceding parable. As Nebuchadnezzar broke off a twig from the top of the cedar and brought it to Babel (ver. 13), so will Jehovah Himself also pluck off a shoot from the top of the high cedar, and plant it upon a high mountain. The *Vav* before לָקַחְתִּי is the *Vav consec.*, and אֲנִי is appended to the verb for the sake of emphasis; but in antithesis to the acting of the eagle, as described in ver. 3, it is placed after it. The cedar, which it designated by the epithet *râmâh*, as rising above the other trees, is the royal house of David, and the tender shoot which Jehovah breaks off and plants is not the Messianic kingdom or sovereignty, so that Zerubbabel could be included, but the Messiah Himself as "a distinct historical personage" (Hävernick). The predicate רַךְ, tender, refers to

Him; also the word יוֹנֵק, a sprout (Isa. liii. 2), which indicates not so much the youthful age of the Messiah (Hitzig) as the lowliness of His origin (compare Isa. xi. 1, liii. 2); and even when applied to David and Solomon, in 2 Sam. iii. 39, 1 Chron. xxii. 5, xxix. 1, expresses not their youthfulness, but their want of strength for the proper administration of such a government. The high mountain, described in ver. 23 as the high mountain of Israel, is Zion, regarded as the seat and centre of the kingdom of God, which is to be exalted by the Messiah above all the mountains of the earth (Isa. ii. 2, etc.). The twig planted by the Lord will grow there into a glorious cedar, under which all birds will dwell. The Messiah grows into a cedar in the kingdom founded by Him, in which all the inhabitants of the earth will find both food (from the fruits of the tree) and protection (under its shadow). For this figure, compare Dan. iv. 8, 9. צִפּוֹר כָּל־כָּנָף, birds of every kind of plumage (cf. ch. xxxix. 4, 17), is derived from Gen. vii. 14, where birds of every kind find shelter in Noah's ark. The allusion is to men from every kind of people and tribe. By this will all the trees of the field learn that God lowers the lofty and lifts up the lowly. As the cedar represents the royal house of David, the trees of the field can only be the other kings or royal families of the earth, not the nations outside the limits of the covenant. At the same time, the nations are not to be entirely excluded because the figure of the cedars embraces the idea of the kingdom, so that the trees of the field denote the kingdoms of the earth together with their kings. The clauses, "I bring down the high tree," contain a purely general thought, as in 1 Sam. ii. 7, 8, and the perfects are not to be taken as preterites, but as statements of practical truths. It is true that the thought of the royal house of David in its previous greatness naturally suggests itself in connection with the high and green tree, and that of Jehoiachin in connection with the dry tree (compare Jer. xxii. 30); and these are not to be absolutely set aside. At the same time, the omission of the article from עֵץ לַח and the objects which follow, is sufficient to show that the words are not to be restricted to these particular persons, but are applicable to every high and green, or withered and lowly tree; *i.e.* not merely to kings alone, but to all men in common, and furnish a parallel to 1 Sam. ii. 4-9, " The bows of the mighty men are broken; and they that stumbled are girded with strength," etc.

CHAP. XVIII. THE RETRIBUTIVE JUSTICE OF GOD.

In the word of God contained in this chapter, the delusion that God visits the sins of fathers upon innocent children is overthrown, and the truth is clearly set forth that every man bears the guilt and punishment of his own sins (vers. 1-4). The righteous lives through his righteousness (vers. 5-9), but cannot save his wicked son thereby (vers. 10-13); whilst the son who avoids the sins and wickedness of his father, will live through his own righteousness (vers. 14-20). The man who repents and avoids sin is not even charged with his own sin; and, on the other hand, the man who forsakes the way of righteousness, and gives himself up to unrighteousness, will not be protected from death even by his own former righteousness (vers. 21-29). Thus will God judge every man according to his way; and it is only by repentance that Israel itself can live (vers. 30-32). The exposition of these truths is closely connected with the substance and design of the preceding and following prophecies. In the earlier words of God, Ezekiel had taken from rebellious Israel every support of false confidence in the preservation of the kingdom from destruction. But as an impenitent sinner, even when he can no longer evade the punishment of his sins, endeavours as much as possible to transfer the guilt from himself to others, and comforts himself with the thought that he has to suffer for sins that others have committed, and hardens himself against the chastisement of God through such false consolation as this; so even among the people of Israel, when the divine judgments burst upon them, the delusion arose that the existing generation had to suffer for the fathers' sins. If, then, the judgment were ever to bear the fruit of Israel's conversion and renovation, which God designed, the impenitent generation must be deprived even of this pretext for covering over its sins and quieting its conscience, by the demonstration of the justice which characterized the government of God in His kingdom.

Vers. 1–4. *The proverb and the word of God.*—Ver. 1. *And the word of Jehovah came to me, saying,* Ver. 2. *Why do you use this proverb in the land of Israel, saying, Fathers eat sour grapes, and the sons' teeth are set on edge.* Ver. 3. *As I live, is the saying of the Lord Jehovah, this proverb shall not be used any more in Israel.* Ver. 4. *Behold, all souls are mine; as the father's soul, so also the soul of the son,—they are mine; the soul which sinneth, it shall die.*—On ver. 2a compare ch. xii. 22. מַה־לָּכֶם, what is to you, what are you thinking of, that …? is a question of amazement. עַל־אַדְמַת, in the land of Israel (ch. xii. 22), not "concerning the land of Israel," as Hävernick assumes. The proverb was not, "The fathers have eaten sour grapes," for we have not אָכְלוּ, as in Jer. xxxi. 29, but יֹאכְלוּ, they eat, are accustomed to eat, and אָבוֹת has no article, because it applies to all who eat sour grapes. *Bōsĕr*, unripe, sour grapes, like *bĕsĕr* in Job xvi. 33 (see the comm. *in loc.*). The meaning of the proverb is self-evident. The sour grapes which the fathers eat are the sins which they commit; the setting of the children's teeth on edge is the consequence thereof, *i.e.* the suffering which the children have to endure. The same proverb is quoted in Jer. xxxi. 29, 30, and there also it is condemned as an error. The origin of such a proverb is easily to be accounted for from the inclination of the natural man to transfer to others the guilt which has brought suffering upon himself, more especially as the law teaches that the sins of the fathers are visited upon the children (Ex. xx. 5), and the prophets announce that the Lord would put away

Judah from before His face on account of the sins of Manasseh (2 Kings xxiv. 3; Jer. xv. 4), while Jeremiah complains in Lam. v. 7 that the people are bearing the fathers' sins. Nevertheless the proverb contained a most dangerous and fatal error, for which the teaching of the law concerning the visitation of the sins of the fathers, etc., was not accountable, and which Jeremiah, who expressly mentions the doctrine of the law (Jer. xxxii. 18), condemns as strongly as Ezekiel. God will visit the sins of the fathers upon the children who hate Him, and who also walk in the footsteps of their fathers' sins; but to those who love Him, and keep His commandments, He will show mercy to the thousandth generation. The proverb, on the other hand, teaches that the children would have to atone for their fathers' sins without any culpability of their own. How remote such a perversion of the truth as to the transmission of sins and their consequences, viz. their punishment, was from the law of Moses, is evident from the express command in Deut. xxiv. 16, that the children were not to be put to death with the fathers for the sins which the latter had committed, but that every one was to die for his own sin. What God here enjoins upon the judicial authorities must apply to the infliction of His own judgments. Consequently what Ezekiel says in the following verses in opposition to the delusion, which this proverb helped to spread abroad, is simply a commentary upon the words, "every one shall die for his own sin," and not a correction of the law, which is the interpretation that many have put upon these prophetic utterances of Jeremiah and Ezekiel. In ver. 3, the Lord declares with an oath that this proverb shall not be used any more. The apodosis to אִם יִהְיֶה וגו׳, which is not expressed, would be an imprecation, so that the oath contains a solemn prohibition. God will take care that this proverb shall not be used any more in Israel, not so much by the fact that He will not give them any further occasion to make use of it, as by the way in which He will convince them, through the judgments which He sends, of the justice of His ways. The following is Calvin's admirable paraphrase: "I will soon deprive you of this boasting of yours; for your iniquity shall be made manifest, so that all the world may see that you are but enduring just punishment, which you yourselves have deserved, and that you cannot cast it upon your fathers, as you have hitherto attempted to do." At the same time, this only gives one side; we must also add the other, which is brought out so prominently in Jer. xxxi. 29 sqq., namely, that after the judgment God will manifest His grace so gloriously in the forgiveness of sins, that those who are forgiven will fully recognise the justice of the judgments inflicted. Experience of the love and compassion of the Lord, manifesting itself in the forgiveness of sin, bows down the heart so deeply that the pardoned sinner has no longer any doubt of the justice of the judgments of God. "*In Israel*" is added, to show that such a proverb is opposed to the dignity of Israel. In ver. 4, the reason assigned for the declaration thus solemnly confirmed by an oath commences with a general thought which contains the thesis for further discussion. All souls are mine, the soul of the father as well as that of the son, saith the Lord. In these words, as Calvin has well said, "God does not merely vindicate His government or His authority, but shows that He is moved with paternal affection toward the whole of the human race which He created and formed." There is no necessity for God to punish the one for the other, the son for the father, say because of the possibility that the guilty person might evade Him; and as the Father of all, He cannot treat the one in a different manner from the other, but can only punish the one by whom punishment has been deserved. The soul that sinneth shall die. הַנֶּפֶשׁ is used here, as in many other passages, for "man," and מוּת is equivalent to suffering death as a punishment. "Death" is used to denote the complete destruction with which transgressors are threatened by the law, as in Deut. xxx. 15 (compare Jer. xxi. 8; Prov. xi. 10). This sentence is explained in the verses which follow (vers. 5-20).

Vers. 5-9. The righteous man shall not die.—Ver. 5. *If a man is righteous, and doeth right and righteousness*, Ver. 6. *And doth not eat upon the mountains, and doth not lift up his eyes to the idols of the house of Israel, and doth not defile his neighbour's wife, and doth not approach his wife in her uncleanness*, Ver. 7. *Oppresseth no one, restoreth his security* (lit. debt-pledge), *committeth no robbery, giveth his bread to the hungry, and covereth the naked with clothes*, Ver. 8. *Doth not give upon usury, and taketh not interest, withholdeth his hand from wrong, executeth judgment of truth between one and another*, Ver. 9. *Walketh in my statutes, and keepeth my rights to execute truth; he is righteous, he shall live, is the saying of the Lord "Jehovah."* —The exposition of the assertion, that God only punishes the sinner, not the innocent, commences with a picture of the righteousness which has the promise of life. The righteousness consists in the fulfilment of the commandments of the law: viz. (1) those relating to religious duties, such as the avoidance of idolatry, whether of the grosser kind, such as eating upon the mountains, *i.e.* observing sacrificial festivals, and therefore sacrificing to idols (cf. Deut. xii. 2 sqq.), or of a more refined description, *e.g.* lifting up the eyes to idols, to look to them, or make them the object of trust, and offer supplication to them (cf. Ps. cxxi. 1; Deut. iv. 19), as Israel had done, and was doing still (cf. ch. vi. 13); and (2) those relating to moral obligations, such as the avoidance of adultery (compare Ex. xx. 14; Lev. xx. 10; Deut. xxii. 22; and for טָמֵא, Gen. xxxiv. 5), and of conjugal intercourse with a wife during menstruation, which was a defilement of the marriage relation (cf. Lev. xviii. 19, xx. 18). All these sins were forbidden in the law on pain of death. To these there are appended duties to a neighbour (vers. 7 sqq.), viz. to abstain from oppressing any one (Ex. xxii. 28; Lev. xxv. 14, 17), to restore the pledge to a debtor (Ex. xxii. 25; Deut. xxiv. 6, 10 sqq.). חוֹב is hardly to be taken in any other sense than as in apposition to חֲבֹלָתוֹ, "his pledge, which is debt," equivalent to his debt-pledge or security, like דַּרְכֵּךְ זִמָּה in ch. xvi. 27. The supposition of Hitzig, that חוֹב is a participle, like קוֹם in 2 Kings xvi. 7, in the sense of debtor, is a far less natural one, and has no valid support in the free rendering of the LXX., ἐνεχυρασμὸν ὀφείλοντος. The further duties are to avoid taking unlawful possession of the property of another (cf. Lev. v. 23); to feed the hungry, clothe the naked (cf. Isa. lviii. 5; Matt. xxv. 26; Jas. ii. 15, 16); to abstain from practising usury (Deut. xxiii. 20; cf. Ex. xxii. 24) and taking interest (Lev. xxv. 36, 37); in judicial sentences, to draw back the hand from wrong, and promote judgment of truth,—a sentence in accordance with the true nature of the case (see the comm. on Zech. vii. 9); and, lastly, to walk in the statutes and rights of the Lord,—an expression which embraces, in conclusion, all that is essential to the righteousness required by the law.—This definition of the idea of true righteousness, which preserves from death and destruction, and ensures life to the possessor, is followed in vers. 10 sqq. by a discussion of the attitude which God sustains towards the sons.

Vers. 10–13. *The righteousness of the father does not protect the wicked, unrighteous son from death.*—Ver. 10. *If, however, he begetteth a violent son, who sheddeth blood, and doeth only one of these things*, Ver. 11. *But he himself hath not done all this,—if he even eateth upon the mountains, and defileth his neighbour's wife*, Ver. 12. *Oppresseth the suffering and poor, committeth robbery, doth not restore a pledge, lifteth up his eyes to idols, committeth abomination*, Ver. 13. *Giveth upon usury, and taketh interest: should he live? He shall not live! He hath done all these abominations; he shall be put to death; his blood shall be upon him.*—The subject to וְהוֹלִיד, in ver. 10, is the righteous man described in the preceding verses. פָּרִיץ, violent, literally, breaking in or through, is rendered more emphatic by the words "shedding blood" (cf. Hos. iv. 2). We regard אָח in the next clause as simply a dialectically different form of writing and pronouncing, for אַךְ, "only," and he doeth only one of these, the sins previously mentioned (vers. 6 sqq.). מֵאַחַד, with a partitive מִן, as in Lev. iv. 2, where it is used in a similar connection; the form מֵאַחַד is also met with in Deut. xv. 7. The explanation given by the Targum, "and doeth one of these to his brother," is neither warranted by the language nor commended by the sense. עָשָׂה is never construed with the accusative of the person to whom anything is done; and the limitation of the words to sins against a brother is unsuitable in this connection. The next clause, והוּא ... לֹא עָשָׂה, which has also been variously rendered, we regard as an adversative circumstantial clause, and agree with Kliefoth in referring it to the begetter (father): "and he (the father) has not committed any of these sins." For it yields no intelligible sense to refer this clause also to the son, since כָּל־אֵלֶּה cannot possibly refer to different things from the preceding מֵאֵלֶּה, and a man cannot at the same time both do and not do the same thing. The כִּי which follows signifies "if," as is frequently the case in the enumeration of particular precepts or cases; compare, for example, Ex. xxi. 1, 7, 17, etc., where it is construed with the imperfect, because the allusion is to things that may occur. Here, on the contrary, it is followed by the perfect, because the sins enumerated are regarded as committed. The emphatic גַּם (even) forms an antithesis to אַח מֵאַחַד (אַךְ), or rather an *epanorthosis* of it, inasmuch as כִּי גַּם resumes and carries out still further the description of the conduct of the wicked son, which was interrupted by the circumstantial clause; and that not only in a different form, but with a gradation in the thought. The thought, for instance, is as follows: the violent son of a righteous father, even if he has committed only one of the sins which the father has not committed, shall die. And if he has committed even the gross sins named, viz. idolatry, adultery, violent oppression of the poor, robbery, etc., should he then continue to live? The ו in וָחַי introduces the apodosis, which contains a question, that is simply indicated by the tone, and is immediately denied. The antique form חַי for חָיָה, 3d pers.

perf., is taken from the Pentateuch (cf. Gen. iii. 22 and Num. xxi. 8). The formulae מוֹת יוּמָת and דָּמָיו בּוֹ are also derived from the language of the law (cf. Lev. xx. 9, 11, 13, etc.).

Vers. 14-20. *The son who avoids his father's sin will live; but the father will die for his own sins.—Ver. 14. And behold, he begetteth a son, who seeth all his father's sins which he doeth; he seeth them, and doeth not such things. Ver. 15. He eateth not upon the mountains, and lifteth not up his eyes to the idols of the house of Israel; he defileth not his neighbour's wife, Ver. 16. And oppresseth no one; he doth not withhold a pledge, and committeth not robbery; giveth his bread to the hungry, and covereth the naked with clothes. Ver. 17. He holdeth back his hand from the distressed one, taketh not usury and interest, doeth my rights, walketh in my statutes; he will not die for the sin of his father; he shall live. Ver. 18. His father, because he hath practised oppression, committed robbery upon his brother, and hath done that which is not good in the midst of his people; behold, he shall die for his sin. Ver. 19. And do ye say, Why doth the son not help to bear the father's sin? But the son hath done right and righteousness, hath kept all my statutes, and done them; he shall live. Ver. 20. The soul that sinneth, it shall die. A son shall not help to bear the father's sin, and a father shall not help to bear the sin of the son. The righteousness of the righteous shall be upon him, and the wickedness of the wicked shall be upon him.*—The case supposed in these verses forms the antithesis to the preceding one; the father is the transgressor in this instance, and the son a keeper of the law. The subject to הוֹלִיד in ver. 14 is not the righteous man described in ver. 15, but a man who is described immediately afterwards as a transgressor of the commandments of God. The *Chetib* וירא in the last clause of ver. 14 is not to be read וַיִּרָא, καὶ φοβηθῇ, *et timuerit*, as it has been by the translators of the Septuagint and Vulgate; nor is it to be altered into וַיִּרְאֶה, as it has been by the Masoretes, to make it accord with ver. 28; but it is the apocopated form וַיֵּרֶא, as in the preceding clause, and the object is to be repeated from what precedes, as in the similar case which we find in Ex. xx. 15 (18). Ewald and Hitzig propose to alter מֵעֲנִי in ver. 17 into מֵעָוֶל after ver. 8, but without the slightest necessity. The LXX. are not to be taken as an authority for this, since the Chaldee and Syriac have both read and rendered עֲנִי; and Ezekiel, when repeating the same sentences, is accustomed to make variations in particular words. Holding back the hand from the distressed, is equivalent to abstaining from seizing upon him for the purpose of crushing him (compare ver. 12); בְּתוֹךְ עַמָּיו, in the midst of his countrymen = בְּתוֹךְ עַמּוֹ, is adopted from the language of the Pentateuch. כִּי after הִנֵּה is a participle. The question, "Why does the son not help to bear?" is not a direct objection on the part of the people, but is to be taken as a pretext, which the people might offer on the ground of the law, that God would visit the sin of the fathers upon the sons in justification of their proverb. Ezekiel cites this pretext for the purpose of meeting it by stating the reason why this does not occur. נָשָׂא בְ, to carry, near or with, to join in carrying, or help to carry (cf. Num. xi. 17). This proved the proverb to be false, and confirmed the assertion made in ver. 4*b*, to which the address therefore returns (ver. 20). The righteousness of the righteous man will come upon him, *i.e.* upon the righteous man, namely, in its consequences. The righteous man will receive the blessing of righteousness, but the unrighteous man the curse of his wickedness. There is no necessity for the article, which the *Keri* proposes to insert before רָשָׁע.

Vers. 21–26. Turning to good leads to life; turning to evil is followed by death.—Ver. 21. *But if the wicked man turneth from all his sins which he hath committed, and keepeth all my statutes, and doeth right and righteousness, he shall live, and not die.* Ver. 22. *All his transgressions which he hath committed, shall not be remembered to him: for the sake of the righteousness which he hath done he will live.* Ver. 23. *Have I then pleasure in the death of the wicked? is the saying of Jehovah: and not rather that he turn from his ways, and live?* Ver. 24. *But if the righteous man turn from his righteousness, and doeth wickedness, and acteth according to all the abominations which the ungodly man hath done, should he live? All the righteousness that he hath done shall not be remembered: for his unfaithfulness that he hath committed, and for his sin that he hath sinned, for these he shall die.* Ver. 25. *And ye say, "The way of the Lord is not right." Hear now, O house of Israel: Is my way not right? Is it not your ways that are not right?* Ver. 26. *If a righteous man turneth from his righteousness, and doeth wickedness, and dieth in consequence, he dieth for his wickedness that he hath done.* —The proof that every one must bear his sin did not contain an exhaustive reply to the question, in what relation the righteousness of God stood to the sin of men? For the cases supposed in vers. 5–20 took for granted that there was a constant persistence in the course once taken, and overlooked the instances, which are by no means rare, when a man's course of life is entirely changed. It still remained, therefore, to take notice of such cases as these, and they are handled in vers. 21–26. The ungodly man, who repents and turns, shall live; and the righteous man, who turns to the way of sin, shall die. "As the righteous man, who was formerly a sinner, is not crushed down by his past sins; so the sinner, who was once a righteous man, is not supported by his early righteousness. Every one will be judged in that state in which he is found" (Jerome). The motive for the pardon of the repenting sinner is given in ver. 23, in the declaration that God has no pleasure in the death of the wicked man, but desires his conversion, that he may live. God is therefore not only just, but merciful and gracious, and punishes none with death but those who either will not desist from evil, or will not persevere in the way of His commandments. Consequently the complaint, that the way of the Lord, *i.e.* His conduct toward men, is not weighed (יִתָּכֵן, see comm. on 1 Sam. ii. 3), *i.e.* not just and right, is altogether unfounded, and recoils upon those who make it. It is not God's ways, but the sinner's, that are wrong (ver. 25). The proof of this, which Hitzig overlooks, is contained in the declarations made in vers. 23 and 26,—viz. in the fact that God does not desire the death of the sinner, and in His mercy forgives the penitent all his former sins, and does not lay them to his charge; and also in the fact that He punishes the man who turns from the way of righteousness and gives himself up to wickedness, on account of the sin which he commits; so that He simply judges him according to his deeds.—In ver. 24, וְעָשָׂה is the continuation of the infinitive שׁוּב, and הֲיִחְיֶה is interrogatory, as in ver. 13.

Vers. 27–32. The vindication of the ways of God might have formed a fitting close to this divine oracle. But as the prophet was not merely concerned with the correction of the error contained in the proverb which was current among the people, but still more with the rescue of the people themselves from destruction, he follows up the refutation with another earnest call to repentance.—Ver. 27. *If a wicked man turneth from his wickedness which he hath done, and doeth right and righteousness, he will keep his soul alive.* Ver. 28. *If he seeth and turneth from all his transgressions which he hath committed, he shall live and not die.* Ver. 29. *And the house of Israel saith, The way of the Lord is not right. Are my ways not right, O house of Israel? Is it not rather your ways that are not right?* Ver. 30. *Therefore, every one according to his ways, will I judge you, O house of Israel, is the saying of the Lord Jehovah. Turn and repent of all your transgressions, that it may not become to you a stumbling-block to guilt.* Ver. 31. *Cast from you all your transgressions which ye have committed, and make yourselves a new heart and a new spirit! And why will ye die, O house of Israel?* Ver. 32. *For I have no pleasure in the death of the dying, is the saying of the Lord Jehovah. Therefore repent, that ye may live.*—For the purpose of securing an entrance into their hearts for the call to repentance, the prophet not only repeats, in vers. 27

and 28, the truth declared in vers. 21 and 22, that he who turns from his sin finds life, but refutes once more in ver. 29, as he has already done in ver. 25, the charge that God's ways are not right. The fact that the singular יִתָּכֵן is connected with the plural דַּרְכֵיכֶם, does not warrant our altering the plural into דַּרְפְּכֶם, but may be explained in a very simple manner, by assuming that the ways of the people are all summed up in one, and that the meaning is this: what you say of my way applies to your own ways,—namely, "it is not right; there is just measure therein." לָכֵן, "therefore, etc.;" because my way, and not yours, is right, I will judge you, every one according to his way. Repent, therefore, if ye would escape from death and destruction. שׁוּבוּ is rendered more emphatic by הָשִׁיבוּ, sc. פְּנֵיכֶם, as in ch. xiv. 6. In the last clause of ver. 30, עָוֹן is not to be taken as the subject of the sentence according to the accents, but is a genitive dependent upon מִכְשׁוֹל, as in ch. vii. 19 and xiv. 3; and the subject is to be found in the preceding clause: that it (the sinning) may not become to you a stumbling-block of iniquity, i.e. a stumbling-block through which ye fall into guilt and punishment.—The appeal in ver. 31 points back to the promise in ch. xi. 18, 19. הַשְׁלִיךְ, to cast away. The application of this word to transgressions may be explained from the fact that they consisted for the most part of idols and idolatrous images, which they had made.—"*Make yourselves* a new heart and a new spirit:" a man cannot, indeed, create either of these by his own power; God alone can give them (ch. xi. 19). But a man both can and should come to God to receive them: in other words, he can turn to God, and let both heart and spirit be renewed by the Spirit of God. And this God is willing to do; for He has no pleasure בְּמוֹת הַמֵּת, in the death of the dying one. In the repetition of the assurance given in ver. 23, הַמֵּת is very appropriately substituted for רָשָׁע, to indicate to the people that while in sin they are lying in death, and that it is only by conversion and renewal that they can recover life again.

CHAP. XIX. LAMENTATION FOR THE PRINCES OF ISRAEL.

Israel, the lioness, brought up young lions in the midst of lions. But when they showed their leonine nature, they were taken captive by the nations and led away, one to Egypt, the other to Babylon (vers. 1-9). The mother herself, once a vine planted by the water with vigorous branches, is torn from the soil, so that her strong tendrils wither, and is transplanted into a dry land. Fire, emanating from a rod of the branches, has devoured the fruit of the vine, so that not a cane is left to form a ruler's sceptre (vers. 10-14). — This lamentation, which bewails the overthrow of the royal house and the banishment of Israel into exile, forms a finale to the preceding prophecies of the overthrow of Judah, and was well adapted to annihilate every hope that things might not come to the worst after all.

Vers. 1-9. CAPTURE AND EXILE OF THE PRINCES.— Ver. 1. *And do thou raise a lamentation for the princes of Israel,* Ver. 2. *And say, Why did thy mother, a lioness, lie down among lionesses; bring up her whelps among young lions?* Ver. 3. *And she brought up one of her whelps: it became a young lion, and he learned to take prey; he devoured man.* Ver. 4. *And nations heard of him; he was caught in their pit, and they brought him with nose-rings into the land of Egypt.* Ver. 5. *And when she saw that her hope was exhausted, overthrown, she took one of her whelps, made it a young lion.* Ver. 6. *And he walked among lionesses, he became a young lion, and learned to take prey. He devoured man.* Ver. 7. *He knew its widows, and laid waste their cities; and the land and its fulness became waste, at the voice of his roaring.* Ver. 8. *Then nations round about from the provinces set up against him, and spread over him their net: he was caught in their pit.* Ver. 9. *And they put him in the cage with nose-rings, and brought him to the king of Babylon: brought him into a fortress, that his voice might not be heard any more on the mountains of Israel.*

The princes of Israel, to whom the lamentation applies, are the kings (נָשִׂיא, as in ch. xii. 10), two of whom are so clearly pointed out in vers. 4 and 9, that there is no mistaking Jehoahaz and Jehoiachin. This fact alone is sufficient to protect the plural נְשִׂיאֵי against the arbitrary alteration into the singular נְשִׂיא, proposed by Houbigant and Hitzig, after the reading of the LXX. The lamentation is not addressed to one particular prince, either Zedekiah (Hitzig) or Jehoiachin (Ros., Maurer), but to Israel as a nation; and the mother (ver. 2) is the national community, the theocracy, out of which the kings were born, as is indisputably evident from ver. 10. The words from מָה אִמְּךָ to רְבָצָה form one sentence. It yields no good sense to separate מָה אִמְּךָ from רְבָצָה, whether we adopt the rendering, "what is thy mother?" or take מָה with לְבִיָּא and render it, "how is thy mother a lioness?" unless, indeed, we supply the arbitrary clause "now, in comparison with what she was before," or change the interrogative into a preterite: "how has thy mother become a lioness?" The lionesses, among which Israel lay down, are the other kingdoms, the Gentile nations. The words have no connection with Gen. xlix. 9, where Judah is depicted as a warlike lion. The figure is a different one here. It is not so much the strength and courage of the lion as its wildness and ferocity that are the points of resemblance in the passage before us. The mother brings up her young ones among young lions, so that they learn to take prey and devour men. גּוּר is the lion's whelp, *catulus;* כְּפִיר, the young lion, which is old enough to go out in search of prey. וַתַּעַל is a *Hiphil*, in the tropical sense, to cause to spring up, or grow up, *i.e.* to bring up. The thought is the following: Why has Israel entered into fellowship with the heathen nations? Why, then, has it put itself upon a level with the heathen nations, and adopted the rapacious and tyrannical nature of the powers of the world? The question "why then?" when taken with what follows, involves the reproof that Israel has struck out a course opposed to its divine calling, and will now have to taste the bitter fruits of this assumption of heathen ways. The heathen nations have taken captive its king, and led him away into heathen lands. יִשְׁמְעוּ אֵלָיו, they heard of him (אֵלָיו for עָלָיו). The fate of Jehoahaz, to which ver. 4 refers, is related in 2 Kings xxiii. 31 sqq.—Vers. 5–7 refer to Jehoiachin, the son of Jehoiakim, and not to Zedekiah, as Hitzig imagines. For the fact that Jehoiachin went out of his own accord to the king of Babylon (2 Kings xxiv. 12), is not at variance with the figure contained in ver. 8, according to which he was taken (as a lion) in a net. He simply gave himself up to the king of Babylon because he was unable to escape from the besieged city. Moreover, Jehoahaz and Jehoiachin are simply mentioned as examples, because they both fell into the hands of the world-powers, and their fate showed clearly enough "what the end must inevitably be, when Israelitish kings became ambitious of being lions, like the kings of the nations of the world" (Kliefoth). Jehoiakim was not so suitable an example as the others, because he died in Jerusalem. נוֹחֲלָה, which has been explained in different ways, we agree with Ewald in regarding as the *Niphal* of יחל = הגל, in the sense of feeling vexed, being exhausted or deceived, like the Syriac ܘܚܠ, *viribus defecit, desperavit*. For even in Gen. viii. 12, נוֹחֶל simply means to wait; and this is inapplicable here, as waiting is not equivalent to waiting in vain. The change from הגל to יָחֵל is established by Judg. iii. 25, where הגל or חיל occurs in the sense of יָחֵל. In ver. 7, the figurative language passes into a literal description of the ungodly course pursued by the king. He knew, *i.e.* dishonoured, its (Israel's, the nation's) widows. The Targum reads וירע here instead of וידע, and renders it accordingly, "he destroyed its palaces;" and Ewald has adopted the same rendering. But רעע, to break, or smash in pieces, *e.g.* a vessel (Ps. ii. 9), is never used for the destruction of buildings; and אַלְמְנוֹת does not mean palaces (אַרְמְנוֹת), but windows. There is nothing in the use of the word in Isa. xiii. 22 to support the meaning " palaces," because the palaces are simply called 'almânōth (widows) there, with a sarcastic side glance at their desolate and widowed condition. Other conjectures are still more inadmissible. The thought is as follows: Jehoiachin went much further than Jehoahaz. He not only devoured men, but laid hands on defenceless widows, and laid the cities waste to such an extent that the land with its inhabitants became perfectly desolate through his rapacity. The description is no doubt equally applicable to his father Jehoiakim, in whose footsteps Jehoiachin walked, since Jehoiakim is described in Jer. xxii. 13 sqq. as a grievous despot and tyrant. In ver. 8 the object רִשְׁתָּם also belongs to יִתְּנוּ : they set up and spread out their net. The plural מְצֹדוֹת is used in a general and indefinite manner: in lofty castles, mountain-fortresses, i.e. in one of them (cf. Judg. xii. 7).

Vers. 10–14. DESTRUCTION OF THE KINGDOM, AND BANISHMENT OF THE PEOPLE.—Ver. 10. *Thy mother was like a vine, planted by the water in thy repose; it became fruitful and rich in tendrils from many waters.* Ver. 11. *And it had strong shoots for rulers' sceptres; and its growth ascended among the clouds, and was visible in its height in the multitude of its branches.* Ver. 12. *Then it was torn up in fury, cast to the ground, and the east wind dried up its fruit; its strong shoots were broken off, and withered; fire devoured them.* Ver. 13. *And now it is planted in the desert, in a dry and thirsty land.* Ver. 14. *There goeth out fire from the shoot of its branches, devoureth its fruit, so that there is no more a strong shoot upon it, a sceptre for ruling.* — *A lamentation it is, and it will be for lamentation.*—From the lamentable fate of the princes transported to Egypt and Babylon, the ode passes to a description of the fate, which the lion-like rapacity of the princes is preparing for the kingdom and people. Israel resembled a vine planted by the water. The difficult word בְּדָמְךָ we agree with Hävernick and Kliefoth in tracing to the verb דָּמָה, to rest (Jer. xiv. 17), and regard it as synonymous with בְּדָמִי in Isa. xxxviii. 10: "in thy repose," *i.e.* in the time of peaceful, undisturbed prosperity. For neither of the other renderings, "in thy blood" and "in thy likeness," yields a suitable meaning. The latter explanation, which originated with Raschi and Kimchi, is precluded by the fact that Ezekiel always uses the word דְּמוּת to express the idea of resemblance. —For the figure of the vine, compare Ps. lxxx. 9 sqq. This vine sent out strong shoots for rulers' sceptres; that is to say, it brought forth powerful kings, and grew up to a great height, even into the clouds. עֲבֹתִים signifies "clouds," lit. thicket of clouds, not only here, but in ch. xxxi. 3, 10, 14. The rendering "branches" or "thicket of foliage" is not suitable in any of these passages. The form of the word is not to be taken as that of a new plural of עָבוֹת, the plural of עָב, which occurs in 2 Sam. xxiii. 4 and Ps. lxxvii. 18; but is the plural of עֲבוֹת, an interlacing or thicket of foliage, and is simply transferred to the interlacing or piling up of the clouds. The clause וַיֵּרָא וגו׳, and it appeared, was seen, or became visible, simply serves to depict still further the glorious and vigorous growth, and needs no such alteration as Hitzig proposes. This picture is followed in ver. 12 sqq., without any particle of transition, by a description of the destruction of this vine. It was torn up in fury by the wrath of God, cast down to the ground, so that its fruit withered (compare the similar figures in ch. xvii. 10). מַטֵּה עֻזָּהּ is used collectively, as equivalent to מַטּוֹת עֹז (ver. 11); and the suffix in אֲכָלָתְהוּ is written in the singular on account of this collective use of מַטֶּה. The uprooting ends in the transplanting of the vine into a waste, dry, unwatered land,—in other words, in the transplanting of the people, Israel, into exile. The dry land is Babylon, so described as being a barren soil in which the kingdom of God could not flourish. According to ver. 14, this catastrophe is occasioned by the princes. The fire, which devours the fruit of the vine so that it cannot send out any more branches, emanates כִּמַטֵּה בַדֶּיהָ, from the shoot of its branches, *i.e.* from its branches, which are so prolific in shoots. מַטֶּה is the shoot which grew into rulers' sceptres, *i.e.* the royal family of the nation. The reference is to Zedekiah, whose treacherous breach of covenant (ch. xvii. 15) led to the overthrow of the kingdom and of the earthly monarchy. The picture from ver. 12 onwards is prophetic. The tearing up of the vine, and its transplantation into a dry land, had already commenced with the carrying away of Jeconiah; but it was not completed till the destruction of Jerusalem and the carrying away of Zedekiah, which were still in the future at the time when these words were uttered.—The clause קִינָה הִיא וגו׳ does not contain a concluding historical notice, as Hävernick supposes, but simply the *finale* of the lamentation, indicating the credibility of the prediction which it contains. וַתְּהִי is prophetic, like the perfects from וַתִּשַּׁע in ver. 12 onwards; and the meaning is this: A lamentation forms the substance of the whole chapter; and it will lead to lamentation, when it is fulfilled.

CHAP. XX. THE PAST, PRESENT, AND FUTURE OF ISRAEL.

The date given in ch. xx. 1 applies not only to ch. xx., but also to ch. xx.-xxiii. (compare ch. xxiv. 1); the prophetic utterances in these four chapters being bound together into a group of connected words of God, both by their contents and by the threefold repetition of the expression, " wilt thou judge?" (*vid.* ch. xx. 4, xxii. 2, and xxiii. 36). The formula הֲתִשְׁפּוֹט, which is only omitted from the threat of punishment contained in ch. xxi., indicates at the same time both the nature and design of these words of God. The prophet is to judge, *i.e.* to hold up before the people once more their sinful abominations, and to predict the consequent punishment. The circumstance which occasioned this is narrated in ch. xx. 1–3. Men of the elders of Israel came to the prophet to inquire of the Lord. The occasion is therefore a similar one to that described in the previous group; for we have already been informed, in ch. xiv. 1, that elders had come to the prophet to hear God's word from him; but they had not gone so far as to inquire. Here, however (ch. xx.), they evidently address a question to the prophet, and through him to the Lord; though the nature of their inquiry is not given, and can only be gathered from the answer, which was given to them by the Lord through the prophet. The ground for the following words of God is therefore essentially the same as for those contained in ch. xiv.–xix.; and this serves to explain the relation in which the two groups stand to each other, namely, that ch. xx.–xxiv. simply contain a further expansion of the reproachful and threatening addresses of ch. xiv.–xix.

In ch. xx. the prophet points out to the elders, in the form of a historical survey, how rebellious Israel had been towards the Lord from the very first, even in Egypt (vers. 5–9) and the desert (vers. 10–17 and 18–26), both the older and later generations, how they had sinned against the Lord their God through their idolatry, and how it was only for His own name's sake that the Lord had not destroyed them in His anger (vers. 27–31). And as Israel hath not given up idolatry even in Canaan, the Lord would not suffer Himself to be inquired of by the idolatrous generation, but would refine it by severe judgments among the nations (vers. 32–38), and sanctify it thereby into a people well-pleasing to Him, and would then gather it again out of the dispersion, and bring it into the land promised to the fathers, where it would serve Him with sacrifices and gifts upon His holy mountain (vers. 39–44). This word of God is therefore a more literal repetition of the allegorical description contained in ch. xvi.

Vers. 1–4. Date, occasion, and theme of the discourse which follows.—Ver. 1. *And it came to pass in the seventh year, in the fifth (moon), on the tenth of the moon, there came men of the elders of Israel, to inquire of Jehovah, and sat down before me.* Ver. 2. *Then the word of Jehovah came to me, saying,* Ver. 3. *Son of man, speak to the elders of Israel, and say to them, Thus saith the Lord Jehovah, Have ye come to inquire of me? As I live, if I suffer myself to be inquired of by you, is the saying of the Lord Jehovah.* Ver. 4. *Wilt thou judge them? Wilt thou judge, O son of man? Make known the abominations of their fathers to them.*—If we compare the date given in ver. 1 with ch. viii. 1, we shall find that this word of God was uttered only eleven months and five days after the one in chap. viii.; two years, one month, and five days after the call of Ezekiel to be a prophet (ch. i. 2); and two years and five months before the blockading of Jerusalem by the Chaldeans (ch. xxiv. 1). Consequently it falls almost in the middle of the first section of Ezekiel's prophetic work. דְּרֹשׁ אֶת יְהוָֹה, to seek Jehovah, *i.e.* to ask a revelation from Him. The Lord's answer in ver. 3 is similar to that in ch. xiv. 3. Instead of giving a revelation concerning the future, especially with regard to the speedy termination of the penal sufferings, which the elders had, no doubt, come to solicit, the prophet is to judge them, *i.e.* as the following clause explains, not only in the passage before us, but also in ch. xxii. 3 and xxiii. 36, to hold up before them the sins and abominations of Israel. It is in anticipation of the following picture of the apostasy of the nation from time immemorial that the sins of the fathers are mentioned here. "No reply is given to the sinners, but chiding for their sins; and He adds the oath, 'as I live,' that the sentence of refusal may be all the stronger" (Jerome). The question הֲתִשְׁפֹּט, which is repeated with emotion, "gives expression to an impatient wish, that the thing could have been done already" (Hitzig). The interrogative form of address is therefore adopted simply as a more earnest mode of giving expression to the command to go and do the thing. Hence the literal explanation of the word הֲתִשְׁפֹּט is also appended in the form of an imperative (הוֹדִיעֵם).—The prophet is to revert to the sins of the fathers, not merely for the purpose of exhibiting the magnitude of the people's guilt, but also to hold up before the sinners themselves, the patience and long-suffering which have hitherto been displayed by the Lord.

Vers. 5-9. Election of Israel in Egypt. Its resistance to the commandments of God.—Ver. 5. *And say to them, Thus saith the Lord Jehovah, In the day that I chose Israel, and lifted my hand to the seed of Jacob, and made myself known to them in the land of Egypt, and lifted my hand to them, saying, I am Jehovah, your God:* Ver. 6. *In that day I lifted my hand to them, to bring them out of the land of Egypt into the land which I sought out for them, which floweth with milk and honey—it is an ornament of all lands:* Ver. 7. *And said to them, Cast away every man the abominations of his eyes, and do not defile yourselves with the idols of Egypt. I am Jehovah, your God.* Ver. 8. *But they were rebellious against me, and would not hearken to me. Not one of them threw away the abominations of his eyes, and they did not forsake the idols of Egypt. Then I thought to pour out my wrath upon them, to accomplish my anger upon them in the midst of the land of Egypt.* Ver. 9. *But I did it for my name's sake, that it might not be profaned before the eyes of the nations, in the midst of which they were, before whose eyes I had made myself known to them, to bring them out of the land of Egypt.*—Vers. 5 and 6 form one period. בְּיוֹם בָּחֳרִי (ver. 5) is resumed in בַּיּוֹם הַהוּא (ver. 6), and the sentence continued. With וָאֶשָּׂא the construction with the infinitive passes over into the finite verb. Lifting the hand, sc. to heaven, is a gesture employed in taking an oath (see the comm. on Ex. vi. 8). The substance of the oath is introduced by the word לֵאמֹר at the close of ver. 5; but the clause וָאִוָּדַע וגו' (and made myself known) is previously inserted, and then the lifting of the hand mentioned again to indicate the importance of this act of divine grace. The contents of vers. 5 and 6 rest upon Ex. vi. 2 sqq., where the Lord makes Himself known to Moses, and through him to the children of Israel, according to the nature involved in the name Jehovah, in which He had not yet revealed Himself to the patriarchs (Ex. vi. 3). Both נָשָׂאתִי יָדִי (I lifted my hand) and אֲנִי יְהֹוָה are taken from Ex. vi. 8. The word תֵּרְתִּי, from תּוּר, to seek out, explore, also belongs to the Pentateuch (compare Deut. i. 33); and the same may be said of the description given of Canaan as "a land flowing with milk and honey" (vid. Ex. iii. 8, etc.). But צְבִי, ornament, as an epithet applied to the land of Israel, is first employed by the prophets of the time of the captivity— namely, in vers. 6 and 15 of this chapter, in Jer. iii. 19, and in Dan. viii. 9, xi. 16, 41. The election of the Israelites to be the people of Jehovah, contained *eo ipso* the command to give up the idols of Egypt, although it was at Sinai that the worship of other gods was for the first time expressly prohibited (Ex. xx. 3), and Egyptian idolatry is only mentioned in Lev. xvii. 7 (cf. Josh. xxiv. 14). Ezekiel calls the idols "abominations of their eyes," because, "although they were abominable and execrable things, they were looked upon with delight by them" (Rosenmüller). It is true that there is nothing expressly stated in the Pentateuch as to the refusal of the Israelites to obey the command of God, or their unwillingness to give up idolatry in Egypt; but it may be inferred from the statements contained in Ex. vi. 9 and 12, to the effect that the Israelites did not hearken to Moses when he communicated to them the determination of God to lead them out of Egypt, and still more plainly from their relapse into Egyptian idolatry, from the worship of the golden calf at Sinai (Ex. xxxii.), and from their repeated desire to return to Egypt while wandering in the desert.[1] Nor is there anything said in the Pentateuch concerning the determination of God to pour out His wrath

---

[1] The remarks of Calvin upon this point are very good. "We do not learn directly from Moses," he says, "that they had been rebels against God, because they would not throw away their idols and superstitions; but the conjecture is a very probable one, that they had always been so firmly fixed in their abominations as to prevent in a certain way the hand of God from bringing them relief. And assuredly, if they had embraced what Moses promised them in the name of God with promptness of mind, the

upon the idolatrous people in Egypt. We need not indeed assume on this account that Ezekiel derived his information from some special traditional source, as Vitringa has done *Observv. ss.* I. 263), or regard the statement as a revelation made by God to Ezekiel, and through him to us. The words do not disclose to us either a particular fact or a definite decree of God; they simply contain a description of the attitude which God, from His inmost nature, assumes towards sinners who rebel against His holy commandments, and which He displayed both in the declaration made concerning Himself as a zealous, or jealous God, who visits iniquities (Ex. xx. 5), and also in the words addressed to Moses when the people fell into idolatry at Sinai, "Let me alone, that my wrath may wax hot against them, and that I may consume them" (Ex. xxxii. 10). All that God expresses here, His heart must have felt in Egypt towards the people who would not desist from idolatry. For the words themselves, compare ch. vii. 8, vi. 12, v. 13. וָאֹמַר (ver. 9), "but I did it for my name's sake." The missing object explaining what He did, namely, abstain from pouring out His wrath, is to be gathered from what follows: "that I might not profane my name." This would have taken place if God had destroyed Israel by pouring out His wrath; in other words, have allowed them to be destroyed by the Egyptians. The heathen might then have said that Jehovah had been unable to liberate His people from their hand and power (cf. Num. xiv. 16 and Ex. xxxii. 12). הֵחֵל is an *infin. Niphal* of הָלַל for חָלַל (cf. Lev. xxi. 4).

Vers. 10–17. Behaviour of Israel in the desert.—Ver. 10. *And I led them out of the land of Egypt, and brought them*

execution of the promise would have been more prompt and swift. But we may learn that it was their own obtuseness which hindered God from stretching out His hand forthwith and actually fulfilling all that He had promised It was necessary, indeed, that God should contend with Pharaoh, that His power might be more conspicuously displayed; but the people would not have been so tyrannically afflicted if they had not closed the door of divine mercy."

into the desert; Ver. 11. *And gave them my statutes, and my rights I made known to them, which man is to do that he may live through them.* Ver. 12. *I also gave them my Sabbaths, that they might be for a sign between me and them, that they might know that I Jehovah sanctify them.* Ver. 13. *But the house of Israel was rebellious against me in the desert: they did not walk in my statutes, and my rights they rejected, which man is to do, that he may live through them, and my Sabbaths they greatly profaned: Then I thought to pour out my wrath upon them in the desert to destroy them.* Ver. 14. *But I did it for my name's sake, that it might not be profaned before the eyes of the nations, before whose eyes I had led them out.* Ver. 15. *I also lifted my hand to them in the desert, not to bring them into the land which I had given (them), which floweth with milk and honey; it is an ornament of all lands,* Ver. 16. *Because they rejected my rights, did not walk in my statutes, and profaned my Sabbaths, for their heart went after their idols.* Ver. 17. *But my eye looked with pity upon them, so that I did not destroy them, and make an end of them in the desert.*—God gave laws at Sinai to the people whom He had brought out of Egypt, through which they were to be sanctified as His own people, that they might live before God. On ver. 11 compare Deut. xxx. 16 and 19. Ver. 12 is taken almost word for word from Ex. xxxi. 13, where God concludes the directions for His worship by urging upon the people in the most solemn manner the observance of His Sabbaths, and thereby pronounces the keeping of the Sabbath the kernel of all divine worship. And as in that passage we are to understand by the Sabbaths the actual weekly Sabbaths, and not the institutions of worship as a whole, so here we must retain the literal signification of the word. It is only of the Sabbath recurring every week, and not of all the fasts, that it could be said it was a sign between Jehovah and Israel. It was a sign, not as a token, that they who observed it were Israelites, as Hitzig supposes, but to know (that they might know) that Jehovah was sanctifying them, namely, by the

Sabbath rest—as a refreshing and elevation of the mind, in which Israel was to have a foretaste of that blessed resting from all works to which the people of God was ultimately to attain (see the comm. on Ex. xx. 11). It is from this deeper signification of the Sabbath that the prominence given to the Sabbaths here is to be explained, and not from the outward circumstance that in exile, when the sacrificial worship was necessarily suspended, the keeping of the Sabbath was the only bond which united the Israelites, so far as the worship of God was concerned (Hitzig). Historical examples of the rebellion of Israel against the commandments of God in the desert are given in Ex. xxxii. 1-6 and Num. xxv. 1-3; and of the desecration of the Sabbath, in Ex. xvi. 27 and Num. xv. 32. For the threat referred to in ver. 13*b*, compare Ex. xxxii. 10; Num. xiv. 11, 12.—Vers. 15 and 16 are not a repetition of ver. 13 (Hitzig); nor do they introduce a limitation of ver. 14 (Kliefoth). They simply relate what else God did to put bounds to the rebellion after He had revoked the decree to cut Israel off, at the intercession of Moses (Num. xiv. 11-19). He lifted His hand to the oath (Num. xiv. 21 sqq.), that the generation which had come out of Egypt should not come into the land of Canaan, but should die in the wilderness. Therewith He looked with pity upon the people, so that He did not make an end of them by following up the threat with a promise that the children should enter the land. עָשָׂה כָלָה, as in ch. xi. 13.

Vers. 18-26. *The generation that grew up in the desert.*— Ver. 18. *And I spake to their sons in the desert, Walk not in the statutes of your fathers, and keep not their rights, and do not defile yourselves with their idols.* Ver. 19. *I am Jehovah your God; walk in my statutes, and keep my rights, and do them,* Ver. 20. *And sanctify my Sabbaths, that they may be for a sign between me and you, that ye may know that I am Jehovah your God.* Ver. 21. *But the sons were rebellious against me; they walked not in my statutes, and did not keep my rights, to do them, which man should do that he may live through them; they pro-*

faned my Sabbaths. Then I thought to pour out my wrath upon them, to accomplish my anger upon them in the desert. Ver. 22. *But I turned back my hand and did it for my name's sake, that it might not be profaned before the eyes of the nations, before whose eyes I had them out.* Ver. 23. *I also lifted my hand to them in the desert, to scatter them among the nations, and to disperse them in the lands;* Ver. 24. *Because they did not my rights, and despised my statutes, profaned my Sabbaths, and their eyes were after the idols of their fathers.* Ver. 25. *And I also gave them statutes, which were not good, and rights, through which they did not live;* Ver. 26. *And defiled them in their sacrificial gifts, in that they caused all that openeth the womb to pass through, that I might fill them with horror, that they might know that I am Jehovah.*—
The sons acted like their fathers in the wilderness. Historical proofs of this are furnished by the accounts of the Sabbath-breaker (Num xv. 32 sqq.), of the rebellion of the company of Korah, and of the murmuring of the whole congregation against Moses and Aaron after the destruction of Korah's company (Num. xvi. and xvii.). In the last two cases God threatened that He would destroy the whole congregation (cf. Num. xvi. 21 and xvii. 9, 10); and on both occasions the Lord drew back His hand at the intercession of Moses, and his actual intervention (Num. xvi. 22 and xvii. 11 sqq.), and did not destroy the whole nation for His name's sake. The statements in vers. 21*b* and 22 rest upon these facts. The words of ver. 23 concerning the oath of God, that He would scatter the transgressors among the heathen, are also founded upon the Pentateuch, and not upon an independent tradition, or any special revelation from God. Dispersion among the heathen is threatened in Lev. xxvi. 33 and Deut. xxviii. 64, and there is no force in Kliefoth's argument that "these threats do not refer to the generation in the wilderness, but to a later age." For in both chapters the blessings and curses of the law are set before the people who were then in the desert; and there is not a single word to intimate that either

blessing or curse would only be fulfilled upon the generations of later times. On the contrary, when Moses addressed to the people assembled before him his last discourse concerning the renewal of the covenant (Deut. xxix. and xxx.), he called upon them to enter into the covenant, " which Jehovah maketh with thee *this day* " (Deut. xxix. 12), and to keep all the words of this covenant and do them. It is upon this same discourse, in which Moses calls the threatenings of the law אָלָה, an oath (Deut. xxix. 13), that "the lifting of the hand of God to swear," mentioned in ver. 23 of this chapter, is also founded. Moreover, it is not stated in this verse that God lifted His hand to scatter among the heathen the generation which had grown up in the wilderness, and to disperse them in the lands before their entrance into the land promised to the fathers; but simply that He had lifted His hand in the wilderness to threaten the people with dispersion among the heathen, without in any way defining the period of dispersion. In the blessings and threatenings of the law contained in Lev. xxvi. and Deut. xxviii.–xxx., the nation is regarded as a united whole; so that no distinction is made between the successive generations, for the purpose of announcing this particular blessing or punishment to either one or the other. And Ezekiel acts in precisely the same way. It is true that he distinguishes the generation which came out of Egypt and was sentenced by God to die in the wilderness from the sons, *i.e.* the generation which grew up in the wilderness; but the latter, or the sons of those who had fallen, the generation which was brought into the land of Canaan, he regards as one with all the successive generations, and embraces the whole under the common name of " fathers " to the generation living in his day (" your fathers " ver. 27), as we may clearly see from the turn given to the sentence which describes the apostasy of those who came into the land of Canaan (עוֹד זֹאת וגו'). In thus embracing the generation which grew up in the wilderness and was led into Canaan, along with the generations which followed and lived in

Canaan, Ezekiel adheres very closely to the view prevailing in the Pentateuch, where the nation in all its successive generations is regarded as one united whole. The threat of dispersion among the heathen, which the Lord uttered in the wilderness to the sons of those who were not to see the land, is also not mentioned by Ezekiel as one which God designed to execute upon the people who were wandering in the desert at the time. For if he had understood it in this sense, he would have mentioned its non-fulfilment also, and would have added a וָאַעַשׂ לְמַעַן שְׁמִי וגו׳, as he has done in the case of the previous threats (cf. vers. 22, 14, and 9). But we do not find this either in ver. 24 or ver. 26. The omission of this turn clearly shows that ver. 23 does not refer to a punishment which God designed to inflict, but did not execute for His name's sake; but that the dispersion among the heathen, with which the transgressors of His commandments were threatened by God when in the wilderness, is simply mentioned as a proof that even in the wilderness the people, whom God had determined to lead into Canaan, were threatened with that very punishment which had now actually commenced, because rebellious Israel had obstinately resisted the commandments and rights of its God.

These remarks are equally applicable to vers. 25 and 26. These verses are not to be restricted to the generation which was born in the wilderness and gathered to its fathers not long after its entrance into Canaan, but refer to their descendants also, that is to say, to the fathers of our prophet's contemporaries, who were born and had died in Canaan. God gave them statutes which were not good, and rights which did not bring them life. It is perfectly self-evident that we are not to understand by these statutes and rights, which were not good, either the Mosaic commandments of the ceremonial law, as some of the Fathers and earlier Protestant commentators supposed, or the threatenings contained in the law; so that this needs no elaborate proof. The ceremonial commandments given by God were good, and had the promise attached to them, that obedience to them would give life; whilst the threats of punishment contained in the law are never called חֻקִּים and מִשְׁפָּטִים. Those statutes only are called "not good" the fulfilment of which did not bring life or blessing and salvation. The second clause serves as an explanation of the first. The examples quoted in ver. 26 show what the words really mean. The defiling in their sacrificial gifts (ver. 26), for example, consisted in their causing that which opened the womb to pass through, i.e. in the sacrifice of the first-born. הַעֲבִיר כָּל־פֶּטֶר רֶחֶם points back to Ex. xiii. 12; only לַיהוָֹה, which occurs in that passage, is omitted, because the allusion is not to the commandment given there, but to its perversion into idolatry. This formula is used in the book of Exodus (l.c.) to denote the dedication of the first-born to Jehovah; but in ver. 13 this limitation is introduced, that the first-born of man is to be redeemed. הַעֲבִיר signifies a dedication through fire (= הַעֲבִיר בָּאֵשׁ, ver. 31), and is adopted in the book of Exodus, where it is joined to לַיהוָֹה, in marked opposition to the Canaanitish custom of dedicating children to Moloch by februation in fire (see the comm. on Ex. xiii. 12). The prophet refers to this Canaanitish custom, and cites it as a striking example of the defilement of the Israelites in their sacrificial gifts (טִמֵּא, to make unclean, not to declare unclean, or treat as unclean). That this custom also made its way among the Israelites, is evident from the repeated prohibition against offering children through the fire to Moloch (Lev. xviii. 21 and Deut. xviii. 10). When, therefore, it is affirmed with regard to a statute so sternly prohibited in the law of God, that Jehovah gave it to the Israelites in the wilderness, the word נָתַן (give) can only be used in the sense of a judicial sentence, and must not be taken merely as indicating divine permission; in other words, it is to be understood, like 2 Thess. ii. 11 ("God sends them strong delusion") and Acts vii. 42 ("God turned, and gave them up to worship the host of heaven"), in the sense of hardening, whereby whoever will not renounce idolatry is so given up to its power, that it draws him deeper and deeper in. This is in perfect keeping with the statement in ver. 26 as the design of God in doing this: "that I might fill them with horror;" *i.e.* might excite such horror and amazement in their minds, that if possible they might be brought to reflect and to return to Jehovah their God.

Vers. 27–31. Israel committed these sins in Canaan also, and to this day has not given them up; therefore God will not allow the idolatrous generation to inquire of Him.—Ver. 27. *Therefore speak to the house of Israel, O son of man, and say to them, Thus saith the Lord Jehovah, Still further have your fathers blasphemed me in this, with the faithlessness which they have shown toward me.* Ver. 28. *When I had brought them into the land, which I had lifted my hand to give them, then they looked out every high hill and every thickly covered tree, and offered their sacrifices there, and gave their irritating gifts there, and presented the fragrance of their pleasant odour there, and poured out their drink-offerings there.* Ver. 29. *And I said to them, What height is that to which ye go? And its name is called Height to this day.* Ver. 30. *Therefore say to the house of Israel, Thus saith the Lord Jehovah, What? Do ye defile yourselves in the way of your fathers; and go whoring after their abominations;* Ver. 31. *And defile yourselves in all your idols to this day, by lifting up your gifts, and causing your sons to pass through the fire; and should I let myself be inquired of by you? As I live, is the saying of the Lord Jehovah, I will not let myself be inquired of by you.* — The לָכֵן in ver. 27 is resumed in ver. 30; and there the answer given by God to the elders, who had come to inquire of Him, is first communicated, after an express declaration of the fact that Israel had continued its idolatry in the most daring manner, even after its entrance into Canaan. But the form in which this is done—עוֹד זֹאת, "still further in this"—is to be understood as intimating that the conduct of the fathers of the existing generation, and therefore not merely of those who grew up in the wilderness, but also of those who had lived in Canaan, has already been described in general terms in the preceding verses, and that what follows simply adds another novel feature. But this can only be the case if vers. 23–26 are taken in the sense given above. זֹאת is an accusative; and נָדַף is construed with the accusative both of the person and thing. The more precise definition of זֹאת is not given in בְּמַעֲלָם בִּי at the end of the verse, but in the idolatry depicted in ver. 28. מָעַל refers to the faithlessness involved in the breach of the covenant and in idolatry. This is the general description; whilst the idolatry mentioned in ver. 28*b* constituted one particular feature, in which the faithlessness appeared in the form of blasphemy. For the fact itself, namely, the worship on high places, which was practised on every hand, see ch. vi. 13, xvi. 24, 25; 1 Kings xiv. 23; 2 Kings xvii. 10. In the enumeration of the offerings, there is something striking in the position in which בַּעַס קָרְבָּנָם stands, namely, between the slaughtered sacrifices (זְבָחִים) and the increase- and drink-offerings; and this is no doubt the reason why the clause וַיִּתְּנוּ שָׁם וגו׳ is omitted from the *Cod. Vat.* and *Alex.* of the LXX.; and even Hitzig proposes to strike it out. But Theodoret found this reading in the Alex. Version; and Hitzig is wrong in affirming that קָרְבָּן is used in connection with sacrifices, meat-offerings, and drink-offerings. The meat-offerings are not expressly named, for רֵיחַ נִיחוֹחַ does not signify meat-offerings, but is used in the law for the odour of all the offerings, both slaughtered sacrifices and meat-offerings, even though in Ezek. xvi. 19 it is applied to the odour of the bloodless offerings alone. And in the same way does קָרְבָּן embrace all the offerings, even the slain offerings, in Ezek. xl. 43, in harmony with Lev. i. 2, ii. 1, and other passages. That it is used in this general signification here, is evident from the introduction of the word בַּעַס, irritation or provocation of their gifts, *i.e.* their gifts which provoked irritation on the part of God, because they were offered to idols. As this sentence applies to all the sacrifices (bloody and bloodless), so also does the clause which follows, וַיָּשִׂימוּ שָׁם וגו׳, refer to all the offerings which were burned upon the altar, without regard to the material employed. Consequently Ezekiel mentions only slain offerings and drink-offerings, and, by the two clauses inserted between, describes the offering of the slaughtered sacrifices as a gift of irritation to God, and of pleasant fragrance to the idolatrous worshippers who presented them. He does not mention the meat-offerings separately, because they generally formed an accompaniment to the slain offerings, and therefore were included in these. But although God had called the people to account for this worship on high places, they had not relinquished it even "to this day." This is no doubt the meaning of ver. 29, which has been interpreted in very different ways. The context shows, in the most conclusive manner, that הַבָּמָה is to be taken collectively, and that the use of the singular is to be explained from the antithesis to the one divinely appointed Holy Place in the temple, and not, as Kimchi and Hävernick suppose, from any allusion to one particular *bâmâh* of peculiar distinction, viz. " the great high place at Gibeon." The question מָה הַבָּמָה is not expressive of contempt (Hitzig), but " is founded upon the assumption that they would have to give an account of their doings; and merely asks, What kind of heights are those to which you are going? Who has directed you to go thither with your worship?" (Kliefoth). There is no need to refute the trivial fancy of J. D. Michaelis, which has been repeated by Hitzig, namely, that Ezekiel has taken בָּמָה as a derivative from בא and מה. Again, the question does not presuppose a word addressed by God to Israel, which Ezekiel only has handed down to us; but is simply a rhetorical mode of presenting the condemnation by God of the worship of the high places, to which both the law and the earlier prophets had given utterance. The next clause, " and their name was called Height" (high place), is not to be regarded as containing merely a historical notice of the name given to these idolatrous places of worship; but the giving of the name is a proof of the continued existence of the thing; so that the words affirm, that notwithstanding the condemnation on the part of God, Israel had retained these high places,—had not abolished them to this day.—Vers. 30 and 31 facilitate the transition from the first part of this word of God to the second. What has already been said in vers. 5–29 concerning the idolatry of the people, from the time of its election onwards, is here expressly applied to the existing generation, and carries with it the declaration to them, that inasmuch as they are defiling themselves by idolatry, as their fathers did, Jehovah cannot permit Himself to be inquired of by them. The thought is couched in the form of a question, to express astonishment that those who denied the Lord, and dishonoured Him by their idolatry, should nevertheless imagine that they could obtain revelations from Him. The lifting up (שְׂאֵת, from נָשָׂא) of gifts signifies the offering of sacrifices upon the altars of the high places. For ver. 31*b*, compare ver. 3.—With this declaration God assigns the reason for the refusal to listen to idolaters, which had already been given in ver. 3. But it does not rest with this refusal. God now proceeds to disclose to them the thoughts of their own hearts, and announces to them that He will refine them by severe judgments, and bring them thereby to repentance of their sins, that He may then gather them out of the dispersion, and make them partakers of the promised salvation as a people willingly serving Him.—In this way do vers. 32–44 cast a prophetic glance over the whole of the future history of Israel.

Vers. 32–38. The judgment awaiting Israel of purification among the heathen.—Ver. 32. *And that which riseth up in your mind shall not come to pass, in that ye say,* We will be like the heathen, like the families of the lands, to serve wood and stone. Ver. 33. *As I live, is the saying of the Lord Jehovah, with strong hand and with outstretched arm, and with wrath poured out, will I rule over you.* Ver. 34. *And I will bring you out of the nations, and gather you out of the lands in which ye have been scattered, with strong hand and with outstretched arm, and with wrath poured out,* Ver. 35. *And will bring you into the desert of the nations, and contend with you there face to face.* Ver. 36. *As I contended with your fathers in the desert of the land of Egypt, so will I contend with you, is the saying of the Lord Jehovah.* Ver. 37. *And I will cause you to pass through under the rod, and bring you into the bond of the covenant.* Ver. 38. *And I will separate from you the rebellious, and those who are apostates from me; out of the land of their sojourning will I lead them out, but into the land of Israel shall they not come; that ye may know that I am Jehovah.*—הָעֹלָה עַל רוּחַ, that which rises up in the spirit, is the thought that springs up in the mind. What this thought was is shown in ver. 32*b*, viz. we will be like the heathen in the lands of the earth, to serve wood and stone; that is to say, we will become idolaters like the heathen, pass into heathenism. This shall not take place; on the contrary, God will rule over them as King with strong arm and fury. The words, "with strong hand and stretched-out arm," are a standing expression in the Pentateuch for the mighty acts by which Jehovah liberated His people from the power of the Egyptians, and led them out of Egypt (cf. Ex. vi. 1, 6; Deut. iv. 34, v. 15, vii. 19, etc.), and are connected in Ex. vi. 6 with וּבִמְשְׁפָּטִים גְּדֹלִים. Here, on the contrary, they are connected with בְּחֵמָה שְׁפוּכָה, and are used in ver. 33 with reference to the government of God over Israel, whilst in ver. 34 they are applied to the bringing out of Israel from the midst of the heathen. By the introduction of the clause "with fury poured out," the manifestation of the omnipotence of God which Israel experienced in its dispersion, and which it was still to experience among the heathen, is described as an emanation of the divine wrath, a severe and wrathful judgment. The leading and gathering of Israel out of the nations (ver. 34) is neither their restoration from the existing captivity in Babylon, nor their future restoration to Canaan on the conversion of the people who were still hardened, and therefore rejected by God. The former assumption would be decidedly at variance with both מִן הָעַמִּים and מִן הָאֲרָצוֹת, since Israel was dispersed only throughout one land and among one people at the time of the Babylonian captivity. Moreover, neither of the assumptions is reconcilable with the context, more especially with ver. 35. According to the context, this leading out is an act of divine anger, which Israel is to feel in connection therewith; and this cannot be affirmed of either the redemption of the people out of the captivity in Babylon, or the future gathering of Israel from its dispersion. According to ver. 35, God will conduct those who are brought out from the nations and gathered together out of the lands into the desert of the nations, and contend with them there. The "desert of the nations" is not the desert lying between Babylonia and Palestine, on the coastlands of the Mediterranean, through which the Israelites would have to pass on their way home from Babylon (Rosenmüller, Hitzig, and others). For there is no imaginable reason why this should be called the desert of the nations in distinction from the desert of Arabia, which also touched the borders of several nations. The expression is doubtless a typical one, the future guidance of Israel being depicted as a repetition of the earlier guidance of the people from Egypt to Canaan; as it also is in Hos. ii. 16. All the separate features in the description indicate this, more especially vers. 36 and 37, where it is impossible to overlook the allusion to the guidance of Israel in the time of Moses. The more precise explanation of the words must depend, however, upon the sense in which we are to understand the expression, "desert of the land of Egypt." Here also the supposition that the Arabian desert is referred to, because it touched the border of Egypt, does not furnish a sufficient explanation. It touched the border of Canaan as well. Why then did not Ezekiel name it after the land of Canaan? Evidently for no other reason than that the time spent by the Israelites in the Arabian desert resembled their sojourn in Egypt much more closely than their settlement in Canaan, because, while there, they were still receiving their training for their entrance into Canaan, and their possession and enjoyment of its benefits, just as much as in the land of Egypt. And in a manner corresponding to this, the "desert of the nations" is a figurative expression applied to the world of nations, from whom they were indeed spiritually distinct, whilst outwardly they were still in the midst of them, and had to suffer from their oppression. Consequently the leading of Israel out of the nations (ver. 34) is not a local and corporeal deliverance out of heathen lands, but a spiritual severance from the heathen world, in order that they might not be absorbed into it or become inseparably blended with the heathen. God will accomplish this by means of severe chastisements, by contending with them as He formerly contended with their fathers in the Arabian desert. God contends with His people when He charges them with their sin and guilt, not merely in words, but also with deeds, *i.e.* through chastening and punishments. The words "face to face" point back to Deut. v. 4 : "Jehovah talked with you face to face in the mount, out of the midst of the fire." Just as at Sinai the Lord talked directly with Israel, and made known to it the devouring fire of His own holy nature, in so terrible a manner that all the people trembled and entreated Moses to act the part of a mediator between them, promising at the same time obedience to him (Ex. xx. 19); so will the Lord make Himself known to Israel in the desert of the world of nations with the burning zeal of His anger, that it may learn to fear Him. This contending is more precisely defined in vers. 37 and 38. I will cause you to pass through under the (shepherd's) rod. A shepherd lets his sheep pass through under his rod for the purpose of counting them, and seeing whether they are in good condition or not (*vid.* Jer. xxxiii. 13). The figure is here applied to God. Like a shepherd, He will cause His flock, the Israelites, to pass through under His rod, *i.e.* take them into His special care, and bring them "into the bond of the covenant" (מָסֹרֶת, not from מסר [Raschi], but from אָסַר, for מַאֲסֹרֶת, a fetter); that is to say, not "I will bind myself to you and you to me by a new covenant" (Bochart, *Hieroz.* I. p. 508), for this is opposed to the context, but, as the Syriac version has rendered it, ܒܡܪܕܘܬܐ (*in disciplina*), "the discipline of the covenant." By this we are not merely to understand the covenant punishments, with which transgressors of the law are threatened, as Hävernick does, but the covenant promises must also be included. For not only the threats of the covenant, but the promises of the covenant, are *bonds* by which God trains His people; and אָסַר is not only applied to burdensome and crushing fetters, but to the bonds of love as well (*vid.* Song of Sol. vii. 6). Kliefoth understands by the fetter of the covenant the Mosaic law, as being the means employed by God to preserve the Israelites from mixing with the nations while placed in the midst of them, and to keep them to Himself, and adds the following explanation,—"this law, through which they should have been able to live, they have now to wear as a fetter, and to feel the chastisement thereof." But however correct the latter thought may be in itself, it is hardly contained in the words, "lead them into the fetter (band) of the law." Moreover, although the law did indeed preserve Israel from becoming absorbed into the world of nations, the fact that the Jews were bound to the law did not bring them to the knowledge of the truth, or bring to pass the purging of the rebellious from among the people, to which ver. 38 refers. All that the law accomplished in this respect in the case of those who lived among the heathen was effected by its threatenings and its promises, and not by its statutes and their faithful observance. This discipline will secure the purification of the people, by severing from the nation the rebellious and apostate. God will bring them forth out of the land of their pilgrimage, but will not bring them into the land of Israel. אֶרֶץ מְגוּרִים is the standing epithet applied in the Pentateuch to the land of

Canaan, in which the patriarchs lived as pilgrims, without coming into actual possession of the land (cf. Gen. xvii. 8, xxviii. 4, xxxvi. 7; Ex. vi. 4). This epithet Ezekiel has transferred to the lands of Israel's exile, in which it was to lead a pilgrim-life until it was ripe for entering Canaan. הוֹצִיא, to lead out, is used here for clearing out by extermination, as the following clause, "into the land of Israel shall they not come," plainly shows. The singular יָבֹא is used distributively: not one of the rebels will enter.

Vers. 39-44. *The ultimate gathering of Israel, and its conversion to the Lord.*—Ver. 39. *Ye then, O house of Israel, thus saith the Lord Jehovah, Go ye, serve every one his idols! but afterwards—truly ye will hearken to me, and no longer desecrate my holy name with your sacrificial gifts and your idols,* Ver. 40. *But upon my holy mountain, upon the high mountain of Israel, is the saying of the Lord Jehovah, there will all the house of Israel serve me, the whole of it in the land; there will I accept them gladly; there will I ask for your heave-offerings and the firstfruits of your gifts in all that ye make holy.* Ver. 41. *As a pleasant odour will I accept you gladly, when I bring you out from the nations, and gather you out of the lands, in which you have been scattered, and sanctify myself in you before the eyes of the heathen nations.* Ver. 42. *And ye shall know that I am Jehovah, when I bring you into the land of Israel, into the land which I lifted up my hand to give to your fathers;* Ver. 43. *And there ye will think of your ways and your deeds, with which ye have defiled yourselves, and will loathe yourselves* (lit. experience loathing before yourselves) *on account of all your evil deeds which ye have performed;* Ver. 44. *And ye will know that I am Jehovah, when I deal with you for my name's sake, not according to your evil ways and according to your corrupt deeds, O house of Israel, is the saying of Jehovah.*—After the Lord has declared to the people that He will prevent its being absorbed into the heathen world, and will exterminate the ungodly by severe judgments, the address passes on, with the direction henceforth to serve idols only, to a prediction of the eventual conversion, and the restoration to Canaan of the purified nation. The direction, " Go ye, serve every one his idols," contains, after what precedes it, a powerful appeal to repent. God thereby gives up the impenitent to do whatever they will, having first of all told them that not one of them will come into the land of Canaan. Their opposition will not frustrate His plan of salvation. The words which follow from וְאַחַר onwards have been interpreted in different ways. It is opposed to the usage of the language to connect וְאַחַר with עִבְדוּ, serve ye hereafter also (De Wette, etc.), for ו has not the force of the Latin *et = etiam*, and still less does it signify " afterwards just as before." Nor is it allowable to connect וְאַחַר closely with what follows, in the sense of " and hereafter also, if ye will hearken to me, profane ye my name no more" (Rosenmüller, Maurer). For if תְּחַלְּלוּ were used as an imperative, either it would have to stand at the beginning of the sentence, or it would be preceded by אַל instead of לֹא. Moreover, the antithesis between not being willing to hear and not profaning the name of God, is imported arbitrarily into the text. The name of the Lord is profaned not only by sacrifices offered in external form to Jehovah and in the heart to idols, but also by disobedience to the word and commandments of God. It is much better to take וְאַחַר by itself, and to render the following particle, אִם, as the ordinary sign of an oath : " but afterwards (*i.e.* in the future) . . . verily, ye will hearken to me ; " that is to say, ye will have been converted from your idolatry through the severe judgments that have fallen upon you. The ground for this thought is introduced in ver. 40 by a reference to the fact that all Israel will then serve the Lord upon His holy mountain. כִּי is not " used emphatically before a direct address" (Hitzig), but has a causal signification. For הַר מְרוֹם יִשׂ', see the comm. on ch. xvii. 23. In the expression " all Israel," which is rendered more emphatic by the addition of כֻּלֹּה, there is an allusion to the eventual termination of the severance of the people of God (compare ch. xxxvii. 22). Then will the Lord accept with delight both them and their sacrificial gifts. תְּרוּמוֹת, heave-offerings (see the comm. on Ex. xxv. 2 and Lev. ii. 9), used here in the broader sense of all the sacrificial gifts, along with which the gifts of first-fruits are specially named. מַשְׂאוֹת, as applied to holy offerings in the sense of ἀναθήματα, belongs to the later usage of the language. בְּכָל־קָדְשֵׁיכֶם, consisting of all your consecrated gifts. קָדָשִׁים, as in Lev. xxii. 15. This promise includes *implicite* the bringing back of Israel from its banishment. This is expressly mentioned in ver. 41; but even there it is only introduced as self-evident in the subordinate clause, whereas the cheerful acceptance of Israel on the part of God constitutes the leading thought. בְּרֵיחַ נִיחֹחַ, as an odour of delight (בְּ, the so-called *Beth essentiae*), will God accept His people. רֵיחַ נִיחֹחַ, odour of satisfaction, is the technical expression for the cheerful (well-pleased) acceptance of the sacrifice, or rather of the feelings of the worshipper presenting the sacrifice, which ascend to God in the sacrificial odour (see the comm. on Gen. viii. 21). The thought therefore is the following: When God shall eventually gather His people out of their dispersion, He will accept them as a sacrifice well-pleasing to Him, and direct all His good pleasure towards them. וְנִקְדַּשְׁתִּי בָכֶם does not mean, I shall be sanctified through you, and is not to be explained in the same sense as Lev. xxii. 32 (Rosenmüller), for בְּ is not equivalent to בְּתוֹךְ; but it signifies "I will sanctify myself on you," as in Num. xx. 13, Lev. x. 3, and other passages, where נִקְדַּשׁ is construed with בְּ *pers.* (cf. Ezek. xxviii. 25, xxxvi. 23, xxxviii. 16, xxxix. 27), in the sense of proving oneself holy, mostly by judgment, but here through having made Israel into a holy nation by the refining judgment, and one to which He can therefore grant the promised inheritance.—Vers. 42 sqq. Then will Israel also recognise its God in His grace, and be ashamed of its former sins. For ver. 43, compare ch. vi. 9 and xvi. 61.—With regard to the fulfilment, as Kliefoth has correctly observed, " in the prediction contained in vers. 32-38, the whole of the searching judgments, by which God would lead Israel to conversion, are summed up in one, which includes not only the Babylonian captivity, the nearest and the first, but the still more remote judgment, namely, the present dispersion; for it is only in the present dispersion of Israel that God has really taken it into the wilderness of the nations, just as it was only in the rejection of Christ that its rebellious attitude was fully manifested. And as the prophecy of the state of punishment combines in this way both the nearer and more remote; so are both the nearer and more distant combined in what vers. 40 to 44 affirm with regard to the ultimate fate of Israel." The gathering of Israel from among the heathen will be fulfilled in its conversion to Christ, and hitherto it has only taken place in very small beginnings. The principal fulfilment is still to come, when Israel, as a nation, shall be converted to Christ. With regard to the bringing back of the people into "the land of Israel," see the comm. on ch. xxxvii., where this promise is more fully expanded.

CHAP. XX. 45 TO CHAP. XXI. 32 (HEB. CHAP. XXI.[1]). PROPHECY OF THE BURNING FOREST AND THE SWORD OF THE LORD.

A fire kindled by the Lord will burn the forest of the south (ch. xx. 45-48). This figurative announcement is explained in what follows, in order that the divine threat may make an impression upon the people (ver. 49). The Lord will draw His sword from its scabbard, and cut off from Jerusalem and the land of Israel both righteous and wicked (ch. xxi. 1-17); that is to say, the king of Babylon will draw his sword against

---

[1] In the Hebrew Bible the previous chapter closes at ver. 44, and ch. xxi. commences there. Keil has adhered to this division of chapters; but for the sake of convenience we have followed the arrangement adopted in the English authorized version.—Tr.

Jerusalem and the sons of Ammon, and will, first of all, put an end to the kingdom of Judah, and then destroy the Ammonites (vers. 18–32). The prophecy divides itself accordingly into three parts : viz. (1) the prediction of the destruction of the kingdom of Judah ; (2) the explanation of this prediction by the threat that the sword of the Lord will smite all the inhabitants of Judah, which threat is divisible into three sections, ch. xxi. 1–7, 8–13, and 14–17 ; (3) the application of what is said with regard to the sword to Nebuchadnezzar's expedition against Jerusalem and the Ammonites, which may also be divided into three sections,—viz. (*a*) the general announcement of Nebuchadnezzar's design (vers. 18–23) and its execution ; (*b*) by his expedition against Jerusalem, to destroy the kingdom of Judah (vers. 24–27) ; and (*c*) by his expedition against the Ammonites (vers. 28–32).—The first four or five verses are taken by many in connection with chap. xx. ; and Kliefoth still maintains that they should be separated from what follows, and attached to that chapter as a second word of God. But neither ch. xx. 49 nor the formula in ch. xxi. 1, "the word of Jehovah came to me," warrants our separating the parabolic prediction in ch. xx. 45–48 from the interpretation in vers. 1–17. And the third part is also connected with what precedes, so as to form one single discourse, by the allusion to the sword in vers. 19 and 28, and by the fact that the figure of the fire is resumed in vers. 31 and 32. And there is all the less ground for taking the formula, " and the word of Jehovah came to me," as determining the division of the several portions in this particular instance, from the circumstance that the section (vers. 1–17) in which it occurs both at the commencement and in the middle (vers. 1 and 8), is obviously divided into the minor sections or turns by the threefold occurrence of the verb וְהִנָּבֵא (" and prophesy : vers. 2, 9, and 14).

Chap. xx. 45–49. The burning forest.—Ver. 45. *And the word of Jehovah came to me, saying,* Ver. 46. *Son of man, direct thy face toward the south, and trickle down towards the south, and prophesy concerning the forest of the field in the south land;* Ver. 47. *And say to the forest of the south land, Hear the word of Jehovah; Thus saith the Lord Jehovah, Behold, I kindle a fire in thee, which will consume in thee every green tree, and every dry tree: the blazing flame will not be extinguished, and all faces from the south to the north will be burned thereby.* Ver. 48. *And all flesh shall see that I, Jehovah, have kindled it: it shall not be extinguished.* Ver. 49. *And I said, Ah, Lord Jehovah! they say of me, Does he not speak in parables?*—The prophet is to turn his face toward the south, and prophesy concerning the forest of the field there. הַטֵּף is used for prophesying, as in Amos vii. 16 and Mic. ii. 6, 11. The distinction between the three epithets applied to the south is the following: תֵּימָן is literally that which lies on the right hand, hence the south is a particular quarter of the heavens; דָּרוֹם, which only occurs in Ezekiel and Ecclesiastes, with the exception of Deut. xxxiii. 23 and Job xxxvii. 17, is derived from דָּרַר, to shine or emit streams of light, and probably signifies the brilliant quarter; נֶגֶב, the dry, parched land, is a standing epithet for the southern district of Palestine and the land of Judah (see the comm. on Josh. xv. 21).—The forest of the field in the south is a figure denoting the kingdom of Judah (נֶגֶב is in apposition to הַשָּׂדֶה, and is appended to it as a more precise definition). שָׂדֶה is not used here for a field, as distinguished from a city or a garden; but for the fields in the sense of country or territory, as in Gen. xiv. 7 and xxxii. 3. In ver. 47, יַעַר הַנֶּגֶב, forest of the south land, is the expression applied to the same object (הַנֶּגֶב, with the article, is a geographical term for the southern portion of Palestine). The forest is a figure signifying the population, or the mass of people. Individual men are trees. The green tree is a figurative representation of the righteous man, and the dry tree of the ungodly (ver. 3, compare Luke xxiii. 31). The fire which Jehovah kindles is the fire of war. The combination of the synonyms לֶהָבָת שַׁלְהֶבֶת, flame of the flaming brightness, serves to strengthen the expression, and is equivalent to the strongest possible flame, the blazing fire. כָּל־פָּנִים, all faces are not human faces or persons, in which case the prophet would have dropped the figure; but *pânim* denotes generally the outside of things, which is the first to feel the force of the flame. "All the faces" of the forest are every single thing in the forest, which is caught at once by the flame. In ver. 4, *kŏl-pânim* (all faces) is interpreted by *kŏl-bâsar* (all flesh). From south to north, *i.e.* through the whole length of the land. From the terrible fierceness of the fire, which cannot be extinguished, every one will know that God has kindled it, that it has been sent in judgment. The words of the prophet himself, in ch. xx. 49, presuppose that he has uttered these parabolic words in the hearing of the people, and that they have ridiculed them as obscure (*mâshâl* is used here in the sense of obscure language, words difficult to understand, as παραβολή also is in Matt. xiii. 10). At the same time, it contains within itself a request that they may be explained. This request is granted; and the simile is first of all interpreted in ch. xxi. 1–7, and then still further expanded in vers. 8 sqq.

Chap. xxi. 1–7. The sword of the Lord and its disastrous effects.—Ver. 1. *And the word of Jehovah came to me, saying,* Ver. 2. *Son of man, set thy face toward Jerusalem, and trickle over the holy places, and prophesy over the land of Israel,* Ver. 3. *And say to the land of Israel, Thus saith Jehovah, Behold, I will deal with thee, and will draw my sword out of its scabbard, and cut off from thee the righteous and the wicked.* Ver. 4. *Because I will cut off from thee the righteous and the wicked, therefore shall my sword go forth from its scabbard against all flesh from south to north.* Ver. 5. *And all flesh shall know that I, Jehovah, have drawn my sword out of its scabbard: it shall not return again.* Ver. 6. *And thou, son of man, sigh! so that the hips break; and with bitter pain sigh before their eyes!* Ver. 7. *And when they say to thee, Wherefore dost thou sigh? say, Because of a report that it is coming; and every heart will sink, and all hands become powerless, and every spirit will become dull, and all knees turn into water: Behold, it cometh, and will happen, is the saying of the Lord Jehovah.*—In the preceding parable, the expression "forest of the field in the south," or "forest of the south-land," was enigmatical. This is explained to signify Jerusalem with its holy places (מִקְדָּשִׁים, see comm. on ch. vii. 24), and the land of Israel, *i.e.* the kingdom of Judah. In accordance with this, the fire kindled by the Lord is interpreted as being the sword of the Lord. It is true that this is a figurative expression; but it is commonly used for war, which brings with it devastation and death, and would be generally intelligible. The sword will cut off both righteous and wicked. This applies to the outer side of the judgment, inasmuch as both good and bad fall in war. This is the only aspect brought into prominence here, since the great purpose was to alarm the sinners, who were boasting of their security; but the distinction between the two, as described in ch. ix. 4 sqq., is not therefore to be regarded as no longer existing. This sword will not return, *sc.* into the scabbard, till it has accomplished the result predicted in ver. 3 (cf. 2 Sam. i. 22; Isa. lv. 11). As Tremellius has aptly observed upon this passage, "the last slaughter is contrasted with the former ones, in which, after the people had been chastened for a time, the sword was returned to its scabbard again." In order to depict the terrors of this judgment before the eyes of the people, the prophet is commanded to groan before their eyes in the most painful way possible (vers. 6 sqq.). בְּשִׁבְרוֹן מָתְנַיִם, with breaking of the hips, *i.e.* with pain sufficient to break the hips, the seat of strength in man (compare Nah. ii. 11; Isa. xxi. 3). מְרִירוּת, bitterness, *i.e.* bitter anguish. The reason which he is to assign to the questioners for this sighing is "on account of the report that is coming,"—an *antiptosis* for "on account of the coming report" (cf. Gen. i. 4, etc.). The report comes when the substance of it is realized. The reference is to the report of the sword of the Lord,—that is to say, of the approach of the Chaldeans to destroy Jerusalem and the kingdom of

Judah. The impression which this disclosure will make upon the hearers will be perfectly paralyzing (ver. 7*b*). All courage and strength for offering resistance will be crippled and broken. נָמֵס כָּל־לֵב (cf. Nah. ii. 11) is strengthened by כֵּהֲתָה כָל־רוּחַ, every spirit will become dull, so that no one will know what counsel to give. כָּל־בִּרְכַּיִם תֵּלַכְנָה וגו׳ corresponds to רָפוּ כָל־יָדַיִם (cf. ch. vii. 17). The threat is strengthened by the words, "behold, it cometh, and will take place." The subject is שְׁמוּעָה, the report, *i.e.* the substance of the report.—This threat is more fully expanded in vers. 8–17; vers. 8–13 corresponding to vers. 1–5, and vers. 14–17 to vers. 6, 7.

Vers. 8–17. *The sword is sharpened for slaying.*—Ver. 8. *And the word of Jehovah came to me, saying,* Ver. 9. *Son of man, prophesy, and say, Thus saith Jehovah, A sword, a sword sharpened and also polished:* Ver. 10. *That it may effect a slaughter is it sharpened; that it may flash is it polished: or shall we rejoice (saying), the sceptre of my son despiseth all wood?* Ver. 11. *But it has been given to be polished, to take it in the hand; it is sharpened, the sword, and it is polished, to give it into the hand of the slayer.* Ver. 12. *Cry and howl, son of man, for it goeth over my people, it goeth over all the princes of Israel: they have fallen by the sword along with my people: therefore smite upon the thigh.* Ver. 13. *For the trial is made, and what if the despising sceptre shall not come? is the saying of the Lord Jehovah.* Ver. 14. *And thou, son of man, prophesy and smite the hands together, and the sword shall double itself into threefold, the sword of the pierced: it is the sword of a pierced one, of the great one, which encircles them.* Ver. 15. *That the heart may be dissolved, and stumbling-blocks may be multiplied, I have set the drawing of the sword against all their gates: Alas! it is made into flashing, drawn for slaying.* Ver. 16. *Gather thyself up to the right hand, turn to the left, whithersoever thine edge is intended.* Ver. 17. *And I also will smite my hands together, and quiet my wrath: I, Jehovah, have spoken it.*—The description of the sword is thrown into a lyrical form (vers. 8–13),—a kind of sword-song, commemorating the terrible devastation to be effected by the sword of the Lord. The repetition of חֶרֶב in ver. 9 is emphatic. הוּחַדָּה is the perfect *Hophal* of חָדַד, to sharpen. מְרוּטָה is the passive participle of מָרַט, to polish; מֹרָטָּה (ver. 10), the participle *Pual*, with מ dropped, and *Dagesh euphon.* הֱיֵה, a rare form of the infinitive for הֱיוֹת. The polishing gives to the sword a flashing brilliancy, which renders the sharpness of its edge still more terrible. The very obscure words, אוֹ נָשִׂישׂ וגו׳, I agree with Schmieder and Kliefoth in regarding as a protest, interposed by the prophet in the name of the people against the divine threat of the sword of vengeance, on the ground of the promises which had been given to the tribe of Judah. אוֹ, or perhaps; introducing an opposite case, or an exception to what has been said. The words שֵׁבֶט בְּנִי וגו׳ are to be taken as an objection, so that לֵאמֹר is to be supplied in thought. The objection is taken from the promise given in Jacob's blessing to the tribe of Judah: "the sceptre will not depart from Judah" (Gen. xlix. 10). שֵׁבֶט בְּנִי points unquestionably to this. בְּנִי is taken from ver. 9, where the patriarch addresses Judah, whom he compares to a young lion, as בְּנִי. Consequently the sceptre of my son is the command which the patriarch holds out to view before the tribe of Judah. This sceptre despises all wood, *i.e.* every other ruler's staff, as bad wood. This view is not rendered a doubtful one by the fact that שֵׁבֶט is construed as a feminine here, whereas it is construed as a masculine in every other case; for this construction is unquestionable in ver. 7 (12), and has many analogies in its favour. All the other explanations that have been proposed are hardly worth mentioning, to say nothing of refuting, as they amount to nothing more than arbitrary conjectures; whereas the assumption that the words are to be explained from Gen. xlix. 10 is naturally suggested by the unquestionable allusion to the prophecy in that passage, which we find in ver. 27 of the present chapter. וַיִּתֵּן in ver. 11 is to be taken adversatively, " but he gave it (the sword) to be sharpened." The subject to וַיְחַד is not Jehovah, but is indefinite, "one" (*man*, Angl. they), although it is actually God who has prepared the sword for the slaughter of Israel. The train of thought is the following: Do not think we have no reason to fear the sharply-ground sword of Jehovah, because Judah has received the promise that the sceptre shall not depart from it; and this promise will certainly be fulfilled, and Judah be victorious over every hostile power. The promise will not help you in this instance. The sword is given to be ground, not that it may be put into the scabbard, but that it may be taken in the hand by a slayer, and smite all the people and all its princes. In the phrase חֶרֶב הוּחַדָּה הִיא, חֶרֶב is in apposition to the subject הִיא, and is introduced to give emphasis to the words. It is not till ver. 19 that it is stated who the slayer is; but the hearers of the prophecy could be in no doubt. Consequently—this is the connection with ver. 12— there is no ground for rejoicing from a feeling of security and pride, but rather an occasion for painful lamentation. This is the meaning contained in the command to the prophet to cry and howl. For the sword will come upon the nation and its princes. It is the simplest rendering to take הִיא as referring to הָיָה בְ חֶרֶב, to be at a person, to fasten to him, to come upon him, as in 1 Sam. xxiv. 14; 2 Sam. xxiv. 17. מְגוּרֵי, not from נוּר, but the passive participle of מָגַר in the *Pual*, to overthrow, cast down (Ps. lxxxix. 45): "fallen by the sword have they (the princes) become, along with my people." The perfects are prophetic, representing that which will speedily take place as having already occurred.—Smiting upon the thigh is a sign of alarm and horror (Jer. xxxi. 19). בֹּחַן, perfect *Pual*, is used impersonally: the trial is made. The words allude to the victories gained already by Nebuchadnezzar, which have furnished tests of the sharpness of his sword. The question which follows וּמָה contains an *aposiopesis*: and what? Even if the despising sceptre shall not come, what will be the case then? שֵׁבֶט מֹאֶסֶת, according to ver. 10, is the sceptre of

Judah, which despises all other sceptres as bad wood. יִהְיֶה, in this instance, is not " to be," in the sense of to remain, but to become, to happen, to come (come to pass), to enter. The meaning is, if the sceptre of Judah shall not display, or prove itself to possess, the strength expected of it.—With ver. 14 the address takes a new start, for the purpose of depicting still further the operations of the sword. Smiting the hands together (smiting hand in hand) is a gesture expressive of violent emotion (cf. ch. vi. 11; Num. xxiv. 10). The sword is to double, *i.e.* multiply itself, into threefold (שְׁלִישִׁתָה, adverbial), namely, in its strength, or its edge. Of course this is not to be taken arithmetically, as it has been by Hitzig, but is a bold paradoxical statement concerning the terrible effect produced by the sword. It is not even to be understood as referring to three attacks made at different times by the Chaldeans upon Jerusalem, as many of the commentators suppose. The sword is called חֶרֶב חֲלָלִים, sword of pierced ones, because it produces the pierced or slain. The following words are rendered by Hitzig and Kliefoth: the great sword of the slain. But apart from the tautology which this occasions, the rendering can hardly be defended on grammatical grounds. For, in the first place, we cannot see why the singular חָלָל should have been chosen, when the expression was repeated, instead of the plural חֲלָלִים; and secondly, הַגָּדוֹל cannot be an adjective agreeing with חֶרֶב, for חרב is a noun of the feminine gender, and is construed here as a feminine, as הַחֹדֶרֶת clearly shows. הַגָּדוֹל is in apposition to חָלָל, " sword of a pierced man, the great one;" and the great man pierced is the king, as Ewald admits, in agreement with Hengstenberg and Hävernick. The words therefore affirm that the sword will not only slay the mass of the people, but pierce the king himself. (See also the comm. on ver. 25.)—Ver. 15a is not dependent upon what precedes, but introduces a new thought, viz. for what purpose the sword is sharpened. God has placed the flashing sword before all the gates of the Israelites, in order that (לְמַעַן, pleonastic for לְמַעַן) the heart may dissolve, the inhabitants may lose all their courage for defence, and to multiply *offendicula*, *i.e.* occasions to fall by the sword. The ἀπ. λεγ. אָבְחַת signifies the rapid motion or turning about of the sword (cf. Gen. iii. 24); אבה, related to הפך, in the *Mishna* אפך. The ἀπ. λεγ. מְעֻטָּה, fem. of מָעֻט, does not mean smooth, *i.e.* sharpened, synonymous with מָרַט, but, according to the Arabic ﺳﻞ, *eduxit e vagina gladium*, drawn (from the scabbard). In ver. 16 the sword is addressed, and commanded to smite right and left. הִתְאַחֲדִי, gather thyself up, *i.e.* turn with all thy might toward the right (Tanchum). To the verb הָשִׂימוּ it is easy to supply פָּנַיִךְ, from the context, "direct thine edge toward the left." אָנָה, whither, without an interrogative, as in Josh. ii. 5 and Neh. ii. 16. מְעָדוֹת, from יָעַד, intended, ordered; not, directed, turned. The feminine form may be accounted for from a construction *ad sensum*, the gender regulating itself according to the חֶרֶב addressed in פָּנַיִךְ. The command to the sword is strengthened by the explanation given by Jehovah in ver. 17, that He also (like the prophet, ver. 14) will smite His hands together and cool His wrath upon them (cf. ch. v. 13).

Vers. 18-22. The sword of the king of Babylon will smite Jerusalem, and then the Ammonites also.—Ver. 18. *And the word of Jehovah came to me, saying*, Ver. 19. *And thou, son of man, make to thyself two ways, that the sword of the king of Babylon may come by them; out of one land shall they both come forth, and draw a hand, at the cross road of the city do thou draw it.* Ver. 20. *Make a way that the sword may come to Rabbah of the sons of Ammon, and to Judah into fortified Jerusalem.* Ver. 21. *For the king of Babylon is stopping at the cross road, at the parting of the two ways, to practise divination. He is shaking the arrows, inquiring of the teraphim, looking at the liver.* Ver. 22. *The divination falls to his right: Jerusalem, to set battering-rams, to open the mouth with a death-cry, to lift up the voice with a war-cry, to set battering-rams at the gates, to heap up a rampart, to build siege towers.*—After the picture of the terrible devastation which the sword of the Lord will produce, the last word of God in this prophecy answers the questions, in whose hand Jehovah will place His sword, and whom it will smite. The slayer into whose hand the sharpened sword is given (ver. 11) is the king of Babylon, and it will smite not only Judah, but the Ammonites also. Jerusalem and Judah will be the first to fall, and then the arch-enemy of the covenant nation, namely Ammon, will succumb to the strokes of the sword of Jehovah, in order that the embittered enemies of the Lord and His people may learn that the fall of Jerusalem is not, as they fancy, a proof of the impotence, but rather of the omnipotence, of its God. In this way does our prophecy expand into a prediction of the judgment which will fall upon the whole of the world in hostility to God. For it is only as the arch-enemies of the kingdom of God that the Ammonites come into consideration here. The parallel between Israel and the sons of Ammon is carried out in such a way as to give constant prominence to the distinction between them. Jerusalem will fall, the ancient theocracy will be destroyed till he shall come who will restore the right (vers. 26 and 27). Ammon, on the other hand, will perish, and not a trace be left (vers. 31, 32).— This prediction is exhibited to the eye by means of a sign. The prophet is to make two ways, *i.e.* to prepare a sketch representing a road leading from a country, viz. Babylon, and dividing at a certain spot into two roads, one of which leads to Rabbath-Ammon, the capital of the kingdom of the Ammonites, the other to Judah, into Jerusalem. He is to draw the ways for the coming (לָבוֹא) of the sword of the king of Babylon. At the fork of the road he is to engrave a hand, יָד, *i.e.* an index. בָּרָא signifies in the *Piel* to cut away (Josh. xvii. 15, 18), to dig or hew (Ezek. xxiii. 47), here to engrave written characters in hard material. The selection of this word shows that Ezekiel was to sketch the ways upon some hard material, probably a brick or tile (cf. ch. iv. 1). יָד does not mean *locus spatium*, but a hand, *i.e.* an index. רֹאשׁ דֶּרֶךְ, the beginning of the road, *i.e.*

the fork of the road (ch. xvi. 25), is explained in ver. 21, where it is called אֵם הַדֶּרֶךְ, mother of the road, inasmuch as the roads start from the point of separation, and רֹאשׁ שְׁנֵי הַדְּרָכִים, beginning of the two roads. דֶּרֶךְ עִיר, the road to a city. For *Rabbath-Ammon*, which is preserved in the ruins of *Ammân*, on the Upper Jabbok (*Nahr Ammân*), see the comm. on Deut. iii. 11. The road to Judah is still more precisely defined by בִּירוּשָׁלַםִ בְּצוּרָה, into fortified Jerusalem, because the conquest of Jerusalem was the purpose of Nebuchadnezzar's expedition. The omission of the article before בְּצוּרָה may be explained from the nature of the participle, in which, even in prose, the article may be left out after a definite noun (cf. Ewald, § 335*a*). The drawing is explained in vers. 21 and 22. The king of Babylon is halting (עָמַד, to stand still, stop) to consult his oracles, and inquire which of the two roads he is to take. קְסָם קֶסֶם, to take in hand, or practise divination. In order that he may proceed safely, he avails himself of all the means of divination at his command. He shakes the arrows (more strictly, the quiver with the arrows). On the practice itself Jerome writes as follows: "He consults the oracle according to the custom of his nation, putting his arrows into a quiver, and mixing them together, with the names of individuals inscribed or stamped upon them, to see whose arrow will come out, and which state shall be first attacked."[1] He consults the *Teraphim*, or Penates, worshipped as oracular deities and gods of good fortune (see the comm. on Gen. xxxi. 19 and my *Biblical Archaeology*, § 90). Nothing is known concerning the way in which these deities were consulted and gave their oracles. He examines the liver. The practice of ἡπατο-

---

[1] The arrow-lot (*Belomantie*) of the ancient Greeks (Homer, *Il.* iii. 324, vii. 182, 183) was similar to this; also that of the ancient Arabs (*vid.* Pococke, *Specim. hist. Arab.* pp. 327 sqq., and the passages from Nuweiri quoted by Reiske, *Samml. einiger Arab. Sprichwörter von den Stecken oder Stäben*, p. 21). Another kind, in which the lot was obtained by shooting off the arrows, was common according to the *Fihrist el Ulum* of En-Nedim among the Hananian Ssabians (see Chwolsohn, *Ssabier*, ii. pp. 26 and 119, 200.

σκοπία, *extispicium*, in which signs of good or bad luck, of the success or failure of any enterprise, were obtained from the peculiar condition of the liver of the sacrificial animals, was a species of divination to which great importance was attached by both the Babylonians (*vid.* Diod. Sic. ii. 29) and the Romans (Cicero, *de divin.* vi. 13), and of which traces were found, according to *Barhebr. Chron.* p. 125, as late as the eighth century of the Christian era among the Ssabians of Haran.—The divination resulted in a decision for Jerusalem. בִּימִינוֹ הָיָה is not to be translated "in his right hand was," but "into his right hand there came." הָיָה: ἐγένετο (LXX.), נְפִיל (Chald.), קֶסֶם does not mean lot (Ges.), but soothsaying, divination. יְרוּשָׁלַיִם is connected with this in the form of a noun in apposition: the divination which indicated Jerusalem. The right hand is the more important of the two. The meaning of the words cannot be more precisely defined, because we are not acquainted with the kind of divination referred to; even if we were to take the words as simply relating to the arrow in this sense, that an arrow with the inscription "Jerusalem" came into his right hand, and thus furnished the decision, which was afterwards confirmed by consulting the Teraphim and examining the liver. But the circumstance itself, that is to say, the fact that the divination coincided with the purpose of God, must not be taken, as Hävernick supposes, as suggesting a point of contact between Hebraism and the soothsaying of heathenism, which was peculiar to Ezekiel or to the time of the captivity. All that is proved by this fact is, that even heathenism is subject to the rule and guidance of Almighty God, and is made subservient to the accomplishment of the plans of both His kingdom and His salvation. In the words, to set battering rams, etc., the substance of the oracle obtained by Nebuchadnezzar is more minutely given. It is a double one, showing what he is to do: viz. (1) to set battering rams, *i.e.* to proceed to the siege of Jerusalem, as still further described in the last portion of the verse (ch. iv. 2); and (2) to raise the war-cry for storming the

CHAP. XXI. 23–27.

city, that is to say, to take it by storm. The two clauses לִפְתֹּחַ וגו׳ and לְהָרִים וגו׳ are synonymous; they are not "pure tautology," however, as Hitzig affirms, but are chosen for the purpose of giving greater emphasis to the thought. The expression בְּרֶצַח creates some difficulty, inasmuch as the phrase "*ut aperiat os in caede*" (Vulg.), to open the mouth in murder or ruin, *i.e.* to put to death or lay in ruins, is a very striking one, and could hardly be justified as an "energetic expression for the battle-cry" (Hävernick). ב does not mean "to," and cannot indicate the intention, all the less because בְּרֶצַח is parallel to בִּתְרוּעָה, where תרועה is that in which the raising of the voice expresses itself. There is nothing left then but to take רֶצַח in the sense of field- or war-cry, and to derive this meaning either from רָצַח or, *per metathesin*, from צָרַח.

Vers. 23–27. This announcement will appear to the Judaeans, indeed, to be a deceptive divination, but nevertheless it will be verified.—Ver. 23. *And it is like deceptive divination in their eyes; sacred oaths are theirs* (lit. to them); *but he brings the iniquity to remembrance, that they may be taken.* Ver. 24. *Therefore thus saith the Lord Jehovah, Because ye bring your iniquity to remembrance, in that your offences are made manifest, so that your sins appear in all your deeds, because ye are remembered ye shall be taken with the hand.* Ver. 25. *And thou pierced one, sinner, prince of Israel, whose day is come at the time of the final transgression,* Ver. 26. *Thus saith the Lord Jehovah, The turban will be removed, the crown taken off. This is not this; the low will be lifted up, and the lofty lowered.* Ver. 27. *Overthrown, overthrown, overthrown will I make it; even this shall not be, till He cometh, to whom is the right, to Him do I give it.*—In ver. 23 (28), לָהֶם, which is more precisely defined by בְּעֵינֵיהֶם, refers to the Israelites, *i.e.* the Judaeans. This also applies to the following לָהֶם, which cannot possibly be taken as referring to a different subject, say, for example, the Chaldeans. It is evident, therefore, that it is impossible to sustain the rendering given in Gesenius' *Thesaurus* (*s.v.*) to the obscure words שְׁבֻעֵי שְׁבֻעוֹת, viz. *qui juramenta jurarunt eis* (sc. Chaldaeis), which Maurer has modified and expounded thus: "they will not fear these auguries; they will swear oaths to them (the Chaldeans), that is to say, according to their usual custom, these truce-breakers will take fresh oaths, hoping that the Chaldeans will be conciliated thereby." Moreover, the thought itself is an unsuitable one, inasmuch as "the defiant attitude of confidence with which they looked such awfully threatening danger in the face must have had some other ground than a reliance upon false oaths and Chaldean credulity" (Hävernick). The common explanation, which Rosenmüller and Kliefoth uphold, is, "because the Chaldeans are sworn allies, sworn confederates of theirs;" or as Kliefoth explains it, "on account of the oath of fealty or vassalage sworn by Zedekiah to Nebuchadnezzar, they have sworn confederates in the Chaldeans, and relying upon this, they are confident that they have no hostile attack to fear from them." But this is altogether untenable, not only because it is perfectly arbitrary to supply "the Chaldeans," but still more for the reason adduced by Maurer. "How," he justly asks, "could the Judaeans despise these auguries *because* the Chaldeans were bound to them by an oath when they themselves had broken faith? When a treaty has been violated by one party, is not the other released from his oath?" We therefore adopt the same explanation as Hävernick: "oaths of oaths are theirs (to them), *i.e.* the most sacred oaths are (made) to them, namely, by God." They rely upon that which God has solemnly sworn to them, without considering upon what this promise was conditional, namely, upon a faithful observance on their part of the commandments of God. For the fact itself, compare ch. xx. 42, and such passages as Ps. cv. 9 sqq., etc. The form שְׁבֻעֵי by the side of שְׁבֻעוֹת may be explained in a very simple way from the relation of the construct state, *i.e.* from the endeavour to secure an obvious form for the construct state, and cannot in any case furnish a well-founded argument against the correctness of our explanation. As Ezekiel uses נְפָשִׁים for נְפָשׁוֹת in ch.

xiii. 20, he may also have formed שְׁבָעִים (שְׁבֻעֵי) by the side of שְׁבֻעוֹת.—As they rely upon the promises of God without reflecting upon their own breach of covenant, God will bring their sin to remembrance through His judgment. וְהוּא is Jehovah, upon whose oaths they rely. עָוֹן must not be restricted to Zedekiah's breach of covenant, since ver. 24 clearly shows that it is the wrong-doing of Judah generally. לְהִתָּפֵשׂ in ver. 24 (29) is also to be understood of the whole nation, which is to be taken and punished by the king of Babylon. For ver. 24 (29) introduces the reason for the statement made in the last clause of ver. 23 (28). God must put the people in remembrance of their iniquity by inflicting punishment, because they have called it to remembrance by sins committed without any shame, and thereby have, so to speak, compelled God to remember them, and to cause the sinners to be grasped by the hand of the slayer. הִזְכִּיר עָוֹן is used in ver. 24 (29) in a different sense from ver. 23 (28), and is therefore explained by בְּהִגָּלוֹת וגו'. בַּכַּף, which is indefinite in itself, points back to יַד הוֹרֵג in ver. 11 (16), and receives from that its more exact definition.

With ver. 25 the address turns to the chief sinner, the godless King Zedekiah, who was bringing the judgment of destruction upon the kingdom by his faithless breach of oath. The words חָלָל, רָשָׁע, and נְשִׂיא יִשׂ' are *asyndeta*, co-ordinate to one another. חָלָל does not mean profane or infamous (βέβηλε, LXX.), but simply pierced, slain. This meaning is to be retained here. This is demanded not only by the fixed usage of the language, but also by the relation in which חָלָל stands both to ver. 14 and to חַלְלֵי רְשָׁעִים in ver. 29 (34). It is true that Zedekiah was not pierced by the sword either at that time or afterwards, but was simply blinded and led in captivity to Babylon, where he died. But all that follows from this is, that חָלָל is used here in a figurative sense, given up to the sword, *i.e.* to death; and Zedekiah is so designated for the purpose of announcing in a more energetic manner the certainty of his fate. The selection of the term חָלָל is the more natural, because throughout the whole prophecy the description of the judgment takes its character from the figure of the sword of Jehovah. As God does not literally wield a sword, so חָלָל is no proof of actual slaying with the sword. יוֹמוֹ, his day, is the day of his destruction (cf. 1 Sam. xxvi. 10), or of the judgment upon him. The time of the final transgression is not the time when the transgression reaches its end, *i.e.* its completion, but the time when the wickedness brings the end, *i.e.* destruction (cf. ch. xxxv. 5, and for קֵץ in this sense, ch. vii. 2, 3). The fact that the end, the destruction, is come, *i.e.* is close at hand, is announced in ver. 26 to the prince, and in his person to the whole nation. If we understand the connection in this way, which is naturally suggested by ver. 25*b*, we get rid of the objection, which led Kliefoth to question the fact that it is the king who is addressed in ver. 25*a*, and to take the words as collective, "ye slaughtered sinners, princes of Israel," and to understand them as referring to the entire body of rulers, including the priests,—an explanation that is completely upset by the words וְנָשִׂיא . . . אַתָּה (thou . . . prince), which are so entirely opposed to the collective view. Again, the remark that "what follows in ver. 26, viz. the statement to be made to the נָשִׂיא, has really nothing to do with him, since the sweeping away of the priesthood did not affect Zedekiah personally" (Kliefoth), is neither correct nor conclusive. For ver. 26 contains an announcement not only of the abrogation of the priesthood, but also of the destruction of the kingdom, which did affect Zedekiah both directly and personally. Moreover, we must not isolate the king addressed, even as an individual, from the position which he occupied, or, at any rate, which he ought to have occupied as a theocratic monarch, so as to be able to say that the abrogation of the priesthood did not affect him. The priesthood was one of the fundamental pillars of the theocracy, the removal of which would necessarily be followed by the collapse of the divine state, and therefore by the destruction of the monarchy. Hence it is that the abolition of the priesthood is mentioned first. The infinitives absolute (not imperatives) הָסִיר and הָרִים are selected for the purpose of expressing the truth in the most emphatic manner; and the verbs are synonymous. הָרִים, to lift up, *i.e.* not to elevate, but to take away, to abolish, as in Isa. lvii. 14; Dan. viii. 11. מִצְנֶפֶת does not mean the royal diadem, like צָנִיף in Isa. lxii. 3, but the tiara of the high priest, as it does in every instance in the Pentateuch, from which Ezekiel has taken the word. הָעֲטָרָה, the king's crown. The diadem of the priest and the regal crown are the insignia of the offices of high priest and king; and consequently their removal is the abolition of both high-priesthood and monarchy. These words contain the sentence of death upon the theocracy, of which the Aaronic priesthood and the Davidic monarchy constituted the foundations.—They predict not merely a temporary, but a complete abolition of both offices and dignities; and their fulfilment took place when the kingdom of Judah was destroyed by the king of Babylon. The earthly sovereignty of the house of David was not restored again after the captivity; and the high-priesthood of the restoration, like the second temple, was only a shadowy outline of the glory and essential features of the high-priesthood of Aaron. As the ark with the Shechinah, or the gracious presence of God, was wanting in the temple of Zerubbabel; so were the Urim and Thummim wanting to the high-priesthood, and these were the only means by which the high priest could really carry out the mediation between the Lord and the people. זֹאת לֹא זֹאת (this is not this) does not refer to the tiara (mitre) and crown. זֹאת is neuter, and therefore construed with the masculine הָיָה. This (mitre and crown) will not be this (הָיָה is prophetic), *i.e.* it will not continue, it will be all over with it (Hävernick, Maurer, and Kliefoth). To this there is appended the further thought, that a general inversion of things will take place. This is the meaning of the words—the low will be lifted up, and the lofty lowered. הַגְבֵּהַּ and הַשְׁפִּיל are infinitives, and are chosen in the same sense as in the first hemistich. The form הַשְׁפָלָה, with ה

without the tone, is masculine; the ־ָה probably serving merely to give greater fulness to the form, and to make it correspond more nearly to הַגְּבֹהַ.[1]—This general thought is expressed still more definitely in ver. 27a. עַוָּה, which is repeated twice to give greater emphasis to the thought, is a noun derived from עָוָה, inversion, overthrow; and the suffix in אֲשִׂימֶנָּה points back to זֹאת in ver. 26 (31). This, the existing state, the high-priesthood and the monarchy, will I make into destruction, or utterly overthrow. But the following זֹאת cannot also refer to the tiara and crown, as Kliefoth supposes, on account of the גַּם which precedes it. This shows that זֹאת relates to the thing last mentioned. Even this, the overthrow, shall have no durability; or, as Tanch. has correctly expressed it, *neque haec conditio erit durabilis*. The following עַד־בֹּא attaches itself not so much to this last clause as to the main thought: overthrow upon overthrow will ensue. The thought is this: "nowhere is there rest, nowhere security; all things are in a state of flux till the coming of the great Restorer and Prince of peace" (Hengstenberg). It is generally acknowledged that the words עַד־בֹּא אֲשֶׁר־לוֹ הַמִּשְׁפָּט contain an allusion to Gen. xlix. 10, עַד כִּי יָבֹא שִׁילֹה; and it is only by a false interpretation of the preceding clauses, wrung from the words by an arbitrary alteration of the text, that Hitzig is able to set this connection aside. At

---

[1] Hitzig has given a most preposterous exposition of this verse. Taking the words הָסִיר and הָרִים as antithetical, in the sense of removing and exalting or sustaining in an exalted position, and regarding the clauses as questions signifying, "Shall the high-priesthood be abolished, and the real dignity, on the contrary, remain untouched?" he finds the answer to these questions in the words זֹאת לֹא זֹאת (this, not this). They contain, in his opinion, an affirmation of the former and a negation of the latter. But he does not tell us how זֹאת לֹא זֹאת without a verb can possibly mean, "the former (the abrogation of the high-priesthood) will take place, but the latter (the exaltation of the monarchy) will not occur." And, finally, the last clause, "the low shall be lifted up," etc., is said to contain simply a watchword, which is not for the time being to be followed by any result. Such trifling needs no refutation. We simply observe, therefore, that there is no ground for the assertion, that הָרִים without כֵּן cannot possibly signify to abolish.

the same time, אֲשֶׁר־לוֹ הַמִּשְׁפָּט is of course not to be taken as a philological explanation of the word שִׁילֹה, but is simply a theological interpretation of the patriarchal prophecy, with direct reference to the predicted destruction of the existing relations in consequence of the ungodliness and unrighteousness of the leaders of the theocracy up to that time. הַמִּשְׁפָּט is not the rightful claim to the mitre and crown, but right in an objective sense, as belonging to God (Deut. i. 17), and entrusted by God to the earthly government as His representative. He then, to whom this right belongs, and to whom God will give it, is the Messiah, of whom the prophets from the times of David onwards have prophesied as the founder and restorer of perfect right on earth (cf. Ps. lxxii.; Isa. ix. 6, xlii. 1; Jer. xxiii. 5, xxxiii. 17). The suffix attached to נְתַתִּיו is not a dative, but an accusative, referring to מִשְׁפָּט (cf. Ps. lxxii. 1). There was no necessity to mention the person again to whom God would give the right, as He had already been designated in the previous expression אֲשֶׁר לוֹ.

Vers. 28–32. *Overthrow of the Ammonites.*—Ver. 28. *And thou, son of man, prophesy and say, Thus saith the Lord Jehovah, concerning the sons of Ammon, and concerning their scorn, sword, sword, drawn to slay, polished, that it may devour, that it may flash!* Ver. 29. *While they prophesy deceit to thee, while they divine lying to thee, it shall lay thee by the necks of the sinners slain, whose day cometh at the time of the final transgression.* Ver. 30. *Put it in its scabbard again. At the place where thou wast created, in the land of thy birth will I judge thee,* Ver. 31. *And pour out my anger upon thee, kindle the fire of my wrath against thee, and give thee into the hand of foolish men, of smiths of destruction.* Ver. 32. *Thou shalt be for the fire to devour; thy blood shall remain in the midst of the land; thou shalt be remembered no more; for I Jehovah have spoken it.*— As Judah in Jerusalem will fall by the sword of the king of Babylon, contrary to all expectation; so will the Ammonites be punished for their scorn with utter extermination. חֶרְפָּה is scorn at the overthrow of Israel (cf. ch. xxv. 3, 6, and Zeph. ii. 8). The sword is already drawn against them. פְּתוּחָה, taken out of the scabbard, as in Ps. xxxvii. 14. לְטֶבַח is to be connected with פְּתוּחָה, notwithstanding the accents, and לְהָכִיל with מְרוּטָה. This is required by the correspondence of the clauses. הָכִיל is regarded as a derivative of כּוּל by Ewald and others, in the sense of *ad sustinendum*, according to capacity, *i.e.* as much as possible. But the adverbial rendering is opposed to the context, and cannot be sustained from ch. xxiii. 32. Moreover, כּוּל, to contain, is applicable enough to goblets and other vessels, but not to a sword. Hitzig therefore explains it from the Arabic كَلَّ, to blunt (*sc.* the eyes), *i.e.* to blind. But this is open to the objection that the form הָכִיל points to the verb כּוּל rather than כָּלַל; and also to a still greater one,—namely, that there is nothing in the Hebrew usage to suggest the use of כלל in such a sense as this, and even if it were used in the sense of blunting, it would be perfectly arbitrary to supply עֵינַיִם; and lastly, that even the flashing of the sword does not suggest the idea of blinding, but is intended to heighten the terror occasioned by the sharpness of the sword. We therefore adhere to the derivation of הָכִיל from אָכַל, and regard it as a defective form for הַאֲכִיל, like אֹמְרוּ for תֹּאמְרוּ in 2 Sam. xix. 14, יָהֵל as syncopated form for יַאֲהֵל (Isa. xiii. 20), and וַתַּחֲזִי for וַתֹּאחֲזִי in 2 Sam. xx. 9; literally, to cause it to eat or devour, *i.e.* to make it fit for the work of devouring. לְמַעַן בָּרָק, literally, for the sake of the lightning (flash) that shall issue therefrom (cf. ver. 10).—In ver. 29 (34), לָתֵת (to lay, or place) is also dependent upon חֶרֶב פְּתוּחָה, drawn to lay thee; so that the first half of the verse is inserted as a parenthesis, either to indicate the occasion for bringing the sword into the land (Hitzig), or to introduce an attendant circumstance, according to the sense in which the ב in בַּחֲזוֹת is taken. The parenthetical clause is understood by most of the commentators as referring to deceptive oracles of Ammonitish soothsayers, which either determined the policy of Ammon, as Hitzig supposes (cf. Jer. xxvii. 9, 10), or inspired the Ammonites with confidence, that they had nothing to fear from the Chaldeans. Kliefoth, on the other hand, refers the words to the oracles consulted by Nebuchadnezzar, according to ver. 23. " These oracles, which directed the king not to march against the Ammonites, but against Jerusalem, proved themselves, according to ver. 29, to be deceptive prophesying to the Ammonites, inasmuch as they also afterwards fell by the sword ; just as, according to ver. 23, they proved themselves to be genuine so far as the Israelites were concerned, inasmuch as they were really the first to be smitten." This view is a very plausible one, if it only answered in any degree to the words. But it is hard to believe that the words, " while it (one) prophesies falsehood to thee," are meant to be equivalent to " while its prophecy proves itself to be false to thee." Moreover, Nebuchadnezzar did not give the Ammonites any oracle, either false or true, by the circumstance that his divination at the cross-road led him to decide in favour of the march to Jerusalem ; for all that he did in consequence was to postpone his designs upon the Ammonites, but not to relinquish them. We cannot understand the words in any other sense, therefore, than as relating to oracles, which the Ammonites received from soothsayers of their own.—Hitzig takes offence at the expression, " that it (the sword) may lay thee by (to) the necks of the sinners slain," because *colla* cannot stand for *corpora decollata*, and consequently proposes to alter אוֹתָךְ into אוֹתָהּ, to put it (the sword) to the necks. But by this conjecture he gets the not less striking thought, that the sword was to be put to the necks of those already slain ; a thing which would be perfectly unmeaning, and is therefore not generally done. The sinners slain are the Judaeans who have fallen. The words point back to ver. 25, the second half of which is repeated here, and predict the same fate to the Ammonites. It is easy to supply חֶרֶב to הָשֵׁב אֶל־תַּעְרָהּ : put the sword into its scabbard again. These words can only be addressed to the Ammonites; not to the Chaldeans, as Kliefoth imagines, for the latter does not harmonize in any way with what follows, viz. in the place of thy birth will I judge thee. God does not execute the judgment independently of the Chaldeans, but through the medium of their sword. The difficulties occasioned by taking the words as referring to the Ammonites are not so great as to necessitate an alteration of the text (Hitzig), or to call for the arbitrary explanation: put it now or for the present into the scabbard (Kliefoth). The use of the masculine הָשֵׁב (with *Patach* for הָשֵׁב, as in Isa. xlii. 22), if Ammon is addressed by the side of the feminine אוֹתָהּ, may be explained in a very simple way, from the fact that the sword is carried by men, so that here the thought of the people, the warriors, is predominant, and the representation of the kingdom of the Ammonites as a woman falls into the background. The objection that the suffix in תַּעְרָהּ can only refer to the sword (of the Chaldean) mentioned in ver. 28, is more plausible than conclusive. For inasmuch as the scabbard presupposes a sword, and every sword has a scabbard, the suffix may be fully accounted for from the thing itself, as the words, "put the sword into its scabbard," would lead any hearer to think at once of the sword of the person addressed, without considering whether that particular sword had been mentioned before or not. The meaning of the words is this: every attempt to defend thyself with the sword and avert destruction will be in vain. In thine own land will God judge thee. For מְכֻרוֹתַיִךְ, see the comm. on ch. xvi. 3. This judgment is still further explained in ver. 31, where the figure of the sword is dropped, and that of the fire of the wrath of God introduced in its place. בְּאֵשׁ ... אָפִיחַ, we render: "the fire of my wrath I blow (kindle) against thee," after Isa. liv. 16, and not "with the fire ... do I blow, or snort, against thee," as others have done; because blowing with the fire is an unnatural figure, and the interpretation of the words in accordance with Isa. *l.c.* is all the more natural, that in the closing words of the verse, הָרָשֵׁי מַשְׁחִית, the allusion to that passage is indisputable, and it is only from this that the combination of the two words can be accounted for.—Different explanations have been given of בֹּעֲרִים. Some render it *ardentes*, and in accordance with Isa. xxx. 27: burning with wrath. But בָּעַר is never used in this sense. Nor can the rendering "scorching men" (Kliefoth) be sustained, for בָּעַר, to burn, only occurs in connection with things which are combustible, *e.g.* fire, pitch, coals, etc. The word must be explained from Ps. xcii. 7, "brutish," foolish, always bearing in mind that the Hebrew associated the idea of godlessness with folly, and that cruelty naturally follows in its train.—Ver. 32. Thus will Ammon perish through fire and sword, and even the memory of it be obliterated. For ver. 32*a* compare ch. xv. 4. The words, "thy blood will be בְּתוֹךְ הָאָרֶץ in the midst of the land," can hardly be understood in any other sense than "thy blood will flow over all the land." For the rendering proposed by Ewald, "remain in the midst of the earth, without thy being mentioned," like that given by Kliefoth, "thy blood will the earth drink," does not harmonize with ch. xxiv. 7, where דָּמָהּ בְּתוֹכָהּ הָיָה is affirmed of blood, which cannot penetrate into the earth, or be covered with dust. For תּוּבְרִי, see ch. xxv. 10. Ammon as the enemy of the kingdom of God will utterly perish, leaving no trace behind, and without any such hope of restoration as that held out in ver. 27 to the kingdom of Judah or the people of Israel.

CHAP. XXII. THE SINS OF JERUSALEM AND ISRAEL.

To the prediction of the judgment in ch. xxi. there is appended another description of the sins of Jerusalem and Israel, by which this judgment is occasioned. The chapter contains three words of God, which are connected together both in substance and design, viz. (1) The blood-guiltiness and idolatry of Jerusalem accelerate the coming of the days when the city will be an object of scorn to all the world (vers. 1–16);

(2) The house of Israel has become dross, and is to be melted in the fire of tribulation (vers. 17–22); (3) All ranks of the kingdom—prophets, priests, princes, and people—are thoroughly corrupt, therefore has the judgment burst upon them (vers. 23–31).

Vers. 1–16. Blood-guiltiness of Jerusalem and the burden of its sins. Vers. 1–5 contain the principal accusation relating to bloodshed and idolatry; and vers. 6–16 a further account of the sins of the people and their rulers, with a brief threatening of punishment.—Ver. 1. *And the word of Jehovah came to me, saying,* Ver. 2. *And thou, son of man, wilt thou judge? wilt thou judge the city of blood-guiltiness? then show it all its abominations,* Ver. 3. *And say, Thus saith the Lord Jehovah, City, which sheddeth blood in the midst of it, that her time may come, and maketh idols within itself for defilement.* Ver. 4. *Through thy blood which thou hast shed hast thou made thyself guilty, and through thine idols which thou hast made hast thou defiled thyself, and hast drawn thy days near, and hast come to thy years; therefore I make thee a scorn to the nations, and ridicule to all lands.* Ver. 5. *Those near and those far off from thee shall ridicule thee as defiled in name, rich in confusion.*—The expression הַתְחִישָׁפֵט וגו׳ proves this address to be a continuation of the reproof of Israel's sins, which commenced in ch. xx. 4. The epithet city of blood-guiltiness, as in ch. xxiv. 6, 9 (compare Nah. iii. 1), is explained in ver. 3. The apodosis commences with וְהוֹדַעְתָּהּ, and is continued in ver. 3 (וְאָמַרְתָּ). לָבוֹא עִתָּהּ, that her time, *i.e.* her time of punishment, may come: עִתָּהּ, like יוֹמוֹ in ch. xxi. 30. וְעָשְׂתָה is not a continuation of the infinitive לָבוֹא, but of the participle שֹׁפֶכֶת. עָלֶיהָ, of which different renderings have been given, does not mean "over itself," *i.e.* as a burden with which it has laden itself (Hävernick); still less "for itself" (Hitzig), a meaning which עַל never has, but literally "upon," *i.e.* in itself, covering the city with it, as it were. וַתִּקְרִיבִי, thou hast brought near, brought on thy days, that is to say, the days of judgment, and hast come to, arrived at thy years, *sc.* the years of visitation and punishment (cf. Jer. xi. 23). This meaning is readily supplied by the context. טְמֵאַת הַשֵּׁם, defiled, unclean with regard to the name, *i.e.* having forfeited the name of a holy city through capital crimes and other sinful abominations. מְהוּמָה is internal confusion, both moral and religious, as in Amos iii. 9 (cf. Ps. lv. 10–12).

In vers. 6–12 there follows an enumeration of a multitude of sins which had been committed in Jerusalem.—Ver. 6. *Behold, the princes of Israel are every one, according to his arm, in thee to shed blood.* Ver. 7. *Father and mother they despise in thee; toward the foreigner they act violently in the midst of thee; orphans and widows they oppress in thee.* Ver. 8. *Thou despisest my holy things, and desecratest my Sabbaths.* Ver. 9. *Slanderers are in thee to shed blood, and they eat upon the mountains in thee; they practise lewdness in thee.* Ver. 10. *They uncover the father's nakedness in thee; they ravish the defiled in her uncleanness in thee.* Ver. 11. *And one committeth abomination with his neighbour's wife, and another defileth his daughter-in-law by incest, and the third ravisheth his sister, his father's daughter in thee.* Ver. 12. *They take gifts in thee to shed blood; interest and usury thou takest, and overreachest thy neighbours with violence, and thou forgettest me, is the saying of the Lord Jehovah.*— By the repetition of the refrain, to shed blood (vers. 6, 9, and 12), the enumeration is divided into three groups of sins, which are placed in the category of blood-guiltiness by the fact that they are preceded by this sentence and the repetition of it after the form of a refrain. The first group (vers. 6–8) embraces sins which are committed in daring opposition to all the laws of morality. By the princes of Israel we are to understand primarily the profligate kings, who caused innocent persons to be put to death, such, for example, as Jehoiakim (2 Kings xxiv. 4), Manasseh (2 Kings xxi. 16), and others. The words אִישׁ לִזְרֹעוֹ הָיוּ are rendered by Hitzig and Kliefoth, they were ready to help one another; and in support of the rendering they appeal to Ps. lxxxiii. 9. But in that case אִישׁ לִזְרֹעוֹ

would stand for לְזְרוֹעַ אִישׁ, or rather for אִישׁ זְרוֹעַ לְאִישׁ,—a substitution which cannot be sustained. Nor can they be taken in the sense proposed by Hävernick, every one relying upon his arm, *i.e.* looking to physical force alone, but simply every one according to his arm, *i.e.* according to his strength or violence, are they in thee. In this case הָיוּ does not require anything to be supplied, any more than in the similar combination in ver. 9. Followed by לְמַעַן with an infinitive, it means to be there with the intention of doing anything, or making an attempt, *i.e.* to direct his efforts to a certain end. In ver. 7 it is not the princes who are the subject, but the ungodly in general. הֵקַלּוּ is the opposite of כַּבֵּד (Ex. xx. 12). In the reproofs which follow, compare Ex. xxii. 20 sqq.; Lev. xix. 13; Deut. xxiv. 14 sqq. With insolence and violence toward men there is associated contempt of all that is holy. For ver. 8*b*, see ch. xx. 13.—In the second group, vers. 9–11, in addition to slander and idolatry, the crimes of lewdness and incest are the principal sins for which the people are reproved; and here the allusion to Lev. xviii. and xix. is very obvious. The reproof of slander also points back to the prohibition in Lev. xix. 16. Slander to shed blood, refers to malicious charges and false testimony in a court of justice (*vid.* 1 Kings xxi. 10, 11). For eating upon the mountains, see ch. xviii. 6. The practice of *zimmâh* is more specifically described in vers. 10 and 11. For the thing itself, compare Lev. xviii. 7, 8, xix. 15 and 9. The threefold אִישׁ in ver. 11 does not mean every one, but one, another, and the third, as the correlative רֵעֵהוּ shows.—The third group, ver. 12, is composed of sins of covetousness. For the first clause, compare the prohibition in Ex. xxiii. 2; for the second, ch. xviii. 8, 13. The reproof finishes with forgetfulness of God, which is closely allied to covetousness.

Vers. 13–16. The Lord is enraged at such abominable doings. He will interfere, and put an end to them by scattering Judah among the heathen.—Ver. 13. *And, behold, I smite my hand because of thy gain which thou hast made, and over thy blood-*

guiltiness which is in the midst of thee. Ver. 14. *Will thy heart indeed stand firm, or will thy hands be strong for the day when I shall deal with thee? I Jehovah have spoken it, and also do it.* Ver. 15. *I will scatter thee among the nations, and disperse thee in the lands, and will utterly remove thine uncleanness from thee.* Ver. 16. *And thou wilt be desecrated through thyself before the eyes of the nations, and know that I am Jehovah.*—Ver. 13 is closely connected with the preceding verse. This serves to explain the fact that the only sins mentioned as exciting the wrath of God are covetousness and blood-guiltiness. הִכָּה כַף, as 2 Kings xi. 12 clearly shows, is a contracted expression for הִכָּה כַף אֶל כַּף (ch. xxi. 19), and the smiting of the hands together is a gesture indicative of wrathful indignation. For the form דָּמֶךְ, contracted from דָּמַיִךְ, see the comm. on ch. xvi. 45.—As ver. 13 leads on to the threatening of judgment, so does ver. 14 point in anticipation to the terrible nature of the judgment itself. The question, "will thy heart stand firm?" involves a warning against security. עָמַד is the opposite of נָמֵס (cf. ch. xxi. 12), as standing forms the antithesis to passing away (cf. Ps. cii. 27). עָשָׂה אוֹתָךְ, as in ch. xvi. 59 and vii. 27. The Lord will scatter them (cf. ch. xii. 15, xx. 23), and remove the uncleanness of sin, namely, by purifying the people in exile (cf. Isa. iv. 4). הֵתֵם, from תָּמַם, to cause to cease, with מִן, to take completely away. נַחֲלְתְּ, *Niphal* of חָלַל, connected with לְעֵינֵי גוֹיִם, as in ch. xx. 9, not from נָחַל, as many of the commentators who follow the Septuagint and Vulgate suppose. בָּךְ, not *in te*, in thyself, but through thee, *i.e.* through thy sinful conduct and its consequences.

Vers. 17–22. Refining of Israel in the furnace of besieged Jerusalem.—Ver. 17. *And the word of Jehovah came to me, saying,* Ver. 18. *Son of man, the house of Israel has become to me as dross; they are all brass, and tin, and iron, and lead in the furnace; dross of silver have they become.* Ver. 19. *Therefore thus saith the Lord Jehovah, Because ye have all become dross, therefore, behold, I gather you together in Jerusalem.* Ver. 20. *As men gather together silver, and brass, and iron, and lead, and tin into the furnace, to blow the fire upon it for melting, so will I gather (you) together in my anger and my wrath, and put you in and melt you.* Ver. 21. *And I will collect you together, and blow the fire of my wrath upon you, that ye may be melted therein.* Ver. 22. *As silver is melted in the furnace, so shall ye be melted therein* (viz. in Jerusalem), *and shall learn that I Jehovah have poured out my wrath upon you.*—This second word of God rests no doubt upon the figure in ver. 15*b*, of the uncleanness or dirt of sin; but it is not an exposition of the removal of the dirt, as predicted there. For that was to be effected through the dispersion of Israel among the nations, whereas the word of God, from ver. 17 onwards, represents the siege awaiting Jerusalem as a melting process, through which God will separate the silver ore contained in Israel from the baser metals mingled with it. In ver. 18 it commences with a description of the existing condition of Israel. It has turned to dross. הָיוּ is clearly a perfect, and is not to be taken as a prophetical future, as Kliefoth proposes. Such a rendering is not only precluded by the clause יַעַן הֱיוֹת וגו' in ver. 19, but could only be made to yield an admissible sense by taking the middle clause of the verse, "all of them brass and tin," etc., as a statement of what Israel had become, or as a preterite in opposition to all the rules of Hebrew syntax, inasmuch as this clause merely furnishes an explanation of הֱיוֹת־לְסוּג. סוּג, which only occurs here, for סִיג signifies dross, not smelting-ore (Kliefoth), literally, *recedanea*, the baser ingredients which are mixed with the silver, and separated from it by smelting. This is the meaning here, where it is directly afterwards interpreted as consisting of brass, tin, iron, and lead, and then still further defined as סִגִים כָּסֶף, dross of silver, *i.e.* brass, tin, iron, and lead, with a mixture of silver. Because Israel had turned into silver-dross of this kind, the Lord would gather it together in Jerusalem, to smelt it there as in a smelting furnace; just as men gather together brass, iron, lead, and tin in a furnace to smelt them, or rather to separate the silver contained therein. קְבֻצַת כֶּסֶף, literally, a collection of silver, etc., for " like a collection." The כ *simil.* is probably omitted for the sake of euphony, to avoid the discord occasioned by prefixing it to קְבֻצַת. Ezekiel mentions the silver as well, because there is some silver contained in the brass, iron, etc., or the dross is silver-dross. הִתּוּךְ, *nomen verbale*, from נָתַךְ in the *Hiphil*, smelting; literally, as the smelting of silver takes place in the furnace. The smelting is treated here simply as a figurative representation of punishment, and consequently the result of the smelting, namely, the refining of the silver by the removal of the baser ingredients, is not referred to any further, as is the case in Isa. i. 22, 25; Jer. vi. 27–30; Mal. iii. 2, 3. This smelting process was experienced by Israel in the last siege of Jerusalem by the Chaldeans.

Vers. 23–31. The corrupt state of all classes in the kingdom is the immediate cause of its destruction.—Ver. 23. *And the word of Jehovah came to me, saying,* Ver. 24. *Son of man, say to it, Thou art a land which is not shined upon, nor rained upon in the day of anger.* Ver. 25. *Conspiracy of its prophets is within it; like a roaring lion, which rends in pieces the prey, they devour souls, take possessions and money; they multiply its widows within it.* Ver. 26. *Its priests violate my law and profane my holy things; they make no distinction between holy and unholy, and do not teach the difference between clean and unclean, and they hide their eyes from my Sabbaths, and I am profaned among them.* Ver. 27. *Its princes in the midst of it are like wolves, which rend prey in pieces, that they may shed blood, destroy souls, to acquire gain.* Ver. 28. *And its prophets plaster it with cement, seeing what is worthless, and divining lies for them, saying, " Thus saith the Lord Jehovah," when Jehovah hath not spoken.* Ver. 29. *The common people offer violence and commit theft; they crush the wretched and the poor, and oppress the foreigner against right.* Ver. 30. *I seek among them for a man who might build a wall and step into the breach before me on behalf of the land, that I might not destroy it, but I find none.* Ver. 31. *Therefore I pour out my anger upon them; I destroy them in the fire of my wrath, I give their way upon their head, is the saying of the Lord Jehovah.* — To show the necessity for the predicted judgment still more clearly, in the third word of God contained in this chapter a description is given of the spread of deep corruption among all classes of the people, and the impossibility of saving the kingdom is plainly shown. The words אֱמָר־לָהּ, " say unto her," are taken by most of the commentators as referring to Jerusalem, the abominations of which the prophet is commanded to declare. But although the clause, " thou art a land," etc. (ver. 24), could unquestionably be made to harmonize with this, yet the words of ver. 30, " I sought for a man who might stand in the gap before Jehovah for the land," indicate most unquestionably that this word of God is directed against the land of Judah, and consequently לָהּ must be taken as referring to אֶרֶץ which follows, the pronoun in this case being placed before the noun to which it refers, as in Num. xxiv. 17. Any allusion to the city of Jerusalem would therefore be somewhat out of place, inasmuch as in the preceding word of God the object referred to was not the city, but the house of Israel, or the nation generally, from which a transition is here made to the land, or the kingdom of Judah. The meaning of ver. 24 is a disputed question. לֹא מְטֹהָרָה הִיא, which is rendered ἡ οὐ βρεχομένη in the Sept., is taken by most of the expositors to mean, " it is not cleansed," the form מְטֹהָרָה being correctly rendered as a participle *Pual* of טָהַר. But this rendering does not furnish any appropriate sense, unless the following words לֹא גֻּשְׁמָהּ are taken as a threat: there shall not be rain, or it shall not be rained upon in the day of wrath. But this view is hardly reconcilable with the form of the word. גֻּשְׁמָהּ, according to the Masoretic pointing with *Mappik* in the ה, is evidently meant to be taken as a noun גֻּשְׁמָהּ = גֶּשֶׁם. In that case, if the words were intended to contain a threat, יִהְיֶה ought not to be omitted. But without a verb the words contain a statement in harmony with what precedes. We regard the *Chetib* נטמה as the perfect *Pual*

נֻשָּׁמָה. And let it not be objected to this that the *Pual* of this verb is not met with elsewhere, for the form of the noun נֻשָּׁם with the *u* sound does not occur anywhere else. As a perfect *Pual*, לֹא נֻשָּׁמָה is a simple continuation of the participial clause לֹא מְטֹהָרָה הִיא, containing like this an affirmation, and cannot possibly be taken as a threat or prediction. But "not cleansed" and "not rained upon" do not agree together, as rain is not a means of purification according to the Hebrew idea. It is true that in the law the withdrawal or suspension of rain is threatened as a punishment from God, and the pouring out of rain is promised as a theocratical blessing. But even if the words are taken in a tropical sense, as denoting a withdrawal of the blessings of divine grace, they will not harmonize with the other clause, "not cleansed." We therefore take מְטֹהָרָה in the sense of "shined upon by the light," or provided with brightness; a meaning which is sustained by Ex. xxiv. 10, where *tohar* occurs in the sense of splendour, and by the kindred word *tzohar*, light. In this way we obtain the suitable thought, land which has neither sunlight nor rain in the day of wrath, *i.e.* does not enjoy a single trace of the divine blessing, but is given up to the curse of barrenness. The reason for this threat is given in vers. 25 sqq., where a picture is drawn of the moral corruption of all ranks; viz. of the prophets (ver. 25), the priests (ver. 26), the princes (ver. 27), and the common people (ver. 29). There is something very striking in the allusion to the prophets in ver. 25, not so much because they are mentioned again in ver. 28,—for this may be accounted for on the ground that in the latter passage they are simply introduced as false advisers of the princes,—as on account of the statement made concerning them in ver. 25, namely, that, like lions tearing their prey, they devour souls, etc.; a description which is not given either in chap. xiii. or elsewhere. Hitzig therefore proposes to alter נְבִיאֶיהָ into נְשִׂיאֶיהָ, after the rendering ἀφηγούμενοι given by the LXX. This alteration of the text, which confines itself to a single letter, is rendered very plausible by the fact that almost the same is affirmed of the persons mentioned in ver. 25 as of the princes in ver. 27, and that in the passage in Zephaniah (iii. 3, 4), which is so similar to the one before us, that Ezekiel appears to have had it in his mind, the princes (שָׂרֶיהָ) and the judges (שֹׁפְטֶיהָ) are called the prophets and the priests. The נְשִׂיאִים here would correspond to the שָׂרִים of Zephaniah, and the שָׂרִים to the שֹׁפְטִים. According to ver. 6, the נְשִׂיאִים would indicate primarily the members of the royal family, possibly including the chief officers of the crown; and the שָׂרִים (ver. 27) would be the heads of tribes, of families, and of fathers' houses, in whose hands the national administration of justice principally lay (cf. Ex. xviii. 19 sqq.; Deut. i. 13–18; and my *Bibl. Archäol.* ii. § 149). I therefore prefer this conjecture, or correction, to the Masoretic reading, although the latter is supported by ancient witnesses, such as the Chaldee with its rendering סָפְרַיָּא, scribes, and the version of Jerome. For the statement which the verse contains is not applicable to prophets, and the best explanation given of the Masoretic text—namely, that by Michaelis, " they have made a compact with one another as to what kind of teaching they would or would not give; and in order that their authority may continue undisturbed, they persecute even to blood those who do not act with them, or obey them, but rather contradict"—does not do justice to the words, but weakens their sense. קֶשֶׁר is not a predicate to 'נב, " they are (*i.e.* form) a conspiracy;" but 'נב is a genitive. At the same time, there is no necessity to take קֶשֶׁר in the sense of " company," a rendering which cannot be sustained. The fact that in what follows, where the comparison to lions is introduced, the נביאים (נְשִׂיאִים) are the subject, simply proves that in the first clause also these men actually form the prominent idea. There is no ground for supplying הֵמָּה to כַּאֲרִי וגו' (they are like, etc.); but the simile is to be linked on to the following clause. נֶפֶשׁ אָכָלוּ is to be explained from the comparison to a lion, which devours the prey that it has captured in its blood, in which is the soul, or *nephesh* (Gen.

ix. 4; Lev. xvii. 11 sqq.). The thought is this: in their insatiable greed for riches they sacrifice men and put them to death, and thereby multiply the number of victims (for the fact, see chap. xix. 5, 7). What is stated in ver. 26 concerning the priests is simply a further expansion of Zeph. iii. 4, where the first two clauses occur word for word; for קֹדֶשׁ in Zephaniah is really equivalent to קָדְשִׁי, holy things and deeds. The desecration of the holy things consisted in the fact that they made no distinction between sacred and profane, clean and unclean. For the fact, compare Lev. x. 10, 11. Their covering their eyes from the Sabbaths showed itself in their permitting the Sabbaths to be desecrated by the people, without offering any opposition (cf. Jer. xvii. 27).—The comparison of the rulers (*sārim*) to ravening wolves is taken from Zeph. iii. 3. For the following clause, compare ver. 12 and ch. xiii. 10. Destroying souls to acquire gain is perfectly applicable to unjust judges, inasmuch as, according to Ex. xviii. 21, the judges were to hate בָּצַע. All that is affirmed in ver. 28 of the conduct of the false prophets is repeated for the most part *verbatim* from ch. xiii. 10, 9, and 7. By לָהֶם, which points back to the three classes of men already mentioned, and not merely to the *sārim*, the prophets are represented as helpers of those who support the ungodly in their wicked ways, by oracles which assured them of prosperity. עַם הָאָרֶץ (ver. 29), as distinguished from the spiritual and secular rulers of the nation, signifies the common people. With reference to their sins and wickedness, see ch. xviii. 7, 12, 18; and for the command against oppressing the poor and foreigners, compare Ex. xxii. 20, 21; Deut. xxiv. 17.—The corruption is so universal, that not a man is to be found who could enter into the gap as a righteous man, or avert the judgment of destruction by his intercession. מֵהֶם refers not merely to the prophets, who did not enter into the gap according to ch. xiii. 5, but to all the classes previously mentioned. At the same time, it does not follow from this, that entering into the gap by means of intercession cannot be the thing intended, as Hitzig supposes. The expression לִפְנֵי בְעַד הָאָרֶץ clearly refers to intercession. This is apparent from the simple fact that, as Hitzig himself observes, the intercession of Abraham for Sodom (Gen. xviii. 13 sqq.) was floating before the mind of Ezekiel, since the concluding words of the verse contain an obvious allusion to Gen. xviii. 28. Because the Lord does not find a single righteous man, who might intercede for the land, He pours out His anger upon it, to destroy the inhabitants thereof. With reference to the fact and the separate words employed, compare ch. xxi. 36, vii. 4, ix. 10, xi. 21, and xvi. 43. It does not follow from the word וָאֶשְׁפֹּךְ, that Ezekiel "is speaking after the catastrophe" (Hitzig). For although וָאֶשְׁפֹּךְ expresses the consequence of Jehovah's seeking a righteous man and not finding one, it by no means follows from the occurrence of the preterite וְלֹא מָצָאתִי that וָאֶשְׁפֹּךְ is also a preterite. וָאֶשְׁפֹּךְ is simply connected with וָאֲבַקֵּשׁ as a consequence; and in both verbs the *Vav consec.* expresses the sequence of thought, and not of time. The seeking, therefore, with the result of not having found, cannot be understood in a chronological sense, *i.e.* as an event belonging to the past, for the simple reason that the preceding words do not record the chronological order of events. It merely depicts the existing moral condition of the people, and ver. 30 sums up the result of the description in the thought that there was no one to be found who could enter in the gap before God. Consequently we cannot determine from the imperfect with *Vav consec.* either the time of the seeking and not finding, or that of the pouring out of the wrath.

CHAP. XXIII. OHOLAH AND OHOLIBAH, THE HARLOTS SAMARIA AND JERUSALEM.

Samaria and Jerusalem, as the capitals and representatives of the two kingdoms Israel and Judah, are two sisters, who have practised whoredom from the days of Egypt onwards (vers. 2–4). Samaria has carried on this whoredom with Assyria and Egypt, and has been given up by God into the power of the Assyrians as a consequent punishment (vers. 5–10). But Jerusalem, instead of allowing this to serve as a warning, committed fornication still more grievously with Assyria and the Chaldeans, and, last of all, with Egypt again (vers. 11–21). In consequence of this, the Lord will permit the Chaldeans to make war upon them, and to plunder and put them to shame, so that, as a punishment for their whoredom and their forgetfulness of God, they may, in the fullest measure, experience Samaria's fate (vers. 22–35). In conclusion, both kingdoms are shown once more, and in still severer terms, the guilt of their idolatry (vers. 36–44), whilst the infliction of the punishment for both adultery and murder is foretold (vers. 45–49).

In its general character, therefore, this word of God is coordinate with the two preceding ones in ch. xxi. and xxii., setting forth once more in a comprehensive way the sins and the punishment of Israel. But this is done in the form of an allegory, which closely resembles in its general features the allegorical description in ch. xvi.; though, in the particular details, it possesses a character peculiarly its own, not only in certain original turns and figures, but still more in the arrangement and execution of the whole. The allegory in ch. xvi. depicts the attitude of Israel towards the Lord in the past, the present, and the future; but in the chapter before us, the guilt and punishment of Israel stand in the foreground of the picture throughout, so that a parallel is drawn between Jerusalem and Samaria, to show that the punishment of destruction, which Samaria has brought upon itself through its adulterous intercourse with the heathen, will inevitably fall upon Jerusalem and Judah also.

Vers. 1–4. The sisters Oholah and Oholibah.—Ver. 1. *And the word of Jehovah came to me, saying,* Ver. 2. *Son of man, two women, daughters of one mother were they,* Ver. 3. *They committed whoredom in Egypt, in their youth they committed whoredom; there were their breasts pressed, and there men handled their virgin bosom.* Ver. 4. *Their names are Oholah, the greater, and Oholibah her sister; and they became mine, and bare sons and daughters. But their names are: Samaria is Oholah, and Jerusalem is Oholibah.*—The name אָהֳלִיבָה is formed from אָהֳלִי בָהּ, "my tent in her;" and, accordingly, אָהֳלָה is to be derived from אָהֳלָהּ, "her tent," and not to be regarded as an abbreviation of אָהֳלָה בָּהּ, "her tent in her," as Hitzig and Kliefoth maintain. There is no ground for this assumption, as "her tent," in contrast with "my tent in her," expresses the thought with sufficient clearness, that she had a tent of her own, and the place where her tent was does not come into consideration. The "tent" is the sanctuary: both tabernacle and temple. These names characterize the two kingdoms according to their attitude toward the Lord. Jerusalem had the sanctuary of Jehovah; Samaria, on the other hand, had her own sanctuary, *i.e.* one invented by herself. Samaria and Jerusalem, as the historical names of the two kingdoms, represent Israel of the ten tribes and Judah. Oholah and Oholibah are daughters of one mother, because they were the two halves of the one Israel; and they are called women, because Jehovah had married them (ver. 4). Oholah is called הַגְּדוֹלָה, the great, *i.e.* greater sister (not the elder, see the comm. on ch. xvi. 46); because ten tribes, the greater portion of Israel, belonged to Samaria, whereas Judah had only two tribes. They committed whoredom even in Egypt in their youth, for even in Egypt the Israelites defiled themselves with Egyptian idolatry (see the comm. on ch. xx. 7). מָעַךְ, to press, to crush: the *Pual* is used here to denote lewd handling. In a similar manner the *Piel* עִשָּׂה is used to signify *tractare, contrectare mammas,* in an obscene sense.

Vers. 5–10. Samaria's whoredom and punishment.—Ver. 5. *And Oholibah played the harlot under me, and burned towards her lovers, even as far as Assyria, standing near;* Ver. 6. *Clothed in purple, governors and officers, all of them choice men of good deportment, horsemen riding upon horses.* Ver. 7. *And she directed her whoredom toward them, to the choice of the sons of Assyria all of them, and with all towards whom she burned, with all their idols she defiled herself.* Ver. 8. *Also her whoredom from Egypt she did not give up; for they had lain with her in her youth, and they had handled her virgin bosom, and had poured out their lust upon her.* Ver. 9. *Therefore I have given her into the hand of her lovers, into the hand of the sons of Assyria, towards whom she was inflamed.* Ver. 10. *They uncovered her nakedness, took away her sons and her daughters, and slew her with the sword, so that she became a legend among the women, and executed judgments upon her.*—Coquetting and whoring with Assyria and Egypt denote religious and political leaning towards and connection with these nations and kingdoms, including idolatry and the formation of alliances with them, as in chap. xvi. תַּחְתַּי is to be interpreted in accordance with תַּחַת אִישָּׁהּ (ch. xvi. 32). עֲגַב, which only occurs in Ezekiel and once in Jeremiah, denotes the eager desire kindled by passionate love towards any one. By the words אֶל־אַשּׁוּר the lovers are more precisely defined. קְרוֹבִים without an article is not an adjective, belonging to מְאַהֲבֶיהָ, but in apposition, which is continued in the next verse. In these appositions the particular features, which excited the ardent passion towards the lovers, are pointed out. קָרוֹב is not to be taken in an outward or local sense, but as signifying inward or spiritual nearness: standing near, equivalent to inwardly related, as in Ps. xxxviii. 12; Job xix. 14. The description given of the Assyrians in ver. 6 contains the thought that Israel, dazzled by Assyria's splendour, and overpowered by the might of that kingdom, had been drawn into intercourse with the Assyrians, which led her astray into idolatry. The predicate, clothed in purple, points to the splendour and glory of this imperial power; the other predicates, to the magnitude of its military force. פַּחוֹת וּסְגָנִים are rulers of higher and lower grades (cf. Jer. li. 57). "Here the expression is a general one, signifying the different classes of office-bearers in the kingdom" (Hävernick). With regard to פֶּחָה, see my comm. on Hag. i. 1; and for סָגָן, see Delitzsch on Isa. xli. 25. "Riding upon horses" is added to פָּרָשִׁים to denote the noblest horsemen, in contrast to riders upon asses and camels (cf. Isa. xxi. 7). In ver. 7*b* בְּכָל־גִּלּוּלֵיהֶם is in apposition to בְּכֹל אֲשֶׁר עָגְבָה, and defines more precisely the instigation to pollution: with all towards whom she burned in love, namely, with all their (the lovers') idols. The thought is as follows: it was not merely through her intercourse with the Assyrians that Israel defiled herself, but also through their idols. At the same time, Samaria did not give up the idolatry which it had derived from Egypt. It was from Egypt that the worship of God under the image of the golden calves had been imported. The words are much too strong for us to understand them as relating simply to political intercourse, as Hitzig has done. We have already observed at ch. xx. 7, that even in Egypt itself the Israelites had defiled themselves with Egyptian idolatry, as is also stated in ver. 8*b*.—Vers. 9, 10. As a punishment for this, God gave Samaria into the power of the Assyrians, so that they executed judgment upon the harlot. In ver. 10*b* the prophecy passes from the figure to the fact. The uncovering of the nakedness consisted in the transportation of the sons and daughters, *i.e.* the population of Samaria, into exile by the Assyrians, who slew the woman herself with the sword; in other words, destroyed the kingdom of Samaria. Thus did Samaria become a name for women; that is to say, her name was circulated among the nations, her fate became an object of conversation and ridicule to the nations, not "a nickname for the nations," as Hävernick supposes (*vid.* ch. xxxvi. 3). שְׁפוּטִים, a later form for שְׁפָטִים (cf. ch. xvi. 41).

Vers. 11–21. *Whoredom of Judah.*—Ver. 11. *And her sister Oholibah saw it, and carried on her coquetry still more wantonly than she had done, and her whoredom more than the whoredom of her sister.* Ver. 12. *She was inflamed with lust towards the sons of Asshur, governors and officers, standing near, clothed in perfect beauty, horsemen riding upon horses, choice men of good deportment.* Ver. 13. *And I saw that she had defiled herself; they both went one way.* Ver. 14. *And she carried her whoredom still further; she saw men engraved upon the wall, figures of Chaldeans engraved with red ochre,* Ver. 15. *Girded about the hips with girdles, with overhanging caps upon their heads, all of them knights in appearance, resembling the sons of Babel, the land of whose birth is Chaldea:* Ver. 16. *And she was inflamed with lust toward them, when her eyes saw them, and sent messengers to them to Chaldea.* Ver. 17. *Then the sons of Babylon came to her to the bed of love, and defiled her with their whoredom; and when she had defiled herself with them, her soul tore itself away from them.* Ver. 18. *And when she uncovered her whoredom, and uncovered her nakedness, my soul tore itself away from her, as my soul had torn itself away from her sister.* Ver. 19. *And she increased her whoredom, so that she remembered the days of her youth, when she played the harlot in the land of Egypt.* Ver. 20. *And she burned toward their paramours, who have members like asses and heat like horses.* Ver. 21. *Thou lookest after the lewdness of thy youth, when they of Egypt handled thy bosom because of thy virgin breasts.*— The train of thought in these verses is the following :—Judah went much further than Samaria. It not only indulged in sinful intercourse with Assyria, which led on to idolatry as the latter had done, but it also allowed itself to be led astray by the splendour of Chaldea, to form alliances with that imperial power, and to defile itself with her idolatry. And when it became tired of the Chaldeans, it formed impure connections with the Egyptians, as it had done once before during its sojourn in Egypt. The description of the Assyrians in ver. 12 coincides with that in vers. 5 and 6, except that some of the predicates are placed in a different order, and לְבֻשֵׁי מִכְלוֹל is substituted for לְבֻשֵׁי תְכֵלֶת. The former expression, which occurs again in ch. xxxviii. 4, must really mean the same as לְבֻשֵׁי תְכֵלֶת. But it does not follow from this that מִכְלוֹל signifies purple, as

Hitzig maintains. The true meaning is perfection; and when used of the clothing, it signifies perfect beauty. The Septuagint rendering, εὐπάρυφα, with a beautiful border,—more especially a variegated one,—merely expresses the sense, but not the actual meaning of מִכְלוֹל. The Chaldee rendering is לְבִישֵׁי גְמַר, *perfecte induti*.—There is great obscurity in the statement in ver. 14 as to the way in which Judah was seduced to cultivate intercourse with the Chaldeans. She saw men engraved or drawn upon the wall (מְחֻקֶּה, a participle *Pual* of חָקַק, engraved work, or sculpture). These figures were pictures of Chaldeans, engraved (drawn) with שָׁשַׁר, red ochre, a bright-red colour. חֲגוֹרֵי, an adjective form חָגוֹר, wearing a girdle. טְבוּלִים, coloured cloth, from טָבַל, to colour; here, according to the context, variegated head-bands or turbans. סְרוּחֵי, the overhanging, used here of the cap. The reference is to the *tiarae tinctae* (Vulgate), the lofty turbans or caps, as they are to be seen upon the monuments of ancient Nineveh. שָׁלִישִׁים, not chariot-warriors, but knights: "*tristatae*, the name of the second grade after the regal dignity" (Jerome. See the comm. on Ex. xiv. 7 and 2 Sam. xxiii. 8). The description of these engravings answers perfectly to the sculptures upon the inner walls of the Assyrian palaces in the monuments of Nimrud, Khorsabad, and Kouyunjik (see Layard's *Nineveh and its Remains*, and Vaux, *Nineveh and Persepolis*). The pictures of the Chaldeans are not mythological figures (Hävernick), but sculptures depicting war-scenes, triumphal processions of Chaldean rulers and warriors, with which the Assyrian palaces were adorned. We have not to look for these sculptures in Jerusalem or Palestine. This cannot be inferred from ch. viii. 10, as Hävernick supposes; nor established by Hitzig's argument, that the woman must have been in circumstances to see such pictures. The intercourse between Palestine and Nineveh, which was carried on even in Jonah's time, was quite sufficient to render it possible for the pictures to be seen. When Israelites travelled to Nineveh, and saw the palaces there, they could easily make the people acquainted with the glory of Nineveh by the accounts they would give on their return. It is no reply to this, to state that the woman does not send ambassadors till afterwards (ver. 16), as Hitzig argues; for Judah sent ambassadors to Chaldea not to view the glories of Assyria, but to form alliances with the Chaldeans, or to sue for their favour. Such an embassy, for example, was sent to Babylon by Zedekiah (Jer. xxix. 3); and there is no doubt that in ver. 16*b* Ezekiel has this in his mind. Others may have preceded this, concerning which the books of Kings and Chronicles are just as silent as they are concerning that of Zedekiah. The thought in these verses is therefore the following:—The acquaintance made by Israel (Judah) with the imperial splendour of the Chaldeans, as exhibited in the sculptures of their palaces, incited Judah to cultivate political and mercantile intercourse with this imperial power, which led to its becoming entangled in the heathen ways and idolatry of the Chaldeans. The Chaldeans themselves came and laid the foundation for an intercourse which led to the pollution of Judah with heathenism, and afterwards filled it with disgust, because it was brought thereby into dependence upon the Chaldeans. The consequence of all this was, that the Lord became tired of Judah (vers. 17, 18). For instead of returning to the Lord, Judah turned to the other power of the world, namely, to Egypt; and in the time of Zedekiah renewed its ancient coquetry with that nation (vers. 19–21 compared with ver. 8). The form וַתַּעְגְּבָה in ver. 20, which the *Keri* also gives in ver. 18, has taken *ah* as a feminine termination (not the cohortative *ah*), like תָּרְנָה in Prov. i. 20, viii. 1 (*vid.* Delitzsch, *On Job*, pp. 117 and 268). פִּלַּגְשִׁים are *scorta mascula* here (Kimchi),—a drastically sarcastic epithet applied to the *sârisim*, the eunuchs, or courtiers. The figurative epithet answers to the licentious character of the Egyptian idolatry. The sexual heat both of horses and asses is referred to by Aristotle, *Hist. anim.* vi. 22, and Columella, *de re rust.* vi. 27; and that of the horse has already been applied to the idolatry of the people by Jeremiah (*vid.* Jer. v. 8). בָּשָׂר, as in ch. xvi. 26. פָּקַד (ver. 21), to look about for anything, *i.e.* to search for it; not to miss it, as Hävernick imagines.

Vers. 22–35. Punishment of the harlot Jerusalem.—Ver. 22. *Therefore, Oholibah, thus saith the Lord Jehovah, Behold, I raise up thy lovers against thee, from whom thy soul has torn itself away, and cause them to come upon thee from every side;* Ver. 23. *The sons of Babel, and all the Chaldeans, rulers, lords, and nobles, all the sons of Assyria with them: chosen men of graceful deportment, governors and officers together, knights and counsellors, all riding upon horses.* Ver. 24. *And they will come upon thee with weapons, chariots, and wheels, and with a host of peoples; target and shield and helmet will they direct against thee round about: and I commit to them the judgment, that they may judge thee according to their rights.* Ver. 25. *And I direct my jealousy against thee, so that they shall deal with thee in wrath: nose and ears will they cut off from thee; and thy last one shall fall by the sword: they will take thy sons and thy daughters; and thy last one will be consumed by fire.* Ver. 26. *They will strip off thy clothes from thee, and take thy splendid jewellery.* Ver. 27. *I will abolish thy lewdness from thee, and thy whoredom from the land of Egypt: that thou mayest no more lift thine eyes to them, and no longer remember Egypt.* Ver. 28. *For thus saith the Lord Jehovah, Behold, I give thee into the hand of those whom thou hatest, into the hand of those from whom thy soul has torn itself away:* Ver. 29. *And they shall deal with thee in hatred, and take all thy gain, and leave thee naked and bare; that thy whorish shame may be uncovered, and thy lewdness and thy whoredom.* Ver. 30. *This shall happen to thee, because thou goest whoring after the nations, and on account of thy defiling thyself with their idols.* Ver. 31. *In the way of thy sister hast thou walked; therefore I give her cup into thy hand.* Ver. 32. *Thus saith the Lord Jehovah, The cup of thy sister thou shalt drink, the deep and broad one; it will be for laughter and for derision, because it contains so much.* Ver. 33. *Thou wilt become full of drunkenness and misery: a cup of desolation and devastation is the cup of thy sister Samaria.* Ver. 34. *Thou wilt drink it up and drain it, and gnaw its fragments, and tear thy breasts (therewith); for I have spoken it, is the saying of the Lord Jehovah.* Ver. 35. *Therefore thus saith the Lord Jehovah, Because thou hast forgotten me, and hast cast me behind thy back, thou shalt also bear thy lewdness and thy whoredom.*—As Jerusalem has given herself up to whoredom, like her sister Samaria, she shall also share her sister's fate. The paramours, of whom she has become tired, God will bring against her as enemies. The Chaldeans will come with all their might, and execute the judgment of destruction upon her.—For the purpose of depicting their great and powerful forces, Ezekiel enumerates in vers. 23 and 24 the peoples and their military equipment: viz. the sons of Babel, *i.e.* the inhabitants of Babylonia, the Chaldeans,—the ruling people of the empire at that time,—and all the sons of Asshur, *i.e.* the inhabitants of the eastern portions of the empire, the former rulers of the world. There is some obscurity in the words פְּקוֹד וְשׁוֹעַ וְקוֹעַ, which the older theologians have almost unanimously taken to be the names of different tribes in the Chaldean empire. Ewald also adopts this view, but it is certainly incorrect; for the words are in apposition to וְכָל־בָּיְשׂדִּים, as the omission of the copula ו before פְּקוֹד is sufficient to show. This is confirmed by the fact that שׁוֹעַ is used, in Isa. xxxii. 5 and Job xxxiv. 19, in the sense of the man of high rank, distinguished for his prosperity, which is quite in harmony with the passage before us. Consequently פְּקוֹד is not to be taken in the sense of visitation or punishment, after Jer. l. 21; but the meaning is to be sought in the verb פָּקַד, to exercise supervision, or lead; and the abstract oversight is used for overseer, or ruler, as an equivalent to פָּקִיד. Lastly, according to Rabbins, the Vulgate, and others, קוֹעַ signifies princes, or nobles. The predicates in ver. 23*b* are repeated from vers. 6

and 12, and קְרוּאִים alone is added. This is a word taken from the Pentateuch, where the heads of the tribes and families, as being members of the council of the whole congregation of Israel, are called קְרוּאֵי הָעֵדָה or קְרוּאֵי מוֹעֵד, persons called or summoned to the meeting (Num. i. 16, xvi. 2). As Michaelis has aptly observed, "he describes them sarcastically in the very same way in which he had previously described those upon whom she doted."—There is a difficulty in explaining the ἅπ. λεγ. הֹגֶן,—for which many MSS. read הֹגֶן,—as regards not only its meaning, but its position in the sentence. The fact that it is associated with רֶכֶב וְגַלְגַּל would seem to indicate that הֹגֶן is also either an implement of war or some kind of weapon. At the same time, the words cannot be the subject to וּבָאוּ; but as the expression וּבִקְהַל עַמִּים, which follows, clearly shows, they simply contain a subordinate definition of the manner in which, or the things with which, the peoples mentioned in vers. 23, 24 will come, while they are governed by the verb in the freest way. The attempts which Ewald and Hitzig have made to remove the difficulty, by means of conjectures, are forced and extremely improbable. נָתַתִּי לִפְנֵיהֶם, I give up to them (not, I place before them) ; נָתַן לִפְנֵי, as in 1 Kings viii. 46, to deliver up, or give a thing into a person's hand or power. לִפְנֵי is used in this sense in Gen. xiii. 9 and xxiv. 51.—In vers. 25, 26, the execution of the judgment is depicted in detail. The words, "they take away thy nose and ears," are not to be interpreted, as the earlier expositors suppose, from the custom prevalent among the Egyptians and other nations of cutting off the nose of an adulteress; but depict, by one particular example, the mutilation of prisoners captured by their enemies. אַחֲרִית : not posterity, which by no means suits the last clause of the verse, and cannot be defended from the usage of the language (see the comm. on Amos iv. 2); but the last, according to the figure employed in the first clause, the trunk; or, following the second clause, the last thing remaining in Jerusalem, after the taking away of the sons and daughters, *i.e.* after the slaying and the deportation of the inhabitants,—viz. the empty houses. For ver. 26, compare ch. xvi. 39.—In ver. 27, "from the land of Egypt" is not equivalent to "dating from Egypt;" for according to the parallel מִמֵּךְ, from thee, this definition does not belong to זְנוּתֵךְ, "thy whoredom," but to הִשְׁבַּתִּי, "I cause thy whoredom to cease from Egypt" (Hitzig).—For ver. 28a, compare ch. xvi. 37; for ver. 28b, vid. ver. 17 above; and for ver. 29, see vers. 25 and 26, and ch. xvi. 39.—Ver. 31 looks back to ver. 13; and ver. 31b is still further expanded in vers. 32-34. Judah shall drink the cup of the wrathful judgment of God, as Samaria has done. For the figure of the cup, compare Isa. li. 17 and Jer. xxv. 15. This cup is described in ver. 32 as deep and wide, i.e. very capacious, so that whoever exhausts all its contents must be thoroughly intoxicated. תִּהְיֶה is the third person; but the subject is מַרְבָּה, and not בּוֹס. The greatness or breadth of the cup will be a subject of laughter and ridicule. It is very arbitrary to supply "*to thee*," so as to read: will be for laughter and ridicule to thee, which does not even yield a suitable meaning, since it is not Judah but the nations who laugh at the cup. Others regard תִּהְיֶה as the second person, thou wilt become; but apart from the anomaly in the gender, as the masculine would stand for the feminine, Hitzig has adduced the forcible objection, that according to this view the words would not only anticipate the explanation given of the figure in the next verse, but would announce the consequences of the שִׁכָּרוֹן וְיָגוֹן mentioned there. Hitzig therefore proposes to erase the words from תִּהְיֶה to וּלְלַעַג as a gloss, and to alter מִרְבָּה into מַרְבָּה: which contains much, is very capacious. But there is not sufficient reason to warrant such critical violence as this. Although the form מִרְבָּה is ἀπ. λεγ., it is not to be rejected as a *nomen subst.*; and if we take מִרְבָּה לְהָכִיל, the magnitude to hold, as the subject of the sentence, it contains a still further description of the cup, which does not anticipate what follows, even though the cup will be an object of laughter and ridicule, not so much for its size, as because of its being destined to be drunk completely empty. In ver. 33 the figure and the fact are combined,— יָגוֹן, lamentation, misery, being added to שִׁכָּרוֹן, drunkenness, and the cup being designated a cup of devastation. The figure of drinking is expanded in the boldest manner in ver. 34 into the gnawing of the fragments of the cup, and the tearing of the breasts with the fragments.—In ver. 35 the picture of the judgment is closed with a repetition of the description of the nation's guilt. For ver. 35*b*, compare ch. xvi. 52 and 58.

Vers. 36–49. Another summary of the sins and punishment of the two women.—Ver. 36. *And Jehovah said to me, Son of man, wilt thou judge Oholah and Oholibah, then show them their abominations;* Ver. 37. *For they have committed adultery, and blood is in their hands; and they have committed adultery with their idols; and their sons also whom they bare to me they have caused to pass through to them to be devoured.* Ver. 38. *Yea more, they have done this to me; they have defiled my sanctuary the same day, and have desecrated my Sabbaths.* Ver. 39. *When they slaughtered their sons to their idols, they came into my sanctuary the same day to desecrate it; and, behold, they have acted thus in the midst of my house.* Ver. 40. *Yea, they have even sent to men coming from afar; to them was a message sent, and, behold, they came, for whom thou didst bathe thyself, paint thine eyes, and put on ornaments,* Ver. 41. *And didst seat thyself upon a splendid cushion, and a table was spread before them, thou didst lay thereon my incense and my oil.* Ver. 42. *And the loud noise became still thereat, and to the men out of the multitude there were brought topers out of the desert, and they put armlets upon their hands, and glorious crowns upon their heads.* Ver. 43. *Then I said to her who was debilitated for adultery, Now will her whoredom itself go whoring,* Ver. 44. *And they will go in to her as they go in to a whore; so did they go in to Oholah and Oholibah, the lewd women.* Ver. 45. *But righteous men, these shall judge them according to the judgment of adulteresses and according to the judgment of murderesses; for they are adulter-*

esses, and there is blood in their hands. Ver. 46. *For thus saith the Lord Jehovah, I will bring up against them an assembly, and deliver them up for maltreating and for booty.* Ver. 47. *And the assembly shall stone them, and cut them in pieces with their swords; their sons and their daughters shall they kill, and burn their houses with fire.* Ver. 48. *Thus will I eradicate lewdness from the land, that all women may take warning and not practise lewdness like you.* Ver. 49. *And they shall bring your lewdness upon you, and ye shall bear the sins of your idols, and shall learn that I am the Lord Jehovah.*—The introductory words וגו הִתְשָׁפוֹט point back not only to ch. xxii. 2, but also to ch. xx. 4, and show that this section is really a summary of the contents of the whole group (ch. xx. 23). The actual subject-matter of these verses is closely connected with ver. 16, more especially in the designation of the sins as adultery and bloodshed (compare vers. 37 and 45 with ch. xvi. 38). נָאַף אֶת־גִּל׳, to commit adultery with the idols, whereby the idols are placed on a par with Jehovah as the husband of Israel (compare Jer. iii. 8 and ii. 27). For the Moloch-worship in ver. 37b, compare ch. xvi. 20, 21, and ch. xx. 31. The desecration of the sanctuary (ver. 38a) is more minutely defined in ver. 39. בַּיּוֹם הַהוּא in ver. 38, which has so offended the LXX. and Hitzig that it is omitted by the former, while the latter proposes to strike it out as a gloss, is added for the purpose of designating the profanation of the sanctuary as contemporaneous with the Moloch-worship of ver. 37b, as is evident from ver. 39. For the fact itself, compare 2 Kings xxi. 4, 5, 7. The desecration of the Sabbaths, as in ch. xx. 13, 16. For ver. 39a, compare ch. xvi. 21. The words are not to be understood as signifying that they sacrificed children to Moloch in the temple, but simply that immediately after they had sacrificed children to Moloch, they went into the temple of Jehovah, that there they might worship Jehovah also, and thus placed Jehovah upon a par with Moloch. This was a profanation (חִלֵּל) of His sanctuary.

In vers. 40-44 the allusion is not to actual idolatry, but to the ungodly alliance into which Judah had entered with Chaldea. Judah sent ambassadors to Chaldea, and for the purpose of receiving the Chaldeans, adorned herself as a woman would do for the reception of her paramours. She seated herself upon a splendid divan, and in front of this there was a table spread, upon which stood the incense and the oil that she ought to have offered to Jehovah. This is the explanation which Kliefoth has correctly given of vers. 40 and 41. The emphatic וְאַף כִּי in ver. 40 is sufficient to show that the reference is to a new crime deserving of punishment. This cannot be idolatry, because the worship of Moloch has already been mentioned in vers. 38 and 39 as the worst of all the idolatrous abominations. Moreover, sending for (or to) men who come from afar does not apply to idolatry in the literal sense of the word; for men to whom the harlot sent messengers to invite them to come to her could not be idols for which she sent to a distant land. The allusion is rather to Assyrians or Chaldeans, and, according to ver. 42, it is the former who are referred to here (compare Isa. xxxix. 3). There is no force in Hitzig's objection, namely, that the one woman sent to these, and that their being sent for and coming have already been disposed of in ver. 16. For the singulars in the last clause of ver. 40 show that even here only one woman is said to have sent for the men. Again, תִּשְׁלַחְנָה might even be the third person singular, as this form does sometimes take the termination נָה (vid. Ewald, § 191c, and Ges. § 47, Anm. 3). At the same time, there is nothing in the fact that the sending to Chaldea has already been mentioned in ver. 16 to preclude another allusion to the same circumstance from a different point of view. The woman adorned herself that she might secure the favour of the men for whom she had sent. כָּחַל is the Arabic كحل, to paint the eyes with stibium (kohol). For the fact itself, see the remarks on 2 Kings ix. 30. She then seated herself upon a cushion (not lay down upon a bed; for יָשַׁב does not mean to lie down), and in front of this there was a table, spread with different kinds of food, upon which she placed incense and oil. The suffix to עָלֶיהָ refers to שֻׁלְחָן, and is to be taken as a neuter, which suits the table as a thing, whilst שֻׁלְחָן generally takes the termination ות in the plural. In ver. 41, Ewald and Hävernick detect a description of the *lectisternia* and of the licentious worship of the Babylonian Mylitta. But neither the sitting (יָשַׁב) upon a cushion (divan), nor the position taken by the woman behind the table, harmonizes with this. As Hitzig has correctly observed, "if she has taken her seat upon a cushion, and has a table spread before her, she evidently intends to dine, and that with the men for whom she has adorned herself. The oil is meant for anointing at meal-time (Amos vi. 6; Prov. xxi. 17; cf. Ps. xxiii. 5), and the incense for burning." "My incense and my oil" are the incense and oil given to her by God, which she ought to have devoted to His service, but had squandered upon herself and her foreign friends (cf. ch. xvi. 18; Hos. ii. 10). The oil, as the produce of the land of Palestine, was the gift of Jehovah; and although incense was not a production of Palestine, yet as the money with which Judah purchased it, or the goods bartered for it, were the gifts of God, Jehovah could also call it His incense. Ver. 42 is very obscure. Such renderings of the first clause as *et vox multitudinis exultantis in ea* (Vulg.), and "the voice of a careless multitude within her" (Hävernick), can hardly be sustained. In every other passage in which קוֹל הָמוֹן occurs, it does not signify the voice of a multitude, but a loud tumult; compare Isa. xiii. 4, xxxiii. 3, Dan. x. 6, and 1 Sam. iv. 14, where קוֹל הֶהָמוֹן is used as synonymous with קוֹל הַצְּעָקָה. Even in cases where הָמוֹן is used for a multitude, it denotes a noisy, boisterous, tumultuous crowd. Consequently שָׁלֵו cannot be taken as an adjective connected with הָמוֹן, because a quiet tumult is a contradiction, and שָׁלֵו does not mean either *exultans* or recklessly breaking loose (Hävernick), but simply living in quiet, peaceful and contented. שָׁלֵו must therefore be the predicate to קוֹל הָמוֹן; the sound of the tumult or the loud noise was (or became) quiet, still. בָּהּ, thereat (neuter, like בָּהּ, thereby, Gen. xxiv. 14). The words which follow, וְאֶל אֲנָשִׁים וגו׳, are not to be taken with the preceding clause, as the connection would yield no sense. They belong to what follows. אֲנָשִׁים מֵרֹב אָדָם can only be the men who came from afar (ver. 40). In addition to these, there were brought, *i.e.* induced to come, topers from the desert. The *Chetib* סוֹבָאִים is no doubt a participle of סָבָא, drinkers, topers; and the *Hophal* מוּבָאִים is chosen instead of the *Kal* בָּאִים, for the sake of the paronomasia, with סוֹבָאִים. The former, therefore, can only be the Assyrians (בְּנֵי אַשּׁוּר, vers. 5 and 7), the latter (the topers) the Chaldeans (בְּנֵי בָבֶל, ver. 15). The epithet drinkers is a very appropriate one for the sons of Babylon; as Curtius (ver. 1) describes the Babylonians as *maxime in vinum et quae ebrietatem sequuntur effusi*. The phrase "from the desert" cannot indicate the home of these men, although כְּמִדְבָּר corresponds to מִמֶּרְחָק in ver. 40, but simply the place from which they came to Judah, namely, from the desert of Syria and Arabia, which separated Palestine from Babylon. These peoples decorated the arms of the harlots with clasps, and their heads with splendid wreaths (crowns). The plural suffixes indicate that the words apply to both women, and this is confirmed by the fact that they are both named in ver. 44. The subject to וַיִּתְּנוּ is not merely the סוֹבָאִים, but also the אֲנָשִׁים מִמֶּרְחָק in ver. 40. The thought is simply that Samaria and Judah had attained to wealth and earthly glory through their intercourse with these nations; the very gifts with which, according to ch. xvi. 11 sqq., Jehovah Himself had adorned His people. The meaning of the verse, therefore, when taken in its connection, appears to be the following:—When the Assyrians began to form alliances with Israel, quiet was the immediate result. The Chaldeans were afterwards added to these, so that through their adulterous intercourse with both these nations Israel and Judah acquired both wealth and glory. The sentence which God pronounced upon this conduct was, that Judah had sunk so deeply into adultery that it would be impossible for it ever to desist from the sin. This is the way in which we understand ver. 43, connecting לַבָּלָה נִאֻפִים with וָאֹמַר: "I said concerning her who was debilitated with whoredom." בָּלָה, feminine of בָּלֶה, used up, worn out; see, for example, Josh. ix. 4, 5, where it is applied to clothes; here it is transferred to persons decayed, debilitated, in which sense the verb occurs in Gen. xviii. 12. נִאֻפִים, which is co-ordinated with בָּלָה, does not indicate the means by which the strength has been exhausted, but is an accusative of direction or reference, debilitated with regard to adultery, so as no longer to be capable of practising it.[1] In the next clause תַּזְנוּתֶיהָ, עַתָּ יִזְנֶה וגו' is the subject to יִזְנֶה, and the *Chetib* is correct, the *Keri* being erroneous, and the result of false exposition. If תזנותה were the object to יִזְנֶה, so that the woman would be the subject, we should have the feminine תִּזְנֶה. But if, on the other hand, תזנותה is the subject, there is no necessity for this, whether we regard the word as a plural, from תַּזְנוּתִים, or take it as a singular, as Ewald (§ 259*a*) has done, inasmuch as in either case it is still an abstract, which might easily be preceded by the verb in the masculine form. וְהִיא gives greater force, not only to the suffix, but also to the noun—and that even she (her whoredom). The sin of whoredom is personified, or regarded as רוּחַ זְנוּנִים (Hos. iv. 12), as a propensity to whoredom, which continues in all its force after the capacity of the woman herself is gone.— Ver. 44 contains the result of the foregoing description of the adulterous conduct of the two women, and this is followed in vers. 45 sqq. by an account of the attitude assumed by God, and the punishment of the sinful women. וַיָּבֹא, with an indefinite subject, they (*man*, one) went to her. אֵלֶיהָ, the one woman,

---

[1] The proposal of Ewald to take לַבָּלָה נִאֻפִים as an independent clause, "adultery to the devil," cannot be defended by the usage of the language; and that of Hitzig, "the withered hag practises adultery," is an unnatural invention, inasmuch as לְ, if taken as *nota dativi*, would give this meaning: the hag has (possesses) adultery as her property—and there is nothing to indicate that it should be taken as a question.

Oholibah. It is only in the apodosis that what has to be said is extended to both women. This is the only interpretation of ver. 44 which does justice both to the verb וַיָּבוֹא (imperfect with *Vav consec.* as the historical tense) and the perfect בָּאוּ. The plural אִשֹּׁת does not occur anywhere else. Hitzig would therefore alter it into the singular, as "unheard of," and confine the attribute to Oholibah, who is the only one mentioned in the first clause of the verse, and also in vers. 43, 40, and 41. The judgment upon the two sisters is to be executed by righteous men (ver. 45). The Chaldeans are not designated as righteous in contrast to the Israelites, but as the instruments of the punitive righteousness of God in this particular instance, executing just judgment upon the sinners for adultery and bloodshed (*vid.* ch. xvi. 38). The infinitives הַעֲלֵה and נָתֹן in ver. 46 stand for the third person future. For other points, compare the commentary on ch. xvi. 40 and 41. The formula נָתֹן לְזַעֲוָה is derived from Deut. xxviii. 25, and has been explained in the exposition of that passage. וּבָרֹא is the *inf. abs. Piel.* For the meaning of the word, see the comm. on ch. xxi. 24. From this judgment all women, *i.e.* all nations, are to take warning to desist from idolatry. נִוַּסְּרוּ is a mixed form, compounded of the *Niphal* and *Hithpael,* for הִתְוַסְּרוּ, like כֻּפַּר in Deut. xxi. 8 (see the comm. *in loc.*).—For ver. 49, *vid.* ch. xvi. 58.—The punishment is announced to both the women, Israel and Judah, as still in the future, although Oholah (Samaria) had been overtaken by the judgment a considerable time before. The explanation of this is to be found in the allegory itself, in which both kingdoms are represented as being sisters of one mother; and it may also be defended on the ground that the approaching destruction of Jerusalem and the kingdom of Judah affected the remnants of the kingdom of the ten tribes, which were still to be found in Palestine; whilst, on the other hand, the judgment was not restricted to the destruction of the two kingdoms, but also embraced the later judgments which fell upon the entire nation.

CHAP. XXIV. PREDICTION OF THE DESTRUCTION OF
JERUSALEM BOTH IN PARABLE AND BY SIGN.

On the day on which the king of Babylon commenced the siege and blockade of Jerusalem, this event was revealed by God to Ezekiel on the Chaboras (vers. 1 and 2); and he was commanded to predict to the people through the medium of a parable the fate of the city and its inhabitants (vers. 3-14). God then foretold to him the death of his own wife, and commanded him to show no sign of mourning on account of it. His wife died the following evening, and he did as he was commanded. When he was asked by the people the reason of this, he explained to them, that what he was doing was symbolical of the way in which they were to act when Jerusalem fell (vers. 15-24). The fall would be announced to the prophet by a fugitive, and then he would no longer remain mute, but would speak to the people again (vers. 25-27).—Apart, therefore, from the last three verses, this chapter contains two words of God, the first of which unfolds in a parable the approaching calamities, and the result of the siege of Jerusalem by the Chaldeans (vers. 1-14); whilst the second typifies by means of a sign the pain and mourning of Israel, namely, of the exiles at the destruction of the city with its sanctuary and its inhabitants. These two words of God, being connected together by their contents, were addressed to the prophet on the same day, and that, as the introduction (vers. 1 and 2) expressly observes, the day on which the siege of Jerusalem by the king of Babylon began.

Ver. 1. *And the word of Jehovah came to me in the ninth year, in the tenth month, on the tenth of the month, saying,* Ver. 2. *Son of man, write for thyself the name of the day, this same day! The king of Babylon has fallen upon Jerusalem this same day.*—The date given, namely, the tenth day of the tenth month of the ninth year after the carrying away of Jehoiachin (ch. i. 2), or what is the same thing, of the reign of Zedekiah, who was appointed king in his stead, is mentioned in Jer. lii. 4, xxxix. 1, and 2 Kings xxv. 1, as the day on which Nebuchadnezzar blockaded the city of Jerusalem by throwing up a rampart; and after the captivity this day was still kept as a fast-day in consequence (Zech. viii. 19). What was thus taking place at Jerusalem was revealed to Ezekiel on the Chaboras the very same day; and he was instructed to announce it to the exiles, "that they and the besieged might learn both from the time and the result, that the destruction of the city was not to be ascribed to chance or to the power of the Babylonians, but to the will of Him who had long ago foretold that, on account of the wickedness of the inhabitants, the city would be burned with fire; and that Ezekiel was a true prophet, because even when in Babylon, which was at so great a distance, he had known and had publicly announced the state of Jerusalem." The definite character of this prediction cannot be changed into a *vaticinium post eventum*, either by arbitrary explanations of the words, or by the unfounded hypothesis proposed by Hitzig, that the day was not set down in this definite form till after the event.—Writing the name of the day is equivalent to making a note of the day. The reason for this is given in ver. 2b, namely, because Nebuchadnezzar had fallen upon Jerusalem on that very day. סָמַךְ signifies to support, hold up (his hand); and hence both here and in Ps. lxxviii. 8 the meaning to press violently upon anything. The rendering "to draw near," which has been forced upon the word from the Syriac (Ges., Winer, and others), cannot be sustained.

Vers. 3–14. PARABLE OF THE POT WITH THE BOILING PIECES.—Ver. 3. *And relate a parable to the rebellious house, and say to them, Thus saith the Lord Jehovah, Set on the pot, set on and also pour water into it.* Ver. 4. *Gather its pieces of flesh into it, all the good pieces, haunch and shoulder, fill it with choice bones.* Ver. 5. *Take the choice of the flock, and also a pile of wood underneath for the bones; make it boil well, also* cook its bones therein. Ver. 6. *Therefore, thus saith the Lord Jehovah, Woe! O city of murders! O pot in which is rust, and whose rust doth not depart from it; piece by piece fetch it out, the lot hath not fallen upon it.* Ver. 7. *For her blood is in the midst of her; she hath placed it upon the naked rock; she hath not poured it upon the ground, that they might cover it with dust.* Ver. 8. *To bring up fury, to take vengeance, I have made her blood come upon the naked rock, that it might not be covered.* Ver. 9. *Therefore thus saith the Lord Jehovah, Woe to the city of murders! I also will make the pile of wood great.* Ver. 10. *Heap up the wood, stir the fire, do the flesh thoroughly, make the broth boil, that the bones may also be cooked away.* Ver. 11. *And set it empty upon the coals thereof, that its brass may become hot and glowing, that the uncleanness thereof may melt within it, its rust pass away.* Ver. 12. *He hath exhausted the pains, and her great rust doth not go from her; into the fire with her rust!* Ver. 13. *In thine uncleanness is abomination; because I have cleansed thee, and thou hast not become clean, thou will no more become clean from thy uncleanness, till I quiet my fury upon thee.* Ver. 14. *I Jehovah have spoken it; it cometh, and I will do it; I will not cease, nor spare, nor let it repent me. According to thy ways, and according to thy deeds, shall they judge thee, is the saying of the Lord Jehovah.*

The contents of these verses are called מָשָׁל, a proverb or parable; and Ezekiel is to communicate them to the refractory generation. It follows from this that the ensuing act, which the prophet is commanded to perform, is not to be regarded as a symbolical act which he really carried out, but that the act forms the substance of the *mâshâl*, in other words, belongs to the parable itself. Consequently the interpretation of the parable in vers. 10 sqq. is clothed in the form of a thing actually done. The pot with the pieces of flesh and the bones, which are to be boiled in it and boiled away, represents Jerusalem with its inhabitants. The fire, with which they are boiled, is the fire of war, and the setting of the pot upon the fire is the commencement of the siege, by which the population of the city is to be boiled away like the flesh and bones in a pot. שְׁפֹת is used, as in 2 Kings iv. 38, to signify the setting of a pot by or upon the fire. אֱסֹף וגו׳: put in its pieces all together. נְתָחֶיהָ, its pieces of flesh, *i.e.* the pieces belonging to the cooking-pot. These are defined still more minutely as the best of the pieces of flesh, and of these the thigh (haunch) and shoulder are mentioned as the most important pieces, to which the choicest of the bones are to be added. This is rendered still more emphatic by the further instruction to take the choice of the flock in addition to these. The choicest pieces of flesh and the pieces of bone denote the strongest and ablest portion of the population of the city. To boil these pieces away, more especially the bones, a large fire is requisite. This is indicated by the words, "and also a pile of wood underneath for the bones." דּוּר in ver. 5, for which מְדוּרָה is substituted in ver. 9, signifies a pile of wood, and occurs in this sense in Isa. xxx. 33, from דּוּר, to lay round, to arrange, pile up. דּוּר הָעֲצָמִים cannot mean a heap of bones, on account of the article, but simply a pile of wood for the (previously mentioned) bones, namely, for the purpose of boiling them away. If we pay attention to the article, we shall see that the supposition that Ezekiel was to place a heap of bones under the pot, and the alteration proposed by Böttcher, Ewald, and Hitzig of הָעֲצָמִים into עֵצִים, are alike untenable. Even if דּוּר in itself does not mean a pile of wood, but simply *strues*, an irregular heap, the fact that it is wood which is piled up is apparent enough from the context. If הָעֲצָמִים had grown out of עֵצִים through a corruption of the text, under the influence of the preceding עצמים, it would not have had an article prefixed. Hitzig also proposes to alter רְתָחֶיהָ into נְתָחֶיהָ, though without any necessity. The fact that רְתָחִים does not occur again proves nothing at all. The noun is added to the verb to intensify its force, and is *plurale tant.* in the sense of boiling. גַּם־בָּשְׁלוּ וגו׳ is dependent upon the previous clause גַּם taking the place of the copulative ¹. On בָּשֵׁל, to be cooked, thoroughly done, see the comm. on Ex. xii. 9.

In vers. 6–8 the interpretation of the parable is given, and that in two trains of thought introduced by לָכֵן (vers. 6 and 9). The reason for commencing with לָכֵן, therefore, may be found in the fact that in the parable contained in vers. 3 sqq., or more correctly in the blockade of Jerusalem, which furnished the occasion for the parable, the judgment about to burst upon Jerusalem is plainly indicated. The train of thought is the following:—Because the judgment upon Jerusalem is now about to commence, therefore woe to her, for her blood-guiltiness is so great that she must be destroyed. But the punishment answering to the magnitude of the guilt is so distributed in the two strophes, vers. 6–8 and vers. 9–13, that the first strophe treats of the punishment of the inhabitants of Jerusalem; the second, of the punishment of the city itself. To account for the latter feature, there is a circumstance introduced which is not mentioned in the parable itself, namely, the rust upon the pot, and the figure of the pot is thereby appropriately extended. Moreover, in the explanation of the parable the figure and the fact pass repeatedly the one into the other. Because Jerusalem is a city of murders, it resembles a pot on which there are spots of rust that cannot be removed. Ver. 6*b* is difficult, and has been expounded in various ways. The ל before the twofold נְתָחֶיהָ is, no doubt, to be taken distributively: according to its several pieces, *i.e.* piece by piece, bring it out. But the suffix attached to הוֹצִיאָהּ cannot be taken as referring to סִיר, as Kliefoth proposes, for this does not yield a suitable meaning. One would not say: bring out the pot by its pieces of flesh, when nothing more is meant than the bringing of the pieces of flesh out of the pot. And this difficulty is not removed by giving to הוֹצִיא the meaning to reach hither. For, apart from the fact that there is nothing in the usage of the language to sustain the meaning, reach it hither for the purpose of setting it upon the fire, one would not say: reach hither the pot according to its several pieces of flesh, piece by piece, when all that was meant was, bring hither the pot filled with pieces of flesh. The suffix to הוֹצִיאָהּ refers to the city (עִיר), *i.e.* to its population, "to which the blood-guiltiness really adhered, and not to its collection of houses" (Hitzig). It is only in appearance also that the suffix to נְתָחֶיהָ refers to the pot; actually it refers to the city, *i.e.* to the whole of its population, the different individuals in which are the separate pieces of flesh. The meaning of the instructions therefore is by no means doubtful: the whole of the population to be found in Jerusalem is to be brought out, and that without any exception, inasmuch as the lot, which would fall upon one and not upon another, will not be cast upon her. There is no necessity to seek for any causal connection between the reference to the rust upon the pot and the bringing out of the pieces of flesh that are cooking within it, and to take the words as signifying that all the pieces, which had been rendered useless by the rust upon the pot, were to be taken out and thrown away (Hävernick); but through the allusion to the rust the interpretation already passes beyond the limits of the figure. The pieces of flesh are to be brought out, after they have been thoroughly boiled, to empty the pot, that it may then be set upon the fire again, to burn out the rust adhering to it (ver. 11). There is no force in Kliefoth's objection, that this exposition does not agree with the context, inasmuch as, "according to the last clause of ver. 5 and vers. 10 and 11, the pieces of flesh and even the bones are not to be taken out, but to be boiled away by a strong fire; and the pot is to become empty not by the fact that the pieces of flesh are taken out and thrown away, but by the pieces being thoroughly boiled away, first to broth and then to nothing." For "boiling away to nothing" is not found in the text, but simply that even the bones are to be thoroughly done, so as to turn into the softness of jelly.—So far as the fact is concerned, we cannot follow the majority of commentators, who suppose that the reference is simply to the carrying away of the inhabitants into exile. Bringing the pieces of flesh out of the pot, denotes the sweeping away of the inhabitants from the city, whether by death (*vid.* ch. xi. 7) or by their being carried away captive. The city is to be emptied of men in consequence of its being blockaded by the king of Babylon. The reason of this is given in vers. 7 and 8, where the guilt of Jerusalem is depicted. The city has shed blood, which is not covered with earth, but has been left uncovered, like blood poured out upon a hard rock, which the stone cannot absorb, and which cries to God for vengeance, because it is uncovered (cf. Gen. iv. 10; Job xvi. 18; and Isa. xxvi. 21). The thought is this: she has sinned in an insolent and shameless manner, and has done nothing to cover her sin, has shown no sign of repentance or atonement, by which she might have got rid of her sin. This has all been ordered by God. He has caused the blood that was shed to fall upon a bare rock, that it might lie uncovered, and He might be able to execute vengeance for the crime.

The second turn in the address (ver. 9) commences in just the same manner as the first in ver. 6, and proceeds with a further picture of the execution of punishment. To avenge the guilt, God will make the pile of wood large, and stir up a fierce fire. The development of this thought is given in ver. 10 in the form of a command addressed to the prophet, to put much wood underneath, and to kindle a fire, so that both flesh and bones may boil away. הָתֵם, from תָּמַם, to finish, complete; with בָּשָׂר, to cook thoroughly. There are differences of opinion as to the true meaning of הָרְקַח הַמֶּרְקָחָה; but the rendering sometimes given to רָקַח, namely, to spice, is at all events unsuitable, and cannot be sustained by the usage of the language. It is true that in Ex. xxx. 25 sqq. the verb רָקַח is used for the preparation of the anointing oil, but it is not the mixing of the different ingredients that is referred to, but in all probability the thorough boiling of the spices, for the purpose of extracting their essence, so that "thorough boiling" is no doubt the true meaning of the word. In Job xli. 23 (31), מְרְקָחָה is the boiling unguent-pot. יֵחַר is a cohortative *Hiphil*, from חָרַר, to become red-hot, to be consumed.—Ver. 11. When the flesh and bones have thus been thoroughly boiled, the pot is to be placed upon the coals empty, that the rust upon it may be burned away by the heat. The emptying of the pot or kettle by pouring out the flesh, which has been boiled to broth, is passed over as self-evident. The uncleanness of the pot is the rust upon it. תִּתֻּם is an Aramaean form for תִּתֹּם = תָּתֹם. Michaelis has given the true explanation of the words: "*civibus caesis etiam urbs consumetur*" (when the inhabitants are slain, the city itself will be destroyed).[1]—In vers. 12 sqq. the reason is given, which rendered it necessary to inflict this exterminating judgment. In ver. 12 the address still keeps to the figure, but in ver. 13 it passes over to the actual fact. It (the pot) has exhausted the pains (תְּאֻנִים, ἀπ. λεγ.), namely, as ver. 13 clearly shows, the pains, or wearisome exertions, to make it clean by milder means, and not (as Hitzig erroneously infers from the following clause) to eat away the rust by such extreme heat. הֶלְאָת, third pers. *Hiphil* of לָאָה, is the earlier form, which fell into almost entire disuse in later times (*vid.*

---

[1] Hitzig discovers a *Hysteronproteron* in this description, because the cleaning of the pot ought to have preceded the cooking of the flesh in it, and not to have come afterwards, and also because, so far as the actual fact is concerned, the rust of sin adhered to the people of the city, and not to the city itself as a collection of houses. But neither of these objections is sufficient to prove what Hitzig wants to establish, namely, that the untenable character of the description shows that it is not really a prophecy; nor is there any force in them. It is true that if one intended to boil flesh in a pot for the purpose of eating, the first thing to be done would be to clean the pot itself. But this is not the object in the present instance. The flesh was simply to be thoroughly boiled, that it might be destroyed and thrown away, and there was no necessity to clean the pot for this purpose. And so far as the second objection is concerned, the defilement of sin does no doubt adhere to man, though not, as Hitzig assumes, to man alone. According to the Old Testament view, it extends to things as well (*vid.* Lev. xviii. 25, xxvii. 28). Thus leprosy, for example, did not pollute men only, but clothes and houses also. And for the same reason judgments were not restricted to men, but also fell upon cities and lands.

Ges. § 75, Anm. 1). The last words of ver. 11, I agree with Hitzig, Hävernick, and others, in taking as an exclamation. Because the pot has exhausted all the efforts made to cleanse it, its rust is to go into the fire. In ver. 13 Jerusalem is addressed, and זִמָּה is not a genitive belonging to בְּטֻמְאָתֵךְ, "on account of thy licentious uncleanness" (Ewald and Hitzig), but a predicate, "in thine uncleanness is (there lies) זִמָּה, i.e. an abomination deserving of death" (see Lev. xviii. 17 and xx. 14, where the fleshly sins, which are designated as *zimmâh*, are ordered to be punished with death). The cleansings which God had attempted, but without Jerusalem becoming clean, consisted in the endeavour, which preceded the Chaldean judgment of destruction, to convert the people from their sinful ways, partly by threats and promises communicated through the prophets (*vid*. 2 Chron. xxxvi. 15), and partly by means of chastisements. For הֵנִיחַ חֵמָה, see ch. v. 13. In ver. 14 there is a summary of the whole, which brings the threat to a close.

Vers. 15-24. THE SIGN OF SILENT SORROW CONCERNING THE DESTRUCTION OF JERUSALEM.—Ver. 15. *And the word of Jehovah came to me, saying*, Ver. 16. *Son of man, behold, I take from thee thine eyes' delight by a stroke, and thou shalt not mourn nor weep, and no tear shall come from thee.* Ver. 17. *Sigh in silence; lamentation for the dead thou shalt not make; bind thy head-attire upon thee, and put thy shoes upon thy feet, and do not cover thy beard, and eat not the bread of men.* Ver. 18. *And I spake to the people in the morning, and in the evening my wife died, and I did in the morning as I was commanded.* Ver. 19. *Then the people said to me, Wilt thou not show us what this signifies to us that thou doest so?* Ver. 20. *And I said to them, The word of Jehovah has come to me, saying,* Ver. 21. *Say to the house of Israel, Thus saith the Lord Jehovah, Behold, I will profane my sanctuary, the pride of your strength, the delight of your eyes, and the desire of your soul; and your* sons and your daughters, whom ye have left, will fall by the sword. Ver. 22. *Then will ye do as I have done, ye will not cover the beard, nor eat the bread of men;* Ver. 23. *And ye will have your head-attire upon your heads, and your shoes upon your feet; ye will not mourn nor weep, but will pine away in your iniquity, and sigh one toward another.* Ver. 24. *Thus will Ezekiel be a sign to you; as he hath done will ye do; when it cometh, ye will know that I the Lord am Jehovah.*—From the statements in ver. 18, to the effect that the prophet spoke to the people in the morning, and then in the evening his wife died, and then again in the (following) morning, according to the command of God, he manifested no grief, and in answer to the inquiry of the people explained to them the meaning of what he did, it is evident that the word of God contained in this section came to him on the same day as the preceding one, namely, on the day of the blockade of Jerusalem; for what he said to the people on the morning of this day (ver. 18) is the prophecy contained in vers. 3–14. Immediately after He had made this revelation to him, God also announced to him the approaching death of his wife, together with the significance which this event would have to the people generally. The delight of the eyes (ver. 16) is his wife (ver. 18) בְּמַגֵּפָה by a stroke, *i.e.* by a sudden death inflicted by God (*vid.* Num. xiv. 37, xvii. 13). On the occurrence of her death, he is neither to allow of any loud lamentings, nor to manifest any sign of grief, but simply to sigh in silence. מֵתִים אֵבֶל does not stand for אֵבֶל מֵתִים, but the words are both accusatives. The literal rendering would be: the dead shalt thou not make an object of mourning, *i.e.* thou shalt not have any mourning for the dead, as Storr (*Observv.* p. 19) has correctly explained the words. On occasions of mourning it was customary to uncover the head and strew ashes upon it (Isa. lxi. 3), to go barefoot (2 Sam. xv. 30; Isa. xx. 2), and to cover the beard, that is to say, the lower part of the face as far as the nose (Mic. iii. 7). Ezekiel is not to do any of these things, but to arrange his head-attire (פְּאֵר, the head-attire generally, or turban, vid. ver. 23 and Isa. lxi. 3, and not specially that of the priests, which is called פַּאֲרֵי הַמִּגְבָּעָה in Ex. xxxix. 28), and to put on his shoes, and also to eat no mourning bread. לֶחֶם אֲנָשִׁים does not mean *panis miserorum, cibus lugentium*, in which case אֲנָשִׁים would be equivalent to אֲנֵשִׁים, but bread of men, *i.e.* of the people, that is to say, according to the context, bread which the people were accustomed to send to the house of mourning in cases of death, to manifest their sympathy and to console and refresh the mourners,—a custom which gave rise in the course of time to that of formal funeral meals. These are not mentioned in the Old Testament; but the sending of bread or food to the house of mourning is clearly referred to in Deut. xxvi. 14, Hos. ix. 4, and Jer. xvi. 7 (see also 2 Sam. iii. 35).— When Ezekiel thus abstained from all lamentation and outward sign of mourning on the death of his dearest one, the people conjectured that such striking conduct must have some significance, and asked him what it was that he intended to show thereby. He then announced to them the word of God (vers. 20–24). As his dearest one, his wife, had been taken from him, so should its dearest object, the holy temple, be taken from the nation by destruction, and their children by the sword. When this occurred, then would they act as he was doing now; they would not mourn and weep, but simply in their gloomy sorrow sigh in silence on account of their sins, and groan one toward another. The profanation (חִלֵּל) of the sanctuary is effected through its destruction (cf. ch. vii. 24). To show the magnitude of the loss, the worth of the temple in the eyes of the nation is dwelt upon in the following clauses. גְּאוֹן עֻזְּכֶם is taken from Lev. xxvi. 19. The temple is called the pride of your strength, because Israel based its might and strength upon it as the scene of the gracious presence of God, living in the hope that the Lord would not give up His sanctuary to the heathen to be destroyed, but would defend the temple, and therewith Jerusalem and its inhabitants also (cf. Jer. vii. 4). מַחְמַל נַפְשְׁכֶם,

the desire or longing of the soul (from חָמַל, in Arabic, *desiderio ferri ad aliquam rem*). The sons and daughters of the people are the relatives and countrymen whom the exiles had been obliged to leave behind in Canaan.—The explanation of this lamentation and mourning on account of the destruction of the sanctuary and death of their relations, is to be found in the antithesis: וּנְמַקֹּתֶם בַּעֲוֹ׳, ye will pine or languish away in your iniquities (compare ch. iv. 17 and Lev. xxvi. 39). Consequently we have not to imagine either "stolid indifference" (Eichhorn and Hitzig), or "stolid impenitence" (Ewald), but overwhelming grief, for which there were no tears, no lamentation, but only deep inward sighing on account of the sins which had occasioned so terrible a calamity. נָהַם, lit. to utter a deep growl, like the bears (Isa. lix. 11); here to sigh or utter a deep groan. "One toward another," *i.e.* manifesting the grief to one another by deep sighs; not "full of murmuring and seeking the sin which occasioned the calamity in others rather than in themselves," as Hitzig supposes. The latter exposition is entirely at variance with the context. This grief, which consumes the bodily strength, leads to a clear perception of the sin, and also to true repentance, and through penitence and atonement to regeneration and newness of life. And thus will they attain to a knowledge of the Lord through the catastrophe which bursts upon them (cf. Lev. xxvi. 40 sqq.). For מוֹפֵת, a sign, see the comm. on Ex. iv. 21.

Vers. 25–27. Sequel of the Destruction of Jerusalem to the Prophet himself.—Ver. 25. *And thou, son of man, behold, in the day when I take from them their might, their glorious joy, the delight of their eyes and the desire of their soul, their sons and their daughters,* Ver. 26. *In that day will a fugitive come to thee, to tell it to thine ears.* Ver. 27. *In that day will thy mouth be opened with the fugitive, and thou wilt speak, and no longer be mute; and thus shalt thou be a sign to them that they may know that I am Jehovah.*—As the destruction of Jerusalem would exert a powerful influence upon the future history of the exiles on the Chaboras, and be followed by most important results, so was it also to be a turning-point for the prophet himself in the execution of his calling. Hävernick has thus correctly explained the connection between these closing verses and what precedes, as indicated by וְאַתָּה in ver. 25. As Ezekiel up to this time was to speak to the people only when the Lord gave him a word for them, and at other times was to remain silent and dumb (ch. iii. 26 and 27); from the day on which a messenger should come to bring him the tidings of the destruction of Jerusalem and the temple, he was to open his mouth, and not continue dumb any longer. The execution of this word of God is related in ch. xxxiii. 21, 22. The words, "when I take from them their strength," etc., are to be understood in accordance with ver. 21. Consequently מָעֻזָּם is the sanctuary, which was taken from the Israelites through the destruction of Jerusalem. The predicates which follow down to מַשָּׂא נַפְשָׁם refer to the temple (cf. ver. 21). מַשָּׂא נֶפֶשׁ, an object toward which the soul lifts itself up (נָשָׂא), i.e. for which it cherishes a desire or longing; hence synonymous with מַחְמַל נַפְשׁוֹ in ver. 21. The sons and daughters are attached ἀσυνδέτως. בַּיּוֹם הַהוּא (in that day), in ver. 26, which resumes the words בְּיוֹם קַחְתִּי וגו׳ (in the day when I take, etc.) in ver. 25, is not the day of the destruction of the temple, but generally the time of this event, or more precisely, the day on which the tidings would reach the prophet. הַפָּלִיט, with the generic article, a fugitive (vid. Gen. xiv. 13). לְהַשְׁמָעוּת אָזְנָיִם, to cause the ears to hear (it), i.e. to relate it, namely to the bodily ears of the prophet, whereas he had already heard it in spirit from God. הַשְׁמָעוּת, a verbal noun, used instead of the infinitive Hiphil. אֶת־הַפָּלִיט, with the escaped one, i.e. at the same time "with the mouth of the fugitive" (Hitzig). אֶת expresses association, or so far as the fact is concerned, simultaneousness. The words, "then wilt thou speak, and no longer be dumb," do not imply that it was only from that time forward that Ezekiel was to keep silence, but point back to ch. iii. 26 and 27, where silence is imposed upon him, with the exceptions mentioned there, from the very commencement of his ministry; and in comparison with that passage, simply involve *implicite* the thought that the silence imposed upon him then was to be observed in the strictest manner from the present time until the receipt of the intelligence of the fall of Jerusalem, when his mouth would be opened once more. Through the "words of God" that were given to His prophet (ch. iv.-xxiv.), the Lord had now said to the people of Israel all that He had to say concerning the approaching catastrophe for them to consider and lay to heart, that they might be brought to acknowledge their sin, and turn with sorrow and repentance to their God. Therefore was Ezekiel from this time forward to keep perfect silence toward Israel, and to let God the Lord speak by His acts and the execution of His threatening words. It was not till after the judgment had commenced that his mouth was to be opened again for still further announcements (*vid.* ch. xxxiii. 22).—Ezekiel was thereby to become a sign to the Israelites. These words have a somewhat different meaning in ver. 27 from that which they have in ver. 24. There, Ezekiel, by the way in which he behaved at the death of his wife, was to be a sign to the people of the manner in which they were to act when the judgment should fall upon Jerusalem; whereas here (ver. 27), לְמוֹפֵת refers to the whole of the ministry of the prophet, his silence hitherto, and that which he was still to observe, as well as his future words. Through both of these he was to exhibit himself to his countrymen as a man whose silence, speech, and action were alike marvellous and full of meaning to them, and all designed to lead them to the knowledge of the Lord, the God of their salvation.

Chap. XXV.–XXXII.—PREDICTIONS OF JUDGMENT UPON THE HEATHEN NATIONS.

While the prophet's mouth was to be mute to Israel, the Lord directed him to speak against the heathen nations, and to foretell to them the judgment of destruction, that they might not be lifted up by the fall of the people and kingdom of God, but might recognise in the judgment upon Israel a work of the omnipotence and righteousness of the Lord, the Judge of the whole earth. There are seven heathen nations whose destruction Ezekiel foretells in this section of his book, viz. (1) Ammon; (2) Moab; (3) Edom; (4) the Philistines (ch. xxv.); (5) Tyre, (6) Sidon (ch. xxvi.-xxviii.); and (7) Egypt (ch. xxix.-xxxii.). These prophecies are divided into thirteen words of God by the introductory formula, "The word of Jehovah came to me," the utterances against Ammon, Moab, Edom, and the Philistines, being all comprehended in one word of God; whereas there are four separate words of God directed against Tyre, one against Sidon, and seven against Egypt. In the seven nations and the seven words of God directed against Egypt we cannot fail to discover an allusion to the symbolical significance of the number. Sidon, which had lost its commanding position and become dependent upon Tyre long before the time of Ezekiel, is evidently selected for a special word of God only for the purpose of making up the number seven. And in order to make it the more apparent that the number has been chosen on account of its significance, Ezekiel divides his announcement of the judgment upon the seventh people into seven words of God. On the basis of Gen. i., seven is the number denoting the completion of the works of God. When, therefore, Ezekiel selects seven nations and utters seven words of God concerning the principal nation, namely Egypt, he evidently intends to indicate thereby that the judgment predicted will be executed and completed upon the heathen world and its peoples through the word and acts of God.—The predictions of judgment upon these seven heathen nations are divisible, accordingly, into two groups. Ammon, Moab, Edom, Philistia, Tyre, and Sidon form one group, while the second treats of Egypt alone. This is certainly the way in which the cycle of these prophecies is to be divided rather than the plan ordinarily adopted, according to which the nations included in ch. xxv., as representatives of the one phase of the world-power, are placed in contrast with the other phase of heathenism represented by Tyre, Sidon, and Egypt. The latter is the opinion entertained by Hävernick, for example, with regard to the " beautiful and symmetrical arrangement" of these prophecies. "First of all," says he, " the prophet shows in one series of nations how the idea of the judgment of God was realized in the case of those nations which rose up in direct and open hostility to the theocracy, and thereby represented the might of heathenism as turned away from God and engaged in downright rebellion against Him (ch. xxv.). The prophecies concerning Tyre and Sidon contemplate heathenism in a second aspect (ch. xxvi.–xxviii.). In Tyre we have an exhibition of pride or carnal security, which looks away from God, and plunges deeper and deeper into the sin and worthlessness of the natural life. Both aspects are then finally combined in Egypt, that ancient foe of the covenant nation, which had grown into a world-power, and while displaying in this capacity unbending arrogance and pride, was now, like all the rest, about to be hurled down from the summit of its ancient glory into a bottomless deep." But this interpretation is, in more than one respect, manifestly at variance with the substance of the prophecies. This applies, in the first place, to the antithesis which is said to exist between the nations threatened in ch. xxv. on the one hand, and Tyre and Sidon on the other. In the case of Ammon, Moab, Edom, and the Philistines, for example, the sins mentioned as those for which they would be overthrown by the judgment are their malicious delight at the fall of Israel, and their revengeful, hostile behaviour towards the covenant nation (ch. xxv. 3, 8, 12, 15). And in the same way, according to ch. xxvi. 2, Tyre had involved itself in guilt by giving utterance to its delight at the destruction of Jerusalem, which inspired the hope that everything would now flow into its own store. On the other hand, nothing is said in the case of Pharaoh and Egypt about malicious pleasure, or hostility, or enmity towards Israel or the kingdom of God; but Pharaoh has rendered himself guilty by saying: the Nile is mine, I have made it for myself; and by the fact that Egypt had become a staff of reed to the house of Israel, which broke when they sought to lean upon it (ch. xxix. 3, 6, 7). According to these obvious explanations, Ezekiel reckoned Tyre and Sidon among the nations that were inimically disposed towards Israel, even though the hostile attitude of the Phoenicians was dictated by different motives from those of Edom and the other nations mentioned in ch. xxv.; and the heathen nations are arranged in two groups, and not in three. This is established beyond all doubt, when we observe that each of these two groups terminates with a promise for Israel. To the threat of judgment uttered against Sidon there is appended the promise: and there shall be no more for Israel a malicious briar and smarting thorn from all that are round about them who despise them; and when the Lord shall gather Israel from its dispersion, then will He cause it to dwell safely and prosperously in His land, inasmuch as He will execute judgment upon all round about them who despise them (ch. xxviii. 24–26). And the prediction of judgment upon Egypt in the last prophecy uttered concerning this land, in the twenty-seventh year of the captivity (ch. xxix. 17), closes in a similar manner, with the promise that at the time when the Lord gives Egypt as spoil to the king of Babylon, He will cause a horn to grow to the house of Israel (ch. xxix. 21). The fact that these two prophecies correspond to each other would not have been overlooked by the commentators if the prophecy concerning Egypt, which was really the last in order of time, had been placed in its proper chronological position in the book of Ezekiel, namely, at the close of the words of God directed against that land.

The date of the great mass of these prophecies falls within the period of the last siege of Jerusalem by the Chaldeans, that is to say, in the interval between ch. xxiv. and ch. xxxiii., as the chronological data in the headings plainly affirm. The first word concerning Tyre is from the eleventh year of the captivity of Jehoiachin (ch. xxvi. 1). Of the prophecies against Egypt, the one in ch. xxix. 1–16 dates from the tenth month of the tenth year; that in ch. xxx. 20–26, from the first month of the eleventh year; that in ch. xxxi., from the third month of the same year; the two in ch. xxxii. 1 sqq. and 17 sqq., from the twelfth month of the twelfth year; and lastly, the brief utterance in ch. xxix. 17–21, from the twenty-seventh year of the captivity. There are no chronological data attached to the others. But the short, threatening words against the Ammonites, Moabites, Edomites, and Philistines in ch. xxv. belong to the time immediately succeeding the fall of Jerusalem, since they presuppose its having occurred. The second and third utterances concerning Tyre in ch. xxvii. and ch. xxviii. 1–19, as well as that concerning Sidon in ch. xxviii. 20 sqq., are closely connected, so far as their contents are concerned, with the first word of God against Tyre belonging to the eleventh year of the captivity. And lastly, the threatening word concerning Egypt in ch. xxx. 1–19, to which no definite chronological data are attached, appears to stand nearer in point of time to ch. xxix. 1–16 than to ch. xxix. 17–21.—Consequently the arrangement is based upon the subject-matter of the prophecies, and the chronological sequence is kept subordinate to this, or rather to the comparative importance of the several nations in relation to the theocracy.

These prophecies evidently rest upon the predictions of the earlier prophets against the same nations, so far as their contents are concerned; and in the threats directed against Tyre and Egypt, more especially, many of the thoughts contained in the prophecies of Isaiah (Isa. xxiii. and xix.) are reproduced and expanded. But notwithstanding this resting upon the utterances of earlier prophets, Ezekiel's prophecy against the heathen nations is distinguished in a characteristic manner from that of the other prophets, by the fact that he does not say a word about the prospect of these nations being ultimately pardoned, or of the remnant of them being converted to the Lord, but stops with the announcement of the utter destruction of the earthly and temporal condition of all these kingdoms and nations. The prophecy concerning Egypt in ch. xxix. 13–16, to the effect that after forty years of chastisement God will turn its captivity, and gather it together again, is only an apparent and not a real exception to this; for this turning of the judgment is not to bring about a restoration of Egypt to its former might and greatness or its glorification in the future; but, according to vers. 14 sqq., is simply to restore a lowly and impotent kingdom, which will offer no inducement to Israel to rely upon its strength. Through this promise, therefore, the threat of complete destruction is only somewhat modified, but by no means withdrawn. The only thing which Ezekiel positively holds out to view before the seven heathen nations is, that in consequence of the judgment falling upon them, they will learn that God is Jehovah, or the Lord. This formula regularly returns in the case of all the nations (*vid.* ch. xxv. 5, 7, 11, 17, xxvi. 6, xxviii. 22, 23, xxix. 6, 9, xxx. 8, 19, 25, 26, xxxii. 15); and we might take it to mean, that through the judgment of their destruction in a temporal respect, these nations will come to the knowledge of the God of salvation. And with this interpretation it would contain a slight allusion to the salvation, which will flourish in consequence of and after the judgment, in the case of those who have escaped destruction. If, however, we consider, on the one hand, that in the case of Edom (ch. xxv. 14) the formula takes a harsher form, namely, not that they shall know Jehovah, but that they shall experience His vengeance; and, on the other hand, that the

mighty Tyre is repeatedly threatened with destruction, even
eternal extinction (ch. xxvi. 20, 21, xxvii. 36, xxviii. 19), and
that the whole cycle of these prophecies closes with a funeral-
dirge on the descent of all the heathen nations into Sheol
(ch. xxxii. 17–32),—we shall see that the formula in question
cannot be taken in the sense indicated above, as Kliefoth maintains, but must be understood as signifying that these nations
will discern in their destruction the punitive righteousness of
God, so that it presents no prospect of future salvation, but
simply increases the force of the threat. There is nothing in
this distinction, however, to establish a discrepancy between
Ezekiel and the earlier prophets; for Ezekiel simply fixes his
eye upon the judgment, which will fall upon the heathen
nations, partly on account of their hostile attitude towards the
kingdom of God, and partly on account of their deification of
their own might, and is silent as to the salvation which will
accrue even to them out of the judgment itself, but without in
the least degree denying it. The reason for his doing this is
not that the contemplation of the particular features, which
form the details of the immediate fulfilment, has led him to
avert his eye from the more comprehensive survey of the entire
future;[1] but that the proclamation of the spread of salvation
among the heathen lay outside the limits of the calling which
he had received from the Spirit of God. The prophetic mission of Ezekiel was restricted to the remnant of the covenant
nation, which was carried into exile, and scattered among the
heathen. To this remnant he was to foretell the destruction

[1] Drechsler (in his commentary on Isa. xxiii.) has given the following
explanation of the distinction to be observed between the prophecies of
Isaiah and those of Ezekiel concerning Tyre,—namely, that in the case of
Isaiah the spirit of prophecy invests its utterances with the character of
totality, in accordance with the position assigned to this prophet at the
entrance upon a new era of the world, embracing the entire future even
to the remotest times, and sketching with grand simplicity the ground-
plan and outline of the whole; whereas in the case of the later prophets,
such as Jeremiah and Ezekiel, who were living in the midst of the historical
execution, the survey of the whole gives place to the contemplation of

of the kingdom of Judah, and after the occurrence of that catastrophe the preservation and eventual restoration of the kingdom of God in a renewed and glorified form. With this commission, which he had received from the Lord, there was associated, it is true, the announcement of judgment upon the heathen, inasmuch as such an announcement was well fitted to preserve from despair the Israelites, who were pining under the oppression of the heathen, and to revive the hope of the fulfilment of the promise held out before the penitent of their future redemption from their state of misery and restoration to the position of the people of God. But this would not apply to the prophecies of the reception of the heathen into the renovated kingdom of God, as they contained no special element of consolation to the covenant people in their depression.

In connection with this we have the equally striking circumstance, that Ezekiel does not mention Babylon among the heathen nations. This may also be explained, not merely from the predominance of the idea of the judgment upon Israel and Jerusalem, which the Chaldeans were to execute as "righteous men" (ch. xxiii. 45), so that they only came before him as such righteous men, and not as a world-power also (Kliefoth), but chiefly from the fact that, for the reason described above, Ezekiel's prophecy of the judgment upon the heathen is restricted to those nations which had hitherto cherished and displayed either enmity or false friendship toward Israel, and the Chaldeans were not then reckoned among the number.— For the further development of the prophecy concerning the future of the whole heathen world, the Lord had called the

particular features belonging to the details of the immediate fulfilment. But this explanation is not satisfactory, inasmuch as Jeremiah, notwithstanding the fact that he lived in the midst of the execution of the judgment, foretold the turning of judgment into salvation at least in the case of some of the heathen nations. For example, in ch. xlviii. 47 he prophesies to the Moabites, and in ch. xlix. 6 to the Ammonites, that in the future time Jehovah will turn their captivity; and in ch. xlvi. 26 he says, concerning Egypt, that after the judgment it will be inhabited as in the days of old.

prophet Daniel at the same time as Ezekiel, and assigned him his post at the seat of the existing heathen imperial power.

CHAP. XXV. AGAINST AMMON, MOAB, EDOM, AND THE PHILISTINES.

The prophecies, comprehended in the heading (ver. 1) in one "word of the Lord," against Ammon (vers. 1–7), Moab (vers. 8–11), Edom (vers. 12–14), and the Philistines (vers. 15–17), those four border-nations of Israel, are very concise, the judgment of destruction being foretold to them, in a few forcible lines, partly on account of their scorn at the fall of the people and kingdom of God, and partly because of actual hostility manifested toward them. The date of these utterances is not given in the heading; but in vers. 3, 6, and 8 the destruction of Jerusalem is presupposed as having already occurred, so that they cannot have been delivered till after this catastrophe.

Vers. 1–7. Against the Ammonites.—Ver. 1. *And the word of Jehovah came to me, saying,* Ver. 2. *Son of man, direct thy face towards the sons of Ammon, and prophesy against them,* Ver. 3. *And say to the sons of Ammon, Hear ye the word of the Lord Jehovah! Thus saith the Lord Jehovah, Because thou sayest, Aha! concerning my sanctuary, that it is profaned; and concerning the land of Israel, that it is laid waste; and concerning the house of Judah, that they have gone into captivity;* Ver. 4. *Therefore, behold, I will give thee to the sons of the east for a possession, that they may pitch their tent-villages in thee, and erect their dwellings in thee; they shall eat thy fruits, and they shall drink thy milk.* Ver. 5. *And Rabbah will I make a camel-ground, and the sons of Ammon a resting-place for flocks; and ye shall know that I am Jehovah.* Ver. 6. *For thus saith the Lord Jehovah, Because thou hast clapped thy hand, and stamped with thy foot, and hast rejoiced in soul with all thy contempt concerning the house of Israel,* Ver. 7. *Therefore, behold, I*

will stretch out my hand against thee, and give thee to the nations for booty, and cut thee off from the peoples, and exterminate thee from the lands; I will destroy thee, that thou mayst learn that I am Jehovah.
—In ch. xxi. 28 sqq., when predicting the expedition of Nebuchadnezzar against Jerusalem, Ezekiel had already foretold the destruction of the Ammonites, so that these verses are simply a resumption and confirmation of the earlier prophecy. In the passage referred to, Ezekiel, like Zephaniah before him (Zeph. ii. 8, 10), mentions their reviling of the people of God as the sin for which they are to be punished with destruction. This reviling, in which their hatred of the divine calling of Israel found vent, was the radical sin of Ammon. On the occasion of Judah's fall, it rose even to contemptuous and malicious joy at the profanation of the sanctuary of Jehovah by the destruction of the temple (a comparison with ch. xxiv. 21 will show that this is the sense in which נֶחֱלָל is to be understood), at the devastation of the land of Israel, and at the captivity of Judah, —in other words, at the destruction of the religious and political existence of Israel as the people of God. The profanation of the sanctuary is mentioned first, to intimate that the hostility to Israel, manifested by the Ammonites on every occasion that presented itself (for proofs, see the comm. on Zeph. ii. 8), had its roots not so much in national antipathies, as in antagonism to the sacred calling of Israel. As a punishment for this, they are not only to lose their land (vers. 4 and 5), but to be cut off from the number of the nations (vers. 6 and 7). The Lord will give up their land, with its productions, for a possession to the sons of the east, *i.e.*, according to Gen. xxv. 13–18, to the Arabs, the Bedouins (for בְּנֵי קֶדֶם, see the comm. on Judg. vi. 3 and Job i. 3). The *Piel* יָשְׁבוּ, although only occurring here, is not to be rejected as critically suspicious, and to be changed into *Kal*, as Hitzig proposes. The *Kal* would be unsuitable, because the subject of the sentence can only be בְּנֵי קֶדֶם, and not טִירוֹתֵיהֶם; and יָשַׁב in the *Kal* has an intransitive sense. For טִירוֹת, tent-villages of nomads, see the comm. on Gen.

xxv. 16. מִשְׁכָּנִים, dwellings, are the separate tents of the shepherds. In the last clauses of ver. 4, הֵמָּה is repeated for the sake of emphasis; and Hitzig's opinion, that the first הֵמָּה corresponds to the subject in the clause 'וְיָשְׁבוּ וגו, the second to that in וְנָתְנוּ, is to be rejected as a marvellous flight of imagination, which approaches absurdity in the assertion that פְּרִי הָאָרֶץ signifies the folds, *i.e.* the animals, of the land. Along with the fruit of the land, *i.e.* the produce of the soil, milk is also mentioned as a production of pastoral life, and the principal food of nomads. On the wealth of the Ammonites in flocks and herds, see Judg. vi. 5. The words are addressed to Ammon, as a land or kingdom, and hence the feminine suffix. The capital will also share the fate of the land. *Rabbah* (see the comm. on Deut. iii. 11) will become a camel-ground, a waste spot where camels lie down and feed. This has been almost literally fulfilled. The ruins of *Ammân* are deserted by men, and Seetzen found Arabs with their camels not far off (*vid.* von Raumer, *Palestine*, p. 268). In the parallel clause, the sons of Ammon, *i.e.* the Ammonites, are mentioned instead of their land.—In vers. 6 and 7, the Lord announces to the nation of the Ammonites the destruction that awaits them, and reiterates with still stronger emphasis the sin which occasioned it, namely, the malicious delight they had manifested at Israel's fall. בְּכָל־שָׁאטְךָ is strengthened by בְּנֶפֶשׁ: with all thy contempt in the soul, *i.e.* with all the contempt which thy soul could cherish. In ver. 7 the ἅπ. λεγ. לְבַג occasions some difficulty. The *Keri* has substituted לָבַז, for booty to the nations (cf. ch. xxvi. 5); and all the ancient versions have adopted this. Consequently בַּג might be a copyist's error for בַּז; and in support of this the circumstance might be adduced, that in ch. xlvii. 13, where בַּה stands for זוֹ, we have unquestionably a substitution of ג for ז. But if the *Chetib* בג be correct, the word is to be explained—as it has been by Benfey (*Die Montasnamen*, p. 194) and Gildemeister (in Lassen's *Zeitschrift für die Kunde des Morgenlandes*, iv. 1, p. 213 sqq.)—from the Sanscrit *bhâga*, *pars, portio*, and has passed into the Semitic languages from the Aryan, like the Syriac ܐܶܣܟܳܐ, *esca*, which P. Boetticher (*Horae aram.* p. 21) has correctly traced to the Sanscrit *bhoj, coquere*.—The executors of the judgment are not named; for the threat that God will give up the land of the Ammonites to the Bedouins for their possession, does not imply that they are to exterminate the Ammonites. On the contrary, a comparison of this passage with Amos i. 13-15 and Jer. xlix. 1-5, where the Ammonites are threatened not only with the devastation of their land, but also with transportation into exile, will show that the Chaldeans are to be thought of as executing the judgment. (See the comm. on ver. 11.)

Vers. 8-11. AGAINST THE MOABITES.—Ver. 8. *Thus saith the Lord Jehovah, Because Moab, like Seir, saith, Behold, like all other nations is the house of Judah:* Ver. 9. *Therefore, behold, I will open the shoulder of Moab from the cities, from its cities even to the last, the ornament of the land, Beth-hayeshimoth, Baal-meon, and as far as Kiryathaim,* Ver. 10. *To the sons of the east, together with the sons of Ammon, and will give it for a possession, that the sons of Ammon may no more be remembered among the nations.* Ver. 11. *Upon Moab will I execute judgments; and they shall learn that I am Jehovah.*—Moab has become guilty of the same sin against Judah, the people of God, as Ammon, namely, of misunderstanding and despising the divine election of Israel. Ammon gave expression to this, when Judah was overthrown, in the malicious assertion that the house of Judah was like all the heathen nations,—that is to say, had no pre-eminence over them, and shared the same fate as they. There is something remarkable in the allusion to Seir, *i.e.* Edom, in connection with Moab, inasmuch as no reference is made to it in the threat contained in vers. 9-11; and in vers. 12, 13, there follows a separate prediction concerning Edom. Hitzig therefore proposes to follow the example of the LXX., and erase it from the text as a gloss, but without being able in the smallest degree to show in what way it is probable that such a gloss could have found admission into an obviously unsuitable place. Seir is mentioned along with Moab to mark the feeling expressed in the words of Moab as springing, like the enmity of Edom towards Israel, from hatred and envy of the spiritual birthright of Israel, *i.e.* of its peculiar prerogatives in sacred history. As a punishment for this, Moab was to be given up, like Ammon, to the Bedouins for their possession, and the people of the Moabites were to disappear from the number of the nations. Vers. 9 and 10 form one period, לִבְנֵי קֶדֶם in ver. 10 being governed by פֹּתֵחַ in ver. 9. The shoulder of Moab is the side of the Moabitish land. In the application of the word כָּתֵף to lands or provinces, regard is had to the position of the shoulder in relation to the whole body, but without reference to the elevation of the district. We find an analogy to this in the use of כָּתֵף in connection with the sides of a building. In מֵהֶעָרִים וגו׳, the כִּי cannot be taken, in a privative sense, for מִהְיוֹת; for neither the article הֶעָרִים, nor the more emphatic מֵעָרָיו מִקָּצֵהוּ, allows this; but כִּי indicates the direction, "from the cities onwards," "from its cities onwards, reckoning to the very last,"—that is to say, in its whole extent. מִקָּצֵהוּ, as in Isa. lvi. 11, Gen. xix. 4, etc. This tract of land is first of all designated as a glorious land, with reference to its worth as a possession on account of the excellence of its soil for the rearing of cattle (see the comm. on Num. xxxii. 4), and then defined with geographical minuteness by the introduction of the names of some of its cities. *Beth-Hayeshimoth, i.e.* house of wastes (see the comm. on Num. xxii. 1), has probably been preserved in the ruins of *Suaime*, which F. de Saulcy discovered on the north-eastern border of the Dead Sea, a little farther inland (*vid. Voyage en terre sainte*, Paris 1865, t. i. p. 315). *Baal-Meon*,—when written fully, *Beth-Baal-Meon* (Josh. xiii. 17),—contracted into *Beth-Meon* in Jer. xlviii. 23, is to be sought for to the south-east of this, in the ruins of

Myun, three-quarters of an hour's journey to the south of Heshbon (see the comm. on Num. xxxii. 38). *Kiryathaim* was still farther south, probably on the site of the ruins of *El Teym* (see the comm. on Gen. xiv. 5 and Num. xxxii. 37). The *Chetib* קריתמה is based upon the form קְרִיָתָם, a secondary form of קִרְיָתַיִם, like דֹּתָה, a secondary form of דֹּתָיִן, in 2 Kings vi. 13. The cities named were situated to the north of the Arnon, in that portion of the Moabitish land which had been taken from the Moabites by the Amorites before the entrance of the Israelites into Canaan (Num. xxi. 13, 26), and was given to the tribe of Reuben for its inheritance after the defeat of the Amoritish kings by the Israelites; and then, still later, when the tribes beyond the Jordan were carried into captivity by the Assyrians, came into the possession of the Moabites again, as is evident from Isa. xv. and xvi., and Jer. xlviii. 1, 23, where these cities are mentioned once more among the cities of the Moabites. This will explain not only the naming of this particular district of the Moabitish country, but the definition, " from its cities." For the fact upon which the stress is laid in the passage before us is, that the land in question rightfully belonged to the Israelites, according to Num. xxxii. 37, 38, xxxiii. 49, Josh. xii. 2, 3, xiii. 20, 21, and that it was therefore unlawfully usurped by the Moabites after the deportation of the trans-Jordanic tribes; and the thought is this, that the judgment would burst upon Moab from this land and these cities, and they would thereby be destroyed (Hävernick and Kliefoth). עַל בְּנֵי־עַמּוֹן, not " over the sons of Ammon," but " in addition to the sons of Ammon." They, that is to say, their land, had already been promised to the sons of the east (ver. 4). In addition to this, they are now to receive Moab for their possession (Hitzig and Kliefoth). Thus will the Lord execute judgments upon Moab. Ver. 11 sums up what is affirmed concerning Moab in vers. 9 and 10, in the one idea of the judgments of God upon this people.—The execution of these judgments commenced with the subjugation of the Ammonites and Moabites by Nebuchadnezzar, five years after the destruction of Jerusalem (*vid.* Josephus, *Antt.* x. 9. 7, and M. von Niebuhr, *Gesch. Assurs*, etc., p. 215). Nevertheless the Ammonites continued to exist as a nation for a long time after the captivity, so that Judas the Maccabaean waged war against them (1 Macc. v. 6, 30–43); and even Justin Martyr speaks of Ἀμμανιτῶν νῦν πολὺ πλῆθος (*Dial. Tryph.* p. 272).—But Origen includes their land in the general name of Arabia (lib. i. *in Job*). The name of the Moabites appears to have become extinct at a much earlier period. After the captivity, it is only in Ezra ix. 1, Neh. xiii. 1, and Dan. xi. 41, that we find any notice of them as a people. Their land is mentioned by Josephus in the *Antiq.* xiii. 14. 2, and xv. 4, and in the *Bell. Jud.* iii. 3. 3.—A further fulfilment by the Messianic judgment, which is referred to in Zeph. ii. 10, is not indicated in these words of Ezekiel; but judging from the prophecy concerning the Edomites (see the comm. on ver. 14), it is not to be excluded.

Vers. 12–14. Against the Edomites.—Ver. 12. *Thus saith the Lord Jehovah, Because Edom acteth revengefully towards the house of Judah, and hath been very guilty in avenging itself upon them,* Ver. 13. *Therefore, thus saith the Lord Jehovah, I will stretch out my hand over Edom, and cut off man and beast from it, and make it a desert from Teman, and unto Dedan they shall fall by the sword.* Ver. 14. *And I will inflict my vengeance upon Edom by the hand of my people Israel, that they may do to Edom according to my anger and my wrath; and they shall experience my vengeance, is the saying of the Lord Jehovah.*—Whilst the Ammonites and the Moabites are charged with nothing more than malicious pleasure at the fall of Israel, and disregard of its divine calling, the Edomites are reproached with revengeful acts of hostility towards the house of Judah, and threatened with extermination in consequence. The עֲשׂוֹת, doing or acting of Edom, is more precisely defined as בִּנְקֹם וגו׳, i.e. as consisting in the taking of vengeance, and designated as very guilty, יַאְשְׁמוּ אָשׁוֹם. עָשָׂה, followed by בְּ with an infinitive, as in ch. xvii. 17. Edom had sought every opportunity of acting thus revengefully towards Israel (vid. Obad. vers. 11 sqq.; Amos i. 11), so that in ch. xxxv. 5 Ezekiel speaks of the "eternal enmity" of Edom against Israel. For this reason we must not restrict the reproach in ver. 12 to particular outbreaks of this revenge at the time of the devastation and destruction of Judah by the Chaldeans, of which the Psalmist complains in Ps. cxxxvii., and for which he invokes the vengeance of God upon Edom. Man and beast are to be cut off from Edom in consequence, and the land to become a desert from Teman to Dedan. These names denote not cities, but districts. *Teman* is the southern portion of Idumaea (see the comm. on Amos i. 12); and *Dedan* is therefore the northern district. *Dedan* is probably not the Cushite tribe mentioned in Gen. x. 7, but the tribe of the same name which sprang from the sons of Abraham by Keturah (Gen. xxv. 3), and which is also mentioned in Jer. xlix. 8 in connection with Edom. דְּדֶנֶה has ה local with *Seghol* instead of *Kametz*, probably on account of the preceding *a* (vid. Ewald, § 216c). There is no necessity to connect מִתֵּימָן with the following clause, as Hitzig and Kliefoth have done, in opposition to the accents. The two geographical names, which are used as a periphrasis for Idumaea as a whole, are distributed equally through the *parallelismus membrorum* between the two clauses of the sentence, so that they belong to both clauses, so far as the sense is concerned. Edom is to become a desert from Teman to Dedan, and its inhabitants from Teman to Dedan are to fall by the sword. This judgment of vengeance will be executed by God through His people Israel. The fulfilment of this threat, no doubt, commenced with the subjugation of the Edomites by the Maccabees; but it is not to be limited to that event, as Rosenmüller, Kliefoth, and others suppose, although the foundation was thereby laid for the disappearance of the national existence of Edom. For it is impossible with this limitation to do justice to the emphatic expression, "*my people* Israel." On the ground, therefore, of the prophecies in Amos ix. 12 and Obad. vers. 17 sqq., that the people of God are to take possession of Edom, when the fallen tabernacle of David is raised up again, *i.e.* in the Messianic times, which prophecies point back to that of Balaam in Num. xxiv. 18, and have their roots, as this also has, in the promise of God concerning the twin sons of Isaac, "the elder shall serve the younger" (Gen. xxv. 23), we must seek for the complete fulfilment in the victories of the people of God over all their foes, among whom Edom from time immemorial had taken the leading place, at the time when the kingdom of God is perfected. For even here Edom is not introduced merely as a single nation that was peculiarly hostile to Judah, but also as a type of the implacable enmity of the heathen world towards the people and kingdom of God, as in ch. xxxv., Isa. xxxiv. 63, etc. The vengeance, answering to the anger and wrath of Jehovah, which Israel, as the people of God, is to execute upon Edom, consists not merely in the annihilation of the national existence of Edom, which John Hyrcanus carried into effect by compelling the subjugated Edomites to adopt circumcision (see the comm. on Num. xxiv. 18), but chiefly in the wrathful judgment which Israel will execute in the person of Christ upon the arch-enemy of the kingdom of God by its complete extinction.

Vers. 15–17. AGAINST THE PHILISTINES.—Ver. 15. *Thus saith the Lord Jehovah, Because the Philistines act with revenge, and avenge themselves with contempt in the soul to destroy in everlasting enmity,* Ver. 16. *Therefore thus saith the Lord Jehovah, Behold, I will stretch out my hand over the Philistines, and cut off the Cretans, and destroy the remnant by the seashore.* Ver. 17. *And I will execute great vengeance upon them through chastisements of wrath, and they shall know that*

I am Jehovah, when I bring my vengeance upon them. — The Philistines resembled the Edomites and Ammonites in their disposition towards the covenant nation, the former in their thirst for revenge, the latter in their malicious rejoicing at Israel's fall. For this reason they had already been classed by Isaiah (xi. 14) with Edom, Moab, and Ammon as enemies, who would be successfully attacked and overcome by Israel, when the Lord had gathered it again from its dispersion. In the description of its sin towards Israel we have a combination of elements taken from the conduct of Edom and Ammon (vers. 12 and 6). They execute revenge with contempt in the soul (שְׁאָט בְּנֶפֶשׁ, as in ver. 6), with the intention to destroy (לְמַשְׁחִית) Israel; and this revenge springs from eternal, never-ending hostility. The Lord will cut off the whole of the people of the Philistines for this. כְּרֵתִים, Cretans, originally a branch of the Philistian people, settled in the south-west of Canaan. The name is used by Ezekiel for the people, as it had already been by Zephaniah (ii. 5), for the sake of the *paronomasia* with הִכְרַתִּי. The origin of the name is involved in obscurity, as the current derivation from *Creta* rests upon a very doubtful combination (cf. Stark, *Gaza*, pp. 66 and 99 sqq.). By the "remnant of the sea-coast," *i.e.* the remnant of the inhabitants of the coast of the Mediterranean, in other words, of the Philistines, the destruction of which had already been predicted by Amos (i. 8), Isaiah (xiv. 30), and Jeremiah (xlvii. 4), we are to understand the whole nation to the very last man, all that was still left of the Philistines (see the comm. on Amos i. 8).—The execution of the vengeance threatened by God began in the Chaldean period, in which Gaza was attacked by Pharaoh, and, judging from Jer. xlvii., the whole of Philistia was laid waste by the Chaldeans (see the fuller comments on this in the exposition of Jer. xlvii.). But the ultimate fulfilment will take place in the case of Philistia also, through the Messianic judgment, in the manner described in the commentary on Zeph. ii. 10.

CHAP. XXVI.-XXVIII.—AGAINST TYRE AND SIDON.

The greater portion of these three chapters is occupied with the prophecy concerning Tyre, which extends from ch. xxvi. 1 to ch. xxviii. 19. The prophecy against Sidon is limited to ch. xxviii. 20-26. The reason for this is, that the grandeur and importance of Phoenicia were concentrated at that time in the power and rule of Tyre, to which Sidon had been obliged to relinquish the hegemony, which it had formerly possessed over Phoenicia. The prophecy against Tyre consists of four words of God, of which the first (ch. xxvi.) contains the threat of destruction to the city and state of Tyre; the second (ch. xxvii.), a lamentation over this destruction; the third (ch. xxviii. 1-10), the threat against the king of Tyre; the fourth (ch. xxviii. 11-19), a lamentation over his fall.

CHAP. XXVI. THE FALL OF TYRE.

In four sections, commencing with the formula, "thus saith the Lord," Tyre, the mistress of the sea, is threatened with destruction. In the first strophe (vers. 2-6) there is a general threat of its destruction by a host of nations. In the second (vers. 7-14), the enemy is mentioned by name, and designated as a powerful one; and the conquest and destruction emanating from him are circumstantially described. In the third (vers. 15-18), the impression which this event would produce upon the inhabitants of the islands and coast-lands is depicted. And in the fourth (vers. 19-21), the threat is repeated in an energetic manner, and the prophecy is thereby rounded off.

This word of God bears in the introduction the date of its delivery to the prophet and enunciation by him.—Ver. 1. *It came to pass in the eleventh year, on the first of the month, that the word of Jehovah came to me, saying.*—The eleventh year of the exile of Jehoiachin was the year of the conquest and destruction of Jerusalem (Jer. lii. 6, 12), the occurrence of which is presupposed in ver. 2 also. There is something striking in the omission of the number of the month both here and in ch. xxxii. 17, as the day of the month is given. The attempt to discover in the words בְּאֶחָד לַחֹדֶשׁ an indication of the number of the month, by understanding לַחֹדֶשׁ as signifying the first month of the year: "on the first as regards the month," equivalent to, "in the first month, on the first day of it" (LXX., Luther, Kliefoth, and others), is as forced and untenable as the notion that that particular month is intended which had peculiar significance for Ezekiel, namely, the month in which Jerusalem was conquered and destroyed. The first explanation is proved to be erroneous by ver. 2, where the destruction of Jerusalem, which occurred in the fifth month of the year named, is assumed to have already happened. The second view is open to the objection that the conquest of Jerusalem happened in the fourth month, and the destruction in the fifth (Jer. lii. 6 and 12); and it cannot be affirmed that the conquest was of less importance to Ezekiel than the destruction. We cannot escape the conclusion, therefore, that the number of the month has been dropped through a corruption of the text, which has occurred in copying; but in that case we must give up all hope of being able to determine what the month really was. The conjecture offered by Ewald and Hitzig, that one of the last months of the year is intended, because Ezekiel could not have known before then what impression the conquest of Jerusalem had made upon Tyre, stands or falls with the naturalistic view entertained by these writers with regard to prophecy.

Vers. 2–6. Tyre shall be broken and utterly destroyed.— Ver. 2. *Son of man, because Tyre saith concerning Jerusalem, "Aha, the door of the nations is broken; it turneth to me; I shall become full; she is laid waste;"* Ver. 3. *Therefore thus saith the Lord Jehovah, Behold, I will come upon thee, O Tyre, and will bring up against thee many nations, as the sea bringing up its waves.* Ver. 4. *They will destroy the walls of Tyre, and throw down her towers; and I will sweep away* her dust from her, and make her a bare rock. Ver. 5. *She shall become a place for the spreading of nets in the midst of the sea, for I have spoken it, is the saying of the Lord Jehovah; and she shall become booty for the nations.* Ver. 6. *And her daughters which are in the land shall be slain with the sword; and they shall learn that I am Jehovah.*—TYRE, as in the prophecy of Isaiah (ch. xxiii.), is not the city of that name upon the mainland, ἡ πάλαι Τύρος or Παλαίτυρος, Old Tyre, which was taken by Shalmaneser and destroyed by Alexander (as Perizon., Marsh, Vitringa, J. D. Michaelis, and Eichhorn supposed), but Insular Tyre, which was three-quarters of a mile farther north, and only 1200 paces from the land, being built upon a small island, and separated from the mainland by a strait of no great depth (*vid.* Movers, *Phoenizier*, II. p. 288 sqq.). This Insular Tyre had successfully resisted the Assyrians (Josephus, *Antt.* ix. 14. 2), and was at that time the market of the nations; and in Ezekiel's day it had reached the summit of its greatness as mistress of the sea and the centre of the commerce of the world. That it is against this Tyre that our prophecy is chiefly directed, is evident from vers. 5 and 14, according to which Tyre is to become a bare rock in the midst of the sea, and from the allusion to the daughter cities, בַּשָּׂדֶה, in the field, *i.e.* on the mainland (in ver. 6), as contrasted with the position occupied by Tyre upon a rocky island in the sea; and, lastly, from the description given in ch. xxvii. of the maritime trade of Tyre with all nations, to which Old Tyre never attained, inasmuch as it possessed no harbour (*vid.* Movers, *l.c.* p. 176). This may easily be reconciled with such passages as vers. 6, 8, and ch. xxvii., xxviii., in which reference is also made to the continental Tyre, and the conquest of Tyre is depicted as the conquest of a land-city (see the exposition of these verses).—The threat against Tyre commences, as in the case of the nations threatened in ch. xxv., with a brief description of its sin. Tyre gave expression to its joy at the fall of Jerusalem, because it hoped to derive profit therefrom through the extension of its commerce and increase of its wealth. Different explanations have been given of the meaning of the words put into the mouth of Tyre. "The door of the nations is broken in pieces." The plural דַּלְתוֹת indicates the folding doors which formed the gate, and are mentioned in its stead. Jerusalem is the door of the nations, and is so called according to the current opinion of expositors, because it was the centre of the commerce of the nations, *i.e.* as a place of trade. But nothing is known to warrant the idea that Jerusalem was ever able to enter into rivalry with Tyre as a commercial city. The importance of Jerusalem with regard to other nations was to be found, not in its commerce, nor in the favourable situation which it occupied for trade, in support of which Hävernick refers to Herodotus, iii. 5, and Hitzig to Ezekiel xxiii. 40, 41, but in its sanctuary, or the sacred calling which it had received for the whole world of nations. Kliefoth has therefore decided in favour of the following view: That Jerusalem is called a gate of the nations, not because it had hitherto been open to the nations for free and manifold intercourse, but for the very opposite reason, namely, because the gate of Jerusalem had hitherto been closed and barred against the nations, but was now broken in pieces through the destruction of the city, and thereby opened to the nations. Consequently the nations, and notably Tyre, would be able to enter now; and from this fact the Tyrians hoped to derive advantage, so far as their commercial interests were concerned. But this view is not in harmony with the text. Although a gate is opened by being broken in pieces, and one may force an entrance into a house by breaking the door (Gen. xix. 9), yet the expression "door of the nations" cannot signify a door which bars all entrance on the part of the nations, inasmuch as doors and gates are not made to secure houses and cities against the forcible entrance of men and nations, but to render it possible for them to go out and in. Moreover, the supposition that "door of the nations" is equivalent to shutting against the nations, is not in harmony with the words נָסֵבָּה אֵלַי which follow. The expression "it has turned to me," or it is turned to me, has no meaning unless it signifies that through the breaking of the door the stream of the nations would turn away from Jerusalem to Tyre, and therefore that hitherto the nations had turned to Jerusalem. נָסֵבָּה is the 3d pers. perf. *Niphal* of סָבַב, for נָסַבָּה, formed after the analogy of נָמֵס, etc. The missing subject to נָסֵבָּה is to be found *ad sensum* in דַּלְתוֹת הָעַמִּים. It is not the door itself, but the entrance and streaming in of the nations, which had previously been directed towards Jerusalem, and would now turn to Tyre. There is no necessity, therefore, for Hitzig's conjecture, that אִמָּלְאָה should be altered into מְלֵאָה, and the latter taken as the subject. Consequently we must understand the words of the Tyrians as signifying that they had regarded the drawing of the nations to Jerusalem, *i.e.* the force of attraction which Jerusalem had hitherto exerted upon the nations, as the seat of the divine revelation of mercy, or of the law and judgment of the Lord, as interfering with their endeavour to draw all nations to themselves and gain them over to their purposes, and that they rejoiced at the destruction of Jerusalem, because they hoped that henceforth they would be able to attract the nations to themselves and enrich themselves with their possessions. This does not require that we should accredit the Tyrians with any such insight into the spiritual calling of Jerusalem as would lie beyond their heathen point of view. The simple circumstance, that the position occupied by Jerusalem in relation to the world apparently interfered with the mercantile interests of the Tyrians, would be quite sufficient to excite a malignant pleasure at the fall of the city of God, as the worship of God and the worship of Mammon are irreconcilably opposed. The source from which the envy and the enmity manifesting itself in this malicious pleasure took their rise, is indicated in the last words: "I shall fill myself, she (Jerusalem) is laid waste," which Jerome has correctly linked together thus: *quia illa deserta est, idcirco ego implebor*. אִמָּלְאָה, to be filled with merchandise and wealth, as in ch. xxvii. 25. On account of this disposition toward the kingdom of God, which led Tyre to expect an increase of power and wealth from its destruction, the Lord God would smite it with ruin and annihilation. הִנְנִי עָלַיִךְ, behold, I will come upon thee, as in ch. xiii. 8; Jer. l. 31, Nah. iii. 5. God will lead a powerful army against Tyre, which shall destroy its walls and towers. Instead of the army, "many nations" are mentioned, because Tyre is hoping to attract more nations to itself in consequence of the destruction of Jerusalem. This hope is to be fulfilled, though in a different sense from that which Tyre intended. The comparison of the advancing army to the advancing waves of the sea is very significant when the situation of Tyre is considered. הַיָּם is the subject to כְּהַעֲלוֹת, and the *Hiphil* is construed with לְ instead of the accusative (compare Ewald, § 292c with § 277e). According to Arrian, ii. 18. 3, and Curtius, iv. 2. 9, 12, and 3. 13, Insular Tyre was fortified all round with lofty walls and towers, which were certainly in existence as early as Nebuchadnezzar's time. Even the dust of the demolished buildings (עֲפָרָהּ) God would sweep away (סִחֵיתִי, ἅπ. λεγ., with a play upon שְׁחִתוֹ), so that the city, *i.e.* the site on which it had stood, would become a bare and barren rock (צְחִיחַ סֶלַע, as in ch. xxiv. 7), a place where fishermen would spread out their nets to dry. "Her daughters" also, that is to say, the towns dependent upon Tyre, "on the field," *i.e.* the open country,—in other words, their inhabitants, —would be slain with the sword.

In vers. 7–14 the threat is carried still further.—Ver. 7. *For thus saith the Lord Jehovah, Behold, I will bring against Tyre Nebuchadnezzar, the king of Babylon, from the north, the king of kings, with horses, and chariots, and horsemen, and a multitude of much people.* Ver. 8. *Thy daughters in the field he will slay with the sword, and he will erect siege-towers against thee, and throw up a rampart against thee, and set up shields against thee,* Ver. 9. *And direct his battering-rams against thy walls, and throw down thy towers with his swords.* Ver. 10. *From the multitude of his horses their dust will cover thee; from the noise of the horsemen, wheels, and chariots, thy walls will shake when he shall enter into thy gates, as they enter a city broken open.* Ver. 11. *With the hoofs of his horses he will tread down all thy streets; thy people he will slay with the sword, and thy glorious pillars will fall to the ground.* Ver. 12. *They will make booty of thy possessions, and plunder thy merchandise, destroy thy walls, and throw down thy splendid mansions, and sink thy stones, thy wood, and thy dust in the water.* Ver. 13. *I will put an end to the sound of thy songs, and the music of thy harps shall be heard no more.* Ver. 14. *I will make thee a bare rock; thou shalt be a place for the spreading of nets, and be built no more; for I Jehovah have spoken it, is the saying of the Lord Jehovah.*—Nebuchadnezzar, the great king of Babylon, —this is the meaning of the rhetorical description in these verses,—will come with a powerful army (ver. 7), smite with the sword the inland cities dependent upon Tyre (ver. 8, compare ver. 6), then commence the siege of Tyre, destroy its walls and towers (vers. 8b and 9), enter with his army the city in which breaches have been made, put the inhabitants to death (vers. 10 and 11), plunder the treasures, destroy walls and buildings, and cast the ruins into the sea (ver. 12). *Nebuchadrezzar*, or *Nebuchadnezzar* (for the name see the comm. on 2 Kings xxiv. 1), is called king of kings, as the supreme ruler of the Babylonian empire, because the kings of conquered provinces and lands were subject to him as vassals (see the comm. on Isa. x. 8). His army consists of war-chariots, and cavalry, and a great multitude of infantry. קָהָל וְעַם־רָב are co-ordinate, so far as the rhetorical style is concerned; but in reality עַם־רָב is subordinate to קָהָל, as in ch. xxiii. 24, inasmuch as the קָהָל consisted of עַם־רָב. On the siege-works mentioned in ver. 8b, see the comm. on ch. iv. 2. הֵקִים צִנָּה signifies the construction of a roof with shields, by which the besiegers were accustomed to defend themselves from the missiles of the defenders of the city wall while pursuing their labours. Herodotus repeatedly mentions such shield-roofs as used by the Persians (ix. 61. 99, 102), though, according to Layard, they are not to be found upon the Assyrian monuments (see the comm. on Nah. ii. 6). There is no doubt that מְחִי קָבְלֹו signifies the battering-ram, called כַּר in ch. xxi. 27, though the meaning of the words is disputed. מְחִי, literally, thrusting or smiting. קבלו, from קְבֵל, to be pointed either קָבְלֹו or קְבָלֹו (the form קְבָלֹו adopted by v. d. Hooght and J. H. Michaelis is opposed to the grammatical rules), has been explained by Gesenius and others as signifying *res opposita*, that which is opposite; hence מחי קבלו, the thrusting or demolishing of that which stands opposite. In the opinion of others, קְבָל is an instrument employed in besieging; but there is nothing in the usage of the language to sustain either this explanation or that adopted by Hävernick, "destruction of his defence." חַרְבוֹתָיו, his swords, used figuratively for his weapons or instruments of war, "his irons," as Ewald has very aptly rendered it. The description in ver. 10 is hyperbolical. The number of horses is so great, that on their entering the city they cover it with dust, and the walls shake with the noise of the horsemen and chariots. כִּמְבוֹאֵי עִיר מְב׳, literally, as the marchings into a broken city, *i.e.* a city taken by storm, generally are. The simile may be explained from the peculiar situation of Insular Tyre. It means that the enemy will enter it as they march into a land-fortress into which a breach has been made by force. The words presuppose that the besieger has made a road to the city by throwing up an embankment or dam. מַצְּבוֹת עֻזֵּךְ, the memorial pillars of thy might, and the pillars dedicated to Baal, two of which are mentioned by Herodotus (ii. 44) as standing in the temple of Hercules at Tyre, one of gold, the other of emerald; not images of gods, but pillars, as symbols of Baal. These sink or fall to the ground before the overwhelming might of the foe (compare Isa. xlvi. 1, xxi. 9, and 1 Sam. v. 3). After the slaughter of the inhabitants and the fall of the gods, the plundering of the treasures begins, and then follows the destruction of the city.

בָּתֵּי הַמְוָּה are not pleasure-houses ("pleasure-towers, or garden-houses of the wealthy merchants," as Ewald supposes), for there was not space enough upon the island for gardens (Strabo, xvi. 2. 23), but the lofty, magnificent houses of the city, the palaces mentioned in Isa. xxiii. 13. Yea, the whole city shall be destroyed, and that so completely that they will sweep stones, wood, and rubbish into the sea.—Thus will the Lord put an end to the exultation and rejoicing in Tyre (ver. 13; compare Isa. xiv. 11 and Amos v. 23).—The picture of the destruction of this powerful city closes with the repetition of the thought from ver. 5, that Tyre shall be turned into a bare rock, and shall never be built again.

Vers. 15–18. The tidings of the destruction of Tyre will produce great commotion in all her colonies and the islands connected with her.—Ver. 15. *Thus saith the Lord Jehovah to Tyre, Will not the islands tremble at the noise of thy fall, at the groaning of the wounded, at the slaughter in the midst of thee?* Ver. 16. *And all the princes of the sea will come down from their thrones, and will lay aside their robes and take off their embroidered clothes, and dress themselves in terrors, sit upon the earth, and they will tremble every moment, and be astonished at thee.* Ver. 17. *They will raise a lamentation for thee, and say to thee: How hast thou perished, thou who wast inhabited from out of the sea, thou renowned city, she who was mighty upon the sea, she and her inhabitants, who inspired all her inhabitants with fear of her!* Ver. 18. *Now do the islands tremble on the day of thy fall, and the islands in the sea are confounded at thy departure.*—הֲלֹא, *nonne*, has the force of a direct affirmation. קוֹל מַפֶּלֶת, the noise of the fall, stands for the tidings of the noise, since the noise itself could not be heard upon the islands. The fall takes place, as is added for the purpose of depicting the terrible nature of the event, at or amidst the groaning of the wounded, and the slaughter in the midst of thee. בֵּהָרֵג is the infinitive *Niphal*, with the accent drawn back on account of the following *Milel*, and should be pointed בְּהָרֵג. The word

אִיִּים, islands, is frequently used so as to embrace the coast lands of the Mediterranean Sea; we have therefore to understand it here as applied to the Phoenician colonies on the islands and coasts of that sea. The "princes of the sea" are not kings of the islands, but, according to Isa. xxiii. 8, the merchants presiding over the colonies of Tyre, who resembled princes. כִּסְאוֹת, not royal thrones, but chairs, as in 1 Sam. iv. 13, etc. The picture of their mourning recalls the description in Jonah iii. 6; it is not derived from that passage, however, but is an independent description of the mourning customs which commonly prevailed among princes. The antithesis introduced is a very striking one: clothing themselves in terrors, putting on terrors in the place of the robes of state which they have laid aside (see the similar trope in ch. vii. 27). The thought is rendered still more forcible by the closing sentences of the verse: they tremble לִרְגָעִים, by moments, *i.e.* as the moments return,—actually, therefore, "every moment" (*vid.* Isa. xxvii. 3).—In the lamentation which they raise (ver. 17), they give prominence to the alarming revolution of all things, occasioned by the fact that the mistress of the seas, once so renowned, has now become an object of horror and alarm. נוֹשֶׁבֶת מִיַּמִּים, inhabited from the seas. This is not to be taken as equivalent to "as far as the seas," in the sense of, whose inhabitants spread over the seas and settle there, as Gesenius (*Thes.*) and Hävernick suppose; for being inhabited is the very opposite of sending the inhabitants abroad. If מִן were to be taken in the geographical sense of direction or locality, the meaning of the expression could only be, whose inhabitants spring from the seas, or have migrated thither from all seas; but this would not apply to the population of Tyre, which did not consist of men of all nations under heaven. Hitzig has given the correct interpretation, namely, from the sea, or out of the seas, which had as it were ascended as an inhabited city out of the bosom of the sea. It is not easy to explain the last clause of ver. 17: who inspired all her inhabitants with their terror, or with terror of them (of themselves); for if the relative אֲשֶׁר is taken in connection with the preceding יֹשְׁבֶיהָ, the thought arises that the inhabitants of Tyre inspired her inhabitants, *i.e.* themselves, with their terror, or terror of themselves. Kimchi, Rosenmüller, Ewald, Kliefoth, and others, have therefore proposed to take the suffix in the second יֹשְׁבֶיהָ as referring to הַיָּם, all the inhabitants of the sea, *i.e.* all her colonies. But this is open to the objection, that not only is יָם of the masculine gender, but it is extremely harsh to take the same suffix attached to the two יֹשְׁבֶיהָ as referring to different subjects. We must therefore take the relative אֲשֶׁר and the suffix in חִתִּיתָם as both referring to הִיא וְיֹשְׁבֶיהָ: the city with its population inspired all its several inhabitants with fear of itself. This is not to be understood, however, as signifying that the inhabitants of Tyre kept one another in a state of terror and alarm; but that the city with its population, through its power upon the sea, inspired all the several inhabitants with fear of this its might, inasmuch as the distinction of the city and its population was reflected upon every individual citizen. This explanation of the words is confirmed by the parallel passages in ch. xxxii. 24 and 26.—This city had come to so appalling an end, that all the islands trembled thereat. The two hemistichs in ver. 18 are synonymous, and the thought returns by way of conclusion to ver. 15. אִיִּין has the Aramaean form of the plural, which is sometimes met with even in the earlier poetry (*vid.* Ewald, § 177*a*). צֵאת, departure, *i.e.* destruction.

Vers. 19-21. Thus will Tyre, covered by the waves of the sea, sink into the region of the dead, and vanish for ever from the earth.—Ver. 19. *For thus saith the Lord Jehovah, When I make thee a desolate city, like the cities which are no longer inhabited, when I cause the deep to rise over thee, so that the many waters cover thee,* Ver. 20. *I cast thee down to those who have gone into the grave, to the people of olden time, and cause thee to dwell in the land of the lower regions, in the ruins from the olden time, with those who have gone into the grave, that thou mayest be no longer inhabited, and I create that which is glorious in the land of the living.* Ver. 21. *I make thee a terror, and thou art no more; they will seek thee, and find thee no more for ever, is the saying of the Lord Jehovah.*—Not only will ruin and desolation come upon Tyre, but it will sink for ever into the region of the dead. In this concluding thought the whole threat is summed up. The infinitive clauses of ver. 19 recapitulate the leading thoughts of the previous strophes, for the purpose of appending the closing thought of banishment to the under-world. By the rising of the deep we are to understand, according to ver. 12, that the city in its ruins will be sunk into the depths of the sea. יוֹרְדֵי בוֹר, those who go down into the pit or grave, are the dead. They are described still further as עַם עוֹלָם, not "those who are sleeping the long sleep of death," or the generation of old whom all must join; but the people of the "old world" before the flood (2 Pet. ii. 5), who were buried by the waters of the flood, in accordance with Job xxii. 15, where עוֹלָם denotes the generations of the primeval world, and after the analogy of the use of עַם עוֹלָם in Isa. xliv. 7, to describe the human race as existing from time immemorial. In harmony with this, חָרְבוֹת מֵעוֹלָם are the ruins of the primeval world which perished in the flood. As עַם עוֹלָם adds emphasis to the idea of יוֹרְדֵי בוֹר, so also does בְּחָרָבוֹת מֵעוֹלָם to that of אֶרֶץ תַּחְתִּיּוֹת. Tyre shall not only descend to the dead in Sheol, but be thrust down to the people of the dead, who were sunk into the depths of the earth by the waters of the flood, and shall there receive its everlasting dwelling-place among the ruins of the primeval world which was destroyed by the flood, beside that godless race of the olden time. אֶרֶץ תַּחְתִּיּוֹת, land of the lowest places (cf. ch. xxxii. 18, 24), is a periphrasis for Sheol, the region of the dead (compare Eph. iv. 9, "the lower parts of the earth"). On וְנָתַתִּי צְבִי וגו׳ Hitzig has observed with perfect correctness: "If we retain the pointing as the first person, with which the place assigned to the *Athnach* (אֶ) coincides, we must at any rate not regard the clause as still dependent upon לְמַעַן, and the force of the לֹא as continued. We should then have to take the clause as independent and affirmative, as the accentuators and the Targum have done." But as this would give rise to a discrepancy between the two halves of the verse, Hitzig proposes to alter נָתַתִּי into the second person וְנָתַתִּי, so that the clause would still be governed by לֹא לְמַעַן. But the want of agreement between the two halves of the verse does not warrant an alteration of the text, especially if it lead to nothing better than the forced rendering adopted by Hitzig, "and thou no longer shinest with glory in the land of the living," which there is nothing in the language to justify. And even the explanation proposed by Hävernick and Kliefoth, "that I no longer produce anything glorious from thee (Tyre) in the land of the living," is open to this objection, that "from thee" is arbitrarily interpolated into the text; and if this were what Ezekiel meant, he would either have added לְךָ or written נְתַתִּיךְ. Moreover, the change of person is a sufficient objection to our taking נָתַתִּי as dependent upon לְמַעַן, and supplying לֹא. וְנָתַתִּי is evidently a simple continuation of וְהוֹשַׁבְתִּיךְ. And nothing but the weightiest objections should lead us to give up a view which so naturally suggests itself. But no such objections exist. Neither the want of harmony between the two halves of the verse, nor the context,—according to which Tyre and its destruction are referred to both before and immediately after,—forces us to the adoption of explanations at variance with the simple meaning of the words. We therefore adhere to the natural interpretation of the words, "and I set (establish) glory in the land of the living;" and understand by the land of the living, not the theocracy especially, but the earth, in contrast to the region of the dead. The words contain the general thought, that on and after the overthrow of the glory of the ungodly power of the world, He will create that which is glorious on the earth to endure for ever; and this He really does by the establishing of His kingdom.—Tyre, on the contrary, shall become, through its fate, an object of terror, or an example of sudden destruction, and pass away with all its glory, not leaving a trace behind. For ver. 21*b*, compare Isa. xli. 12 and Ps. xxxvii. 36. וַתֵּבָקְשִׁי, imperf. *Pual*, has *Chateph-patach* between the two *u*, to indicate emphatically that the syllable is only a very loosely closed one (*vid.* Ewald, § 31*b*, p. 95).

CHAP. XXVII. LAMENTATION OVER THE FALL OF TYRE.

The lamentation commences with a picture of the glory of the city of Tyre, its situation, its architectural beauty, its military strength and defences (vers. 3–11), and its wide-spread commercial relations (vers. 12–25); and then passes into mournful lamentation over the ruin of all this glory (vers. 26–36).

Vers. 1–11. Introduction and description of the glory and might of Tyre.—Ver. 1. *And the word of Jehovah came to me, saying,* Ver. 2. *And do thou, O son of man, raise a lamentation over Tyre,* Ver. 3. *And say to Tyre, Thou who dwellest at the approaches of the sea, merchant of the nations to many islands, thus saith the Lord Jehovah, Tyre, thou sayest, I am perfect in beauty.* Ver. 4. *In the heart of the seas is thy territory; thy builders have made thy beauty perfect.* Ver. 5. *Out of cypresses of Senir they built all double-plank-work for thee; they took cedars of Lebanon to make a mast upon thee.* Ver. 6. *They made thine oars of oaks of Bashan, thy benches they made of ivory set in box from the islands of the Chittaeans.* Ver. 7. *Byssus in embroidery from Egypt was thy sail, to serve thee for a banner; blue and red purple from the islands of Elishah was thine awning.* Ver. 8. *The inhabitants of Sidon and Arvad were thy rowers; thy skilful men, O Tyre, were in thee, they were thy sailors.* Ver. 9. *The elders of Gebal and its skilful men were with thee to repair thy leaks; all the ships of the sea and their mariners were in thee to barter thy goods.* Ver. 10. *Persian and Lydian and Libyan were in thine army, thy men of war; shield and helmet they hung up in thee; they gave brilliancy to thee.* Ver. 11. *The sons of Arvad and thine army were upon thy walls round about, and brave men were upon thy towers; they hung up their shields upon thy walls round about; they have made thy beauty perfect.*—The lamentation commences with an address to Tyre, in which its favourable situation for purposes of trade, and the perfect beauty of which she was conscious, are placed in the foreground (ver. 3). Tyre is sitting, or dwelling, at the approaches of the sea. מְבוֹאֹת יָם, approaches or entrances of the sea, are harbours into which ships sail and from which they depart, just as מְבוֹא הָעִיר, the gate of the city, is both entrance and exit. This description does not point to the city on the mainland, or Old Tyre, but answers exactly to Insular Tyre with its two harbours.[1] יֹשַׁבְתִּי, with the connecting *i*, which is apparently confounded here after the Aramaean fashion with the *i* of the feminine pronoun, and has therefore been marked by the Masora as superfluous (vid. Ewald, § 211*b*). The combination of רֹכֶלֶת with אֶל אִיִּים ר may be accounted for from the primary meaning of רָכַל, to travel about as a merchant: thou who didst go to the nations on many shores to carry on thy trade. Tyre itself considers that she is perfect in her beauty, partly on account of her strong position in the sea, and partly because of her splendid edifices.[2] In the description which follows of this

---

[1] Insular Tyre possessed two harbours, a northern one called the Sidonian, because it was on the Sidonian side, and one on the opposite or south-eastern side, which was called the Egyptian harbour from the direction in which it pointed. The Sidonian was the more celebrated of the two, and consisted of an inner harbour, situated within the wall of the city, and an outer one, formed by a row of rocks, which lay at a distance of about three hundred paces to the north-west of the island, and ran parallel to the opposite coast of the mainland, so as to form a roadstead in which ships could anchor (*vid.* Arrian, ii. 20; Strabo, xvi. 2. 23). This northern harbour is still held by the city of *Sur*, whereas the Egyptian harbour with the south-eastern portion of the island has been buried by the sand driven against the coasts by the south winds, so that even the writers of the Middle Ages make no allusion to it. (See Movers, *Phönizier*, II. 1, pp. 214 sqq.)

[2] Curtius, iv. 2: *Tyrus et claritate et magnitudine ante omnes urbes Syriae Phoenicesque memorabilis.* (Cf. Strabo, xvi. 2. 22.)

beauty and glory, from ver. 4 onwards, Tyre is depicted allegorically as a beautiful ship, splendidly built and equipped throughout, and its destruction is afterwards represented as a shipwreck occasioned by the east wind (vers. 26 sqq.).[1] The words, "in the heart of the seas is thy territory" (ver. 4a), are equally applicable to the city of Tyre and to a ship, the building of which is described in what follows. The comparison of Tyre to a ship was very naturally suggested by the situation of the city in the midst of the sea, completely surrounded by water. As a ship, it must of necessity be built of wood. The shipbuilders selected the finest kinds of wood for the purpose; cypresses of Antilibanus for double planks, which formed the sides of the vessel, and cedar of Lebanon for the mast. *S'nir*, according to Deut. iii. 9, was the Amoritish name of *Hermon* or *Antilibanus*, whereas the Sidonians called it *Sirion*. On the other hand, *S'nir* occurs in 1 Chron. v. 23, and *Sh'nir* in Song of Sol. iv. 8, in connection with *Hermon*, where they are used to denote separate portions of Antilibanus. Ezekiel evidently uses *Senir* as a foreign name, which had been retained to his own time, whereas *Sirion* had possibly become obsolete, as the names had both the same meaning (see the comm. on Deut. iii. 9). The naming of the places from which the several materials were obtained for the fitting out of the ship, serve to heighten the glory of its construction and give an ideal character to the picture. All lands have contributed their productions to complete the glory and might of Tyre. Cypress-wood was frequently used by the ancients for buildings and (according to Virgil, *Georg.* ii. 443) also for ships, because it was

---

[1] Jerome recognised this allegory, and has explained it correctly as follows: " He (the prophet) speaks τροπικῶς, as though addressing a ship, and points out its beauty and the abundance of everything. Then, after having depicted all its supplies, he announces that a storm will rise, and the south wind (*auster*) will blow, by which great waves will be gathered up, and the vessel will be wrecked. In all this he is referring to the overthrow of the city by King Nabuchodonosor," etc. Raschi and others give the same explanation.

exempt from the attacks of worms, and was almost imperishable, and yet very light (Theophr. *Hist. plant.* v. 8; Plinii *Hist. nat.* xvi. 79). לֻחֹתַיִם, a dual form, like הֹמֹתַיִם in 2 Kings xxv. 4, Isa. xxii. 11, double-planks, used for the two side-walls of the ship. For oars they chose oaks of Bashan (מָשׁוֹט as well as מָשׁוֹט in ver. 29 from שׁוּט, to row), and the rowing benches (or deck) were of ivory inlaid in box. קֶרֶשׁ is used in Ex. xxvi. 15 sqq. for the boards or planks of the wooden walls of the tabernacle; here it is employed in a collective sense, either for the rowing benches, of which there were at least two, and sometimes three rows in a vessel, one above another, or more properly, for the deck of the vessel (Hitzig). This was made of *shen*, or ivory, inlaid in wood. The ivory is mentioned first as the most valuable material of the קֶרֶשׁ, the object being to picture the ship as possessing all possible splendour. The expression בַּת־אֲשֻׁרִים occasions some difficulty, partly on account of the use of the word בַּת, and partly in connection with the meaning of אֲשֻׁרִים, although so much may be inferred from the context, that the allusion is to some kind of wood inlaid with ivory, and the custom of inlaying wood with ivory for the purpose of decoration is attested by Virgil, *Aen.* x. 137:

> " *Vel quale per artem*
> *Inclusum buxo, aut Oricia terebintho*
> *Lucet ebur.*"

But the use of בַּת does not harmonize with the relation of the wood to the ivory inserted in wood; nor can it be defended by the fact that in Lam. iii. 3 an arrow is designated "the son of the quiver." According to this analogy, the ivory ought to have been called the son of the Ashurim, because the ivory is inserted in the wood, and not the wood in the ivory.[1] We must therefore adopt the solution proposed by R. Salomo and others, —namely, that the Masoretic division of בת־אשרים into two words is founded upon a mistake, and that it should be read as

[1] The Targum has paraphrased it in this way: דַּפִּין דְּאֹשִׁכְרְעִין מְכַבְּשִׁין בְּשֵׁן דְּפִיל, *i.e.* planks of box or pine inlaid with ivory.

one word בִּתְאַשֻּׁרִים, ivory in תְּאַשֻּׁרִים, *i.e.* either sherbin-cedar (according to more recent expositors), or box-wood, for which Bochart (*Phal.* III. 5) has decided. The fact that in Isa. lx. 13 the תְּאַשּׁוּר is mentioned among the trees growing upon Lebanon, whereas here the תְּאַשֻּׁרִים are described as coming from the islands of the כִּתִּים, does not furnish a decisive argument to the contrary. We cannot determine with certainty what species of tree is referred to, and therefore it cannot be affirmed that the tree grew upon Lebanon alone, and not upon the islands of the Mediterranean. כִּתִּים are the Κιτιεῖς, the inhabitants of the port of Κίτιον in Cyprus; then the Cyprians generally; and here, as in Jer. ii. 10, where אִיֵּי of the כִּתִּים are mentioned, in a still broader sense, inhabitants of Cyprus and other islands and coast-lands of the Mediterranean. In 1 Macc. i. 1 and viii. 5, even Macedonia is reckoned as belonging to the γῆ Χεττειείμ or Κιτιέων. Consequently the place from which the תְּאַשֻּׁרִים were brought does not furnish any conclusive proof that the Cyprian pine is referred to, although this was frequently used for ship-building. There is just as much ground for thinking of the box, as Bochart does, and we may appeal in support of this to the fact that, according to Theophrastus, there is no place in which it grows more vigorously than on the island of Corsica. In any case, Ezekiel mentions it as a very valuable kind of wood; though we cannot determine with certainty to what wood he refers, either from the place where it grew or from the accounts of the ancients concerning the kinds of wood that ship-builders used. The reason for this, however, is a very simple one,—namely, that the whole description has an ideal character, and, as Hitzig has correctly observed, " the application of the several kinds of wood to the different parts of the ship is evidently only poetical."

The same may be said of the materials of which, according to ver. 7, the sails and awning of the ship were made. *Byssus* in party-coloured work (רִקְמָה, see comm. on Ex. xxvi. 36), *i.e.*

woven in mixed colours, probably not merely in stripes, but woven with figures and flowers.[1] "From Egypt;" the byssus-weaving of Egypt was celebrated in antiquity, so that byssus-linen formed one of the principal articles of export (*vid.* Movers, *ut supra*, pp. 317 sqq.). מִפְרָשׂ, literally, spreading out, evidently signifies the sail, which we expect to find mentioned here, and with which the following clause, "to serve thee for a banner," can be reconciled, inasmuch as it may be assumed either that the sails also served for a banner, because the ships had no actual flag, like those in Wilkinson's engraving, or that the flag (נֵס) being also extended is included under the term מִפְרָשׂ (Hitzig). The covering of the ship, *i.e.* the awning which was put up above the deck for protection from the heat of the sun, consisted of purple (תְּכֵלֶת and אַרְגָּמָן, see the comm. on Ex. xxv. 4) from the islands of *Elishah*, *i.e.* of the Grecian Peloponnesus, which naturally suggests the Laconian purple so highly valued in antiquity on account of its splendid colour (Plin. *Hist. nat.* ix. 36, xxi. 8). The account of the building of the ship is followed by the manning, and the attention paid to its condition. The words of ver. 8*a* may be taken as referring quite as much to the ship as to the city, which was in possession of ships, and is mentioned by name in ver. 8*b*. The reference to the *Sidonians* and *Arvad*, *i.e.* to the inhabitants of *Aradus*, a rocky island to the north of Tripolis, as rowers, is not at variance with the latter; since there is no need to understand by the rowers either slaves or servants employed to row, and the Tyrians certainly drew their rowers from the whole of the Phoenician population, whereas the chief men in command of

---

[1] See Wilkinson, *Manners and Customs*, III. Pl. xvi., where engravings are given of Egyptian state-ships with embroidered sails. On one ship a large square sail is displayed in purple-red and purple-blue checks, surrounded by a gold border. The vessel of Antony and Cleopatra in the battle of Actium had also purple sails; and in this case the purple sails were the sign of the admiral's ship, just as in Ezekiel they serve as a mark of distinction (נֵס). See Movers, II. 3, p. 165, where the accounts of ancient writers concerning such state-ships are collected together.

the ships, the captain and pilot (חֹבְלִים), were no doubt as a rule citizens of Tyre. The introduction of the inhabitants of *Gebal*, *i.e.* the *Byblos* of the Greeks, the present *Jebail*, between Tripolis and Berytus (see the comm. on Josh. xiii. 5), who were noted even in Solomon's time as skilful architects (1 Kings v. 32), as repairers of the leak, decidedly favours the supposition that the idea of the ship is still kept in the foreground; and by the naming of those who took charge of the piloting and condition of the vessel, the thought is expressed that all the cities of Phoenicia assisted to maintain the might and glory of Tyre, since Tyre was supreme in Phoenicia. It is not till ver. 9*b* that the allegory falls into the background. Tyre now appears no longer as a ship, but as a maritime city, into which all the ships of the sea sail, to carry on and improve her commerce.—Vers. 10, 11. Tyre had also made the best provision for its defence. It maintained an army of mercenary troops from foreign countries to protect its colonies and extend its settlements, and entrusted the guarding of the walls of the city to fighting men of Phoenicia. The hired troops specially named in ver. 10 are *Pharas*, *Lud*, and *Phut*. פּוּט is no doubt an African tribe, in Coptic *Phaiat*, the Libyans of the ancients, who had spread themselves over the whole of North Africa as far as Mauretania (see the comm. on Gen. x. 6). לוּד is not the Semitic people of that name, the Lydians (Gen. x. 22), but here, as in ch. xxx. 5, Isa. lxvi. 19, and Jer. xlvi. 9, the Hamitic people of לוּדִים (Gen. x. 13), probably a general name for the whole of the Moorish tribes, since לוּד (ch. xxx. 5) and לוּדִים (Jer. xliv. 9) are mentioned in connection with פּוּט as auxiliaries in the Egyptian army. There is something striking in the reference to פָּרַס, the Persians. Hävernick points to the early intercourse carried on by the Phoenicians with Persia through the Persian Gulf, through which the former would no doubt be able to obtain mercenary soldiers, for which it was a general rule to select tribes as remote as possible. Hitzig objects to this, on the ground that there is no proof that this intercourse with Persia through the Persian Gulf was carried on in Ezekiel's time, and that even if it were, it does not follow that there were any Persian mercenaries. He therefore proposes to understand by פרס, Persians who had settled in Africa in the olden time. But this settlement cannot be inferred with sufficient certainty either from Sallust, *Jug.* c. 18, or from the occurrence of the African Μάκαι of Herodotus, iv. 175, along with the Asiatic (Ptol. vi. 7. 14), to take it as an explanation of פָּרַס. If we compare ch. xxxviii. 5, where *Pâras* is mentioned in connection with *Cush* and *Phut*, *Gomer* and *Togarmah*, as auxiliaries in the army of *Gog*, there can be no doubt that Asiatic Persians are intended there. And we have to take the word in the same sense here; for Hitzig's objections consist of pure conjectures which have no conclusive force. Ezekiel evidently intends to give the names of tribes from the far-off east, west, and south, who were enlisted as mercenaries in the military service of Tyre. Hanging the shields and helmets in the city, to ornament its walls, appears to have been a Phoenician custom, which Solomon also introduced into Judah (1 Kings x. 16, 17; Song of Sol. iv. 4), and which is mentioned again in the times of the Maccabees (1 Macc. iv. 57).—A distinction is drawn in ver. 11 between the mercenary troops on the one hand, and the Aradians, and חֵילֵךְ, thine army, the military corps consisting of Tyrians, on the other. The latter appear upon the walls of Tyre, because native troops were employed to watch and defend the city, whilst the mercenaries had to march into the field. The ἀπ. λεγ. גַּמָּדִים (*Gammâdim*) signifies brave men, as Roediger has conclusively shown from the Syrian usage, in his *Addenda* to Gesenius' *Thes.* p. 70 seq. It is therefore an *epitheton* of the native troops of Tyre.—With the words, "they (the troops) completed thy beauty," the picture of the glory of Tyre is rounded off, returning to its starting-point in vers. 4 and 5.

Vers. 12–25. This is followed by a description of the commerce of Tyre with all nations, who delivered their productions in the market of this metropolis of the commerce of the world, and received the wares and manufactures of this city in return. —Ver. 12. *Tarshish traded with thee for the multitude of goods of all kinds; with silver, iron, tin, and lead they paid for thy sales.* Ver. 13. *Javan, Tubal, and Meshech, they were thy merchants; with souls of men and brazen vessels they made thy barter.* Ver. 14. *From the house of Togarmah they paid horses, riding-horses, and mules for thy sales.* Ver. 15. *The sons of Dedan were thy merchants; many islands were at thy hand for commerce; ivory horns and ebony they brought thee in payment.* Ver. 16. *Aram traded with thee for the multitude of thy productions; with carbuncle, red purple, and embroidery, and byssus, and corals, and rubies they paid for thy sales.* Ver. 17. *Judah and the land of Israel, they were thy merchants; with wheat of Minnith and confectionery, and honey and oil, and balsam they made thy barter.* Ver. 18. *Damascus traded with thee in the multitude of thy productions, for the multitude of goods of all kinds, with wine of Chelbon and white wool.* Ver. 19. *Vedan and Javan from Uzal gave wrought iron for thy sales; cassia and calamus were for thy barter.* Ver. 20. *Vedan was thy merchant in cloths spread for riding.* Ver. 21. *Arabia and all the princes of Kedar, they were at thy hand for commerce; lambs and rams and he-goats, in these they traded with thee.* Ver. 22. *The merchants of Sheba and Ragmah, they were thy merchants; with all kinds of costly spices and with all kinds of precious stones and gold they paid for thy sales.* Ver. 23. *Haran, and Canneh, and Eden, the merchants of Sheba, Asshur, Chilmad, were thy merchants;* Ver. 24. *They were thy merchants in splendid clothes, in purple and embroidered robes, and in treasures of twisted yarn, in wound and strong cords for thy wares.* Ver. 25. *The ships of Tarshish were thy caravans, thy trade, and thou wast filled and glorious in the heart of the seas.*—The enumeration of the different peoples, lands, and cities, which carried on trade with Tyre, commences with Tarshish (Tartessus) in the extreme west, then turns to the north, passes through the different lands of Anterior Asia and the Mediterranean to the remotest north-east, and ends by mentioning Tarshish again, to round off the list. But the lands and peoples, which are mentioned in vers. 5-11 as furnishing produce and manufactures for the building of Tyre, viz. Egypt and the tribes of Northern Africa, are left out.—To avoid wearisome uniformity in the enumeration, Ezekiel has used interchangeably the synonymous words which the language possessed for trade, besides endeavouring to give life to the description by a variety of turns of expression. Thus סֹחַרְתֵּךְ (vers. 12, 16, 18), סֹחֲרַיִךְ (ver. 21), and סֹחֲרַת יָדֵךְ (ver. 15), or סֹחֲרֵי יָדֵךְ (ver. 21), are interchanged with רֹכְלַיִךְ (vers. 13, 15, 17, 22, 24), רֹכַלְתֵּךְ (vers. 20, 23), and מַרְכֻּלְתֵּךְ (ver. 24); and, again, נָתַן עִזְבוֹנַיִךְ (vers. 12, 14, 22) or נָתַן בְּעִזְבוֹנַיִךְ (vers. 16, 19) with נָתַן מַעֲרָבֵךְ (vers. 13, 17), and בְּמַעֲרָבֵךְ הָיָה (ver. 19), and הֵשִׁיב אֶשְׁכָּרֵךְ (ver. 15). The words סֹחֵר, participle of סָחַר, and רֹכֵל, from רָכַל, signify merchants, traders, who travel through different lands for purposes of trade. סֹחֶרֶת, literally, the female trader; and סְחֹרָה, literally, trade; then used as abstract for concrete, the tradesman or merchant. רֹכֵל, the travelling merchant.—רֹכֶלֶת, the female trader, a city carrying on trade. מַרְכֹּלֶת, trade or a place of trade, a commercial town. עִזְבוֹנִים (pluralet.) does not mean a place of trade, market, and profits (Gesenius and others); but according to its derivation from עָזַב, to leave, relinquish, literally, leaving or giving up, and as Gusset. has correctly explained it, "that which you leave with another in the place of something else which he has given up to you." Ewald, in accordance with this explanation, has adopted the very appropriate rendering *Absatz*, or sale. נָתַן עִזְבוֹנַיִךְ, with בְּ, or with a double accusative, literally, to make thy sale with something, *i.e.* to pay or to give, *i.e.* pay, something as an equivalent for the sale; נָתַן בְּעִזְבוֹ, to give something for the sale, or the goods to be sold. מַעֲרָב, barter, goods bartered with נָתַן, to give bartered goods, or carry on trade by barter.

The following are the countries and peoples enumerated:—
תַּרְשִׁישׁ, the Tyrian colony of *Tarshish* or *Tartessus*, in *Hispania Baetica*, which was celebrated for its wealth in silver (Jer. x. 9), and, according to the passage before us, also supplied iron, tin, and lead (*vid.* Plin. *Hist. nat.* iii. 3 (4), xxxiii. 6 (31), xxxiv. 14 (41); Diod. Sic. v. 38). Further particulars concerning Tarshish are to be found in Movers, *Phoeniz.* II. 2, pp. 588 sqq., and II. 3, p. 36.—*Javan*, *i.e.* Jania, Greece or Greeks.—*Tubal* and *Meshech* are the *Tibareni* and *Moschi* of the ancients between the Black and Caspian Seas (see the comm. on Gen. x. 2). They supplied souls of men, *i.e.* slaves, and things in brass. The slave trade was carried on most vigorously by the Ionians and Greeks (see Joel iv. 6, from which we learn that the Phoenicians sold prisoners of war to them); and both Greeks and Romans drew their largest suplies and the best slaves from the Pontus (for proofs of this, see Movers, II. 3, pp. 81 seq.). It is probable that the principal supplies of brazen articles were furnished by the Tibareni and Moschi, as the Colchian mountains still contain an inexhaustible quantity of copper. In Greece, copper was found and wrought in *Euboea* alone; and the only other rich mines were in Cyprus (*vid.* Movers, II. 3, pp. 66, 67).—Ver. 14. "From the house of *Togarmah* they paid," *i.e.* they of the house of Togarmah paid. *Togarmah* is one of the names of the *Armenians* (see the comm. on Gen. x. 3); and Strabo (XI. 14. 9) mentions the wealth of Armenia in horses, whilst that in asses is attested by Herodotus (i. 194), so that we may safely infer that mules were also bred there.—Ver. 15. The sons of *Dedan*, or the Dedanites, are, no doubt, the Dedanites mentioned in Gen. x. 7 as descendants of Cush, who conducted the carrying trade between the Persian Gulf and Tyre, and whose caravans are mentioned in Isa. xxi. 13. Their relation to the Semitic Dedanites, who are evidently intended in ver. 20, and by the inhabitants of *Dedan* mentioned in connection with Edom in ch. xxv. 13 and Jer. xlix. 8, is involved in obscurity (see the

comm. on Gen. x. 7). The combination with אִיִּים רַבִּים and the articles of commerce which they brought to Tyre, point to a people of southern Arabia settled in the neighbourhood of the Persian Gulf. The many אִיִּים are the islands and coasts of Arabia on the Persian Gulf and Erythraean Sea.¹ סְחֹרַת יָדֵךְ, the commerce of thy hand, *i.e.* as *abstr. pro concr.*, those who were ready to thy hand as merchants. קַרְנוֹת שֵׁן, ivory horns. This is the term applied to the elephants' tusks (*shēn*) on account of their shape and resemblance to horns, just as Pliny (*Hist. nat.* xviii. 1) also speaks of *cornua elephanti*, although he says, in viii. 3 (4), that an elephant's weapons, which Juba calls *cornua*, are more correctly to be called *dentes*.² The ἀπ. λεγ. הוֹבְנִים, *Keri* הָבְנִים, signifies ἔβενος, *hebenum*, ebony. The ancients obtained both productions partly from India, partly from Ethiopia (Plin. xii. 4 (8)). According to Dioscor. i. 130, the Ethiopian ebony was preferred to the Indian. הֵשִׁיב אֶשְׁכָּר, to return payment (see the comm. on Ps. lxxii. 10).—In ver. 16, J. D. Michaelis, Ewald, Hitzig, and others read אֱדֹם for אֲרָם, after the LXX. and Pesh., because Aram did not lie in the road from Dedan and the אִיִּים to Israel (ver. 17), and it is not till ver. 18 that Ezekiel reaches Aram. Moreover, the corruption ארם for אדום could arise all the more readily from the simple fact that the defective form אֱדֹם only occurs in Ezekiel (xxv. 14), and is altogether an extraordinary one. These reasons are undoubtedly worthy of consideration; still they are not conclusive, since the enumeration does not follow a strictly geographical

---

¹ Movers (II. 3, pp. 303 sqq.) adduces still further evidence in addition to that given above, namely, that "unquestionable traces of the ancient name have been preserved in the region in which the ancient Dedanites are represented as living, partly on the coast in the names *Attana*, *Attene*, which have been modified according to well-known laws,—the former, a commercial town on the Persian Gulf, visited by Roman merchants (Plin. vi. 32, § 147); the latter, a tract of country opposite to the island of Tylos (Plin. *l.c.* § 49),—and partly in the islands of the Persian Gulf" (p. 304).

² The Ethiopians also call ivory *Karna nage*, i.e. *cornu elephanti*, and suppose that it is from horns, and not from tusks, that ivory comes (*vid.* Hiob Ludolph, *Hist. Aeth.* I. c. 10)

order, inasmuch as Damascus is followed in vers. 19 sqq. by many of the tribes of Southern Arabia, so that *Aram* might stand, as Hävernick supposes, for Mesopotamian Aram, for which the articles mentioned in ver. 16 would be quite as suitable as for Edom, whose chief city *Petra* was an important place of commerce and emporium for goods. רֹב מַעֲשַׂיִךְ, the multitude of thy works, thy manufactures. Of the articles of commerce delivered by אֲרָם, the red purple, embroidery, and בּוּץ (the Aramaean name for byssus, which appears, according to Movers, to have originally denoted a species of cotton), favour Aram, particularly Babylonia, rather than Edom. For the woven fabrics of Babylonia were celebrated from the earliest times (*vid.* Movers, II. 3, pp. 260 sqq.); and Babylon was also the oldest and most important market for precious stones (*vid.* Movers, p. 266). נֹפֶךְ is the carbuncle (see the comm. on Ex. xxviii. 18). כַּדְכֹּד, probably the ruby; in any case, a precious stone of brilliant splendour (*vid.* Isa. liv. 12). רָאמוֹת, corals or pearls (*vid.* Delitzsch on Job xxviii. 18).—*Judah* (ver. 17) delivered to Tyre wheat of *Minnith*, *i.e.* according to Judg. xi. 33, an Ammonitish place, situated, according to the *Onomast.*, four Roman miles from Heshbon in the direction of Philadelphia. That Ammonitis abounded in wheat, is evident from 2 Chron. xxvii. 5, although the land of Israel also supplied the Tyrians with wheat (1 Kings v. 25). The meaning of the ἅπ. λεγ. פַּנַּג cannot be definitely ascertained. The rendering confectionery is founded upon the Aramaean פְּנַג, *deliciari*, and the Chaldee translation, קוֹלְיָא, *i.e.* κολία, according to Hesychius, τὰ ἐκ μέλιτος τρωγάλια, or sweetmeats made from honey. Jerome renders it *balsamum*, after the μύρων of the LXX.; and in Hitzig's opinion, *Pannaga* (literally, a snake) is a name used in Sanscrit for a sweet-scented wood, which was employed in medicine as a cooling and strengthening drug (?). Honey (from bees) and oil are well-known productions of Palestine. צֳרִי is balsam; whether *resina* or the true balsam grown in gardens about Jericho (*opobalsamum*), it is impossible to decide (see my *Bibl. Archäol.* I. p. 38, and Movers, II. 3, pp. 220 sqq.). *Damascus* supplied Tyre with wine of *Chelbon.* חֶלְבּוֹן still exists in the village of *Helbôn,* a place with many ruins, three hours and a half to the north of Damascus, in the midst of a valley of the same name, which is planted with vines wherever it is practicable, from whose grapes the best and most costly wine of the country is made (*vid.* Robinson, *Biblical Researches*). Even in ancient times this wine was so celebrated, that, according to Posidonius (in *Athen. Deipnos.* i. 22), the kings of Persia drank only Chalybonian wine from Damascus (*vid.* Strabo, XV. 3. 22). צֶמֶר צָחַר, wool of dazzling whiteness; or, according to others, wool of *Zachar,* for which the Septuagint has ἔρια ἐκ Μιλήτου, Milesian wool.[1]—Ver. 19. Various explanations have been given of the first three words. וְדָן is not to be altered into וְדָן, as it has been by Ewald, both arbitrarily and unsuitably with ver. 20 immediately following; nor is it to be rendered "*and Dan.*" It is a decisive objection to this, that throughout the whole enumeration not a single land or people is introduced with the copula ו. *Vedan,* which may be compared with the *Vaheb* of Num. xxi. 14, a place also mentioned only once, is the name of a tribe and tract of land not mentioned elsewhere in the Old Testament. Movers (p. 302) conjectures that it is the celebrated city of *Aden* (عدن). *Javan* is also the name of an Arabian place or tribe; and, according to a notice in the *Kamus,* it is a place in *Yemen.* Tuch (*Genesis,* p. 210) supposes it to be a Greek (Ionian) settlement, the founders of which had been led by their enterprising spirit to cross the land of Egypt into Southern Arabia. For the purpose of distinguishing this Arabian *Javan* from Greece itself, or in order to define it more precisely, מְעוּזָּל is

---

[1] According to Movers (II. 3, p. 269), צָחַר is the *Sicharia of Aethicus* (Cosm. § 108): SICHARIA *regio, quae postea Nabathaea, nuncupatur, silvestris valde, ubi Ismaelitae eminus,*—an earlier name for the land of the Nabathaeans, who dwelt in olden time between Palestine and the Euphrates, and were celebrated for their wealth in flocks of sheep.

appended, which all the older translators have taken to be a proper name. According to the Masoretic pointing מְאוּזָּל, the word is, no doubt, to be regarded as a participle *Pual* of אָזַל, in the sense of spun, from אָזַל, to spin. But apart from the fact that it would be a surprising thing to find spun goods mentioned in connection with the trade of the Arabian tribes, the explanation itself could not be sustained from the usage of the language; for there is nothing in the dialects to confirm the idea that אזל is a softened form of עזל, inasmuch as they have all עזל (Aram.) and غَزل (Arab.), and the Talmudic אזל, *texere*, occurs first of all in the Gemara, and may possibly have been derived in the first instance from the Rabbinical rendering of our מאוזל by "spun." Even the fact that the word is written with *Shurek* is against this explanation rather than in its favour; and in all probability its origin is to be traced to the simple circumstance, that in vers. 12, 14, 16 the articles of commerce are always mentioned before נָתְנוּ עִזְבוֹנָיִךְ, and in this verse they would appear to be omitted altogether, unless they are covered by the word מאוזל. But we can very properly take the following words בַּרְזֶל עָשׁוֹת as the object of the first hemistich, since the Masoretic accentuation is founded upon the idea that מאזל is to be taken as the object here. We therefore regard מְאוּזָּל as the only admissible pointing, and take אוּזָל as a proper name, as in Gen. x. 27: "from *Uzal*," the ancient name of *Sanaa*, the subsequent capital of *Yemen*. The productions mentioned bear this out. Forged or wrought iron, by which Tuch (*l.c.* p. 260) supposes that sword-blades from Yemen are chiefly intended, which were celebrated among the Arabs as much as the Indian. Cassia and calamus (see the comm. on Ex. xxx. 23 and 24), two Indian productions, as Yemen traded with India from the very earliest times.—*Dedan* (ver. 20) is the inland people of that name, living in the neighbourhood of Edom (cf. ch. xxv. 13; see the comm. on ver. 15). They furnished בִּגְדֵי חֹפֶשׁ, *tapetes straguli*, cloths for spreading out, most likely costly riding-cloths, like the *middin* of Judg. v. 10.

עֲרָב and קֵדָר represent the nomad tribes of Central Arabia, the Bedouins. For עֲרָב is never used in the Old Testament for the whole of Arabia; but, according to its derivation from עֲרָבָה, a steppe or desert, simply for the tribes living as nomads in the desert (as in Isa. xiii. 20; Jer. iii. 2; cf. Ewald, *Grammat. Arab.* I. p. 5). *Kedar*, descended from Ishmael, an Arabian nomad tribe, living in the desert between Arabia Petraea and Babylonia, the *Cedrei* of Pliny (see the comm. on Gen. xxv. 13). They supplied lambs, rams, and he-goats, from the abundance of their flocks, in return for the goods obtained from Tyre.— Ver. 22. Next to these the merchants of *Sheba* and *Ragmah* (רַעְמָה) are mentioned. They were Arabs of Cushite descent (Gen. x. 7) in south-eastern Arabia (*Oman*); for רַעְמָה, Ῥέγμα, was in the modern province of Oman in the bay of the same name in the Persian Gulf. Their goods were all kinds of spices, precious stones, and gold, in which southern Arabia abounded. רֹאשׁ כָּל־בֹּשֶׂם, the chief or best of all perfumes (on this use of רֹאשׁ, see the comm. on Ex. xxx. 23; Song of Sol. iv. 14), is most likely the genuine balsam, which grew in *Yemen* (*Arabia felix*), according to Diod. Sic. iii. 45, along with other costly spices, and grows there still; for Forskal found a shrub between Mecca and Medina, called *Abu sham*, which he believed to be the true balsam, and of which he has given a botanical account in his *Flora Aeg.* pp. 79, 80 (as *Amyris opobalsamum*), as well as of two other kinds. Precious stones, viz. onyx-stones, rubies, agates, and cornelians, are still found in the mountains of Hadramaut; and in Yemen also jaspers, crystals, and many good rubies (*vid.* Niebuhr, *Descript.* p. 125, and Seetzen in Zach's *Monatl. Corresp.* xix. p. 339). And, lastly, the wealth of Yemen in gold is too strongly attested by ancient writers to be called in question (cf. Bochart, *Phal.* II. 28), although this precious metal is not found there now.—In vers. 23, 24 the trade with Mesopotamia is mentioned. חָרָן, the *Carrhae* of the Romans in north-western Mesopotamia (see the comm. on Gen. xi. 31), was situated at the crossing of the caravan-roads which intersect Mesopotamia; for it was at this point that the two caravan routes from Babylonia and the Delta of the Persian Gulf joined the old military and commercial road to Canaan (Movers, p. 247). The eastern route ran along the Tigris, where *Calneh*, the later *Ktesiphon*, was the most important commercial city. It is here called כַּנֵּה (Canneh), contracted from כַּלְנֵה (see the comm. on Gen. x. 10; Amos vi. 2). The western route ran along the Euphrates, past the cities mentioned in ver. 23*b*. עֶדֶן is not the Syrian, but the Mesopotamian *Eden* (2 Kings xix. 12; Isa. xxxvii. 12), the situation of which has not yet been determined, though Movers (p. 257) has sought for it in the Delta of the Euphrates and Tigris. The singular circumstance that the merchants of Sheba should be mentioned in connection with localities in Mesopotamia, which has given rise both to arbitrary alterations of the text and to various forced explanations, has been explained by Movers (p. 247 compared with p. 139) from a notice of Juba in Pliny's *Hist. nat.* xii. 17 (40), namely, that the Sabaeans, the inhabitants of the spice country, came with their goods from the Persian Gulf to Carrhae, where they held their yearly markets, and from which they were accustomed to proceed to Gabba (Gabala in Phoenicia) and Palestinian Syria. Consequently the merchants of Sabaea are mentioned as those who carried on the trade between Mesopotamia and Tyre, and are not unsuitably placed in the centre of those localities which formed the most important seats of trade on the two great commercial roads of Mesopotamia. *Asshur* and *Chilmad*, as we have already observed, were on the western road which ran along the Euphrates. כִּלְמַד has already been discovered by Bochart (*Phal.* I. 18) in the *Charmande* of Xenophon (*Anab.* i. 5. 10), and Sophaenetus (see Steph. Byz. *s.v.* Χαρμάνδη), a large and wealthy city in a desert region "beyond the river Euphrates." The *Asshur* mentioned along with *Chilmad*, in the midst of purely commercial cities, cannot be the land of Assyria, but must be the emporium *Sura* (Movers, p. 252), the present

Essurieh, which stands upon the bank on this side of the Euphrates above Thapsacus and on the caravan route, which runs from Palmyra past Rusapha (*Rezeph*, Isa. xxxvii. 12; 2 Kings xix. 12) to Nicephorium or Rakka, then in a northerly direction to Haran, and bending southwards, runs along the bank of the river in the direction of Chilmad or Charmande (Ritter, *Erdk.* XI. pp. 1081 sqq.). The articles of commerce from these emporia, which were brought to Tyre by Sabaean caravans, consisted of מִכְלָלִים, literally, articles of perfect beauty, either state-dresses (cf. מִכְלָל, ch. xxiii. 12 and xxxiv. 4), or more generally, costly works of art (Hävernick). The omission of the copula ו before בִּגְלוֹמֵי is decisive in favour of the former, as we may infer from this that בגל is intended as an explanatory apposition to מִכְלָלִים. גְּלוֹמֵי תְכֵלֶת וְרִקְמָה, cloaks (גְּלוֹם connected with χλαμύς) of hyacinth-purple and embroidery, for which Babylonia was celebrated (for proofs of this, see Movers, pp. 258 sqq.). The words which follow cannot be explained with certainty. All that is evident is, that בַּחֲבָלִים חב' וגו' is appended to בְּגִנְזֵי בְרוֹמִים without a copula, as בִּגְלוֹמֵי וגו' is to בְּמִכְלָלִים in the first hemistich, and therefore, like the latter, is intended as an explanatory apposition. חֲבָלִים does not mean either cloths or threads, but lines or cords. חֲבֻשִׁים signifies literally bound or wound up; probably twisted, *i.e.* formed of several threads wound together or spun; and אֲרָזִים, firm, compact, from اَرَزَ, to be drawn together. Consequently גִּנְזֵי בְרוֹמִים וגו' can hardly have any other meaning than treasures of spun yarns, *i.e.* the most valuable yarns formed of different threads. For "treasures" is the only meaning which can be assigned to גְּנָזִים with any certainty on philological grounds, and בְּרוֹמִים, from בָּרַם, برم, *contorsit*, is either yarn spun from several or various threads, or cloth woven from such threads. But the latter would not harmonize with חֲבָלִים. Movers (II. 3, pp. 263 sqq.) adopts a similar conclusion, and adduces evidence that silk yarn, bombyx, and cotton came to Tyre through the Mesopotamian trade, and were there dyed in the splendid Tyrian purples, and woven into cloths, or brought for sale with the dyeing complete. All the other explanations which have been given of these difficult words are arbitrary and untenable; not only the Rabbinical rendering of גִּנְזֵי בְּרוֹמִים, viz. chests of damask, but that of Ewald, "pockets of damask," and that proposed by Hartmann, Hävernick, and others, viz. girdles of various colours, ζῶναι σκιωταί. In ver. 25 the description is rounded off with a notice of the lever of this world-wide trade. שָׂרוֹת cannot mean "walls" in this instance, as in Jer. v. 10, and like שָׂרוֹת in Job xxiv. 11, because the ships, through which Tyre became so rich, could not be called walls. The word signifies "caravans," after שׁוּר = سار (Isa. lvii. 9), corresponding to the Aramaean שְׁיָרָא. מַעֲרָבֵךְ might be regarded as an accusative of more precise definition: caravans, with regard to (for) thy bartering trade. At the same time it is more rhetorical to take מַעֲרָבֵךְ as a second predicate: they were thy trade, *i.e.* the carriers of thy trade. What the caravans were for the emporia of trade on the mainland, the ships of Tarshish were for Tyre, and these on the largest sea-going ships are mentioned *instar omnium*. By means of these vessels Tyre was filled with goods, and rendered weighty (וַתִּכְבְּדִי), *i.e.* rich and glorious.—But a tempest from the east would destroy Tyre with all its glory.

Vers. 26–36. Destruction of Tyre.—Ver. 26. *Thy rowers brought thee into great waters: the east wind broke thee up in the heart of the seas.* Ver. 27. *Thy riches and thy sales, thy bartering wares, thy seamen and thy sailors, the repairers of thy leaks and the traders in thy wares, and all thy fighting men in thee, together with all the multitude of people in thee, fell into the heart of the seas in the day of thy fall.* Ver. 28. *At the noise of the cry of thy sailors the places tremble.* Ver. 29. *And out of their ships come all the oarsmen, seamen, all the sailors of the sea; they come upon the land,* Ver. 30. *And make their voice heard over thee, and cry bitterly, and put dust upon their heads, and cover themselves with ashes;* Ver. 31. *And shave themselves bald on thy account, and gird on sackcloth, and weep for thee in anguish of soul a bitter wailing.* Ver. 32. *They raise over thee in their grief a lamentation, and lament over thee: Who is like Tyre! like the destroyed one in the midst of the sea!* Ver. 33. *When thy sales came forth out of the seas, thou didst satisfy many nations; with the abundance of thy goods and thy wares thou didst enrich kings of the earth.* Ver. 34. *Now that thou art wrecked away from the seas in the depths of the water, thy wares and all thy company are fallen in thee.* Ver. 35. *All the inhabitants of the islands are amazed at thee, and their kings shudder greatly; their faces quiver.* Ver. 36. *The traders among the nations hiss over thee; thou hast become a terror, and art gone for ever.*—The allusion to the ships of Tarshish, to which Tyre was indebted for its glory, serves as an introduction to a renewal in ver. 26 of the allegory of vers. 5–9a; Tyre is a ship, which is wrecked by the east wind (cf. Ps. xlviii. 8). In Palestine (Arabia and Syria) the east wind is characterized by continued gusts; and if it rises into a tempest, it generally causes great damage on account of the violence of the gusts (see Wetzstein in Delitzsch's commentary on Job xxvii. 1). Like a ship broken in pieces by the storm, Tyre with all its glory sinks into the depths of the sea. The repetition of בְּלֵב יַמִּים in vers. 26 and 27 forms an effective contrast to ver. 25; just as the enumeration of all the possessions of Tyre, which fall with the ship into the heart of the sea, does to the wealth and glory in ver. 25b. They who manned the ship also perish with the cargo,—" the seamen," *i.e.* sailors, rowers, repairers of leaks (calkers), also the merchants on board, and the fighting men who defended the ship and its goods against pirates,—the whole *qâhâl*, or gathering of people, in the ship. The difficult expression בְּכָל־קְהָלֶךְ can only be taken as an explanatory apposition to אֲשֶׁר בָּךְ: all the men who are in thee, namely, in the multitude of people in thee. Ver. 28. When the vessel is wrecked, the managers of the ship raise such a cry that the *migreshôth* tremble. מִגְרָשׁ is used in Num. xxxv. 2 for the precincts around the Levitical cities, which were set apart as pasture ground for the flocks; and in Ezek. xlv. 2, xlviii. 17, for the ground surrounding the holy city. Consequently מִגְרָשׁוֹת cannot mean the suburbs of Tyre in the passage before us, but must signify the open places on the mainland belonging to Tyre, *i.e.* the whole of its territory, with the fields and villages contained therein. The rendering "fleet," which Ewald follows the Vulgate in adopting, has nothing to support it.—Vers. 29 sqq. The ruin of this wealthy and powerful metropolis of the commerce of the world produces the greatest consternation among all who sail upon the sea, so that they forsake their ships, as if they were no longer safe in them, and leaving them for the land, bewail the fall of Tyre with deepest lamentation. הִשְׁמִיעַ with בְּקוֹל, as in Ps. xxvi. 7; 1 Chron. xv. 19, etc. For the purpose of depicting the lamentation as great and bitter in the extreme, Ezekiel groups together all the things that were generally done under such circumstances, viz. covering the head with dust (cf. Josh. vii. 6; 1 Sam. iv. 12; and Job ii. 12) and ashes (הִתְפַּלֵּשׁ, to strew, or cover oneself, not to roll oneself: see the comm. on Mic. i. 10); shaving a bald place (see ch. vii. 18 and the comm. on Mic. i. 16); putting on sackcloth; loud, bitter weeping (בְּמַר נֶפֶשׁ, as in Job vii. 11 and x. 1); and singing a mournful dirge (vers. 32 sqq.). בְּנִיהֶם, *in lamento eorum;* נִי contracted from נְהִי (Jer. ix. 17, 18; cf. הִי, ch. ii. 10). The reading adopted by the LXX., Theodot., Syr., and eleven Codd. (בְּנֵיהֶם) is unsuitable, as there is no allusion to sons, but the seamen themselves raise the lamentation. The correction proposed by Hitzig, בְּפִיהֶם, is altogether inappropriate. The exclamation, Who is like Tyre! is more precisely defined by כְּדֻמָּה, like the destroyed one in the midst of the sea. דֻּמָּה, participle *Pual*, with the מ dropt, as in 2 Kings ii. 10, etc. (*vid.* Ges. § 52. 2, Anm. 6). It is quite superfluous to assume that there was a noun דֻּמָּה signifying destruction. בְּצֵאת עִזְבוֹנַיִךְ has been aptly explained by Hitzig: "inasmuch as thy wares sprang out of the sea, like the plants and field-fruits out of the soil" (the selection of the word הִשְׂבַּעַתְּ also suggested this simile); "not as being manufactured at Tyre, and therefore in the sea, but because the sea floated the goods to land for the people in the ships, and they satisfied the desire of the purchasers." Tyre satisfied peoples and enriched kings with its wares, not only by purchasing from them and paying for their productions with money or barter, but also by the fact that the Tyrians gave a still higher value to the raw material by the labour which they bestowed upon them. הוֹנַיִךְ in the plural is only met with here.—Ver. 34. But now Tyre with its treasures and its inhabitants has sunk in the depths of the sea. The antithesis in which ver. 34 really stands to ver. 33 does not warrant our altering עֵת נִשְׁבֶּרֶת into עַתְּ נִשְׁבֶּרֶתְּ, as Ewald and Hitzig propose, or adopting a different division of the second hemistich. עֵת is an adverbial accusative, as in ch. xvi. 57: "at the time of the broken one away from the seas into the depth of the waters, thy wares and thy people have fallen, *i.e.* perished." עֵת נִשְׁבֶּרֶת, *tempore quo fracta es.* נִשְׁבֶּרֶת מִיַּמִּים is intentionally selected as an antithesis to יֹשֶׁבֶת מִיַּמִּים in ch. xxvi. 17.—Ver. 35. All the inhabitants of the islands and their kings, *i.e.* the inhabitants of the (coast of the) Mediterranean and its islands, will be thrown into consternation at the fall of Tyre; and (ver. 36) the merchants among the nations, *i.e.* the foreign nations, the rivals of Tyre in trade, will hiss thereat; in other words, give utterance to malicious joy. שָׁמֵם, to be laid waste, or thrown into perturbation with terror and amazement. רָעַם פָּנִים, to tremble or quiver in the face, *i.e.* to tremble so much that the terror shows itself in the countenance.—In ver. 36*b* Ezekiel brings the lamentation to a close in a similar manner to the threat contained in ch. xxvi. (*vid.* ch. xxvi. 21).

CHAP. XXVIII. 1-19. AGAINST THE PRINCE OF TYRE.

As the city of Tyre was first of all threatened with destruction (ch. xxvi.), and then her fall was confirmed by a lamentation (ch. xxvii.), so here the prince of Tyre is first of all forewarned of his approaching death (vers. 1-10), and then a lamentation is composed thereon (vers. 11-19).

Vers. 1-10. FALL OF THE PRINCE OF TYRE.—Ver. 1. *And the word of Jehovah came to me, saying,* Ver. 2. *Son of man, say to the prince of Tyre, Thus saith the Lord Jehovah, Because thy heart has lifted itself up, and thou sayest, " I am a God, I sit upon a seat of Gods, in the heart of the seas," when thou art a man and not God, and cherishest a mind like a God's mind,* Ver. 3. *Behold, thou art wiser than Daniel; nothing secret is obscure to thee;* Ver. 4. *Through thy wisdom and thy understanding hast thou acquired might, and put gold and silver in thy treasuries;* Ver. 5. *Through the greatness of thy wisdom hast thou increased thy might by thy trade, and thy heart has lifted itself up on account of thy might,* Ver. 6. *Therefore thus saith the Lord Jehovah, Because thou cherishest a mind like a God's mind,* Ver. 7. *Therefore, behold, I will bring foreigners upon thee, violent men of the nations; they will draw their swords against the beauty of thy wisdom, and pollute thy splendour.* Ver. 8. *They will cast thee down into the pit, that thou mayest die the death of the slain in the heart of the seas.* Ver. 9. *Wilt thou indeed say, I am a God, in the face of him that slayeth thee, when thou art a man and not God in the hand of him that killeth thee?* Ver. 10. *Thou wilt die the death of the uncircumcised at the hand of foreigners; for I have spoken it, is the saying of the Lord Jehovah.*—This threat of judgment follows in general the same course as those addressed to other nations (compare especially ch. xxv.), namely, that the sin is mentioned first (vers. 2-5), and then the punishment consequent upon the sin (vers. 6-10). In ver. 12 מֶלֶךְ is used instead of נָגִיד, *dux.* In the use of the term נָגִיד to designate the king,

Kliefoth detects an indication of the peculiar position occupied by the prince in the commercial state of Tyre, which had been reared upon municipal foundations; inasmuch as he was not so much a monarch, comparable to the rulers of Babylon or to the Pharaohs, as the head of the great mercantile aristocracy. This is in harmony with the use of the word נָגִיד for the prince of Israel, David for example, whom God chose and anointed to be the *nâgîd* over His people; in other words, to be the leader of the tribes, who also formed an independent commonwealth (*vid.* 1 Sam. xiii. 14; 2 Sam. vii. 8, etc.). The pride of the prince of Tyre is described in ver. 2 as consisting in the fact that he regarded himself as a God, and his seat in the island of Tyre as a God's seat. He calls his seat מוֹשַׁב אֱלֹהִים, not "because his capital stood out from the sea, like the palace of God from the ocean of heaven" (Ps. civ. 3), as Hitzig supposes; for, apart from any other ground, this does not suit the subsequent description of his seat as God's mountain (ver. 16), and God's holy mountain (ver. 14). The God's seat and God's mountain are not the palace of the king of Tyre, but Tyre as a state, and that not because of its firm position upon a rocky island, but as a holy island (ἁγία νῆσος, as Tyre is called in Sanchun. ed. Orelli, p. 36), the founding of which has been glorified by myths (*vid.* Movers, *Phoenizier*, I. pp. 637 sqq.). The words which Ezekiel puts into the mouth of the king of Tyre may be explained, as Kliefoth has well expressed it, "from the notion lying at the foundation of all natural religions, according to which every state, as the production of its physical factors and bases personified as the native deities of house and state, is regarded as a work and sanctuary of the gods." In Tyre especially the national and political development went hand in hand with the spread and propagation of its religion. "The Tyrian state was the production and seat of its gods. He, the prince of Tyre, presided over this divine creation and divine seat; therefore he, the prince, was himself a god, a manifestation of the deity, having its work and home in the state of Tyre." All heathen rulers looked upon themselves in this light; so that the king of Babylon is addressed in a similar manner in Isa. xiv. 13, 14. This self-deification is shown to be a delusion in ver. 2*b*; He who is only a man makes his heart like a God's heart, *i.e.* cherishes the same thought as the Gods. לֵב, the heart, as the seat of the thoughts and imaginations, is named instead of the disposition. This is carried out still further in vers. 3–5 by a description of the various sources from which this imagination sprang. He cherishes a God's mind, because he attributes to himself superhuman wisdom, through which he has created the greatness, and might, and wealth of Tyre. The words, " behold, thou art wiser," etc. (ver. 3), are not to be taken as a question, " art thou indeed wiser?" as they have been by the LXX., Syriac, and others; nor are they ironical, as Hävernick supposes; but they are to be taken literally, namely, inasmuch as the prince of Tyre was serious in attributing to himself supernatural and divine wisdom. Thou art, *i.e.* thou regardest thyself as being, wiser than Daniel. No hidden thing is obscure to thee (עָמַם, a later word akin to the Aramaean, " to be obscure"). The comparison with Daniel refers to the fact that Daniel surpassed all the magi and wise men of Babylon in wisdom through his ability to interpret dreams, since God gave him an insight into the nature and development of the power of the world, such as no human sagacity could have secured. The wisdom of the prince of Tyre, on the other hand, consisted in the cleverness of the children of this world, which knows how to get possession of all the good things of the earth. Through such wisdom as this had the Tyrian prince acquired power and riches. חַיִל, might, possessions in the broader sense; not merely riches, but the whole of the might of the commercial state of Tyre, which was founded upon riches and treasures got by trade. In ver. 5 בְּרֻכָלָּתְךָ is in apposition to בְּרֹב חָכְמָתְךָ, and is introduced as explanatory. The fulness of its wisdom showed itself in its commerce and the manner in which it conducted it, whereby Tyre had become rich and powerful. It is not till we reach ver. 6 that we meet with the apodosis answering to יַעַן גָּבַהּ וגו׳ in ver. 2, which has been pushed so far back by the intervening parenthetical sentences in vers. 2b–5. For this reason the sin of the prince of Tyre in deifying himself is briefly reiterated in the clause יַעַן תִּתְּךָ וגו׳ (ver. 6b, compare ver. 2b), after which the announcement of the punishment is introduced with a repetition of לָכֵן in ver. 7. Wild foes approaching with barbarous violence will destroy all the king's resplendent glory, slay the king himself with the sword, and hurl him down into the pit as a godless man. The enemies are called עָרִיצֵי גּוֹיִם, violent ones of the peoples,—that is to say, the wild hordes composing the Chaldean army (cf. ch. xxx. 11, xxxi. 12). They drew the sword "against the beauty (יְפִי, the construct state of יֳפִי) of thy wisdom," *i.e.* the beauty produced by thy wisdom, the beautiful Tyre itself, with all that it contains (ch. xxvi. 3, 4). יִפְעָה, splendour; it is only here and in ver. 17 that we meet with it as a noun. The king himself they hurl down into the pit, *i.e.* the grave, or the nether world. כְּמוֹתֵי חָלָל, the death of a pierced one, substantially the same as מוֹתֵי עֲרֵלִים. The plural מְמוֹתֵי and מוֹתֵי here and Jer. xvi. 4 (*mortes*) is a *pluralis exaggerativus*, a death so painful as to be equivalent to dying many times (see the comm. on Isa. liii. 9). In ver. 9 Ezekiel uses the *Piel* מְחַלֵּל in the place of the *Poel* מְחוֹלֵל, as חָלַל in the *Piel* occurs elsewhere only in the sense of *profanare*, and in Isa. li. 9 the *Poel* is used for piercing. But there is no necessity to alter the pointing in consequence, as we also find the *Pual* used by Ezekiel in ch. xxxii. 26 in the place of the *Poal* of Isa. liii. 5. The death of the uncircumcised is such a death as godless men die—a violent death. The king of Tyre, who looks upon himself as a god, shall perish by the sword like a godless man. At the same time, the whole of this threat applies, not to the one king, *Ithobal*, who was reigning at the time of the siege of Tyre by the Chaldeans, but to the king as the founder and creator of the might of Tyre (vers. 3–5), *i.e.* to the supporter of that royalty which was to perish along with Tyre itself.—It is to the king, as the representative of the might and glory of Tyre, and not merely to the existing possessor of the regal dignity, that the following lamentation over his fall refers.

Vers. 11–19. LAMENTATION OVER THE KING OF TYRE.—
Ver. 11. *And the word of Jehovah came to me, saying,* Ver. 12. *Son of man, raise a lamentation over the king of Tyre, and say to him, Thus saith the Lord Jehovah, Thou seal of a well-measured building, full of wisdom and perfect in beauty.* Ver. 13. *In Eden, the garden of God, wast thou; all kinds of precious stones were thy covering, cornelian, topaz, and diamond, chrysolit*, *beryl, and jasper, sapphire, carbuncle, and emerald, and gold: the service of thy timbrels and of thy women was with thee; on the day that thou wast created, they were prepared.* Ver. 14. *Thou wast a cherub of anointing, which covered, and I made thee for it; thou wast on a holy mountain of God; thou didst walk in the midst of fiery stones.* Ver. 15. *Thou wast innocent in thy ways from the day on which thou wast created, until iniquity was found in thee.* Ver. 16. *On account of the multitude of thy commerce, thine inside was filled with wrong, and thou didst sin: I will therefore profane thee away from the mountain of God; and destroy thee, O covering cherub, away from the fiery stones!* Ver. 17. *Thy heart has lifted itself up because of thy beauty, thou hast corrupted thy wisdom together with thy splendour: I cast thee to the ground, I give thee up for a spectacle before kings.* Ver. 18. *Through the multitude of thy sins in thine unrighteous trade thou hast profaned thy holy places; I therefore cause fire to proceed from the midst of thee, which shall devour thee, and make thee into ashes upon the earth before the eyes of all who see thee.* Ver. 19. *All who know thee among the peoples are amazed at thee: thou hast become a terror, and art gone for ever.*—The lamentation over the fall of the king of Tyre commences with a picture of the super-terrestrial glory of his position, so as to correspond to his self-deification as depicted in the fore-

going word of God. In ver. 12 he is addressed as חֹתֵם תָּכְנִית. This does not mean, "artistically wrought signet-ring;" for חֹתֵם does not stand for חָתָם, but is a participle of חָתַם, to seal. There is all the more reason for adhering firmly to this meaning, that the following predicate, מָלֵא חָכְמָה, is altogether inapplicable to a signet-ring, though Hitzig once more scents a corruption of the text in consequence. תָּכְנִית, from תָּכַן, to weigh, or measure off, does not mean perfection (Ewald), beauty (Ges.), façon (Hitzig), or symmetry (Hävernick); but just as in ch. xliii. 10, the only other passage in which it occurs, it denotes the measured and well-arranged building of the temple, so here it signifies a well-measured and artistically arranged building, namely, the Tyrian state in its artistic combination of well-measured institutions (Kliefoth). This building is sealed by the prince, inasmuch as he imparts to the state firmness, stability, and long duration, when he possesses the qualities requisite for a ruler. These are mentioned afterwards, namely, "full of wisdom, perfect in beauty." If the prince answers to his position, the wisdom and beauty manifest in the institutions of the state are simply the impress received from the wisdom and beauty of his own mind. The prince of Tyre possessed such a mind, and therefore regarded himself as a God (ver. 2). His place of abode, which is described in vers. 13 and 14, corresponded to his position. Ezekiel here compares the situation of the prince of Tyre with that of the first man in Paradise; and then, in vers. 15 and 16, draws a comparison between his fall and the fall of Adam. As the first man was placed in the garden of God, in Eden, so also was the prince of Tyre placed in the midst of paradisaical glory. עֵדֶן is shown, by the apposition בְּ אֱלֹהִים, to be used as the proper name of Paradise; and this view is not to be upset by the captious objection of Hitzig, that Eden was not the garden of God, but that this was situated in Eden (Gen. ii. 8). The fact that Ezekiel calls Paradise גַּן־עֵדֶן in ch. xxxvi. 35, proves nothing more than that the terms *Eden* and *Garden of*

God do not cover precisely the same ground, inasmuch as the garden of God only occupied one portion of Eden. But notwithstanding this difference, Ezekiel could use the two expressions as synonymous, just as well as Isaiah (Isa. li. 3). And even if any one should persist in pressing the difference, it would not follow that בְּעֶדֶן was corrupt in this passage, as Hitzig fancies, but simply that גַּן אלהים defined the idea of עֵדֶן more precisely—in other words, restricted it to the garden of Paradise. There is, however, another point to be observed in connection with this expression, namely, that the epithet גַּן אלהים is used here and in ch. xxxi. 8, 9; whereas, in other places, Paradise is called גַּן יהוה (*vid.* Isa. li. 3; Gen. xiii. 10). Ezekiel has chosen Elohim instead of Jehovah, because Paradise is brought into comparison, not on account of the historical significance which it bears to the human race in relation to the plan of salvation, but simply as the most glorious land in all the earthly creation. The prince of Tyre, placed in the pleasant land, was also adorned with the greatest earthly glory. Costly jewels were his coverings, that is to say, they formed the ornaments of his attire. This feature in the pictorial description is taken from the splendour with which Oriental rulers are accustomed to appear, namely, in robes covered with precious stones, pearls, and gold. מְסֻכָּה, as a noun ἅπ. λεγ., signifies a covering. In the enumeration of the precious stones, there is no reference to the breastplate of the high priest. For, in the first place, the order of the stones is a different one here; secondly, there are only nine stones named instead of twelve; and lastly, there would be no intelligible sense in such a reference, so far as we can perceive. Both precious stones and gold are included in the glories of Eden (*vid.* Gen. ii. 11, 12). For the names of the several stones, see the commentary on Ex. xxviii. 17–20. The words מְלֶאכֶת תֻּפֶּיךָ וגו׳—which even the early translators have entirely misunderstood, and which the commentators down to Hitzig and Ewald have made marvellous attempts to explain—present no peculiar difficulty, apart from the plural נְקָבֶיךָ, which is only met with here. As the meaning timbrels, tambourins (*aduffa*), is well established for תֻּפִּים, and in 1 Sam. x. 5 and Isa. v. 12 flutes are mentioned along with the timbrels, it has been supposed by some that נְקָבִים must signify flutes here. But there is nothing to support such a rendering either in the Hebrew or in the other Semitic dialects. On the other hand, the meaning *pala gemmarum* (Vulgate), or ring-casket, has been quite arbitrarily forced upon the word by Jerome, Rosenmüller, Gesenius, and many others. We agree with Hävernick in regarding נְקָבִים as a plural of נְקֵבָה (*foeminae*), formed, like a masculine, after the analogy of נָשִׁים, פִּלַגְשִׁים, etc., and account for the choice of this expression from the allusion to the history of the creation (Gen. i. 27). The service (מְלָאכָת, performance, as in Gen. xxxix. 11, etc.) of the women is the leading of the circular dances by the odalisks who beat the timbrels: "the harem-pomp of Oriental kings." This was made ready for the king on the day of his creation, *i.e.* not his birthday, but the day on which he became king, or commenced his reign, when the harem of his predecessor came into his possession with all its accompaniments. Ezekiel calls this the day of his creation, with special reference to the fact that it was God who appointed him king, and with an allusion to the parallel, underlying the whole description, between the position of the prince of Tyre and that of Adam in Paradise.[1] The next verse (ver. 14) is a more difficult one. אַתְּ is an abbreviation of אַתָּ, אַתָּה, as in Num. xi. 15; Deut. v. 24 (see Ewald, § 184a). The ἀπ. λεγ. מִמְשַׁח has been explained in very different ways, but mostly according to the Vulgate rendering,

---

[1] In explanation of the fact alluded to, Hävernick has very appropriately called attention to a passage of Athen. (xii. 8, p. 531), in which the following statement occurs with reference to Strato, the Sidonian king: "Strato, with flute-girls, and female harpers and players on the cithara, made preparations for the festivities, and sent for a large number of *hetaerae* from the Peloponnesus, and many singing-girls from Ionia, and young *hetaerae* from the whole of Greece, both singers and dancers." See also other passages in Brissonius, *de regio Pers. princ.* pp. 142–3.

tu Cherub extentus et protegens, as signifying spreading out or extension, in the sense of "with outspread wings" (Gesenius and many others). But מָשַׁח does not mean either to spread out or to extend. The general meaning of the word is simply to anoint; and judging from מִשְׁחָה and מָשְׁחָה, *portio*, Lev. vii. 35 and Num. xviii. 8, also to measure off, from which the idea of extension cannot possibly be derived. Consequently the meaning "anointing" is the only one that can be established with certainty in the case of the word מִמְשַׁח. So far as the form is concerned, מִמְשַׁח might be in the construct state; but the connection with הַסּוֹכֵךְ, anointing, or anointed one, of the covering one, does not yield any admissible sense. A comparison with ver. 16, where כְּרוּב הַסּוֹכֵךְ occurs again, will show that the מִמְשַׁח, which stands between these two words in the verse before us, must contain a more precise definition of כְּרוּב, and therefore is to be connected with כְּרוּב in the construct state: cherub of anointing, *i.e.* anointed cherub. This is the rendering adopted by Kliefoth, the only commentator who has given the true explanation of the verse. מִמְשַׁח is the older form, which has only been retained in a few words, such as מִרְמָס in Isa. x. 6, together with the tone-lengthened *a* (*vid.* Ewald, § 160*a*). The prince of Tyre is called an anointed cherub, as Ephraem Syrus has observed, because he was a king even though he had not been anointed. הַסּוֹכֵךְ is not an abstract noun, either here or in Nah. ii. 6, but a participle; and this predicate points back to Ex. xxv. 20, "the cherubim covered (סוֹכְכִים) the capporeth with their wings," and is to be explained accordingly. Consequently the king of Tyre is called a cherub, because, as an anointed king, he covered or overshadowed a sanctuary, like the cherubim upon the ark of the covenant. What this sanctuary was is evident from the remarks already made at ver. 2 concerning the divine seat of the king. If the "seat of God," upon which the king of Tyre sat, is to be understood as signifying the state of Tyre, then the sanctuary which he covered or overshadowed as a cherub will also be the Tyrian state, with its holy places and sacred things. In the next clause, וּנְתַתִּיךָ is to be taken by itself according to the accents, "and I have made thee (so)," and not to be connected with בְּהַר קֹדֶשׁ. We are precluded from adopting the combination which some propose—viz. "I set thee upon a holy mountain; thou wast a God"—by the incongruity of first of all describing the prince of Tyre as a cherub, and then immediately afterwards as a God, inasmuch as, according to the Biblical view, the cherub, as an angelic being, is simply a creature and not a God; and the fanciful delusion of the prince of Tyre, that he was an *El* (ver. 2), could not furnish the least ground for his being addressed as *Elohim* by Ezekiel. And still more are we precluded from taking the words in this manner by the declaration contained in ver. 16, that Jehovah will cast him out "from the mountain of Elohim," from which we may see that in the present verse also *Elohim* belongs to *har*, and that in ver. 16, where the mountain of God is mentioned again, the predicate קֹדֶשׁ is simply omitted for the sake of brevity, just as מִמְשַׁח is afterwards omitted on the repetition of כְּרוּב הַסּוֹכֵךְ. The missing but actual object to נְתַתִּיךָ can easily be supplied from the preceding clause,—namely, this, *i.e.* an overshadowing cherub, had God made him, by placing him as king in paradisaical glory. The words, "thou wast upon a holy mountain of God," are not to be interpreted in the sense suggested by Isa. xiv. 13, namely, that Ezekiel was thinking of the mountain of the gods (Alborj) met with in Asiatic mythology, because it was there that the cherub had its home, as Hitzig and others suppose; for the Biblical idea of the cherub is entirely different from the heathen notion of the griffin keeping guard over gold. It is true that God placed the cherub as guardian of Paradise, but Paradise was not a mountain of God, nor even a mountainous land. The idea of a holy mountain of God, as being the seat of the king of Tyre, was founded partly upon the natural situation of Tyre itself, built as it was upon one or two rocky islands of the Mediterranean, and partly upon the heathen notion of the sacredness of this island as the seat of the Deity, to which the Tyrians attributed the grandeur of their state. To this we may probably add a reference to Mount Zion, upon which was the sanctuary, where the cherub covered the seat of the presence of God. For although the comparison of the prince of Tyre to a cherub was primarily suggested by the description of his abode as Paradise, the epithet הַסּוֹכֵךְ shows that the place of the cherub in the sanctuary was also present to the prophet's mind. At the same time, we must not understand by הַר קֹדֶשׁ Mount Zion itself. The last clause, "thou didst walk in the midst of (among) fiery stones," is very difficult to explain. It is admitted by nearly all the more recent commentators, that "stones of fire" cannot be taken as equivalent to "every precious stone" (ver. 13), both because the precious stones could hardly be called stones of fire on account of their brilliant splendour, and also being covered with precious stones is not walking in the midst of them. Nor can we explain the words, as Hävernick has done, from the account given by Herodotus (II. 44) of the two emerald pillars in the temple of Hercules at Tyre, which shone resplendently by night; for pillars shining by night are not stones of fire, and the king of Tyre did not walk in the temple between these pillars. The explanation given by Hofmann and Kliefoth appears to be the correct one, namely, that the stones of fire are to be regarded as a wall of fire (Zech. ii. 9), which rendered the cherubic king of Tyre unapproachable upon his holy mountain.

In ver. 15, the comparison of the prince of Tyre to Adam in Paradise is brought out still more prominently. As Adam was created sinless, so was the prince of Tyre innocent in his conduct in the day of his creation, but only until perverseness was found in him. As Adam forfeited and lost the happiness conferred upon him through his fall, so did the king of Tyre forfeit his glorious position through unrighteousness and sin, and cause God to cast him from his eminence down to the ground.

He fell into perverseness in consequence of the abundance of his trade (ver. 16a). Because his trade lifted him up to wealth and power, his heart was filled with iniquity. מָלוּ for מָלְאוּ, like מְלֹו for מְלֹוא in ch. xli. 8, and נָשׂוּ for נָשְׂאוּ in ch. xxxix. 26. תּוֹכְךָ is not the subject, but the object to מָלוּ; and the plural מָלוּ, with an indefinite subject, "they filled," is chosen in the place of the passive construction, because in the Hebrew, as in the Aramaean, active combinations are preferred to passive whenever it is possible to adopt them (vid. Ewald, § 294b and 128b). מָלֵא is used by Ezekiel in the transitive sense "to fill" (ch. viii. 17 and xxx. 11). תָּוֶךְ, the midst, is used for the interior in a physical sense, and not in a spiritual one; and the expression is chosen with an evident allusion to the history of the fall. As Adam sinned by eating the forbidden fruit of the tree, so did the king of Tyre sin by filling himself with wickedness in connection with trade (Hävernick and Kliefoth). God would therefore put him away from the mountain of God, and destroy him. חִלֵּל with מִן is a pregnant expression: to desecrate away from, i.e. to divest of his glory and thrust away from. וָאַבֶּדְךָ is a contracted form for וָאֲאַבֶּדְךָ (vid. Ewald, § 232h and § 72c).—Vers. 17 and 18 contain a comprehensive description of the guilt of the prince of Tyre, and the approaching judgment is still further depicted. עַל יִפְעָתֶךָ cannot mean, "on account of thy splendour," for this yields no appropriate thought, inasmuch as it was not the splendour itself which occasioned his overthrow, but the pride which corrupted the wisdom requisite to exalt the might of Tyre,—in other words, tempted the prince to commit iniquity in order to preserve and increase his glory. We therefore follow the LXX., Syr., Ros., and others, in taking עַל in the sense of *una cum*, together with. רַאֲוָה is an infinitive form, like אַהֲבָה for ראוֹת, though Ewald (§ 238e) regards it as so extraordinary that he proposes to alter the text. רָאָה with בְ is used for looking upon a person with malicious pleasure. בְּעָוֶל רְכֻלָּתְךָ shows in what the guilt (עָוֹן) consisted (עֲוֹל is the construct state of עָוֶל). The sanctuaries (*miqdâshim*) which the king of Tyre desecrated by the unrighteousness of his commerce, are not the city or the state of Tyre, but the temples which made Tyre a holy island. These the king desecrated by bringing about their destruction through his own sin. Several of the codices and editions read מִקְדָּשְׁךָ in the singular, and this is the reading adopted by the Chaldee, Syriac, and Vulgate versions. If this were the true reading, the sanctuary referred to would be the holy mountain of God (vers. 14 and 16). But the reading itself apparently owes its origin simply to this interpretation of the words. In the clause, "I cause fire to issue from the midst of thee," מִתּוֹכְךָ is to be understood in the same sense as תּוֹכְךָ in ver. 16. The iniquity which the king has taken into himself becomes a fire issuing from him, by which he is consumed and burned to ashes. All who know him among the peoples will be astonished at his terrible fall (ver. 19, compare ch. xxvii. 36).

If we proceed, in conclusion, to inquire into the fulfilment of these prophecies concerning Tyre and its king, we find the opinions of modern commentators divided. Some, for example Hengstenberg, Hävernick, Drechsler (on Isa. xxiii.), and others, assuming that, after a thirteen years' siege, Nebuchadnezzar conquered the strong Island Tyre, and destroyed it; while others—viz. Gesenius, Winer, Hitzig, etc.—deny the conquest by Nebuchadnezzar, or at any rate call it in question; and many of the earlier commentators suppose the prophecy to refer to Old Tyre, which stood upon the mainland. For the history of this dispute, see Hengstenberg, *De rebus Tyriorum comment.* (Berol. 1832); Hävernick, *On Ezekiel*, pp. 420 sqq.; and Movers, *Phoenizier*, II. 1, pp. 427 sqq.—The denial of the conquest of Insular Tyre by the king of Babylon rests partly on the silence which ancient historians, who mention the siege itself, have maintained as to its result; and partly on the statement contained in Ezek. xxix. 17–20.—All that Josephus (*Antt.* x. 11. 1) is able to quote from the ancient historians on this point is the following:—In the first place, he states, on the authority of the third book of the Chaldean history of Berosus, that when the father of Nebuchadnezzar, on account of his own age and consequent infirmity, had transferred to his son the conduct of the war against the rebellious satrap in Egypt, Coelesyria, and Phoenicia, Nebuchadnezzar defeated him, and brought the whole country once more under his sway. But as the tidings reached him of the death of his father just at the same time, after arranging affairs in Egypt, and giving orders to some of his friends to lead into Babylon the captives taken from among the Judaeans, the Phoenicians, the Syrians, and the Egyptians, together with the heavy armed portion of the army, he himself hastened through the desert to Babylon, with a small number of attendants, to assume the government of the empire. Secondly, he states, on the authority of the Indian and Phoenician histories of Philostratus, that when Ithobal was on the throne, Nebuchadnezzar besieged Tyre for thirteen years. The accounts taken from Berosus are repeated by Josephus in his *c. Apion* (i. § 19), where he also adds (§ 20), in confirmation of their credibility, that there were writings found in the archives of the Phoenicians which tallied with the statement made by Berosus concerning the king of Chaldea (Nebuchadnezzar), viz. "that he conquered all Syria and Phoenicia;" and that Philostratus also agrees with this, since he mentions the siege of Tyre in his histories ($\mu\epsilon\mu\nu\eta\mu\acute{\epsilon}\nu\sigma$ $\tau\hat{\eta}s$ $T\acute{\nu}\rho\sigma\nu$ $\pi\sigma\lambda\iota\sigma\rho\kappa\acute{\iota}as$). In addition to this, for synchronistic purposes, Josephus (*c. Ap.* i. 21) also communicates a fragment from the Phoenician history, containing not only the account of the thirteen years' siege of Tyre by Nebuchadnezzar in the reign of Ithobal, but also a list of the kings of Tyre who followed Ithobal, down to the time of Cyrus of Persia.[1] The siege of Tyre is

---

[1] The passage reads as follows: "In the reign of Ithobal the king, Nebuchadnezzar besieged Tyre for thirteen years. After him judges were appointed. Ecnibalus, the son of Baslachus, judged for two months; Chelbes, the son of Abdaeus, for ten months; Abbarus, the high priest, for three months; Myttonus and Gerastartus, the sons of Abdelemus, for

therefore mentioned three times by Josephus, on the authority of Phoenician histories; but he never says anything of the conquest and destruction of that city by Nebuchadnezzar. From this circumstance the conclusion has been drawn, that this was all he found there. For if, it is said, the siege had terminated with the conquest of the city, this glorious result of the thirteen years' exertions could hardly have been passed over in silence, inasmuch as in *Antt.* x. 11. 1 the testimony of foreign historians is quoted to the effect that Nebuchadnezzar was "an active man, and more fortunate than the kings that were before him." But the argument is more plausible than conclusive. If we bear in mind that Berosus simply relates the account of a subjugation and devastation of the whole of Phoenicia, without even mentioning the siege of Tyre, and that it is only in Phoenician writings therefore that the latter is referred to, we cannot by any means conclude, from their silence as to the result or termination of the siege, that it ended gloriously for the Tyrians and with humiliation to Nebuchadnezzar, or that he was obliged to relinquish the attempt without success after the strenuous exertions of thirteen years. On the contrary, considering how all the historians of antiquity show the same anxiety, if not to pass over in silence such events as were unfavourable to their country, at all events to put them in as favourable a light as possible, the fact that the Tyrian historians observe the deepest silence as to the result of the thirteen years' siege of Tyre would rather force us to the conclusion that it was very humiliating to Tyre. And this could only be the case if Nebuchadnezzar really conquered Tyre at the end of thirteen years. If he had been obliged to relinquish the siege because he found himself unable to conquer so strong a city, the Tyrian historians would most assuredly have related

six years; after whom Balatorus reigned for one year. When he died, they sent for and fetched Merbalus from Babylon, and he reigned four years. At his death they sent for his brother Eiramus, who reigned twenty years. During his reign, Cyrus ruled over the Persians."

this termination of the thirteen years' strenuous exertions of the great and mighty king of Babylon.

The silence of the Tyrian historians concerning the conquest of Tyre is no proof, therefore, that it did not really take place. But Ezek. xxix. 17–20 has also been quoted as containing positive evidence of the failure of the thirteen years' siege; in other words, of the fact that the city was not taken. We read in this passage, that Nebuchadnezzar caused his army to perform hard service against Tyre, and that neither he nor his army received any recompense for it. Jehovah would therefore give him Egypt to spoil and plunder as wages for this work of theirs in the service of Jehovah. Gesenius and Hitzig (on Isa. xxiii.) infer from this, that Nebuchadnezzar obtained no recompense for the severe labour of the siege, because he did not succeed in entering the city. But Movers (*l.c.* p. 448) has already urged in reply to this, that " the passage before us does not imply that the city was not conquered any more than it does the opposite, but simply lays stress upon the fact that it *was not plundered*. For nothing can be clearer in this connection than that what we are to understand by the wages, which Nebuchadnezzar did not receive, notwithstanding the exertions connected with his many years' siege, is simply the treasures of Tyre;" though Movers is of opinion that the passage contains an intimation that the siege was brought to an end with a certain compromise which satisfied the Tyrians, and infers, from the fact of stress being laid exclusively upon the neglected plundering, that the termination was of such a kind that plundering might easily have taken place, and therefore that Tyre was either actually conquered, but treated mildly from wise considerations, or else submitted to the Chaldeans upon certain terms. But neither of these alternatives can make the least pretension to probability. In Ezek. xxix. 20 it is expressly stated that " as wages, for which he (Nebuchadnezzar) has worked, I give him the land of Egypt, because they (Nebuchadnezzar and his army) have done it for me ;" in other words, have done the work for me. When, therefore, Jehovah promises to give Egypt to Nebuchadnezzar as a reward or wages for the hard work which has been done for Him at Tyre, the words presuppose that Nebuchadnezzar had really accomplished against Tyre the task entrusted to him by God. But God had committed to him not merely the siege, but also the conquest and destruction of Tyre. Nebuchadnezzar must therefore have executed the commission, though without receiving the expected reward for the labour which he had bestowed; and on that account God would compensate him for his trouble with the treasures of Egypt. This precludes not only the supposition that the siege was terminated, or the city surrendered, on the condition that it should not be plundered, but also the idea that for wise reasons Nebuchadnezzar treated the city leniently after he had taken possession. In either case Nebuchadnezzar would not have executed the will of Jehovah upon Tyre in such a manner as to be able to put in any claim for compensation for the hard work performed. The only thing that could warrant such a claim would be the circumstance, that after conquering Tyre he found no treasures to plunder. And this is the explanation which Jerome has given of the passage *ad litteram*. "Nebuchadnezzar," he says, "being unable, when besieging Tyre, to bring up his battering-rams, besieging towers, and *vineae* close to the walls, on account of the city being surrounded by the sea, employed a very large number of men from his army in collecting rocks and piling up mounds of earth, so as to fill up the intervening sea, and make a continuous road to the island at the narrowest part of the strait. And when the Tyrians saw that the task was actually accomplished, and the foundations of the walls were being disturbed by the shocks from the battering-rams, they placed in ships whatever articles of value the nobility possessed in gold, silver, clothing, and household furniture, and transported them to the islands; so that when the city was taken, Nebuchadnezzar found nothing to compensate him for all his labour. And because he had done the will of God in all this, some years after the conquest of Tyre, Egypt was given to him by God."[1] It is true that we have no historical testimony from any other quarter to support this interpretation. But we could not expect it in any of the writings which have come down to us, inasmuch as the Phoenician accounts extracted by Josephus simply contain the fact of the thirteen years' siege, and nothing at all concerning its progress and result. At the same time, there is the greatest probability that this was the case. If Nebuchadnezzar really besieged the city, which was situated upon an island in the sea, he could not have contented himself with cutting off the supply of drinking water from the city simply on the land side, as Shalmanezer, the king of Assyria, is said to have done (*vid.* Josephus, *Antt.* ix. 14. 2), but must have taken steps to fill up the strait between the city and the mainland with a mound, that he might construct a road for besieging and assaulting the walls, as Alexander of Macedonia afterwards did. And the words of Ezek. xxix. 18, according to which every head was bald, and the skin rubbed off every shoulder with the severity of the toil, point indisputably to the undertaking of some such works as these. And if the Chaldeans really carried out their operations upon the city in this way, as the siege-works advanced, the Tyrians would not neglect any precaution to defend themselves as far as possible, in the event of the capture of the city. They would certainly send the possessions and treasures of the city by ship into the colonies, and thereby place them in security; just as, according to Curtius, iv. 3, they sent off their families to Carthage, when the city was besieged by Alexander.

This view of the termination of the Chaldean siege of Tyre receives a confirmation of no little weight from the fragment of Menander already given, relating to the succession of rulers in Tyre after the thirteen years' siege by Nebuchadnezzar. It is there stated that after Ithobal, Baal reigned for ten years,

[1] Cyrill. Alex. gives the same explanation in his commentary on Isa. xxiii.

that judges (*suffetes*) were then appointed, nearly all of whom held office for a few months only; that among the last judges there was also a king *Balatorus*, who reigned for a year; that after this, however, the Tyrians sent to Babylon, and brought thence *Merbal*, and on his death *Hiram*, as kings, whose genuine Tyrian names undoubtedly show that they were descendants of the old native royal family. This circumstance proves not only that Tyre became a Chaldean dependency in consequence of the thirteen years' siege by Nebuchadnezzar, but also that the Chaldeans had led away the royal family to Babylonia, which would hardly have been the case if Tyre had submitted to the Chaldeans by a treaty of peace.

If, however, after what has been said, no well-founded doubt can remain as to the conquest of Tyre by Nebuchadnezzar, our prophecy was not so completely fulfilled thereby, that Tyre became a bare rock on which fishermen spread their nets, as is threatened in ch. xxvi. 4, 5, 14. Even if Nebuchadnezzar destroyed its walls, and laid the city itself in ruins to a considerable extent, he did not totally destroy it, so that it was not restored. On the contrary, two hundred and fifty years afterwards, we find Tyre once more a splendid and powerful royal city, so strongly fortified, that Alexander the Great was not able to take it till after a siege of seven months, carried on with extraordinary exertions on the part of both the fleet and army, the latter attacking from the mainland by means of a mound of earth, which had been thrown up with considerable difficulty (Diod. Sic. xvii. 40 sqq.; Arrian, *Alex.* ii. 17 sqq.; Curtius, iv. 2–4). Even after this catastrophe it rose once more into a distinguished commercial city under the rule of the Seleucidae and afterwards of the Romans, who made it the capital of Phoenicia. It is mentioned as such a city in the New Testament (Matt. xv. 21; Acts xxi. 3, 7); and Strabo (xvi. 2. 23) describes it as a busy city with two harbours and very lofty houses. But Tyre never recovered its ancient grandeur. In the first centuries of the Christian era, it is frequently mentioned as an archbishop's see. From A.D. 636 to A.D. 1125 it was under the rule of the Saracens, and was so strongly fortified, that it was not till after a siege of several months' duration that they succeeded in taking it. Benjamin of Tudela, who visited Tyre in the year 1060, describes it as a city of distinguished beauty, with a strongly fortified harbour, and surrounded by walls, and with the best glass and earthenware in the East. " Saladin, the conqueror of Palestine, broke his head against Tyre in the year 1189. But after Acre had been taken by storm in the year 1291 by the Sultan El-Ashraf, on the day following this conquest the city passed without resistance into the hands of the same Egyptian king; the inhabitants having forsaken Tyre by night, and fled by sea, that they might not fall into the power of such bloodthirsty soldiers" (Van de Velde). When it came into the hands of the Saracens once more, its fortifications were demolished; and from that time forward Tyre has never risen from its ruins again. Moreover, it had long ceased to be an insular city. The mound which Alexander piled up, grew into a broader and firmer tongue of land in consequence of the sand washed up by the sea, so that the island was joined to the mainland, and turned into a peninsula. The present *Sûr* is situated upon it, a market town of three or four thousand inhabitants, which does not deserve the name of a city or town. The houses are for the most part nothing but huts; and the streets are narrow, crooked, and dirty lanes. The ruins of the old Phoenician capital cover the surrounding country to the distance of more than half an hour's journey from the present town gate. The harbour is so thoroughly choked up with sand, and filled with the ruins of innumerable pillars and building stones, that only small boats can enter. The sea has swallowed up a considerable part of the greatness of Tyre; and quite as large a portion of its splendid temples and fortifications lie buried in the earth. To a depth of many feet the soil trodden at the present day is one solid mass of building stones, shafts of pillars, and rubbish composed of marble, porphyry, and granite. Fragments of pillars of the costly *verde antiquo* (green marble) also lie strewn about in large quantities. The crust, which forms the soil that is trodden to-day, is merely the surface of this general heap of ruins. Thus has Tyre actually become "a bare rock, and a place for the spreading of nets in the midst of sea;" and "the dwelling-places, which are now erected upon a portion of its former site, are not at variance with the terrible decree, 'thou shalt be built no more'" (compare Robinson's *Palestine*, and Van de Velde's *Travels*).—Thus has the prophecy of Ezekiel been completely fulfilled, though not directly by Nebuchadnezzar; for the prophecy is not a bare prediction of historical details, but is pervaded by the idea of the judgment of God. To the prophet, Nebuchadnezzar is the instrument of the punitive righteousness of God, and Tyre the representative of the ungodly commerce of the world. Hence, as Hävernick has already observed, Nebuchadnezzar's action is more than an isolated deed in the prophet's esteem. "In his conquest of the city he sees the whole of the ruin concentrated, which history places before us as a closely connected chain. The breaking of the power of Tyre by Nebuchadnezzar stands out before his view as inseparably connected with its utter destruction. This was required by the internal theocratic signification of the fact in its relation to the destruction of Jerusalem." Jerusalem will rise again to new glory out of its destruction through the covenant faithfulness of God (ch. xxviii. 25, 26). But Tyre, the city of the world's commerce, which is rejoicing over the fall of Jerusalem, will pass away for ever (ch. xxvi. 14, xxvii. 36).

CHAP. XXVIII. 20–26. PROPHECY AGAINST SIDON AND PROMISE FOR ISRAEL.

The threatening word against Sidon is very brief, and couched in general terms, because as a matter of fact the prophecy against Tyre involved the announcement of the fall of Sidon, which was dependent upon it; and, as we have already observed, Sidon received a special word of God simply for the purpose of making up the number of the heathen nations mentioned to the significant number seven. The word of God against Sidon brings to a close the cycle of predictions of judgment directed against those heathen nations which had given expression to malicious pleasure at the overthrow of the kingdom of Judah. There is therefore appended a promise for Israel (vers. 25, 26), which is really closely connected with the threatening words directed against the heathen nations, and for which the way is prepared by ver. 24. The correspondence of נִקְדַּשְׁתִּי בָהּ (I shall be sanctified in her) in ver. 22 to נִקְדַּשְׁתִּי בָם (I shall be sanctified in them) in ver. 25, serves to place the future fate of Israel in antithesis not merely to the future fate of Sidon, but, as vers. 24 and 26 clearly show, to that of all the heathen nations against which the previous threats have been directed.

Ver. 20. *And the word of Jehovah came to me, saying,* Ver. 21. *Son of man, direct thy face towards Sidon, and prophesy against it,* Ver. 22. *And say, Thus saith the Lord Jehovah, Behold, I will be against thee, O Sidon, and will glorify myself in the midst of thee; and they shall know that I am Jehovah, when I execute judgments upon it, and sanctify myself upon it.* Ver. 23. *I will send pestilence into it, and blood into its streets; slain will fall in the midst of it by the sword, which cometh upon it from every side; and they shall learn that I am Jehovah.* Ver. 24. *And there shall be no more to the house of Israel a malignant thorn and smarting sting from all round about them, who despise them; but they shall learn that I am the Lord Jehovah.*
—Jehovah will glorify Himself as the Lord upon Sidon, as He did before upon Pharaoh (compare Ex. xiv. 4, 16, 17, to which the word נִכְבַּדְתִּי in ver. 22, an unusual expression for Ezekiel, evidently points). The glorification is effected by judgments, through which He proves Himself to be holy upon the enemies of His people. He executes the judgments through

pestilence and blood (*vid.* ch. v. 17, xxxviii. 22), *i.e.* through disease and bloodshed occasioned by war, so that men fall, slain by the sword (cf. ch. vi. 7). Instead of נָפַל we have the intensive form נְפַל, which is regarded by Ewald and Hitzig as a copyist's error, because it is only met with here. Through these judgments the Lord will liberate His people Israel from all round about, who increase its suffering by their contempt. These thoughts sum up in ver. 24 the design of God's judgments upon all the neighbouring nations which are threatened in ch. xxv.–xxviii., and thus prepare the way for the concluding promise in vers. 25 and 26. The figure of the sting and thorn points back to Num. xxxiii. 55, where it is said that the Canaanites whom Israel failed to exterminate would become thorns in its eyes and stings in its sides. As Israel did not keep itself free from the Canaanitish nature of the heathen nations, God caused it to feel these stings of heathenism. Having been deeply hurt by them, it was now lying utterly prostrate with its wounds. The sins of Canaan, to which Israel had given itself up, had occasioned the destruction of Jerusalem (chap. xvi.). But Israel is not to succumb to its wounds. On the contrary, by destroying the heathen powers, the Lord will heal His people of the wounds which its heathen neighbours have inflicted upon it. סִלּוֹן, synonymous with סַלּוֹן in ch. ii. 6, a word only found in Ezekiel. מַמְאִיר, on the contrary, is taken from Lev. xiii. 51 and xiv. 44, where it is applied to malignant leprosy (see the comm. on the former passage).—For הַשָּׁאטִים אֹתָם, see ch. xvi. 57 and xxv. 6.

Ver. 25. *Thus saith the Lord Jehovah, When I shall gather the house of Israel out of the peoples among whom they have been scattered, I shall sanctify myself upon them before the eyes of the heathen nations, and they will dwell in their land which I have given to my servant Jacob.* Ver. 26. *They will dwell there securely, and build houses and plant vineyards, and will dwell securely when I execute judgments upon all who despise them of those round about them; and they shall learn that I Jehovah am their God.*—Whilst the heathen nations succumb to the judgments of God, Israel passes on to a time of blessed peace. The Lord will gather His people from their dispersion among the heathen, bring them into the land which He gave to the patriarch Jacob, His servant, and give them in that land rest, security, and true prosperity. (For the fact itself, compare ch. xi. 17, xx. 41, xxxvi. 22 sqq.)

END OF VOL. I.

This day, in demy 8vo, price 9s.,

A CHRONOLOGICAL AND GEOGRAPHICAL INTRODUCTION TO THE LIFE OF CHRIST.

By C. E. CASPARI.

TRANSLATED FROM THE GERMAN, WITH ADDITIONAL NOTES, BY

M. J. EVANS, B.A.

Revised by the Author.

'The work is handy and well suited for the use of the student. It gives him in very reasonable compass, and in well digested forms, a great deal of information respecting the dates and outward circumstances of our Lord's life, and materials for forming a judgment upon the various disputed points arising out of them.'—*Guardian.*

'In this work the author affords us the results of many-sided study on one of the most important objects of theological inquiry, and on a knot of problems which have been so often treated and which are of so complex a nature. The author is unquestionably right in supposing that the so-called outworks of the life of Jesus have their value, by no means to be lightly esteemed. Their examination must be returned to ever afresh, until the historic or unhistoric character of the substance of the gospel narrative has been brought out as the result of scientific examination. . . . In conclusion, we believe we can with full conviction characterise the whole work as a real gain to the scientific literature of the question and a great advance on previous investigations; not doubting that the most important positions maintained by the author will in all essential points win the approbation of the student.'—*Jahrbucher für Deutsche Theologie.*

'A thoroughly scholarlike treatise, in which every point of criticism is weighed with the utmost exactness, every phase of doubt examined with the nicest precision, and every proof that can be furnished for the authenticity and truth of the gospel history, sought after and produced with unfaltering accuracy. . . . No Bible student should fail to make this treatise his constant friend and companion, and no honest man can read, mark, learn, and digest its contents, without being persuaded that its value is priceless.'—*Bell's Weekly Messenger.*

'The volume before us is to be regarded as an exceedingly valuable contribution to the extensive literature we already possess, and it combines the two advantages of large chronological and typographical knowledge with careful exegesis. . . . The fruits of this conscientious study are here stored in goodly abundance and ripeness. . . . The translator deserves more than any ordinary word of commendation, for it is evident that he has entered upon his task *con amore*; and has furnished us not only with a satisfactory rendering of the original, but also added some notes of great value.'—*English Independent.*

'Taking up the different events in the life of Christ, every incident is dwelt upon in connection with the place and time of its occurrence; and the student and the expounder of Scripture will find in these chapters a complete guide to the surroundings of the life of Christ, and much that will throw a vivid light upon His words and actions.'—*Courant.*

'This is in every way a remarkable work, and one that cannot fail to prove of great value to biblical students.'—*Rock.*

Just published, in crown 8vo, price 6s.,

THE SENSUALISTIC PHILOSOPHY
OF
THE NINETEENTH CENTURY
CONSIDERED.

By R. L. DABNEY, D.D., LL.D.

'The volume is marked by discriminating criticism, and clear, strong exposition and defence of the intuitional theory of knowledge.'—*Daily Review.*

Just published, Fourth Edition, price 6s.,

THE TRIPARTITE NATURE OF MAN,
SPIRIT, SOUL, AND BODY,

Applied to Illustrate and Explain the Doctrines of Original Sin, the New Birth, the Disembodied State, and the Spiritual Body.

By Rev. J. B. HEARD, M.A.

With an Appendix on the FATHERHOOD OF GOD.

'The author has got a striking and consistent theory. Whether agreeing or disagreeing with that theory, it is a book which any student of the Bible may read with pleasure.'—*Guardian.*

'A valuable and interesting treatise on the "Tripartite Nature of Man," the first English theological work of any pretensions which has dealt with the subject in a methodical and systematic manner.'—DEAN OF NORWICH.

'It is with considerable satisfaction we note the issue of a fourth edition of this most original and valuable treatise, which, without exaggeration, may be described as one of the ablest contributions to our theological literature which has been published of late years.'—*English Independent.*

In crown 8vo, price 5s.,

VOICES OF THE PROPHETS.

Twelve Lectures Preached in the Chapel of Lincoln's Inn, in the Years 1870-74, on the Foundation of Bishop Warburton.

By EDWARD HAMILTON GIFFORD, D.D.

'The author has long ago attained high position as a scholar, a man of science, and a theologian, and in the volume before us he offers his readers some of the best fruits of these varied accomplishments.'—*Standard.*

'We have not for many years met with a book dealing with the important question of prophecy in all respects so satisfactory, so reverent in its treatment of the written word, so fair in argument, so courteous and dignified withal in its replies to the objections of "science falsely so called."'—*Daily Review.*

'This volume deals with the subject of prophecy in a clear and forcible manner. The objections to a belief in prophetic utterances are ably met, and much light is thrown upon the matter, which has here been dealt with in a scholarly and Christian spirit.'—*Rock.*

In crown 8vo, price 4s.,

PRINCIPLES

OF

NEW TESTAMENT QUOTATION

Established and Applied to Biblical Science.

BY REV. JAMES SCOTT, M.A., B.D.

'Mr. Scott's very exhaustive essay is quite a masterpiece of pithy compression. Theological students will find the book to be one of great value, not only for its direct help, but for its lucid example of method. It does not contain a specific criticism of every Old Testament citation found in the New Testament, but deals with the whole question of quotation in general, and thus exhibits the principles of the Biblical quotation, and vindicates them with a masterly force.'—*English Churchman.*

'The book is thoughtful, learned, conscientious, and painstaking, and performs a service which ought to be heartily recognised.'—*Baptist Magazine.*

'The treatment throughout is reverent, scholarly, and satisfactory.'—*Freeman.*

'A thoughtful attempt to arrange and systematize the various forms of quotation . . . in which the author has been highly successful.'—*Scotsman.*

'The work is a valuable contribution to the external defences of the faith.'—*Methodist Recorder.*

'Much solid learning and sound philosophy in the work.'—*London Weekly Review.*

In Two Vols., demy 8vo, price 21s.,

History of Protestant Theology,

PARTICULARLY IN GERMANY,

Viewed according to its Fundamental Movement, and in connection with the Religious, Moral, and Intellectual Life.

TRANSLATED FROM THE GERMAN OF

DR. J. A. DORNER, PROFESSOR OF THEOLOGY, BERLIN.

With a Preface to the Translation by the Author.

'This work, which may be called a History of Modern Theology, is one of the most important, interesting, and useful that Messrs. Clark have ever issued. A careful study of it would systematize on the reader's mind the whole round of evangelical truth. In fact, it is, in a certain sense, a comprehensive view of historical theology, written on a new plan—not in the form of the tabulated summary, but as traced in the living history of those whose struggles won for us the truth, and whose science formulated it for posterity.'—*London Quarterly Review.*

'We earnestly recommend this most valuable and important work to the attention of all theological students. So great a mass of learning and thought so ably set forth has never before been presented to English readers, at least on this subject.'—*Journal of Sacred Literature.*

Just published, in demy 8vo, price 9s.,

St. John the Author of the Fourth Gospel.

By Professor C. E. LUTHARDT, Author of 'Fundamental Truths of Christianity,' etc. Translated and the Literature enlarged by C. R. GREGORY, Leipzig.

'A work of thoroughness and value; the translator has added a lengthy Appendix containing a very complete account of the literature bearing on the controversy respecting this Gospel. The indices which close the volume are well ordered and add greatly to its value.'—*Guardian.*

'In this work, from the pen of one of the greatest divines of Germany, the facts are made to speak for themselves, and the result is a complete refutation of the Anti-Johannine school of criticism, and a correspondingly complete establishment of the truth on which the unanimous testimony of the ancient Church is shown to rest. . . . Such a work as this was much needed.'—*Dickinson's Quarterly.*

BY THE SAME AUTHOR.
Fourth edition, crown 8vo, 6s.,

The Fundamental Truths of Christianity.

The Antagonistic Views of the World in their Historical Development; The Anomalies of Existence; The Personal God; The Creation of the World; Man; Religion; Revelation; History of Revelation—Heathenism and Judaism; Christianity in History; The Person of Jesus Christ.

BY THE SAME AUTHOR.
Third edition, crown 8vo, 6s.,

Apologetic Lectures on the Saving Truths
of Christianity.

The Nature of Christianity; Sin; Grace; The God-Man; The Work of Jesus Christ; The Trinity; The Church; Holy Scripture; The Means of Grace; The Last Things.

BY THE SAME AUTHOR.
Second edition, crown 8vo, 6s.,

Apologetic Lectures on the Moral Truths
of Christianity.

The Nature of Christian Morality; Man; The Christian, and the Christian Virtues; The Devotional Life of the Christian, and his Attitude towards the Church; Christian Marriage; The Christian Home; The State and Christianity; The Life of the Christian in the State; Culture and Christianity; Humanity and Christianity.

'From Dr. Luthardt's exposition even the most learned theologians may derive invaluable criticism, and the most acute disputants supply themselves with more trenchant and polished weapons than they have as yet been possessed of.'—*Bell's Weekly Messenger.*

'We do not know any volumes so suitable in these times for young men entering on life, or, let us say, even for the library of a pastor called to deal with such, than the three volumes of this series. We commend the whole of them with the most cordial satisfaction. They are altogether quite a specialty in our literature.'—*Weekly Review.*

Crown 8vo, 5s.,

Luthardt, Kahnis, and Bruckner—The
Church: Its Origin, its History, and its present Position.

'A comprehensive review of this sort, done by able hands, is both instructive and suggestive.'—*Record.*

Just published, Second Edition, *in crown 8vo, price 7s. 6d.*,

DAVID, THE KING OF ISRAEL:
A PORTRAIT DRAWN FROM BIBLE HISTORY AND THE BOOK OF PSALMS.

By F. W. KRUMMACHER, D.D.,

Author of 'Elijah the Tishbite.'

'Dr. Krummacher's work on David's life resembles that of his "Elijah" in its eloquence, its graphic description, its devout and earnest spirit, and will be widely welcomed.'—*Evangelical Magazine.*

At the close of two articles reviewing this work, the *Christian Observer* says: 'Our space will not permit us to consider more at large this very interesting work, but we cannot do less than cordially commend it to the attention of our readers. It affords such an insight into King David's character as is nowhere else to be met with; it is therefore most instructive.'

'This will be a pleasant household reading-book for many people.'—*Literary Churchman.*

BY THE SAME AUTHOR.

In crown 8vo, Eighth Edition, price 7s. 6d.,

THE SUFFERING SAVIOUR;
OR, MEDITATIONS ON THE LAST DAYS OF THE SUFFERINGS OF CHRIST.

'A book which has reached its eighth edition needs no introduction to the reading public. And yet the very circumstance of its repeated publication entitles it to popularity. There is a richness in these meditations which wins and warms the heart.'—*Nonconformist.*

'A book of inestimable value.'—*John Bull.*

'The reflections are of a pointed and practical character, and are eminently calculated to inform the mind and improve the heart. To the devout and earnest Christian the volume will be a treasure indeed.'—*Wesleyan Times.*

'The work will be prized by experienced Christians throughout the world; and is destined, we trust, to as wide a circulation and as long a life as the gifted author's "Elijah."'—*English Presbyterian Messenger.*

In crown 8vo, price 7s. 6d.,

THE FOOTSTEPS OF CHRIST.

Translated from the German of A. CASPERS.

'It is a book of solid thought and solid learning, and should find a considerable publicity in its English dress.'—*Nonconformist.*

'A very interesting and instructive book. Its style is quaint and antithetic; it abounds in bright thoughts, presents striking views of Scripture facts and doctrines, and is altogether eminently fitted to refresh and edify believers.'—*Family Treasury.*

'Eminently evangelical, and distinguished also by great originality and terseness.'—*Baptist Magazine.*

'There is much deeply experimental truth and precious spiritual love in Caspers' book. I do not always agree with his theology, but I own myself much profited by his devout utterances.'—Rev. C. H. SPURGEON.

Just published, in Two Vols., large crown 8vo, price 7s. 6d. each,

THE YEAR OF SALVATION.
WORDS OF LIFE FOR EVERY DAY.
A BOOK OF HOUSEHOLD DEVOTION.

By J. J. van OOSTERZEE, D.D.

'A work of great value and interest. To the clergy these readings will be found full of suggestive hints for sermons and lectures; while for family reading or for private meditation they are most excellent. The whole tone of the work is thoroughly practical, and never becomes controversial.'—*Church Bells.*

'The text is illustrated by apposite and thoughtful remarks, which will be found both convenient and profitable not only in the family circle, but also for private meditation.' —*Christian Observer.*

'The *very best* religious exposition for every-day use that has ever fallen in our way.'— *Bell's Weekly Messenger.*

'The author's mind is deeply imbued with Scripture principles, and overflows with words, rich, warm, and devotional in their character.'—*Ecclesiastical Gazette.*

'This charming and practical book of household devotion will be welcomed on account of its rare intrinsic value, as one of the most practical devotional books ever published.' —*Standard.*

'Massive of thought, persuasive, earnest, and eloquent.'—*Literary Churchman.*

'Simple, terse, and practical; and will, we are sure, be read with profit and pleasure by many.'—*Leeds Mercury.*

'Every page breathes a spirit of deep piety and earnest faith.'—*Scotsman.*

BY THE SAME AUTHOR.

Just published, in crown 8vo, price 6s.,

MOSES:
A BIBLICAL STUDY.

'Our author has seized, as with the instinct of a master, the great salient points in the life and work of Moses, and portrayed the various elements of his character with vividness and skill. . . . The work will at once take its place among our ablest and most valuable expository and practical discourses.'—*Baptist Magazine.*

'The treatise is practical, not scientific; the study is a study of character for spiritual purposes. This is conducted with much elaboration, judgment, and piety.'—*Daily Review.*

'Few men have proved themselves more competent to write such a life than Dr. Oosterzee. On the oldest subjects he never writes platitudes; on the most simple he never writes stupidly. He is always scholarly, scriptural, and devout.'—*Homilist.*

'An original, beautiful, and striking work.'—*Christian Treasury.*

Just published, in demy 8vo, price 12s.,

INTRODUCTION
TO
THE PAULINE EPISTLES.

By PATON J. GLOAG, D.D.,

Author of a 'Critical and Exegetical Commentary on the Acts of the Apostles.'

'Those acquainted with the author's previous works will be prepared for something valuable in his present work; and it will not disappoint expectation, but rather exceed it. The most recent literature of his subject is before him, and he handles it with ease and skill. . . . It will be found a trustworthy guide, and raise its author's reputation in this important branch of biblical study.'—*British and Foreign Evangelical Review.*

'A work of uncommon merit. He must be a singularly accomplished divine to whose library this book is not a welcome and valuable addition.'—*Watchman.*

'It will be found of considerable value as a handbook to St. Paul's Epistles. The dissertations display great thought as well as research. The author is fair, learned, and calm, and his book is one of worth.'—*Church Bells.*

'A capital book, full, scholarly, and clear. No difficulty is shirked, but dealt with fairly, and in an evangelical spirit. To ministers and theological students the book will be of great value.'—*Evangelical Magazine.*

'It bears the stamp of study, and of calm, critical power. It is a good defence of the orthodox views, written in a style which combines dignity, strength, and clearness. It may be read with pleasure by any lover of theology, and will be a valuable addition to the book-shelf as a book of reference.'—*Glasgow Herald.*

Recently published, in demy 8vo, price 14s.,

THE APOCALYPSE
TRANSLATED AND EXPOUNDED.

By JAMES GLASGOW, D.D.,

Irish General Assembly's Professor of Oriental Languages, etc. etc.

'A book which sober scholars will not despise, and which intelligent Christians will highly value. . . . It has substantial merits, and cannot be read without great profit.'—*Watchman.*

'A goodly volume, . . . replete with the fruits of learning and profound research, . . . characterized by independence of thought, originality and even singularity of view, and decision in grasping and enunciating results.'—*Evangelical Witness.*

'A most elaborate work, the result of careful thought, wide reading, and patient industry.'—*English Independent.*

'The book is very able, and is well worthy the study of those who are seeking to know the meaning of the Word of God.'—*Princeton Review.*

Just published, in demy 8vo, price 10s. 6d.,

DELIVERY AND DEVELOPMENT

OF

CHRISTIAN DOCTRINE.

The Fifth Series of the Cunningham Lectures.

By ROBERT RAINY, D.D.,

PRINCIPAL AND PROFESSOR OF DIVINITY AND CHURCH HISTORY, NEW COLLEGE, EDINBURGH.

'We gladly acknowledge their high excellence and the extensive learning which they all display. They are *able* to the last degree; and the author has in an unusual measure the power of acute and brilliant generalization. He handles his array of multifarious facts with ease and elegance; and we must needs acknowledge (and we do it willingly) that the Lectures are a real contribution to the settlement of the vast and obscure question with which they are occupied.'—*Literary Churchman.*

'It is a rich and nutritious book throughout, and in temper and spirit beyond all praise.'—*British and Foreign Evangelical Review.*

'The subject is treated with a comprehensive grasp, keen logical power, clear analysis and learning, and in a devout spirit.'—*Evangelical Magazine.*

In crown 8vo, Second Edition, price 4s. 6d.,

AIDS TO THE STUDY

OF

GERMAN THEOLOGY.

By Rev. GEORGE MATHESON, M.A., B.D.,

MINISTER OF INNELLAN.

'The writer of this treatise has formed to himself singularly clear conceptions, and he possesses in a remarkable degree the faculty of lucid exposition. . . . Besides serving as an admirable introduction to the study of German theology, this little volume will be valuable to the general reader, as furnishing an intelligible and interesting account of the principal phases which theological speculation has assumed in Germany in modern times.' —*Scotsman.*

'This little volume is a valuable and instructive introduction to a department of theological literature that every student is now compelled to examine.'—*British Quarterly Review.*

'A helpful little volume; helpful to the student of German theology, and not less so to the careful observer of the tendencies of English religious thought.'—*Freeman.*

'The writer or compiler deserves high praise for the clear manner in which he has in a brief compass stated these opinions.'—*Christian Observer.*

www.ingramcontent.com/pod-product-compliance
Lightning Source LLC
Chambersburg PA
CBHW032130010526
44111CB00034B/572